VFX Made Easy with Houdini

A mesmerizing journey into procedural modeling, simulations, visual effects, and rendering

Alasgar Hasanov

<packt>

VFX Made Easy with Houdini

Portfolio Director: Rohit Rajkumar
Relationship Lead: Neha Pande
Program Manager: Sandeep Tadge
Content Engineer: Shreya Sarkar
Technical Editor: Tejas Mhasvekar
Copy Editor: Safis Editing
Indexer: Rekha Nair
Proofreader: Shreya Sarkar
Production Designer: Shantanu Zagade
Growth Lead: Lee Booth

First published: September 2025

Production reference: 1290825

Published by Packt Publishing Ltd.
Grosvenor House
11 St Paul's Square
Birmingham
B3 1RB, UK.

ISBN 978-1-83588-290-0
www.packtpub.com

Foreword

When I first started my career in animation and VFX nearly 35 years ago—long before founding Jellyfish Pictures—I remember the excitement of learning new 3D software. Every time a new version of Softimage was released, we eagerly anticipated the tools and advances, often helping to shape and implement them. With each release came the challenge of mastering new features so that our creativity could flourish. A book like *VFX Made Easy with Houdini* would have been priceless to us then.

My journey led to setting up Jellyfish Pictures in 2001, and that same spirit of curiosity and innovation has stayed with me ever since. In the early days, Softimage laid the foundation of our CG pipeline. As the industry evolved, we moved through XSI and Maya, eventually adopting a combination of Maya and Houdini. This evolution reflected our commitment to pushing creative boundaries and delivering exceptional work. Houdini, with its procedural approach, played a big role. Suddenly, we could create effects and simulations with a speed and flexibility that had previously been out of reach.

VFX Made Easy with Houdini is a celebration of that power and versatility. Alasgar Hasanov brings to this book more than a decade of high-end production experience and years of teaching and mentoring. His ability to demystify complex workflows and break them into clear, digestible steps makes this an invaluable resource for artists at every level. From procedural modelling and workflows to dynamic simulations and rendering in Karma, Alasgar guides readers with a structured, practical approach that steadily builds confidence.

At Jellyfish, I could see how Houdini's procedural mindset can transform workflows, helping artists iterate faster, tackle challenges with flexibility, and allowing creativity to be predominant. This book captures that same journey, beginning with the fundamentals and advancing to intricate effects like pyro simulations, water dynamics, and disintegration, giving the reader confidence to create demanding and complex effects.

Whether you are just starting out in Houdini or looking to refine your craft, this book will be an invaluable companion. It is more than a guide—it is an invitation to explore, to experiment, and to create. With it, you will be able to unlock Houdini's full potential and have the ability to take your artistry to new heights. The very thing that drew me into the VFX world many years ago.

Philip Dobree,

Founder of Jellyfish Pictures and Creative Entrepreneur and Consultant to the Animation and VFX sector

Author's Note

When I first discovered Houdini, I was struck by its unique mix of technical depth and artistic freedom. At first, it felt hard to learn, but soon I realized it was a tool of endless creativity, capable of solving problems and unlocking possibilities that no other software could match.

This book was written to show that learning Houdini can be easy, fun, and rewarding. My aim is to remove some of the mystery and help readers gain confidence by breaking down core concepts into approachable lessons. With a solid foundation, I believe anyone can find joy in exploring Houdini and applying it to their own creative projects.

The examples and techniques shared here come from both production experience and years of teaching, distilled into practical workflows that can be adapted across many contexts. Whether you are new to visual effects or looking to expand your skills, Houdini has something valuable to offer.

I invite you to experiment, explore, and most importantly, enjoy the process of learning Houdini.

Contributors

About the author

Alasgar Hasanov is a CG and VFX artist with over a decade of professional experience, specializing in complex dynamics simulations created entirely in Houdini. His work spans a wide range of effects, including large- and small-scale water simulations, advanced pyro FX, abstract particle systems, and both rigid and soft body dynamics. While FX remains his primary focus, Alasgar brings a broad, multidisciplinary skill set that includes modeling, look development, rendering, and compositing, enabling him to contribute effectively to multiple stages of the production process.

His work has been featured in major feature films such as *Doctor Strange*, *Thor*, *Ant-Man*, *Ms. Marvel*, *X-Men: Dark Phoenix*, *It Chapter Two*, *Bad Boys for Life*, and *Snake Eyes (G.I. Joe)*. He has also contributed to acclaimed television series, including *Game of Thrones*, *American Gods*, *The Boys*, *Vikings: Valhalla*, and *Jupiter's Legacy*. Beyond film and television, Alasgar has created high-end FX and look development for global brands such as Nike, Dolby Digital, and Proline, among many others.

In addition to his production work, Alasgar has been actively involved in education, serving as a professor, program supervisor, and lead at Think Tank Training Centre, Technicolor Academy, and Humber College. He has also developed professional courses for Gnomon Workshop.

With a passion for pushing technical and artistic boundaries, Alasgar continues to blend creativity with precision, delivering cinematic, high-quality visual effects that bring stories and worlds to life for global audiences.

Writing this book has been both an exciting challenge and a rewarding journey, and it would not have been possible without the support of so many people. I am grateful to the SideFX team for creating Houdini and continually pushing the boundaries of procedural workflows, and to my colleagues, mentors, and students whose insights helped shape this work. I owe deep thanks to my family and friends for their patience and encouragement throughout the process, and to the Houdini community for their creativity, curiosity, and passion that continues to inspire me every day.

About the reviewers

Matthias Villemont is a senior Houdini FX artist and technical director from Reunion Island with extensive experience in visual effects for film, television, and high-end advertising. Amongst the numerous studios he has collaborated with are MPC, Trixter, and UPP. He has also worked on major international productions across Canada and Europe. He specializes in advanced and complex simulations, pipeline integration, and custom FX tool development.

Passionate about procedural workflows, mentoring, and technical artistry, Matthias offers consulting services to studios looking to build robust, scalable, and efficient visual effects tailored to their unique production needs.

Thanks to the author, Alasgar Hasanov, for making technical FX topics accessible, and to Packt for the opportunity to contribute. It was a pleasure to help shape this valuable resource for aspiring Houdini artists!

Christopher Akpala is a senior VFX artist with expertise in simulation and procedural animation for live broadcasts, in-game visuals, and cinematics. He specializes in creating live augmented reality (AR) graphics, bringing dynamic effects to high-profile productions. At WWE, Christopher played a key role in the virtual graphics department, delivering pyro, particle, and fluid simulations in Houdini and Unreal Engine. His work contributed to projects that earned two gold and two silver Telly Awards in 2023. He currently focuses on freelance contracts while continuing to use Houdini and Unreal Engine in his daily workflows.

Table of Contents

Part 2: Heart of Houdini: FX Simulations 89

Chapter 3: Unleashing the Power of Particles 91

Chapter 4: Igniting Pyro Effects 139

Chapter 6: Diving into Water FX 207

Chapter 11: The Big Finale: Part 3 339

Chapter 12: Best Practices for Houdini Artists 359

Preface

Houdini is widely recognized as one of the most versatile tools for creating digital content. From visual effects and animation to games, design, and visualization, it offers unmatched flexibility for artists and technical creators. Yet many learners struggle with where to begin and how to turn its procedural, node-based approach into practical results. *VFX Made Easy with Houdini* was written to provide a clear and structured path, showing that learning Houdini can be straightforward, creative, fun, and rewarding.

The book's content spans Houdini's most essential areas, starting with procedural modeling and workflow fundamentals before moving into particles, pyro, rigid and soft body dynamics, and fluid simulations. It then introduces shading, lighting, and rendering with Karma, alongside workflow efficiency techniques, project organization, and professional best practices. Each topic is presented at a level that builds both technical understanding and creative confidence.

VFX Made Easy with Houdini follows a hands-on, project-based approach. Each chapter includes step-by-step instructions, illustrated guides, and practical exercises that gradually increase in complexity. Insights and tips drawn from years of production and teaching experience help explain not only *how* to achieve results but also *why* certain approaches are effective. The learning journey culminates in a large-scale project that combines multiple disciplines into a cinematic volcanic eruption.

By the end of this book, you will be equipped with a strong foundation in Houdini and the ability to create a wide variety of effects and procedural setups. Whether your goal is to design simulations, develop interactive content, or explore procedural art, you will gain both the practical skills and the inspiration to continue building your own projects with confidence.

Who this book is for

This book is written for beginner Houdini users who want to strengthen their understanding of visual effects and procedural workflows. It is also well suited for FX artists, lighting artists, compositors, motion designers, 3D animators, and game artists who wish to integrate Houdini into their creative pipeline. A basic familiarity with 3D content creation tools is recommended, but no prior experience with Houdini is required.

What this book covers

Chapter 1, Introducing Houdini, introduces the interface, navigation tools, and node-based workflow fundamentals.

Chapter 2, Demystifying Procedural Modeling, explains proceduralism, creating flexible assets, and organizing networks.

Chapter 3, Unleashing the Power of Particles, covers particle emitters, forces, and configuring simulation settings.

Chapter 4, Igniting Pyro Effects, teaches how to create smoke, fire, and explosions using Houdini's Pyro FX tools.

Chapter 5, Breaking through Rigid Body Dynamics, focuses on fracturing models, RBD simulations, and secondary details.

Chapter 6, Diving into Water FX, explores fluid simulations, water surfaces, splashes, and interaction.

Chapter 7, Effects Case Study: Disintegration FX, shows how to build a stylized disintegration effect using particles.

Chapter 8, Effects Case Study: Explosion FX, demonstrates fast, art-directable methods for creating cinematic explosions.

Chapter 9, The Big Finale: Part 1, begins a large-scale project, with part one focusing on layout and sourcing.

Chapter 10, The Big Finale: Part 2, continues the project with pyro simulations, layering, and scale control.

Chapter 11, The Big Finale: Part 3, completes the project with debris, shading, lighting, and rendering.

Chapter 12, *Best Practices for Houdini Artists*, reviews workflows, optimization, and tips for working efficiently in production.

To get the most out of this book

To follow along successfully, you should have a basic understanding of 3D concepts, such as geometry, materials, and animation. Prior Houdini experience is not essential, but familiarity with other digital content creation tools will help you progress more quickly.

Additional knowledge in rendering, compositing, or scripting may be beneficial but is not required.

Software/hardware requirements

To follow along with the projects in this book, you'll need the following setup:

Software/hardware covered in the book	Operating system requirements
Houdini version 20 or later	A Windows, macOS, or Linux machine capable of running Houdini FX
SideFX Labs (installed with Houdini)	Sufficient RAM and GPU resources for simulations and rendering

You can download Houdini from the official website at `https://www.sidefx.com/download/`.

I recommend working through each chapter step by step and taking time to experiment with variations. Whenever possible, type parameters manually instead of copy-pasting to reinforce learning. Use the provided project files and resources, and explore additional documentation and the GitHub repository (link is available in the next section) for extended examples.

Note that the author acknowledges the use of cutting-edge AI, such as ChatGPT, with the sole aim of enhancing the language and clarity within the book, thereby ensuring a smooth reading experience for readers. It's important to note that the content itself has been crafted by the author and edited by a professional publishing team.

Download the example project files

The project files for the book are hosted on GitHub at `https://github.com/PacktPublishing/VFX-Made-Easy-with-Houdini`.

We also have other code bundles from our rich catalog of books and videos available at `https://github.com/PacktPublishing`. Check them out!

Download the color images

We also provide a PDF file that has color images of the screenshots used in this book. Please note that the screenshots in this book are meant to show you the overall workflow and node layout, not every tiny parameter. Houdini's interface is wide and detail-heavy, which makes print images hard to read.

To address this, we've included two resources: QR codes to view the chapter screenshots in better clarity and full Houdini project files via GitHub. By using the QR codes and files, you can inspect every node, parameter, and setting in Houdini—the best way to truly understand how the setups work.

You can download the PDF file here: `https://packt.link/gbp/9781835882900`.

Conventions used

There are a number of text conventions used throughout this book.

`CodeInText`: Indicates code words in text, database table names, folder names, filenames, file extensions, pathnames, dummy URLs, user input, and X (formerly Twitter) handles. For example: "Rename the newly created node from `geo1` to `particle_fx` and double-click on the node to dive inside."

A block of code is set as follows:

```
@v *= fit(@pscale, 0.0025, 0.0125, 0.1, 0.5);
```

Bold: Indicates a new term, an important word, or words that you see on the screen. For instance, words in menus or dialog boxes appear in the text like this. For example: "Add a **POP Properties** node after **POP Drag** and enable the **Mass** checkbox."

Warnings or important notes appear like this.

Tips and tricks appear like this.

Get in touch

Feedback from our readers is always welcome.

General feedback: If you have questions about any aspect of this book or have any general feedback, please email us at `customercare@packt.com` and mention the book's title in the subject of your message.

Errata: Although we have taken every care to ensure the accuracy of our content, mistakes do happen. If you have found a mistake in this book, we would be grateful if you reported this to us. Please visit `http://www.packt.com/submit-errata`, click **Submit Errata**, and fill in the form.

Piracy: If you come across any illegal copies of our works in any form on the internet, we would be grateful if you would provide us with the location address or website name. Please contact us at `copyright@packt.com` with a link to the material.

If you are interested in becoming an author: If there is a topic that you have expertise in and you are interested in either writing or contributing to a book, please visit `http://authors.packt.com/`..

Share your thoughts

Once you've read *VFX Made Easy with Houdini, First Edition*, we'd love to hear your thoughts! Scan the QR code below to go straight to the Amazon review page for this book and share your feedback.

`https://packt.link/r/1835882919`

Your review is important to us and the tech community and will help us make sure we're delivering excellent quality content.

Part 1

Learning the Fundamentals

Every journey in Houdini begins with mastering its unique environment and understanding how its procedural system works. This part introduces you to the user interface, the different contexts in which tasks are performed, and the node networks that define every workflow. You will also complete your first Houdini project: creating a fun procedural effect of colorful magical particles without using any simulation methods, alongside your first steps into lighting and rendering. These exercises will establish a foundation that carries across all future projects.

With these basics in place, the focus shifts to procedural modeling. You'll start by creating shapes with curve tools, then refine them using groups, polygon modeling operations, and alignment tools. As your models grow more complex, you'll learn how subnetworks streamline node organization, how duplication and variation are managed with **Copy** tools, and how Boolean and volume operations expand your creative possibilities. The section concludes by bringing your models into Solaris for rendering and presentation.

By the end of this part, you will have a strong grasp of Houdini's core workspace and the principles of proceduralism, equipping you with the skills to build and present flexible, procedural assets.

This part has the following chapters:

- *Chapter 1, Introducing Houdini*
- *Chapter 2, Demystifying Procedural Modeling*

1

Introducing Houdini

Hello everyone, and welcome to an exciting adventure into the art of crafting mesmerizing visual effects in Houdini – made easier than you might think. In this book, we'll explore the world of Houdini, the industry's leading software for creating everything from complex procedural environments to dynamic, high-quality visual effects and animation.

Whether you're a curious newcomer or with some experience, prepare to unlock the secrets of this powerful toolset as we delve into the art and science of creating spectacular visual effects. From procedural modeling to particle systems, from smoke, fire, and destruction to fluid water effects, this book equips you with the knowledge and techniques essential for unleashing the full potential of Houdini FX.

In the first chapter, you will learn how to navigate Houdini's **user interface** (**UI**), as well as create your first project. If you are coming from another software package, you will find that Houdini's user interface is similar to those of many other 3D content creation applications. The biggest power of Houdini comes from its procedural approach and the flexibility to create complex systems that can give you a lot of control over the creation of different effects.

In this chapter, we will cover the following topics:

- Exploring the Houdini UI
- Understanding Houdini contexts
- Diving into node networks
- Lighting and rendering

By the end of this chapter, you will have a solid understanding of how to navigate Houdini's UI, build node networks, and create your first fully rendered project in Houdini.

Getting the most out of this book – get to know your free benefits

Unlock exclusive **free** benefits that come with your purchase, thoughtfully crafted to supercharge your learning journey and help you learn without limits.

Here's a quick overview of what you get with this book:

Next-gen reader

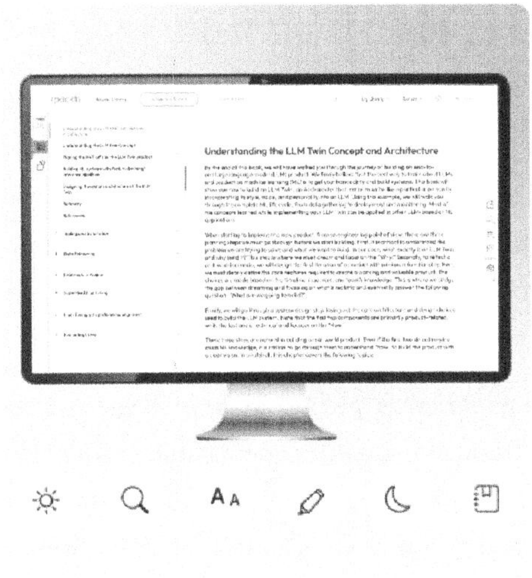

Figure 1.1: Illustration of the next-gen Packt Reader's features

Our web-based reader, designed to help you learn effectively, comes with the following features:

Multi-device progress sync: Learn from any device with seamless progress sync.

Highlighting and notetaking: Turn your reading into lasting knowledge.

Bookmarking: Revisit your most important learnings anytime.

Dark mode: Focus with minimal eye strain by switching to dark or sepia mode.

Interactive AI assistant (beta)

Figure 1.2: Illustration of Packt's AI assistant

Our interactive AI assistant has been trained on the content of this book, to maximize your learning experience. It comes with the following features:

✦ **Summarize it**: Summarize key sections or an entire chapter.

✦ **AI code explainers**: In the next-gen Packt Reader, click the **Explain** button above each code block for AI-powered code explanations.

Note: The AI assistant is part of next-gen Packt Reader and is still in beta.

DRM-free PDF or ePub version

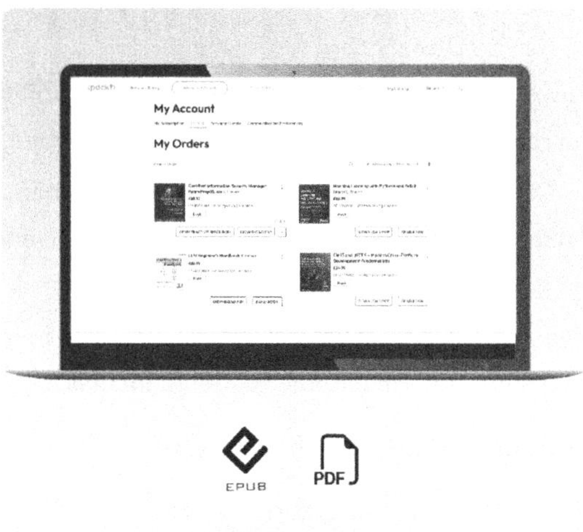

Figure 1.3: Free PDF and ePub

Learn without limits with the following perks included with your purchase:

Learn from anywhere with a DRM-free PDF copy of this book.

Use your favorite e-reader to learn using a DRM-free ePub version of this book.

Technical requirements

For all the content and projects in this book, I will be using **Houdini version 20** and **SideFX Labs**, which you can download for free at `www.sidefx.com/download/`. Some chapters will also use features available in Houdini 20.5.

Note that at the time of writing this book, versions 20 and 20.5 were in use. However, the projects and workflows detailed in the book are compatible with Houdini 21 as well.

Here are the hardware requirements for running Houdini:

- **CPU**: A four-core Intel or AMD CPU is the minimum. For the best performance in CPU-based rendering and simulations, I recommend a core amount of eight or higher with a high clock speed.
- **RAM**: A minimum of 4 GB is required; however, for the best performance and the ability to create highly detailed simulations and renders, I recommend at least 32 GB or more.
- **GPU**: A graphics card with a minimum of 4 GB of VRAM is needed. For the best performance and GPU acceleration in simulation and rendering, 8 GB and higher VRAM on higher-end cards is recommended.
- **HDD**: At least 4.5 GB of disk space is needed for installation, as well as 250 GB or more disk space is recommended for geometry/simulation caches and rendered images.

Additionally, you can find the project file for this chapter in the GitHub repository:

`https://github.com/PacktPublishing/VFX-Made-Easy-with-Houdini`

Houdini's interface is wide and detail-heavy, which can make print images hard to read. To view the chapter images in better clarity, scan the provided QR code or see the *Preface* for the link to the color images. It will direct you to a dedicated link where you can take a look at the images.

Exploring the Houdini UI

Let's start by breaking down the important parts of Houdini's interface. To start, please open a new Houdini file, and refer to *Figure 1.4*:

Figure 1.4 – An overview of the Houdini interface

I have placed numbered markers near each tab of the main UI elements. Now let's explore each of these elements in detail:

1. **Viewport**: This is your window into the magical 3D world. It is used to see everything you create, from 2D shapes and images to complex 3D objects and simulations.
2. **Node network pane**: This is your main building playground. It is used to create, connect, and manipulate nodes to build networks that define the behavior and appearance of objects, effects, and simulations in a Houdini project.

3. **Parameters pane**: This is your control panel with inputs and sliders. It is used to control and adjust the settings of nodes within the network.
4. **Selector, handle, and view tab**: Interactively transform the objects in your 3D scene and access extra elements using these options. They are used to provide specific controls and settings for you to interact with objects and elements in your scene.
5. **Timeline and animation playbar**: This is your time control machine. It is utilized to manage playback and animation within the viewport.
6. **File menu bar**: Navigate to this menu bar to save your progress and much more. It is used to access a wide range of tools for Houdini file management, project settings, scripting, UI preferences, and much more.
7. **Display options**: Use these options to preview anything from the world grid to secret attributes.
8. **Scene update**: The power of making heavy calculations light on your viewport and computer lies here. It is used to switch the viewport update mode and dynamics on/off mode.
9. **Shelf tools bar**: This bar is fun to look at, explore, and can be useful for quick access to presets, commonly used tools, scripts, and workflows.

> Further reading
>
> If you would like a more comprehensive description of Houdini's UI elements, I recommend the *Houdini Foundations* book by Robert Magee.

I will be going over many different settings as we progress through our projects. For now, I would like you to focus on the first three markers: the **Viewport**, **Node Network** pane, and **Parameters** pane, as we will be spending most of our time working with them.

Navigating the viewport

As the first step, let's create our first 3D object in Houdini to navigate around it. Follow these steps to create a 3D object:

1. Put your mouse cursor on the viewport, press *Tab* on your keyboard, navigate to **Geometry**| **Polygons** | **Sphere**, click on the highlighted **Sphere** text with the mouse, and press *Enter* to place it.

2. Alternatively, you can also follow a more standardized way of adding nodes and geometry in Houdini:

    1. Put your mouse cursor on the node network view and press *Tab*.
    2. Type `sphere` near the **search** icon (type to search). You can also type at least the first three letters of the node you are looking for and a list of available nodes will pop up for selection.
    3. If you use **TAB Menu** to create 3D objects in the viewport, you will have the ability to place the object anywhere in the 3D space of your scene. However, it is best to create and develop your 3D scene/effects from the origin of the 3D space.
    4. Creating objects from the network view will automatically put any created 3D geometry in the origin of your 3D scene.

Figure 1.5 – Placing a sphere object in the viewport area

You will notice that three things happened once we placed the sphere:

1. 3D sphere geometry appeared in the viewport
2. The **sphere_object1** node appeared in the network view
3. Basic object node parameters appeared in the **Parameters** pane

I would like you to get very excited about this sphere, because by the end of this chapter, we will transform it into a magical particle entity and render it out as your first Houdini project, as shown in *Figure 1.6*:

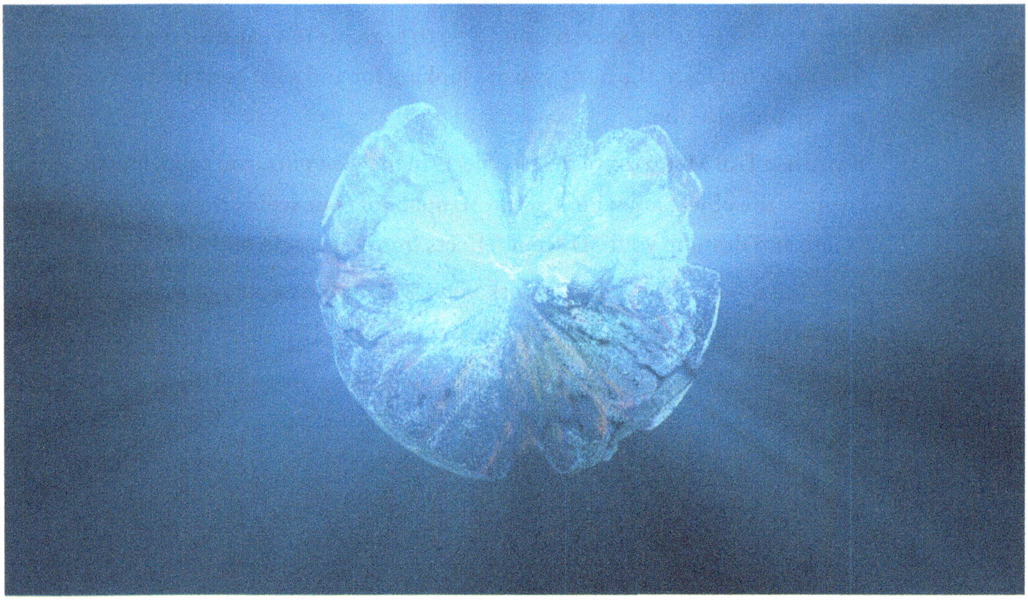

Figure 1.6 – Example of the magic sphere that we will create

Let's look at viewport navigation first, though:

- You can tumble around the object when you press *Spacebar* or *Alt/Opt* + the *left mouse button*
- If you want to pan in the viewport, you can press *Spacebar* or *Alt/Opt* + the *middle mouse button*
- Finally, for dolly or to zoom in on the 3D objects, press *Spacebar* or *Alt/Opt* + the *right mouse button*

I prefer doing all button combinations through the *Alt* (*Opt* on Mac) button, since it is similar to navigation in other 3D packages.

Also, some of the useful viewport navigation shortcuts are *Spacebar + G* to focus on the selected object, and *Spacebar + A* to frame all the objects in your scene. Take a moment to try and test all these viewport navigation controls, since these will be used most of the time during our projects.

Customizing the UI

For the next steps, I will show you how I prefer to organize and change my UI to make the most of space and accessibility.

Let's follow the steps shown in *Figures 1.7*, *1.8*, and *1.9* to organize the UI:

1. With your mouse over the viewport, press the *D* key to bring up the **Display Options**. Following the *white arrows*, navigate to the **Background** tab and select **Dark Grey** from the **Color Scheme** dropdown to make the background dark gray. This color makes it much easier to see effects and attributes in contrast.

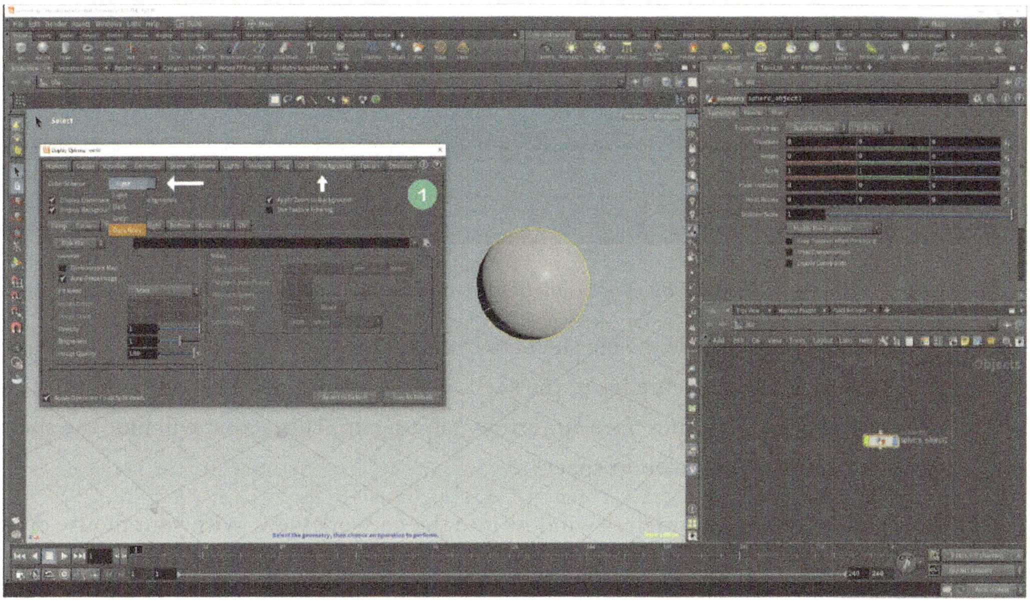

Figure 1.7 – Organizing UI to be more compact and efficient

2. We will hide the **Parameters** window to maximize the network view, but don't worry – we will bring it as a smaller flexible panel to the network nodes. Following the *green arrow*, navigate to the lower part of the **Parameters** window and click on the *left-up-looking pointer near the green arrow*, as shown in *Figure 1.8*:

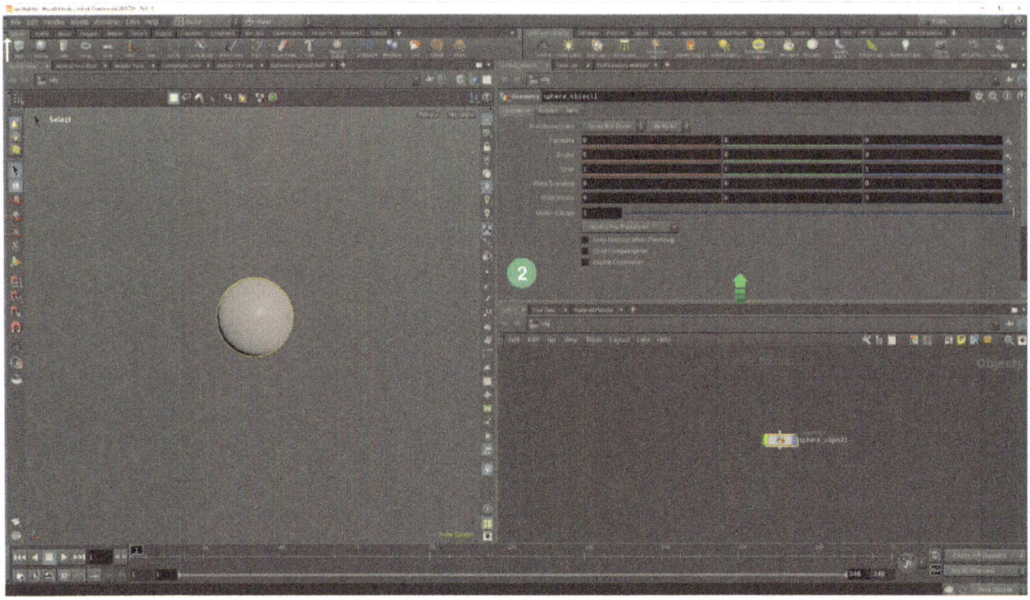

Figure 1.8 – Organizing UI to be more compact and efficient

Additionally, you can hide the big shelf tab by following the *white arrow* (top-left). With your cursor over to the left edge of the shelf tools, click on the tiny section right at the edge of the screen showing the *white* arrow pointing up. This action will hide the shelf tools, maximizing the viewport space.

3. Let's now bring the **Parameters** window into the network view. With your mouse over the network view, press the *p* key, and you should see the **Parameters** window appear as in *Figure 1.9*:

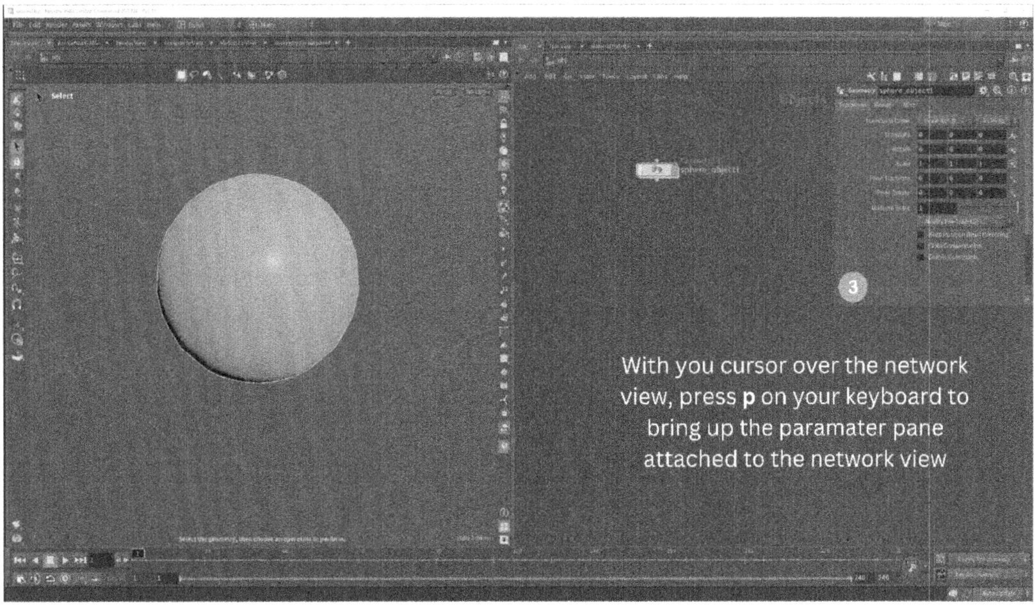

Figure 1.9 – Organizing UI to be more compact and efficient

The last screen in *Figure 1.9* showcases what your optimized UI should look like. Overall, the Houdini UI is highly customizable, and there are variations you can come up with by using the presets of other artists. This gives great flexibility in many pipelines and projects. I will mostly use this custom layout for all this book's projects.

Let's move on to creating our first project in Houdini.

Setting up the folder structure

Every time you start a new project in Houdini, it is always a good idea to be organized and set the project folder structure containing all assets and files in one place.

This is exactly what we are going to do by following these steps:

1. At the top of your Houdini window, click on **File | New Project**. You will see a new window pop up where you can enter the project name and choose in which directory to save all the project folders listed in the window.

2. You can choose any name for your project as long as it has a good description and is aligned with industry standards. I recommend calling this project `myFirstHoudiniProject`.
3. For the project path, you can choose any directory with enough disk space for project files and 3D geometry/simulation/render data cache.
4. After you set the project name and path, click **Accept** and Houdini will create a folder structure for you.
5. The final step would be saving your file into the project directory by clicking on **File** | **Save as** and choosing a filename. Usually, the industry standard would be the effect name and version, which could be `magic_sphere_v001`.

You can also name this file `myFirstHoudiniProject_v001`. *Figure 1.10* shows all the steps we took, as well as how your project and Houdini file will look on your computer:

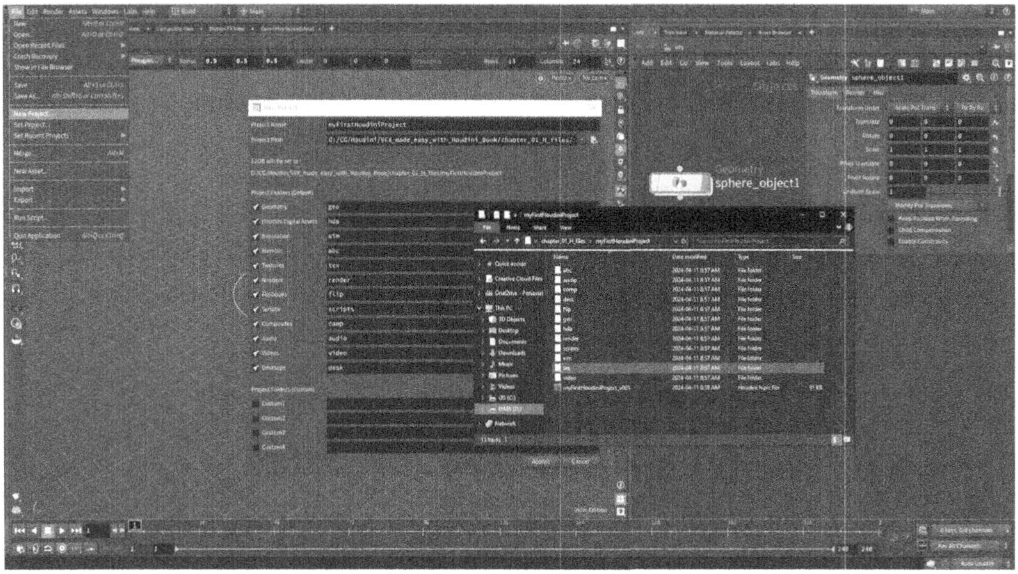

Figure 1.10 – Setting up a new project in Houdini

Next, we will learn about different contexts in Houdini and where to use them.

Understanding Houdini contexts

Let's now take a closer look at how you are going to transform the basic 3D sphere into a magical entity. Most of the work will happen in the node network, where we will change and modify the sphere with every new node and attribute.

If you take a look at your node network's top-right corner in *Figure 1.10*, you will see **Objects** written in light gray. This refers to the **obj context**, where you build and organize 3D objects in your scene. Think of it as a place where each 3D object container (like a car, a character, or a building) gets its own space to live and be edited.

Inside the **obj** context, each object has its own **geometry network**, where you can model, animate, or simulate it using **Surface Operators** (**SOPs**). So, while the **obj** level helps you organize your scene, the real building happens inside each object's node.

It's a bit like a folder structure:

- **obj level** = folders (objects in the scene)
- **SOP level** = files inside the folders (actual geometry and effects)

Overall, Houdini has eight main contexts handling different environments, nodes, and operations. Every context has unique nodes available only for its environment and performing certain tasks.

You can preview all of these contexts by pressing *Shift* + *W* with your mouse over the network view. Refer to *Figure 1.11* to see the contexts:

Figure 1.11 – Houdini Contexts

I am going to give a brief description of every context and its applications:

- **obj**: This is a fundamental context where you create and organize objects within your 3D scene. It serves as the top-level hierarchy for the nodes in your project and plays a crucial role in structuring and managing the elements of your scene. The main purpose of the **obj** context is to manage everything you create in Houdini, from geometry to lights and cameras.
- **mat**: This is a context where you create and define materials for rendering objects in your scenes. It is an important context for developing the visual appearance of surfaces, as well as defining their color, reflectivity, transparency, and other material properties. Within the **mat** context, you can create custom materials, apply textures, add procedural shader effects, and control how objects interact with light sources.
- **out**: This is a context where you can set up render outputs, define render settings, and manage the process of outputting the result of your scene into an image sequence that will be rendered to the disk.
- **stage**: This is a relatively new context that provides a powerful and flexible environment for creating, assembling, and editing **Universal Scene Description (USD)** in Houdini. Think of it like a big workspace where you can bring or create 3D models, add materials, set up lighting, and even render your final image—all in one place. It's a newer part of Houdini that combines the jobs of several older parts (like **obj** for geometry, **mat** for materials, and **out** for rendering), so you can do everything together more smoothly and in a more organized way.
- **tasks**: This is also a relatively new context that is designed to manage and distribute parallel workloads across multiple processors or machines. It is particularly useful for handling tasks that can be computed independently, such as simulations, rendering, and other computationally intensive operations.
- **img**: This is a context designed to handle image files and processing in Houdini. This context allows artists and technical users to work with images, perform various image manipulation tasks, make color corrections, create procedural textures, and prepare images for compositing and rendering.
- **ch**: This is a context for creating and manipulating animation channels. Channels represent animated attributes such as position, rotation, scale, and any other parameter that changes over time. The **ch** context provides a powerful and flexible environment for working with these animated channels, allowing artists to create complex motion, procedural animations, and more.

- **shop**: This is a context where materials and shaders were traditionally created in Houdini. It let you build how surfaces look by connecting shader nodes. It's now mostly replaced by newer systems like **MaterialX** in **stage** context which are more modern and easier to use.

Moving forward, we will focus mainly on **obj** and **stage** contexts, where we can create any 3D objects or effects and render them into a final image.

Let's take a look at how the contexts are connected to each other and how the hierarchy works.

Context hierarchy

As mentioned earlier, most of the time during our projects will be spent in the **obj** context. A very common workflow is also to create reference links to other contexts such as shaders and rendering. The **obj context** organizes objects in a hierarchical manner, allowing for parent-child relationships between nodes. Any 3D transformations performed at the **obj** level are global and affect entire groups of nodes living inside geometry containers.

You can easily see how the context hierarchy is organized if you hover your mouse over the **Tools** menu that is located at the top of your node network, between the **View** and **Layout** menus. Click on **Tools** and select the **Show Operator tree** checkbox. Alternatively, you can use *Shift* + *W* with your mouse over the node network view. What you are going to see on the left side of the network view is all the Houdini contexts and their hierarchy. You will notice that the **obj** node has a little + sign next to it, which means that it contains more levels inside.

Geometry containers

If you expand all the levels in **obj**, it will look like this: **obj** | **sphere_object1** | **sphere1**. This means that the actual sphere geometry that we should work with is located inside the **sphere_object1** container.

This is a fundamental concept describing how Houdini contexts and levels work. All the geometry we see at the top level of the **obj** context is just the object container, and the actual geometry editing and effects creation will happen to everything inside the container.

Also, there is going to be a big difference in the nodes that you can access inside the **sphere_object1** container and outside of it. All the necessary nodes for your 3D effects creation will only be available inside the geometry container.

Please see *Figure 1.12* for reference. If you follow the *white arrows*, you can see that we no longer have **Objects** written at the top right of our node network. Instead, we have **Geometry**, which means that we are inside the geometry container and have access to all the nodes that can help us create, modify, and customize geometry attributes and effects.

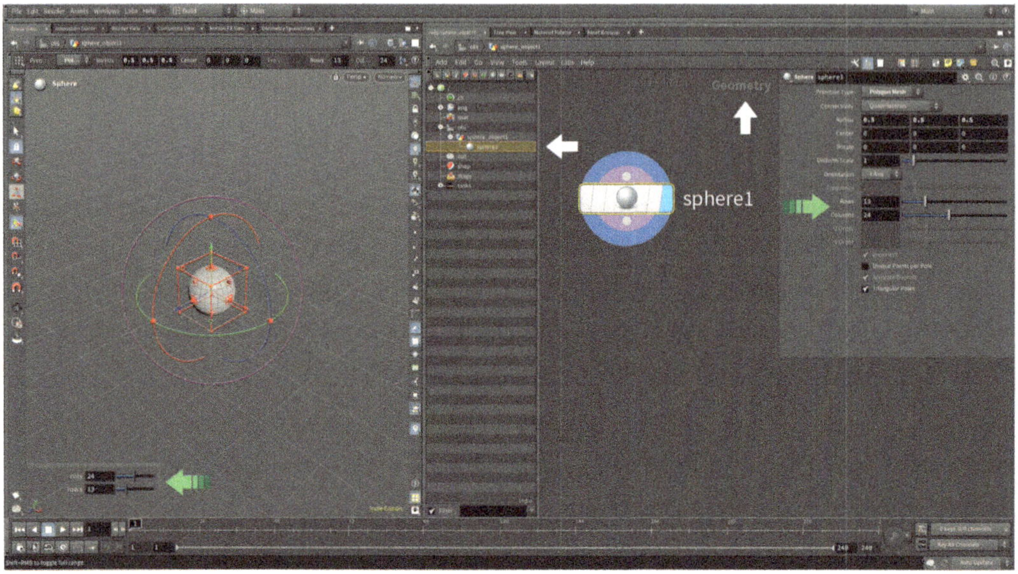

Figure 1.12 – Network view elements

Moreover, the **Parameters** window, instead of showing the global object transform controls, now shows us sphere geometry controls to change the radius, topology, initial poly count, and so on.

At last, we are at the stage where we can start creating the magic sphere effect step by step:

1. In the **Parameters** window, change **Primitive Type** to **Polygon** instead of **Polygon mesh**. The **Polygon** type will change the sphere topology to triangles and will have one slider for global resolution, which will be easier to control.
2. Sphere polygon resolution can be adjusted in the **Frequency** parameter. Let's set it to 96. You will notice that the sphere has many more polygons now and that they are all uniformly spaced, which will be important for the next steps.

We'll now move on to creating procedural setups with nodes as building blocks.

Diving into node networks

We will start by adding one of the first fundamental geometry nodes: the **mountain** node.

Adding nodes

Let's start adding new nodes to modify our sphere into a magic entity:

1. With your mouse over at the network view, press *Tab* and type `mountain` in the search box. After the node is found, it will be colored orange in the **TAB Menu** and ready to be placed in the scene.
2. To place a new node, press *Enter* once to get the node out of the **TAB Menu**, and then press *Enter* again to place it into the network view.
3. Now we need to connect the output of the sphere node to the input of the **mountain** node. You can click on the *white dot* at the bottom of the sphere node and drag a connector to the *white dot* located at the top of the **mountain** node.
4. To disconnect a node, the easiest way is to click, hold, and shake it off the connection. Alternatively, you can *right click* on the connector line and choose **Disconnect** option.

Next, let's take a look at how to use different flags on geometry nodes.

Understanding node display flags

Let's preview the result of applying the **mountain** node to the sphere. If you noticed, there is a *blue colored flag* enabled on the right edge of the sphere node (see *Figure 1.13*). This is the node visibility and evaluation flag. Basically, when the node has it enabled, you will see the result of the node calculation in the viewport.

Let's now click on the right edge of the newly connected **mountain** node to switch the visibility and calculate its result. You will now see that the sphere has changed and looks like a small, displaced 3D object resembling a rock.

The other thing that has changed is the **Parameters** window, which shows the settings and parameters for the **mountain** node now. However, first, let's take a moment and explore **node flags**.

Each node at the **Geometry** level has flags on each side that help to choose how it will be visualized, give access to an information box about the attributes and geometry, and give toggle freeze and bypass controls to bake the node into the scene or ignore its evaluation.

Figure 1.13 depicts everything that's been created and explained:

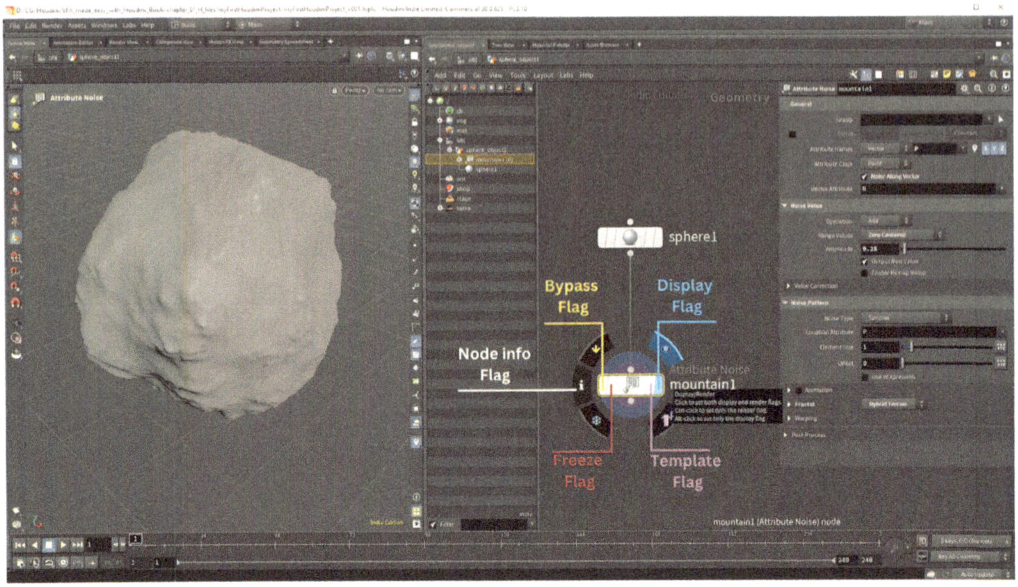

Figure 1.13 – Exploring node flags

If you use your mouse to hover over any node, you will see the flags as a ring around a node. Let's discuss these flags in more detail as follows:

- **Display flag**: This is one of the most commonly used flags while dynamically building and updating the node tree. It's used to visualize and evaluate the result of each node. At the **Geometry** level, all the nodes are evaluated starting from the top, down to the node that has the display flag on.
- **Template flag**: This is useful to preview other nodes as a reference or for snapping, while the main display flag is set to the working node.
- **Bypass flag**: This is used to disable or ignore the node evaluation, but still keep it in the network in case it will be needed in the future. You can also toggle the bypass flag on and off to dynamically see what has been modified in the selected node.
- **Freeze flag**: This is used for locking the cached result of the current node and all nodes above into the file. It is useful for baking data into the Houdini files that is hard to transfer otherwise. However, it can also significantly increase the size of your saved files.

- **Node info flag**: This is used for quickly viewing important information about a node without having to dive into its parameters or settings. The most useful data that can be found in the node info is geometry polycount/point/vertex count, all the attributes or groups that are present on the geometry, as well as any error or warning messages about the node.

  Note that **Node info** as a flag is only accessible when you have your mouse over the actual node. Otherwise, you can middle-mouse-click on the node to preview the node info.

For the next steps, we will concentrate on the **mountain** node as it will be the main driving force for the magic sphere project.

Exploring the mountain node

The **mountain** node is one of the most powerful nodes for adding different noise functions to position or other attributes. This node has many settings to give you lots of control over how the geometry is going to be displaced, reshaped, and even procedurally animated.

The **mountain** node can turn a simple-looking primitive shape such as a sphere, grid, plane, or cylinder into a realistic rock, island, terrain, or even an abstract-looking shape.

Here are some of the examples of what you can do with just a simple **mountain** node:

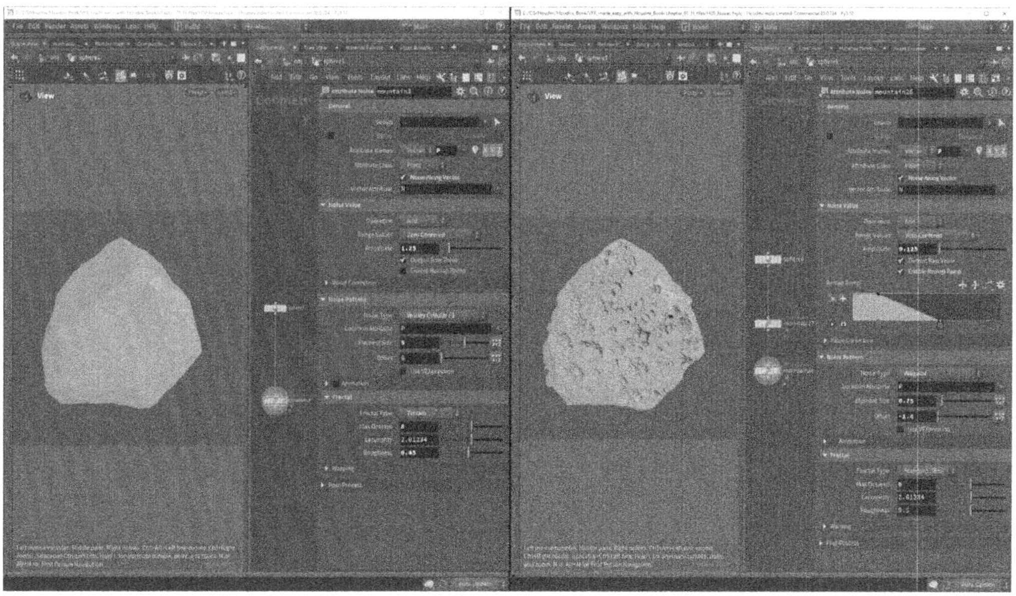

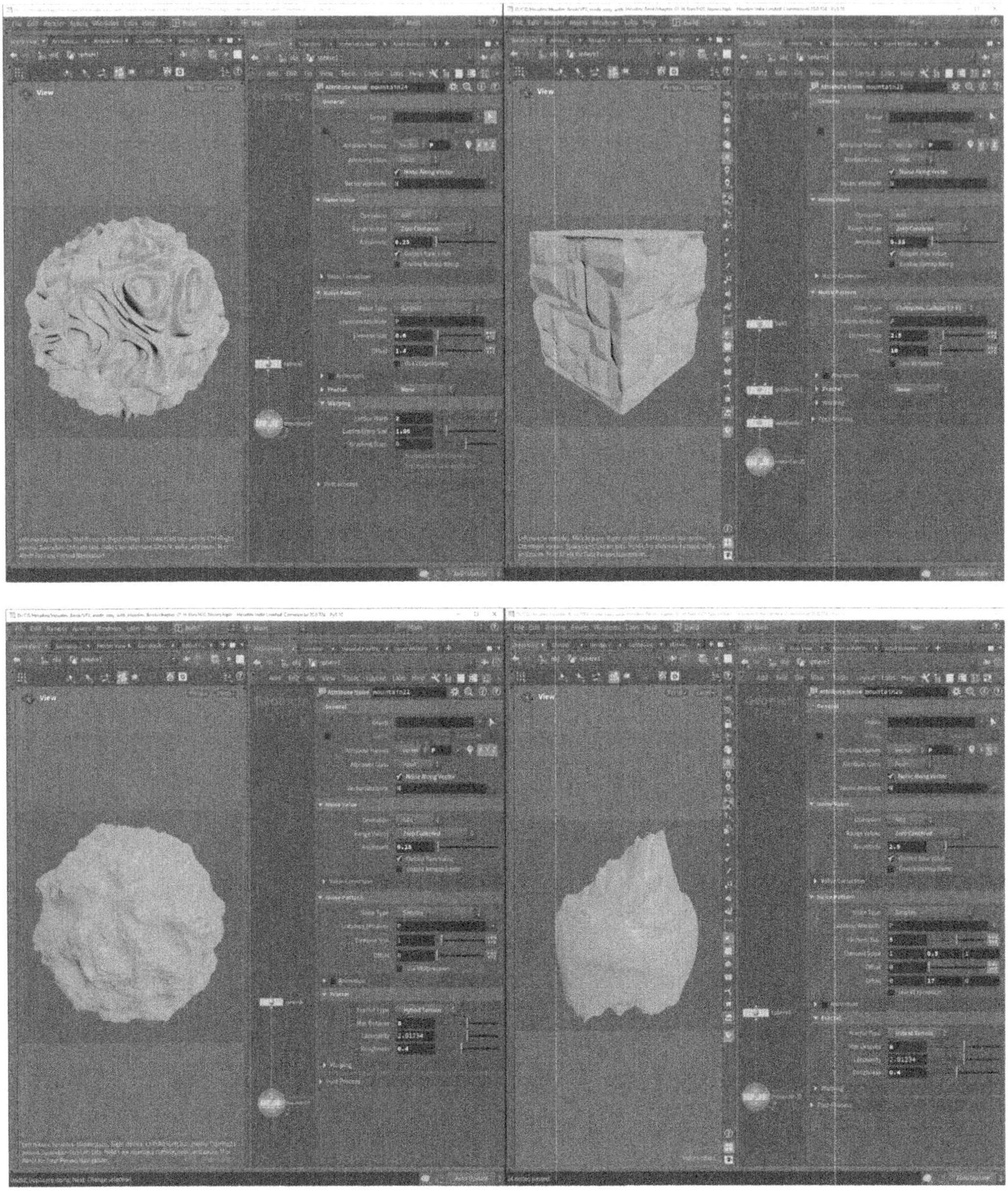

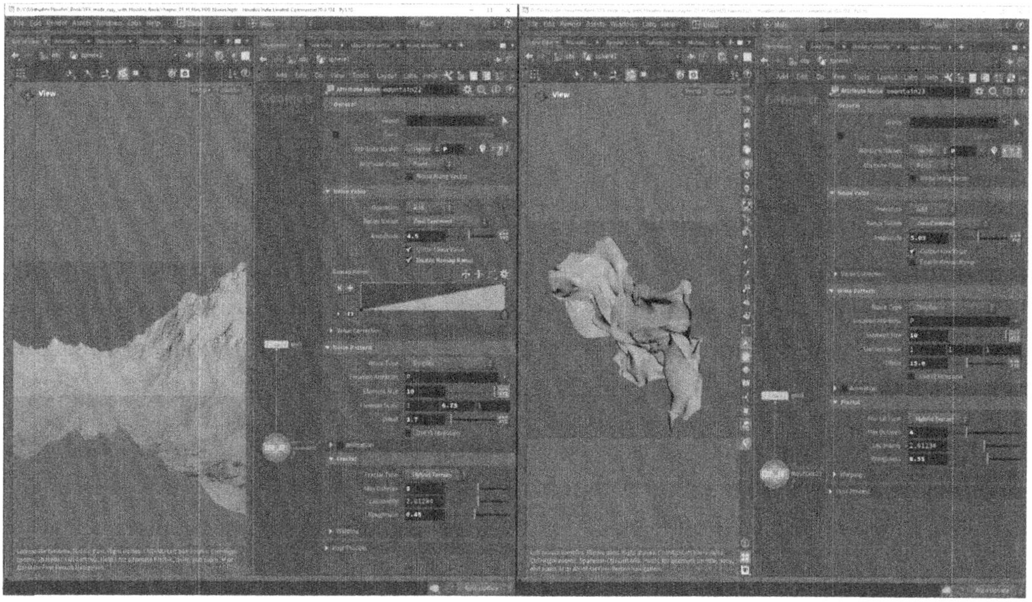

Figure 1.14 – Examples of different noise settings

Quick tip: Need to see a high-resolution version of this image? Open this book in the next-gen Packt Reader or view it in the PDF/ePub copy.

The next-gen Packt Reader and a **free PDF/ePub copy** of this book are included with your purchase. Scan the QR code OR visit `packtpub.com/unlock`, then use the search bar to find this book by name. Double-check the edition shown to make sure you get the right one.

In *Figure 1.14*, you can see the amount of variation you can get by just changing some parameters on the **mountain** node. The key is to have geometry with enough polygons to be able to displace in the highest resolution possible.

I encourage you to go ahead and test some of these parameters and see the level of control you can get. All the shapes use the basic sphere or cube with a high number of polygons, except in the *last two images*, where these shapes have been generated from the input grid geometry.

Modifying the mountain node

Once you have experimented enough and gotten the gist of how the **mountain** node works, you can refer to *Figure 1.15* for mountain settings and start modifying it to achieve a more abstract magical sphere look that we need for our project. We are mainly going to modify **Amplitude** in the **Noise Value** section, as well as **Noise Type** and **Element size** in the **Noise Pattern** section. These two settings are the main drivers of how geometry is going to be displaced.

Secondary settings to control would include checking the **Enable Remap Ramp** checkbox and adding more contracts to the ramp, as well as clicking on the **Animation** checkbox to make the noise change over time. The pulse duration setting in the animation section controls how fast the noise values will change over time. Note that values below 1 will make the noise change faster, whereas values above 1 will make the noise pulse slower. Animated procedural noise can give very convincing results both in geometry motion and simulations.

You can see how the motion changes frame by frame if you click on a specific frame number on the timeline at the bottom of your screen or click the **Play** button on the lower left of the screen.

Figure 1.15 shows the abstract spherical shape and the noise displacement settings:

Figure 1.15 – Adding unique shape noise with the mountain node

Attribute Names

First, I would like to draw your attention to the **Attribute Names** section setting of the **mountain** node. By default, when you create a **mountain** node, it will displace every point on the sphere with 3D noise value applied to the **P** point position attribute.

Attributes play a huge role in Houdini, and we are just scratching the surface of what the attributes can do here. Mainly, attributes allow you to attach additional information to the geometry components within your scene. Attributes provide a flexible and powerful way to control various aspects of how geometry behaves, looks, interacts with forces, and is processed throughout the entire production pipeline.

Some of the most common attribute types are as follows:

- **Vector (3 floats) type**: For example, position (x,y,z) or color (r,g,b)
- **Float type**: For example, **pscale** can only take one-dimensional float value
- **Integer type**: For example, the **id** attribute can hold only integer numbers
- **String type**: It allows you to store and manipulate text data exclusively associated with geometry data or any other elements within your scenes

Some of the very common global attributes that we will be working on in this chapter will be as follows:

- **P**: This refers to *position*
- **Cd**: This refers to *color diffuse*
- **v**: This refers to *velocity*
- **pscale**: This refers to *particle scale*

Important note

Attributes are case-sensitive, so for Houdini to recognize the global attributes you want to create or modify, you need to type the exact name according to upper or lower case. It is also important to set the correct attribute type.

Let's move on to manipulating the sphere position (**P**) attribute with 3D noise.

Shaping the sphere with noise settings

We are back at the original sphere that we have created and now will adjust the mountain settings to get a unique noise and shape.

Let's follow the next steps to make the noise look more abstract:

1. In the **Noise Value** rollout, set **Amplitude** to `0.75` and click the **Enable Remap Ramp** checkbox.
2. Make the ramp like the one in *Figure 1.16* by clicking on endpoints and moving them closer together.
3. In the **Noise Pattern** rollout, set **Noise type** to **Manhattan Cellular F1**.
4. In **Noise Pattern**, set **Element Size** to `0.5`.

Figure 1.16 shows the final noise settings and the result. You can see how our sphere already starts obtaining the shape of the final render provided at the beginning of the chapter.

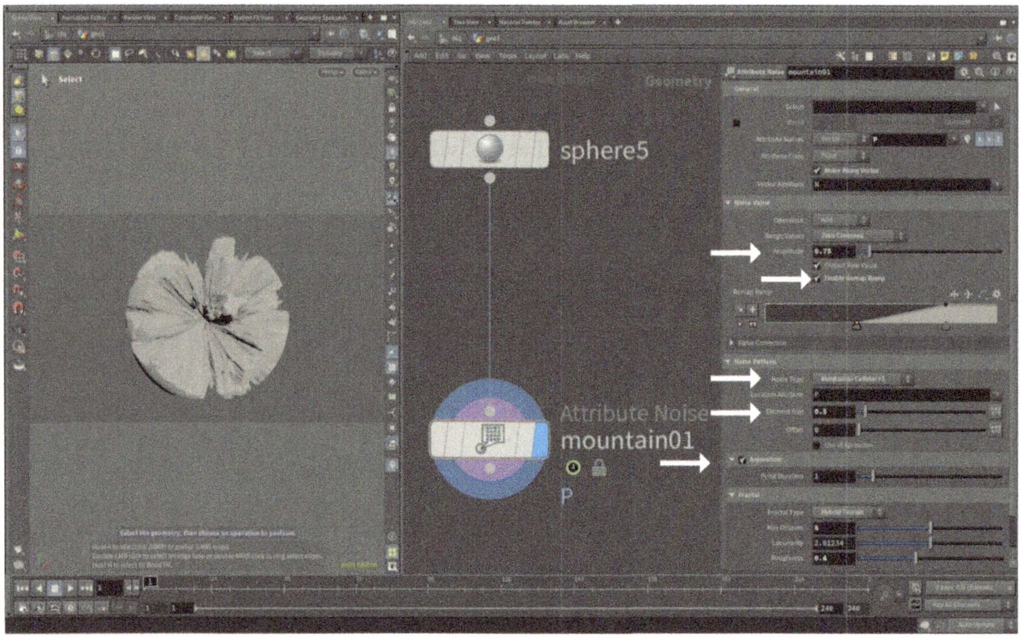

Figure 1.16 – Adding unique shape noise with the mountain node

For the next steps, we are going to calculate the velocity of the noise motion and will use the velocity magnitude to drive the colors, so the faster-moving areas will have a specific color different from slow-moving areas.

Then we are going to convert the polygons to points that will inherit all the attributes created upstream.

For the final steps, we are going to add a **pscale** attribute to the points to have control over how big each particle is going to be. Finally, we are going to add a **retime** node to gain control over the speed of our effect and transition into the rendering context.

Let's go ahead and add a **Point Velocity** node after the **mountain** node:

1. With your mouse over the network view, press *Tab* and type `point velocity` in the search area. After the node appears highlighted in orange, we can place it under the mountain by pressing *Enter* twice.
2. Let's connect the output of the **mountain** node to the input of the **point velocity** node. The **point velocity** node could be used to either compute the **v** attribute from geometry deformation or to create a custom direction or noise-based vector velocity. This node has many options and settings and will be heavily used in this book. For this project, we are only going to use the point velocity node to calculate **v** of the sphere based on its noise deformation.
3. The only options we are going to adjust are setting **Frame sample** to 2 for more accurate computation and setting **Velocity Approximation** to **Central Difference**.

   After **point velocity**, we will be using some of the new **Attribute Adjust** nodes to adjust and modify attributes. One of these nodes is used to modify and adjust vector attributes:

4. Press *Tab* and type `attribute adjust vector`, then press *Enter* twice to place the node after the point velocity. Just like with the **point velocity** node, **Attribute Adjust Vector** has many options and applications. However, currently, we are only going to use one useful function that it provides, which is calculating the length of the velocity vector.
5. Notice that the **Attribute Name** section of **Attribute Adjust Vector** is operating directly on the **v** attribute. The only thing you need to do is to click on the **Length** checkbox in the **Output Attributes** section.

   The **Length** operation will calculate the magnitude or speed of the velocity vector and store it in the dedicated float type length attribute.

In the next section, we will learn how to add color to the 3D object.

Adding color

There are many ways of adding color attributes to geometry and objects in Houdini. However, the most basic method is just placing the **color** node from the **TAB Menu**. *Figure 1.17* shows the steps that we are following:

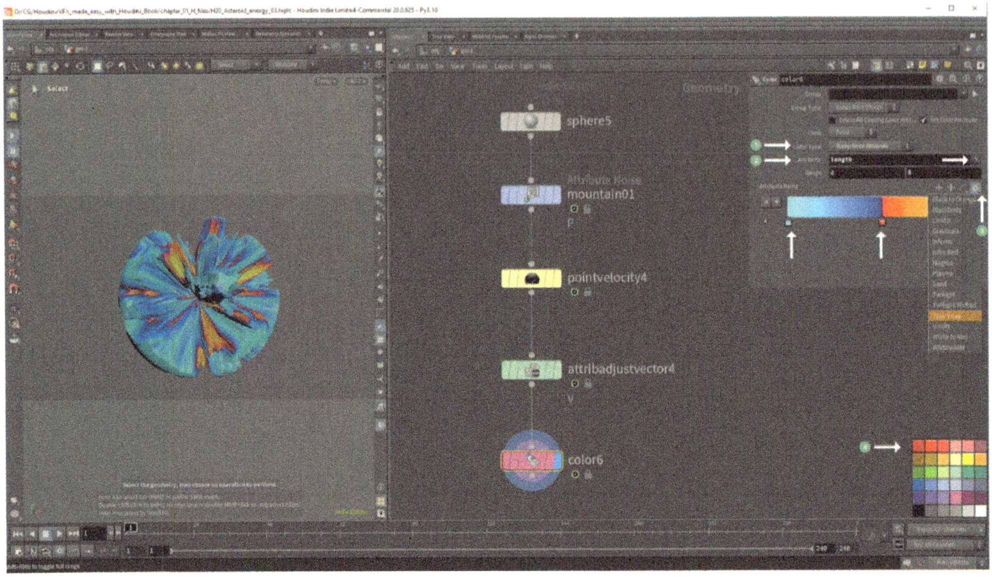

Figure 1.17 – Adding color by velocity

Let's follow these steps to add color to our sphere:

1. Add a **Color** node from the **TAB Menu** and connect it after the last node.
2. Set **Color Type** to **Ramp from Attribute**. This will allow us to use any float attribute and map its values into the color gradient.
3. In the **Attribute** box, you can either type `length` or click on the drop-down button and choose the length as the attribute near the *white arrow*.
4. Click on the **gear** icon, following the arrow in *Step 3*, and you will have access to some of the common color ramp presets. You can also create a completely custom color ramp by double-clicking on the gradient box and choosing the colors from the menu.
5. You can also add custom colors to the nodes, so it is easier to identify them when you have a bigger node tree. With your mouse over the network view, press *C* on the keyboard, and you will see a color palette appear in the bottom-right corner of the network view.

The next big step would be converting the sphere polygons to points. Follow these steps to carry out this task:

1. Press *Tab* and find `Add` node in the search bar.
2. Connect the **Color** node to the **Add** node and click on the **Delete Geometry But Keep The Points** checkbox in the **Points** tab of the **Add** node. This action will keep all the points that contain color, velocity, length, and mountain displacement attributes and delete all the polygons with edges in between.

We can make the points look more organic and interesting by clumping them together. One of the common workflows to add quick clumping to the disconnected points is to blur their position in 3D space. Houdini has just the right node for this action, which is called **Attribute Blur**.

Let's find a node called **Attribute Blur** in the **TAB Menu** and connect it after the **Add** node. **Attribute Blur**, by default, operates on the geometry position **P** attribute. However, you can use this node to blur any other attribute as long as its name is placed into the **Attributes** box correctly.

You are not going to see any change with default settings because the points are disconnected from each other. Therefore, the correct option to blur the position would be to set **Influence Type** to **Proximity**.

Depending on the **Blurring iterations** amount and **Max Neighbors** number, you can get a different look as a result of the blurred position. For this effect, I have set **Blurring Iterations** to 5 and **Max Neighbors** to 25.

Refer to *Figure 1.18* for **Attribute Blur** settings:

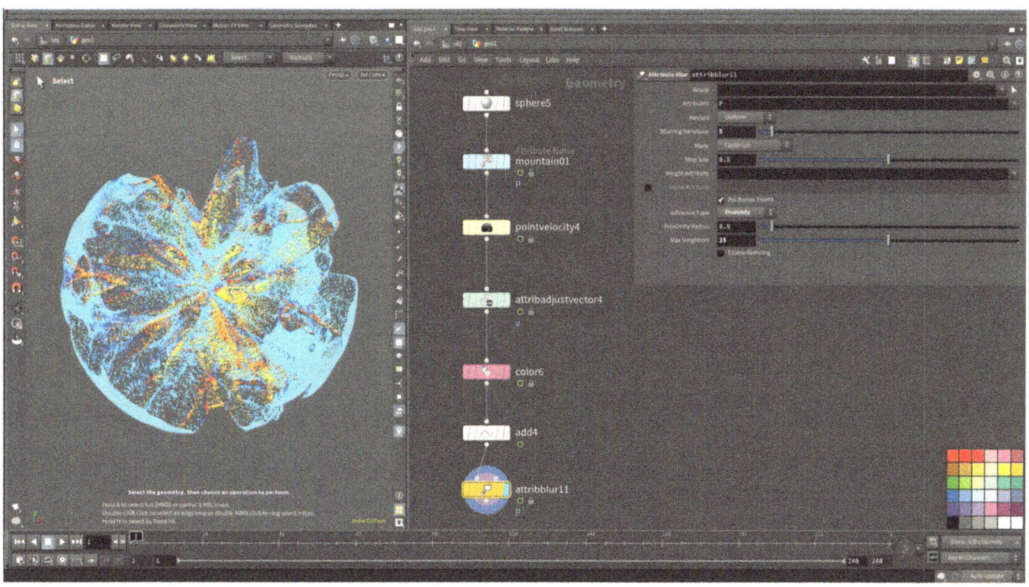

Figure 1.18 – Adding position blur for better clumping

Notice how with every node, we are getting closer to the final result while maintaining control at every level, which is the main power of the procedural workflow. For the next steps, we will mainly focus on creating and manipulating the particle scale attribute and preparing our geometry for rendering.

Using code expressions to create and adjust attributes

Geometry attributes and other parameters can easily be modified with code. You can write simple expressions or full code blocks and functions depending on your coding knowledge and working style.

Let's find the **Attribute Expression** node in the **TAB Menu** and connect it after **Attribute Blur**. The **Attribute Expression** node is used for creating different existing or custom attributes on different parts of geometry.

In this case, since we need to create the particle scale attribute, we have to click on the drop-down menu by the **Attribute Position (P)** section and choose **Scale (pscale)** instead of **P** from the list. Now you need to be able to add values to the newly created **pscale** attribute. However, the **Constant Value** box is grayed out and disabled. In order to enable the **Constant Value** box, you need to click on the **VEXpression** box's drop-down menu and choose **Constant Value**. Alternatively, you can just type `value` in the **VEXpression** box to enable the **Constant Value slider**. You will now notice that we are able to modify **Constant Value** by setting it to a certain number.

VEX is Houdini's high-performance programming language used to control geometry, materials, particles, and more by writing custom logic directly into nodes for faster, more flexible effects.

Usually, the **pscale** attribute is used to define the radius of a particle and, depending on the scene scale, it could have different values. Since our sphere is around 0.5 meters by default primitive settings, we can have the particle scale at least 100 times smaller to achieve good-looking results. This means that in the **Constant Value** box, you can set **pscale** to 0.5/100, which will be `0.005`.

Additionally, you can create a little expression where the particle scale will be further multiplied by the length of the velocity in a certain range. Houdini has a set of nodes called **wrangles** that allow the user to type code in big or small snippets to get even more control over the attribute manipulation.

Search for the **Attribute Wrangle** node in the **TAB Menu** and connect it after the **Attribute Expression** node. Then, in the **VEXpression** section, type the following code:

```
@pscale *= fit(@length, 0, 1, 0.75, 1.25);
```

Now, I'm going to break down this code for you:

- `@pscale`: This means that we are calling the **pscale** attribute into the code expression and multiplying it by the result of the following function.
- `fit`: This is a function that will take a float attribute or variable in a specific input range of values and remap this attribute or variable to the new output range of values.
- `@length`: In our case, the `fit` function takes the length attribute (that we calculated from velocity) by calling it `@length` and sets the input and output range values.

Quick tip: Enhance your coding experience with the **AI Code Explainer** and **Quick Copy** features. Open this book in the next-gen Packt Reader. Click the **Copy** button

(1) to quickly copy code into your coding environment, or click the **Explain** button

(2) to get the AI assistant to explain a block of code to you.

The next-gen Packt Reader is included for free with the purchase of this book. Scan the QR code OR go to `packtpub.com/unlock`, then use the search bar to find this book by name. Double-check the edition shown to make sure you get the right one.

By typing `0, 1` after `@length`, we are setting the minimum and maximum input values for the velocity length and then remapping those values to become `0.75` as the new minimum and `1.25` as the new maximum.

In other words, when the velocity is `0`, we reduce the **pscale** by multiplying it by `0.75`. When the velocity is `1` or higher, we increase the **pscale** by multiplying it by `1.25`.

Figure 1.19 shows the **Attribute Wrangle** code in the **VEXpression** section:

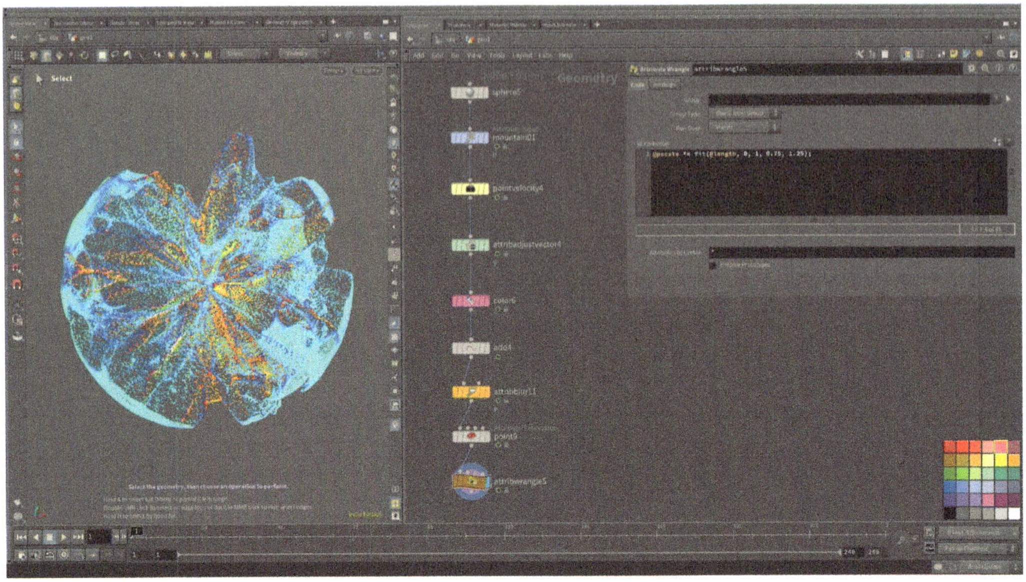

Figure 1.19 – Setting up the particle scale with the pscale attribute

Congratulations on writing your first line of code in Houdini's VEX coding language! This technique will be commonly used throughout the book in multiple scenarios and examples. So, it will become clearer after we use it a couple of times.

Motion retiming

We are at the final steps of the effect creation and will add one more node to our setup. This node will help us to speed up or slow down the motion of the effect.

Follow these steps to add the node to our setup:

1. Add the **Retime** node through the **TAB Menu** and add it to the end of the network tree. The **Retime** node has multiple options to time shift, or adjust the speed of incoming motion in a specific frame range.
2. Set **Input Frame Range** to be the same as **Output Frame Range** and change the **Interpolation** method to **Subdivision**, which is the most accurate.
3. After setting all these base settings, you can now adjust the **Speed** parameter to make the motion faster or slower. I have set my speed value to `0.25` since I wanted the effect to progress more slowly. You can see how the motion changes frame by frame if you click on a specific frame number on the timeline at the bottom of your screen or press the **Play** button on the animation timeline in the lower left of the screen.

Now that we know how to add the **Retime** node, we will learn how to create viewport flipbooks in the next section.

Creating viewport flipbooks

Before we get to the rendering stage, it is always a good idea to make a quick **flipbook preview** (see the *white arrow* in *Figure 1.20*) of the effect to see whether everything behaves correctly. Once the flipbook starts, you can play the effect in real time and see whether you would like to further adjust the speed, colors, or noise values.

Figure 1.20 shows the full effect node tree and the **Retime** node parameters:

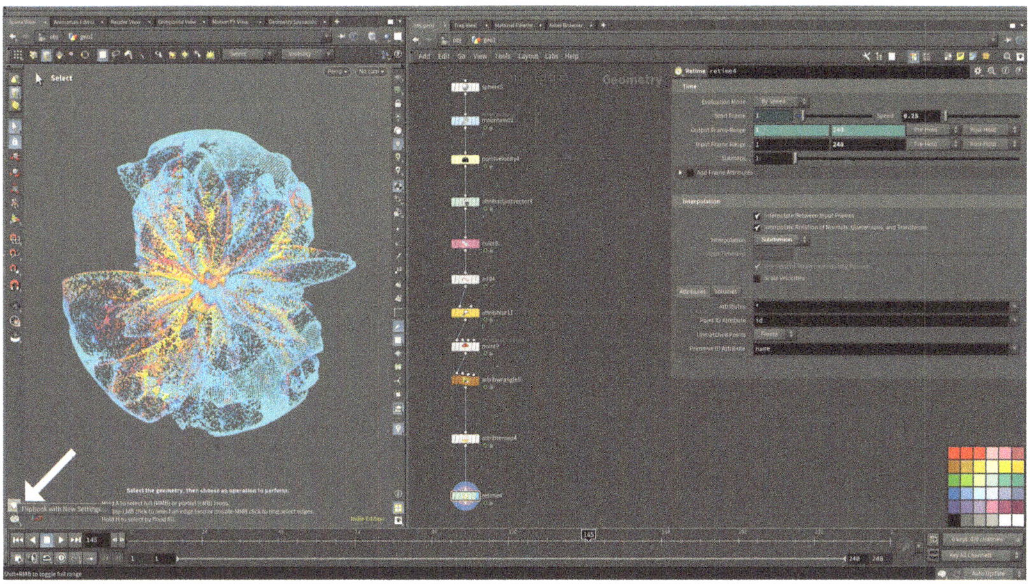

Figure 1.20 – Retiming the speed of the magic sphere effect

Otherwise, if you are happy with the look, then find the **Output** node in the **TAB Menu** and place it as the final node of your setup.

I recommend renaming the **Output** node `OUT_magic_sphere_for_render`. You can rename any node by clicking on its original name once, and it will become editable.

Let's save the file and move to the next stage!

Lighting and rendering

You have made it! We are now ready to move to a different stage of our first project in Houdini: the rendering stage. I will be using the new **Houdini Solaris stage** context for lighting, shading, and rendering.

We will jump between the **obj** and **stage** contexts during the lighting and rendering processes. The easiest way to access the **Solaris** environment is to use **Tree View** or the hierarchy view, which is accessible by pressing *Shift* + *W*.

Click on the **stage** icon that is in the hierarchy view of your node network. Refer to *Figure 1.21* for jumping from **obj** to the **stage** context:

Figure 1.21 – Switching to the stage context

You will notice that we are no longer at the **Geometry** level. Instead, the top-right corner of the network view is named **Solaris**.

Also, our particle sphere has disappeared from the viewport since it only exists at the **Geometry** level and we need to import it back into the **Solaris** level. Follow these steps to carry out this task:

1. Press *Tab*, type `sop import` in the search box, and press *Enter* twice to place the **SOP Import** node into the scene. The **SOP Import** node is used to bring any geometry from the **obj** context to the **Solaris** level.

2. You can bring the sphere particles if you provide the path to the **Output** node that we have created at the **Geometry** level. A very easy way to get the path of any node into **SOP Import** is to select the node from the hierarchy view and drag it into the path box.
3. Select **OUT_magic_sphere** located under **sphere_object1** in the hierarchy view.
4. Click and hold the *left mouse button* on the selection and drag it to the **SOP Path** box of the **SOP Import** node.

Figure 1.22 shows the result of linking the sphere particles into **Solaris** from the **obj** context:

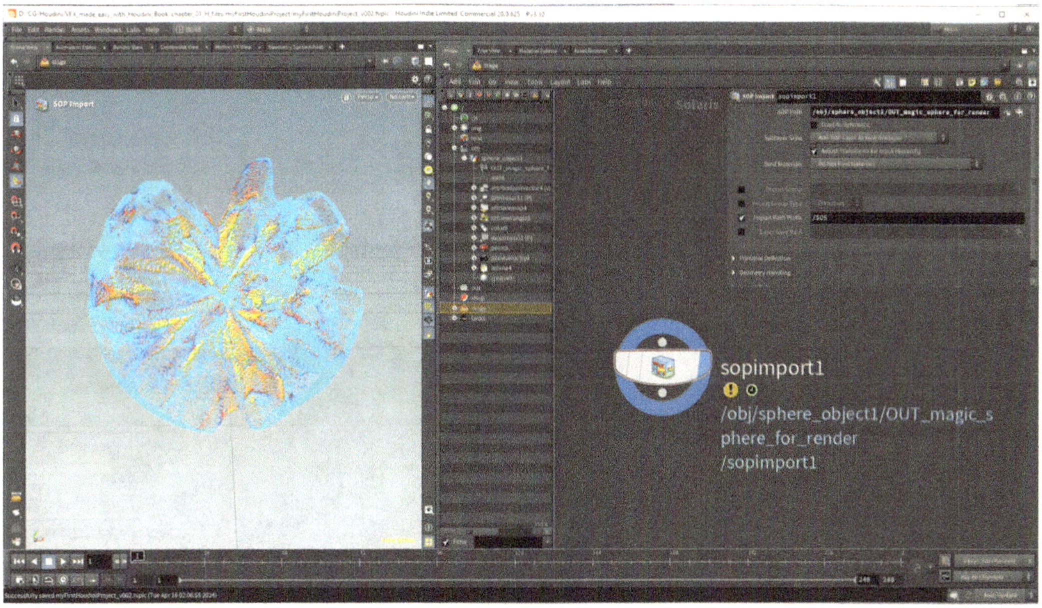

Figure 1.22 – Importing geometry from obj into stage

Next, we'll be moving on to creating lights and adding a rendering camera to our scene.

Adding lights and cameras

The next step would be to create a light source and a camera for the scene. Follow these steps to add a light source and a camera to the scene:

1. Find the **Light** node in the **TAB Menu** and connect it to the output of the **sopimport1** node.

   Set the light type to **Sphere**, the **Exposure** parameter to `15`, and the **Radius** parameter to `0.05`. To achieve strong volumetric rays coming from the sphere, the key is to have a very small light shape with a very high power.

2. Additionally, you can set the light to any color you like.
3. Let's create our first camera by searching for `camera` in the **TAB Menu**, and connecting it to the output of the **light1** node.
4. You can then adjust the camera position if you click on the **lock** icon in the **Display** panel in the right corner of the viewport and use viewport navigation to position the camera framing the effect. Don't forget to turn the **lock** icon back off (follow the *white arrow* in *Figure 1.21*) after you are happy with the camera adjustments.

Figure 1.23 shows the result of adding a camera and light to our scene:

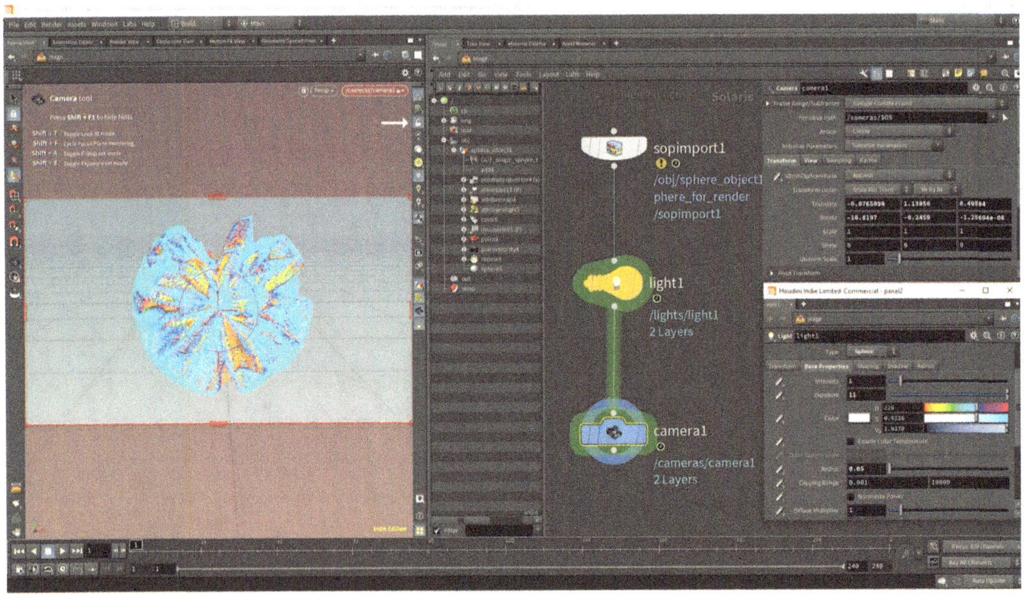

Figure 1.23 – Adding lights and cameras

Now we'll move on to adding the volumetric fog effect.

Increasing realism with volumetric fog

To achieve the volumetric light rays effect coming through the particles, we will need a uniform volume, with density covering the area around the sphere:

1. Search for the `karma fog box` node in the **TAB Menu** and place it next in the network chain.
2. Set the fog's **Shape** value to **Sphere** and increase the **Uniform Scale** value to `10`.

Refer to the parameters in *Figure 1.24* for the volumetric fog effect:

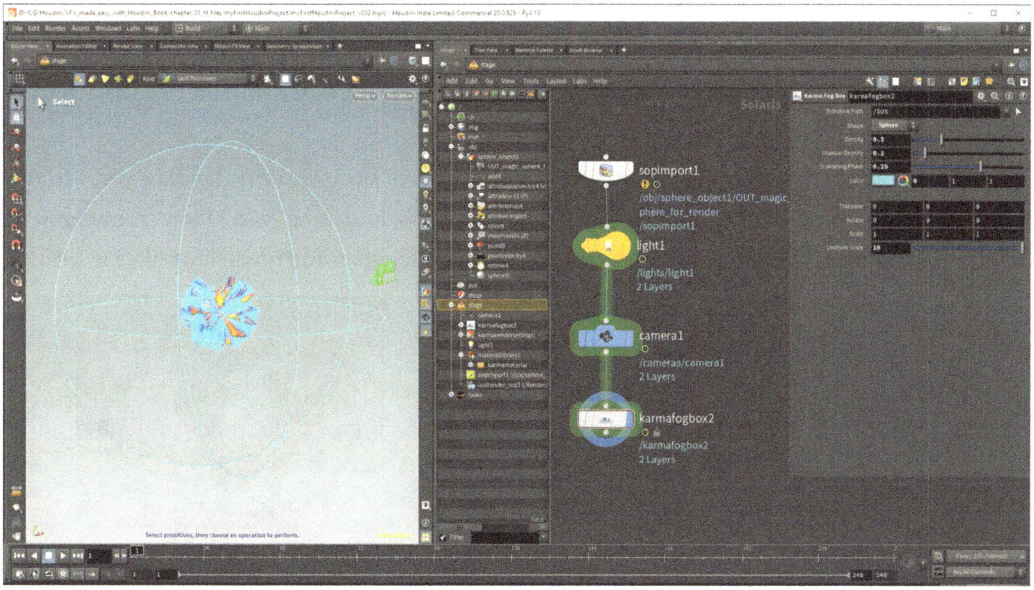

Figure 1.24 – Setting up volumetric fog

Adding render engine and fine-tuning settings

Finally, let's place the main engine that will combine all the elements and nodes together into a rendered image. Follow these steps to carry out this task:

1. Search for the `karma` node in the **TAB Menu** and place connect it after the **Karma Fog Box** node. You will notice that the **Karma** render engine will come as two connected nodes, one for render settings and another for saving the images to the disk.
2. In the **Karma Render Settings** node, I recommend setting **Rendering Engine** to **XPU**, since it will utilize both the power of your CPU and GPU for rendering. You will notice significantly faster renders in the **XPU** mode, especially if you have a fast video card. If you are facing any artifacts or slowdowns with the **XPU** engine, use the **CPU**-only engine.
3. The **XPU** engine works with unified global path-traced samples that, by default, are set to 128. The basic rule is the more samples the more quality renders, the slower the rendering times become. Since our scene isn't very heavy, you can set **Path Trace Samples** to 256 to clean up the image noise and get a smoother result.

4. Additionally, you can set the samples to a lower amount of 64 and utilize the **Denoiser** in the **Image Output**'s **Filters** tab to get a good balance of render speed vs. quality.
5. Since we have computed the velocity **v** attribute, it can be used to achieve realistic motion blur. In the **Karma Render Settings | Camera effects** tab, make sure that **Velocity Blur** is set to the **Velocity Blur** option.
6. We are finally ready to make our first render! Make sure your display flag is set to the **karmarendersettings** node, go to the viewport top, and change the view from **Persp** to **Karma XPU**. The viewport will now become a render view and it will look like *Figure 1.25*:

Figure 1.25 – Rendering the final result

Congratulations on your first render and completed project in Houdini for this chapter!

Summary

As we conclude this chapter, you should now have a foundational understanding of Houdini's unique and powerful workspace. We began by exploring the overall layout, delving into each primary component that you'll interact with daily. The network pane, as the heart of Houdini's procedural workflow, was introduced, illustrating how nodes serve as building blocks for complex 3D scenes.

We navigated through the viewport, mastering the basic controls essential for viewing and manipulating your 3D models. We explored the parameters pane and network view and fine-tuned the properties of each node to achieve a specific look in the project.

We also covered the fundamentals of scene management, ensuring you know how to create, save, and organize your projects efficiently.

Lastly, we utilized all the fundamental tools and knowledge in your first rendered image out of Houdini.

With these essential elements in hand, you are well-equipped to navigate Houdini's interface with confidence. This foundational knowledge will support your journey as you dive deeper into the software's advanced capabilities.

The next chapters will build on this groundwork, guiding you through more complex tasks and unlocking the full potential of Houdini's procedural approach to 3D creation. Continue exploring, experimenting, and creating – your adventure with Houdini has just begun.

2

Demystifying Procedural Modeling

In this chapter, you will learn how to use a variation of **procedural modeling tools** and will create an interesting architectural and organic structure.

Modeling in Houdini might feel different than modeling in other 3D software; however, the procedural modeling tools are very powerful and can create complex geometry structures that are easy to control and edit in a non-destructible way.

In this chapter, we will cover the following main topics:

- Modeling with custom-drawn curve tools
- Exploring procedural groups and poly modeling tools
- Aligning 3D objects and elements together
- Utilizing subnetworks of nodes
- Modeling using **Copy** node tools
- Using Boolean tools for extra detailing and cutting holes
- Organic modeling using volume tools
- Rendering and presenting your model

By the end of this chapter, you will be able to combine the variety of modeling tools learned and create your own custom architectural and organic 3D model, as shown in *Figure 2.1*:

Figure 2.1 – Procedural Greek rotunda temple on a procedural rock

Whenever you are starting a new project, it is always a good idea to gather some sources of inspiration, reference images, and mood boards.

The main inspiration for this project was elements of ancient architecture such as pillars, pedestals, rotundas, and even small Parthenon-like temples, mainly from a Google image search. You can use the provided techniques to build many different procedural elements of interior or exterior architecture, as well as complex organic shapes such as rocks and mountains.

Technical requirements

You will have access to the Houdini file with the completed effect on the GitHub link at `https://github.com/PacktPublishing/VFX-Made-Easy-with-Houdini`. You can keep the file open while you follow along with the steps and build everything in the scene, or use it to study the node network in detail.

For this chapter, I will be using **Houdini 20** for modeling and **Houdini 20.5** for rendering the 3D models.

To view the chapter images in better clarity, scan the provided QR code. It will direct you to a dedicated link where you can take a look at the images.

In every chapter, we will start by creating a new project, the same way we did in the first chapter. To streamline the process and avoid repeating the steps in every chapter, I will instead ask you to create a new project with a specific name and continue with a Houdini file saved in the project directory.

Create a new project and name it `procedural_modeling`, then save the empty Houdini file in the root project directory as `procedural_modeling_v001`.

Modeling with custom-drawn curve tools

After creating the Houdini file, for the next steps in our procedural modeling journey, we are going to start creating the upper and lower base of a procedural pillar:

1. Press *Tab* in the network view and create a geometry container.
2. Double-click on the geometry container to get into **Geometry** | **SOP** level.
3. Press *Tab* and type `curve bezier` in the search bar to place a **Curve** node that has the option to produce rounded corners.
4. Select the **Curve** node and, with the display flag enabled, and press *Enter* to go into **Interactive draw** | **Create** mode.
5. Put your mouse into the viewport and press *Spacebar* + *4* to get into the orthographic front view so it is easier to draw the object profile.

While in **Interactive draw** mode, you will see some useful shortcuts and hints on the left side of the viewport.

I also recommend turning on grid snapping by clicking on the **red magnet** icon. With this workflow, you usually start by clicking at **0,0** to put your first point and then draw the profile shape by placing points one by one and then closing the shape by placing the last point aligned with the first one in a parallel axis.

While holding the *Shift* key, you can keep the curve to snap to either a 90-degree angle or a 45-degree angle. Using the preceding steps, go ahead and draw the profile shape, as shown in *Figure 2.2*:

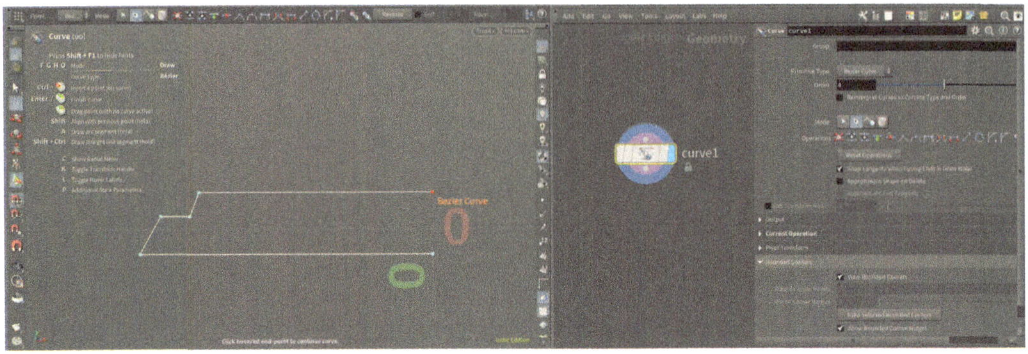

Figure 2.2 – Creating curve profile

After creating this main sharp profile, press *F* to enter **Edit** mode. In the **Edit** mode, you can adjust the positions of drawn points, rearrange them, and even make corners curved.

Select each point that you would like to have a round corner and adjust the **Round Corner Radius** parameter for those points, as shown in *Figure 2.3*. You can select multiple points at the same time by holding *Shift* and clicking on each of the points.

In *Figure 2.3*, you can see how the corner edges will look when you make them rounded and smooth:

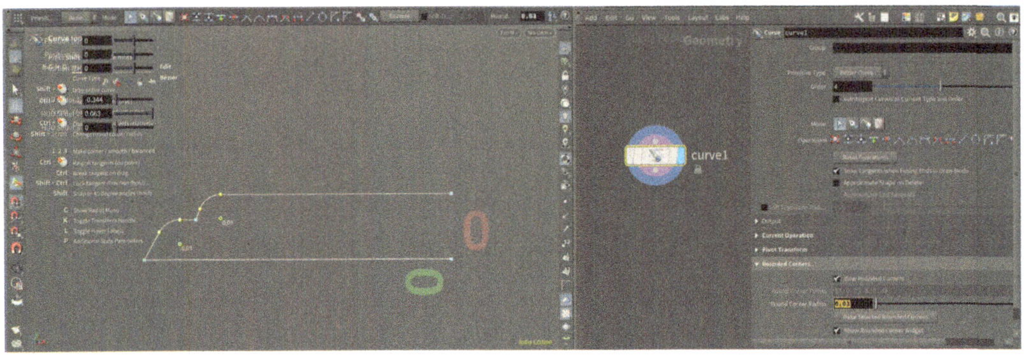

Figure 2.3 – Smoothing curve edges

Now, after successfully creating the profile shape we are ready to make a 3D object with the next magic node called **Revolve**.

Converting 2D profiles to 3D geometry using the Revolve node

The main benefit of curve modeling tools is that you can draw any 2D profile shape, and then with the help of a **Revolve** node, you can turn it into a full 3D enclosed shape with nice topology and UV coordinates.

For the next steps, you are going to switch back to the 3D perspective viewport from orthographic and convert the 2D shape into a 3D object with the help of the **Revolve** node (see *Figure 2.4*):

1. Press *Spacebar+ 1* to switch to the perspective view.
2. Press *Tab*, search for `Revolve` node and connect it after the **Curve** node.
3. Adjust divisions on the **Revolve** node to 64 to get a more detailed mesh.
4. Press *Tab* and add a **Convert** node to convert the curve surface into polygons.
5. The **U** and **V** settings on the **Convert** node will define the resolution of the generated mesh. For optimal quality, click on the **Divisions per Span** tab.

Figure 2.4 shows how the curve profile is going to look when converted into 3D geometry using the **Revolve** node:

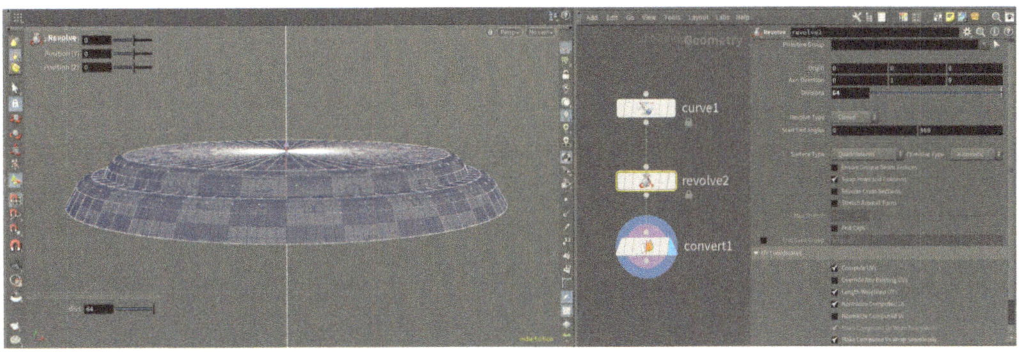

Figure 2.4 – Revolving into polygons

Congratulations, you have just created your first procedural model that can be used as the base for the pillars, and if turned upside down it can be used as the top connector. Since everything is procedural, you can always go back to the first **Curve** node and adjust or add points of the shape and all the nodes down the chain will update nondestructively.

If the polygons are *purple* instead of *gray*, you can use the **Reverse Cross Section** checkbox to invert their orientation.

You may also notice the *checker pattern* on the polygons after the **Revolve** node. This pattern represents the texture coordinates, also called the UV coordinates, that are used in the texturing process and applying image-based maps for shading.

Some geometry creation nodes, such as **Revolve**, will create automatic UV; however, in many cases, the user will have to use specific tools such as **UV Texture**, **UV Project**, and **Labs Auto UV** to create the texture coordinates.

The more complex your 3D model is, in terms of details and shapes, the more complex the UV generation process will be.

Now, after creating our first procedural pillar base, we are ready to start creating all the other elements of the pillar asset and rotunda.

Creating other architectural elements

Now by using the same technique, let's create some more profiles of the objects that we can use. You don't have to follow the shape design exactly; feel free to find a reference of some interesting architectural element that can use a simple shape as a profile and get revolved around to create a 3D surface. The screenshot shown in *Figure 2.5* is for extra reference.

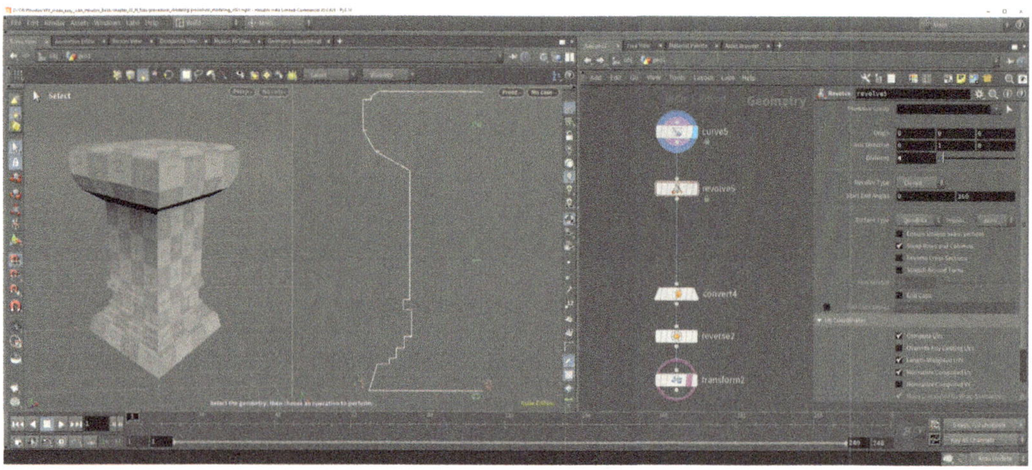

Figure 2.5 – Extra assets technique

You can also combine sharp and round curve points to achieve more complexity in the profile and get a more interesting and detailed mesh in the end. Some of the benefits of the **procedural revolve technique** is that you can go back and start making changes to the curve points and see the live update on the revolved 3D mesh.

Two of the other useful features found in the parameters of the **Revolve** node are **Reverse Cross Sections** and **End Caps**. The **Reverse Cross Sections** checkbox makes sure the created polygons are oriented in the correct way that can affect the shading. On the other hand, the **End Caps** checkbox makes sure that there are no open holes in the generated mesh.

In the screenshot shown in *Figure 2.6*, you can see that I am reverse-orienting the polygons in a separate node called **Reverse**, which can be useful if the mesh generation node does not provide a checkbox for changing polygon orientation.

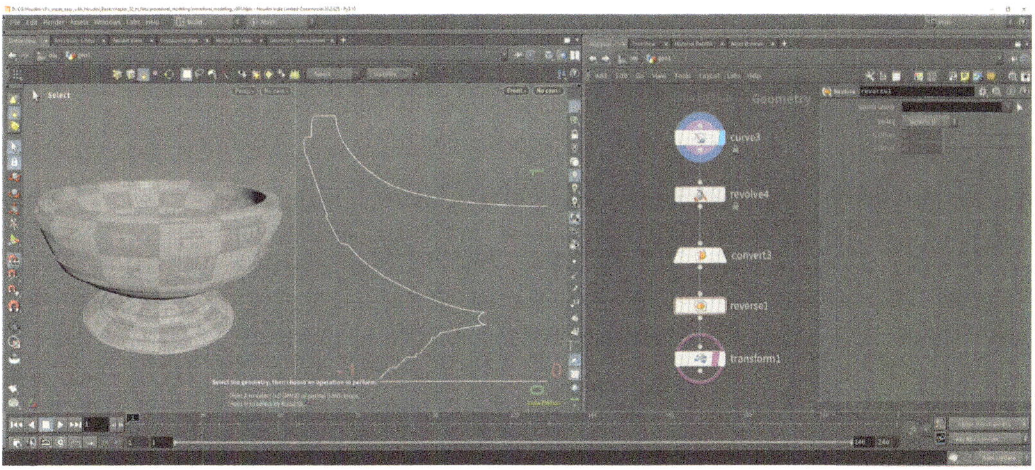

Figure 2.6 – Creating the central altar asset

Advanced techniques and tips

Another useful technique, especially with the **Curve** and **Revolve** modeling workflow, is setting a **profile reference image** in the background to follow the shapes more efficiently.

For this workflow, it is recommended that you split your viewport into two views, one of which is an orthographic flat view of the front, the side, or the top, and the other half is the 3D perspective view.

In order to achieve this, you can either press *Ctrl + 2* or put your mouse in the top-right corner of the viewport where the **white window** icon is located, click on the icon, and choose one of the splitting modes, as shown in *Figure 2.7*:

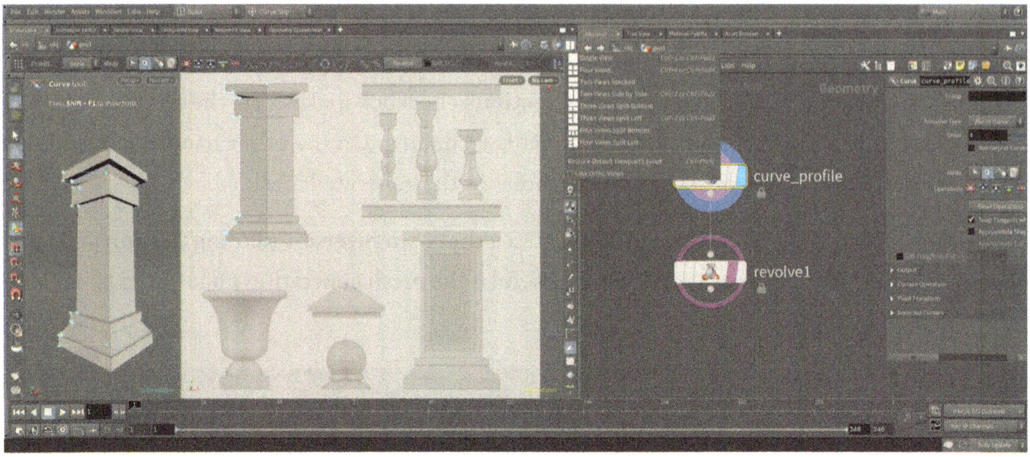

Figure 2.7 – Setting up viewport references

You can also split your viewport into three or four sections by pressing *Ctrl + 3* or *Ctrl + 4*, respectively. If you would like to go back to the single view, you can press *Ctrl + 1*.

Once you have split your viewport into desirable sections, you can set each section to a specific view by putting your mouse over that view and following these shortcuts:

- *Spacebar + 1* for 3D perspective view
- *Spacebar + 2* for top view
- *Spacebar + 3* for front view
- *Spacebar + 4* for right-side view

In *Figure 2.7*, I have set my right side to be **3D Perspective** and my left side to be **Front View**.

For the next step, you can import a background image from the internet of an object shape that you want to follow with the **Curve** tool. By following the steps below, we will prepare the viewports to use background image as a guide for modeling.

1. Put your mouse over the **Front View** side.
2. Press *D* on your keyboard to load **Display Options**.
3. Navigate to the **Background** tab of the **Display Options**.
4. In the **Disc File** empty box, choose the image blueprint file that you have on your computer.

5. Adjust the **Image Offset, Image Scale, Opacity**, and **Brightness**, by using the settings in the **Display Options**.
6. Close **Display Options** and start following the blueprint using the **Curve** tool.

Figure 2.8 shows the reference visibility settings as follows:

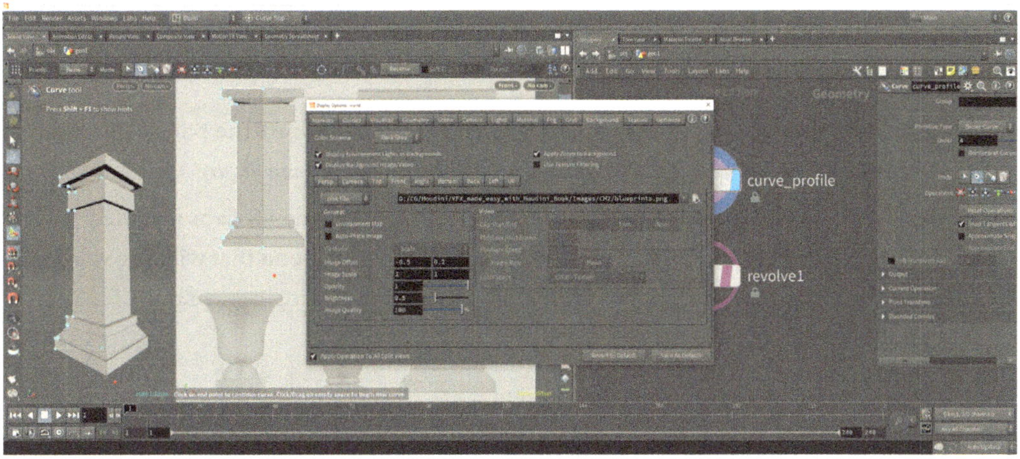

Figure 2.8 – Reference visibility settings

By using all the techniques involving the **Curve** tool, you can create some assets that will be copied and placed around the bigger scene of the 3D environment that we are creating.

All the assets shown in *Figure 2.9*, except for the yellow pillar were created using just the **Curve** and **Revolve** tool combination. We will create the middle part of the pillar using polygon modeling and procedural groups.

Figure 2.9 – 3D asset elements

After you create enough assets and variations using curve modeling tools, we can transition to using groups and polygonal modeling nodes.

Exploring procedural groups and poly modeling tools

The next couple of assets we are going to build by using the combination of groups and poly modeling nodes such as **Extrude**, **Bevel**, and **Polyfill**.

Let's start by building the central part of the pillar. When building cylindrical structures from primitives, you can use the following methods:

- Start with a **Tube (Polygons)** from the **TAB Menu** and adjust the parameters so that **Radius** is `0.5`, **Height** is `8.5`, **Rows** is 2, and **Columns** is 32 (see *Figure 2.10*)
- Start with a **Labs Cylinder Generator** (you need to have **Side FX Labs** installed for this; see the *Technical requirements* section in *Chapter 1*) for **TAB Menu** that will give you access to many settings that a simple **Tube** doesn't have, including curve ramps for specific cylinder profile shapes

Figure 2.10 shows the settings you need to follow:

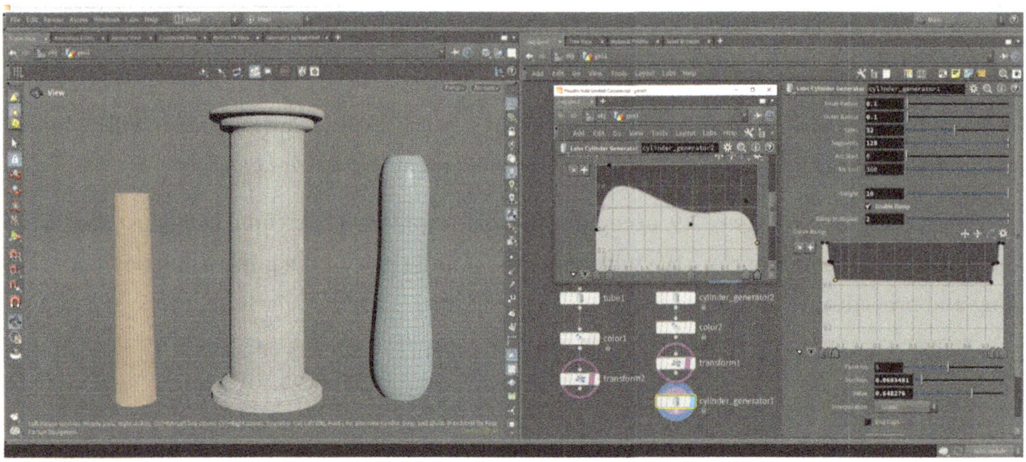

Figure 2.10 – Polygonal modeling

The brown pillar cylinder in *Figure 2.10* is created from a simple **Tube** and the other two pillars were created from the **Labs Cylinder Generator** node. Depending on the design of your pillars or the complexity you need in the side profile, you can choose any of the methods mentioned before.

For the purpose of our project, I am going to proceed with the simple **Tube** pillar since I don't need the top or bottom details or curvature as these elements were already created as separate parts.

For the next steps I am going to group every other row of polygons and extrude them in a way that will create inserted details (see *Figure 2.11*):

1. Press *Tab*, search for `group by range` node, and connect it after the **tube1** node.
2. In the **Group by Range** node, navigate to **Range Filter** and set **Select** to 1 and **of** to 2. This will create a procedural group selecting every other row of polygons and assign them a name of `group1`.

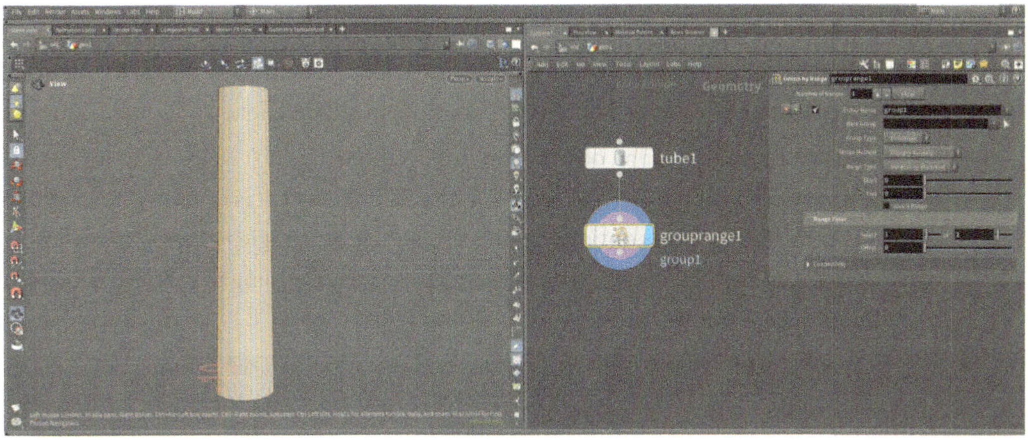

Figure 2.11 – Grouping by range

3. Use the **TAB Menu** to connect **PolyExtrude** node after the **grouprange1**.
4. In the empty **Group** box of the **PolyExtrude** node, type `group1` and use the **Distance** and **Inset** sliders to adjust the depth of the extrusion (see *Figure 2.12*).

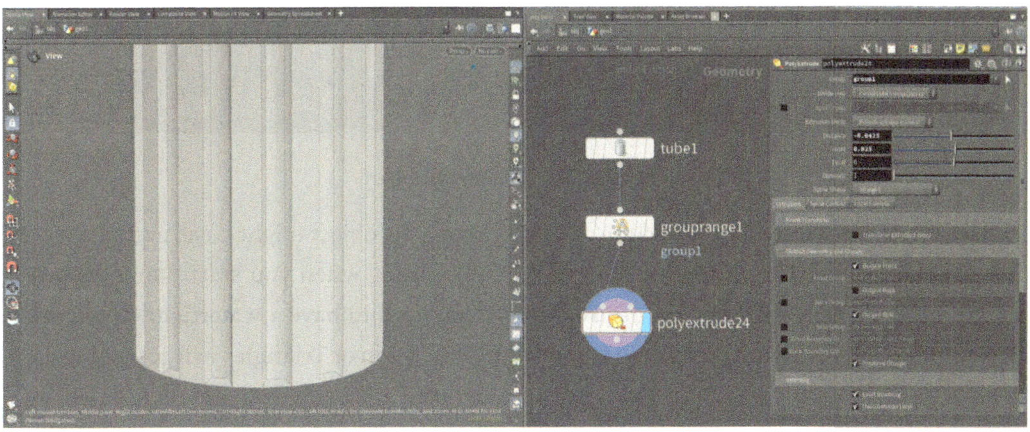

Figure 2.12 – Extruding and insetting polygons

You could add additional detail to this simple angular pillar model by beveling the edges. **Bevel** is an important step during both procedural and non-procedural modeling that can add angular details to the sharp edges and make the model look much more realistic, especially during the shading and rendering, since the beveled edges would catch nice highlights from the light source.

Now, let's connect a **PolyBevel** node after the **Poly Extrude** node and adjust the three important settings as follows (see *Figure 2.13*):

- **Offsetting rollout**: We use the **Distance** option to define the amount of bevel.
- **Fillet rollout**: We use the **Shape** and **Divisions** options to define the shape of the bevel and extra polygons to be added for either curvature or subdivision.
- **Exclusions rollout**: This is one of the most important settings. It helps us to only bevel the edges that fall within a certain angle. For procedural bevel, it is usually very useful to check the **Ignore Flat Edges** option and use a relatively low angle to only capture edges with extruded or inserted details. Otherwise, all the edges are going to get beveled, which we definitely don't want.

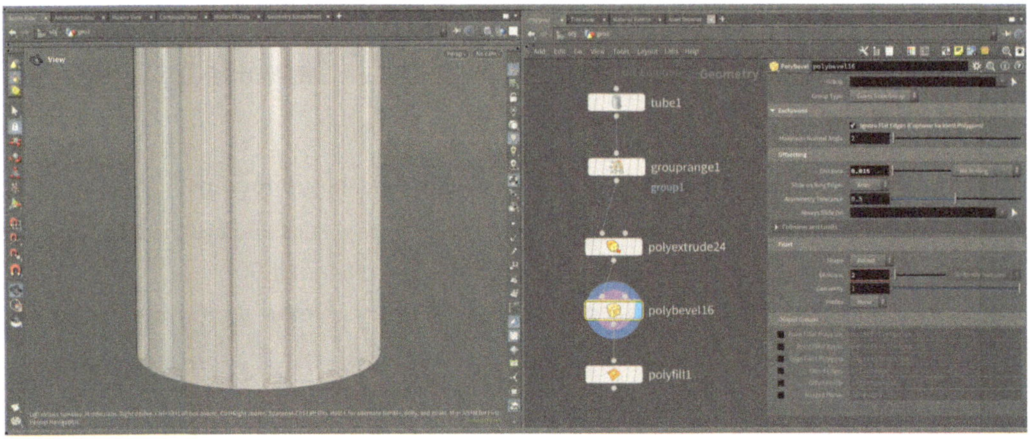

Figure 2.13 – Beveling the edges

Finally, it is always a good idea to close any holes that a 3D object might have, even if they are not directly visible. This workflow is especially important when you start doing geometry fracturing, collision generation, or destruction, which need to have a watertight closed mesh. Adding a **PolyFill** node with the **Fill** mode set to **Single Polygon** or **Triangles** will get the job done.

We should now have the pillar base and capital elements built with curve modeling tools, as well as the central pillar built with poly modeling tools. Now, it is time to align and combine them into a completed pillar asset.

Aligning 3D objects and elements together

In this section, we'll bring together the pillar elements: the bottom and top built using the **Curve** and **Revolve** tools and the pillar middle column built with poly modeling. So far, you should have the elements, as shown in *Figure 2.14*:

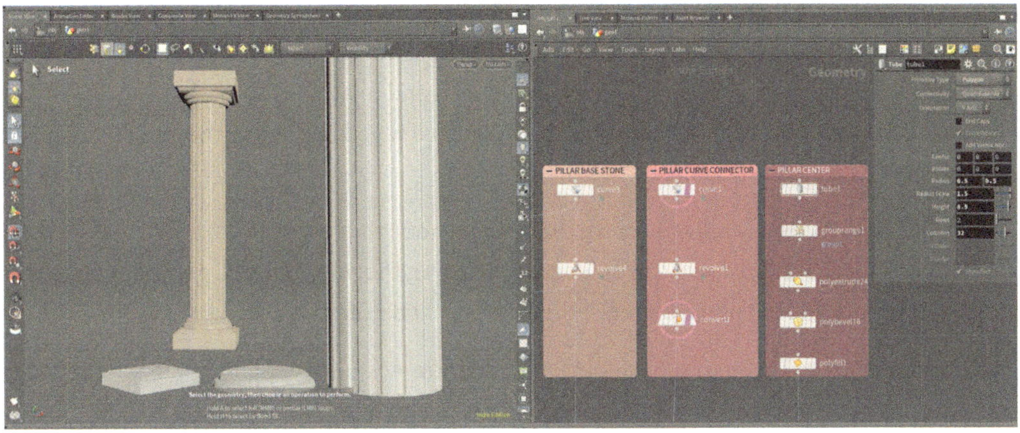

Figure 2.14 – Pillar separate elements

The elements that we have are *gray*, and the final result that is a combination of the elements is *light brown*. Also notice that the scale isn't exactly correct on all the elements, which is fine and can be fixed very easily with a **Transform** node, as we will see later.

For the next steps, we are going to carry out the following tasks:

1. Add **Bevel** to the **BASE STONE**.
2. Scale up and rotate the **BASE STONE**.
3. Align the **PILLAR CURVE CONNECTOR** on top of the **BASE STONE**.
4. Scale the **BASE STONE**and **PILLAR CURVE CONNECTOR** to be bigger than the **PILLAR CENTER** radius.
5. Transform the **BASE STONE**and **PILLAR CURVE CONNECTOR** (I will be calling this **PILLAR BASE** from now on) upside down as a copy.
6. Align the upside-down **PILLAR BASE** copy on top of the pillar.
7. Align the **PILLAR CENTER** combined with **PILLAR CURVE CONNECTOR** on top of the **PILLAR BASE** bottom.

This may look like a lot of steps; however, it is a part of the procedural workflow and will let us have control over each element and section and change them dynamically while having the final assembled pillar update non-destructively.

Now, follow these steps to complete the pillar:

1. Let's place the **PolyBevel** node after the **Revolve** node and give the edges of the pillar base some **Offsetting Distance** of `0.005` while checking the **Ignore Flat Edges** option. You will notice that the stone base shading has changed and looks a lot smoother. Since we have added new polygons, the polygon normal got averaged and made the stone look much smoother than it should be.

   This could be easily adjusted with the **Normal** node that we connect after the **PolyBevel**. If you set the normal angle to 30 degrees or lower, the polygons will get the sharp edges back and will look much better in the viewport and during rendering.

2. Our next step is going to be adding a **Transform** node after the **Normal**, to orient and scale the base stone for a better look.

   Refer to *Figure 2.15*, which shows the **Transform** settings and the updated scale and orientation of the base stone compared to the original position after **Curve** and **Revolve**:

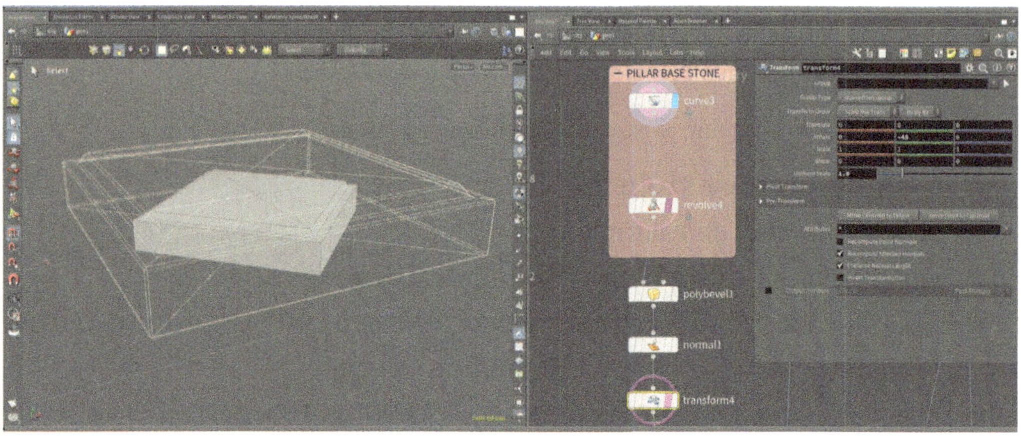

Figure 2.15 – Pillar base scale reference

3. This step is going to be one of the fundamental actions that we are going to use over and over to align objects and make them sit exactly on top of each other or other objects. One of the most useful nodes for geometry alignment in Houdini is the **Match Size** node. This node has two inputs, one of them being the object that we want to align or adjust and the other input being the reference object, the dimensions of which will be matched.

In our case, we don't want to scale one object to match the other—what we need is to translate one object exactly to the top of the other. In other words, we need to match the **PILLAR CURVE CONNECTOR**'s **Minimum** position in the **Y** axis to the **PILLAR BASE STONE**'s **Maximum** position in **Y**, as shown in *Figure 2.16*:

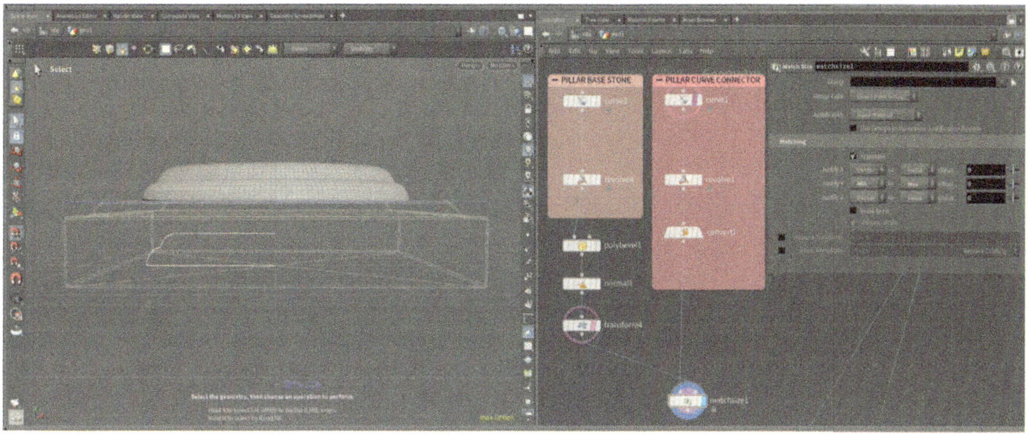

Figure 2.16 – Using match size for object alignment

Notice how the bottom of the curve connector is sitting exactly on the top of the base stone after the **Match Size** node. You can also notice how I'm able to preview different objects at the same time with node flags by having the main display flag on the **Match Size** node, the reference flag on the **Transform** node, and the shaded visible reference on **curve1** (this can be achieved by holding *Ctrl* and clicking on the reference flag of any other object).

4. In this step, we are going to adjust the scale of the pillar base to be bigger in radius than the pillar center and copy it with orientation upside down to use as the top of the pillar.

   Before we do the transformation, though, we need to combine the **PILLAR BASE STONE** and the **PILLAR CURVE CONNECTOR** into a pillar base, so that the **Transform** operations happen on both objects at the same time. You can combine two or more objects with the help of the **Merge** node. This way, any node or operation we apply down the chain will be happening on both objects that are merged.

Figure 2.17 shows the entire node tree for assembling and aligning the pillar elements together:

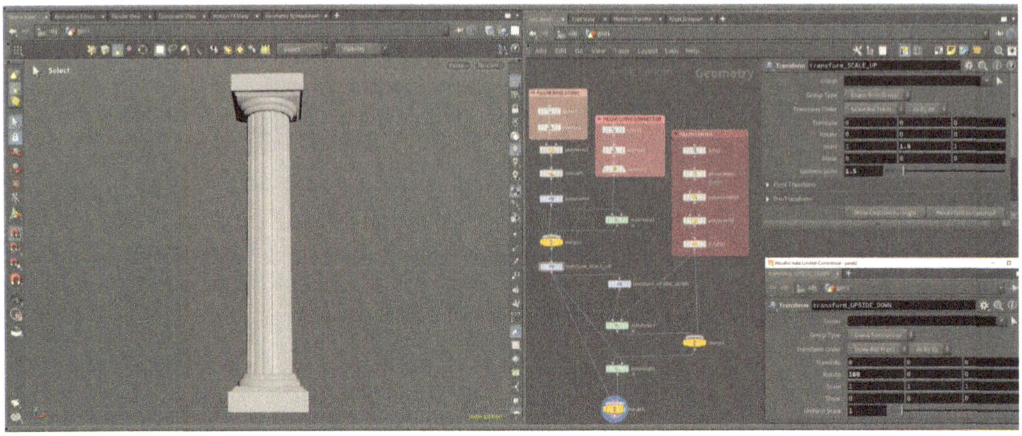

Figure 2.17 – Combining all pillar elements

After you combine the pillar elements with **merge1** node, look at the *purple* **Transform** node that is named **transform_SCALE_UP**. In the transformation parameters, I have increased the **Scale** in the **T** axis `1.5` times and the **Uniform Scale** also `1.5` times, which will respectively stretch the pillar base up and make it bigger than the radius of the pillar center.

5. After the scale up, we will be copying the combined pillar base and orienting the copy upside down to be attached to the top of the pillar center. Take a look at the *purple* node named **transform_UPSIDE_DOWN** and notice that **Rotation** in the **X** axis is set to `180`. We will do exactly what we need to turn the base upside down.
6. For the next step, we are going to place a **Match Size** node with the same settings for **Justify Y Min** and **Max** as the first **matchsize1**. By connecting the upside-down pillar base to the first input and the pillar center to the second input, we will be placing the pillar base on top of the pillar center. Before the next match size alignment, we will need to merge the pillar center and the pillar top elements.
7. As the final step, we will place the pillar center combined with pillar top onto the pillar base with the help of the *green* **matchsize3** node. The settings for **Justify Y Min** and **Max** will be the same as for the previous match size nodes. You can now merge all the aligned pillar elements in the final **merge2** node.

After you have completed all of the steps, the pillar is now complete and ready to be turned into a procedural subnetwork asset, where we will be able to change the scale, height, and other elements non-destructively.

Utilizing subnetworks of nodes

The next steps are not *absolutely necessary* for every modeling project, but rather explained to showcase how to create subnetworks of multiple nodes combined into one asset node with parameters.

We can take our procedural system further and wrap it into a subnetwork that will be compact, take up less space in the node graph, and have only the parameters that we need for control over the pillar look.

Don't forget to save your file before we continue!

To create a digital asset, select all the nodes used for pillar creation and press *Shift* + *C*, as shown in *Figure 2.18*:

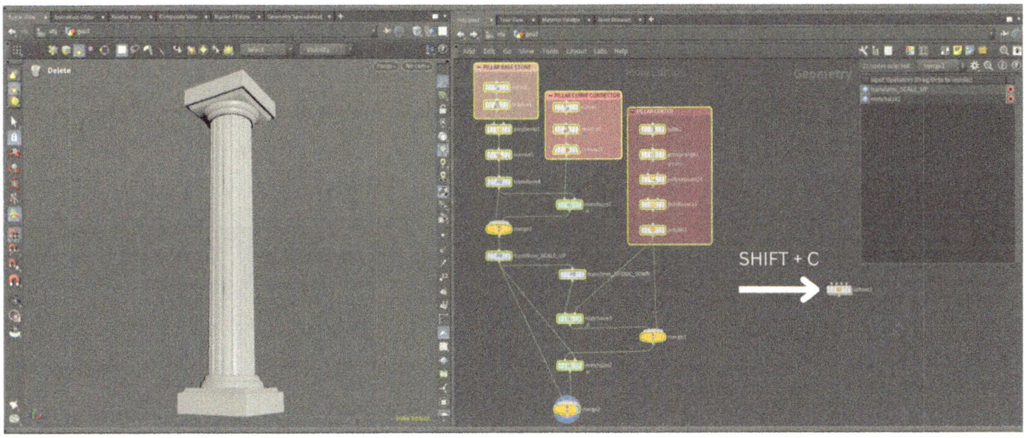

Figure 2.18 – Creating a subnetwork

We adjusted many parameters to create all the elements of the pillar; however, some of the main ones that we might want to modify in the future are as follows:

- Pillar height
- Pillar base height (**Y** scale)
- Overall pillar radius scale
- Pillar global scale

These parameters don't exist in one place but are rather located in different nodes as specific parameters.

The main goal of a subnetwork is as follows:

- Define the main modification settings
- Create the corresponding parameters in the subnet UI
- Link the newly created modification settings to the actual parameters of the nodes inside the subnet

In the next section, we'll learn how to create custom parameters.

Creating custom parameters

We have already defined some of the main parameter modification settings that we will need to adjust in the preceding paragraphs. Now, to create custom parameters for these modifiers, we can follow the next steps:

1. Select the **Subnet** node and click on the **gear** icon at the top of the **Parameters** pane. After clicking on the **gear** icon, a new drop-down menu will appear with some settings related to digital assets and their UI. Select **Edit Parameter Interface...** from the drop-down menu and you should see a new window pop up on the screen to the left, as shown in *Figure 2.19*:

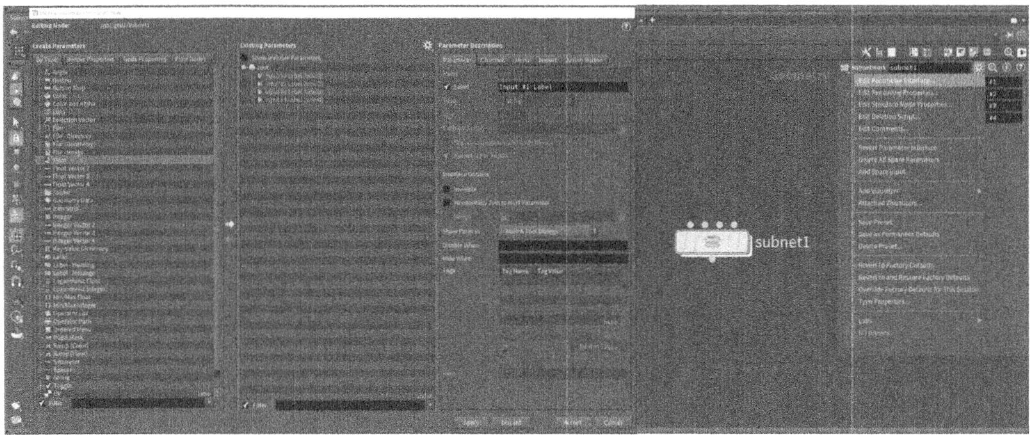

Figure 2.19 – Editing the parameter interface

This editing mode window of the parameter interface will let us create custom modification settings and link them to the actual parameters inside the nodes of the subnet.

2. On the **Create Parameters | By Type** tab, you will see a list of many modifiers that can hold certain data types. For our pillar subnetwork, we are going to mainly need the **Float** type, which can hold float numbers that can be linked to our parameters. Select **Float** from the list and drag it to the window called **Existing Parameters**. You can place it under the **Input #4 Label** parameter.
3. Alternatively, you can click on **Float** and then click on the small *white arrow* that is between the **Create Parameters** and **Existing Parameters** windows. You will notice that now there is a new parameter in the **Existing Parameters** called **Label** (new parameter).

   The **Parameter Description** window now also has new settings related to the **Float** type. When creating new parameters, some of the most common settings you usually want to change are **Name**, **Label**, and **Range**.

   Let's examine these settings:

   - **Name** is going to hold the parameter's variable name, which could be called in expressions or references.
   - **Label** is mainly what you are going to see as the name of the parameter near the settings slider.
   - **Range** is there to define what values the parameter can take from minimum to maximum. Take a look at *Figure 2.20* and notice all the changes I made to the **Parameter Description**:

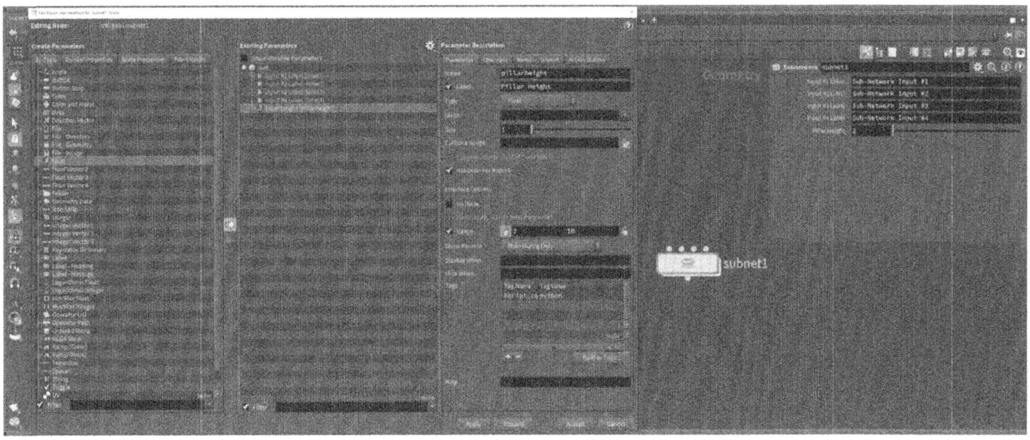

Figure 2.20 – Adding extra parameters

After you fill in all the necessary fields in the **Parameter Description**, you can click **Apply** at the bottom of the window. Notice that now our **subnet1** has a new parameter named **Pillar Height** that has a default value of **2**.

Now this parameter by itself is not going to have any effect on the pillar until you link it with the corresponding parameter inside the subnet that will transform the pillar every time you adjust the height.

4. You can create a reference link from any parameter in Houdini to any other parameter or sets of parameters in any node. This is a very powerful and fundamental concept that lets you drive any parameters with one master parameter.

   To create a reference link, follow these steps:

   1. Right-click on the master parameter that will be used to drive the others and choose **Copy Parameter**.
   2. Select the node that will have dependent parameters then right-click on any parameter that needs to be linked to the master and choose **Paste Relative References**.

   In our case, the newly created **Pillar Height** parameter is going to be the master parameter. Right-click on **Pillar Height** and choose the **Copy Parameter** setting from the menu (see *Figure 2.21*).

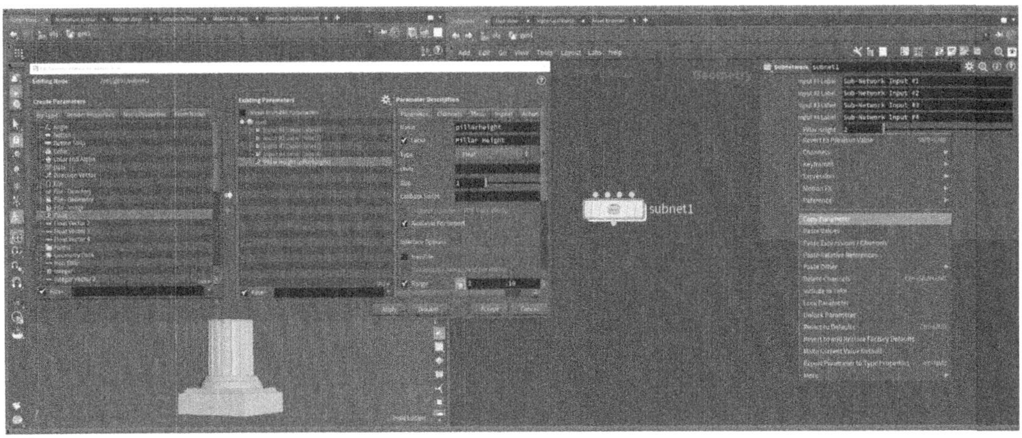

Figure 2.21 – Linking parameters to the asset UI

5. If you double-click on the created node called **subnet1**, inside, you will see all the nodes that were used to create the pillar. You will need to link the **Pillar Height** parameter to the **Height** parameter that could be found in the **tube1** node that was used to create the **PILLAR CENTER** cylinder.

6. Select the **tube1** node, colored *red* in *Figure 2.22*, and right-click on the **Height** parameter that currently has **8.5** as its value. **Choose Paste Relative References** from the **Options** menu, and you will see instead of **8.5** there is now a *green* expression `ch("../pillarheight")` linking the two parameters:

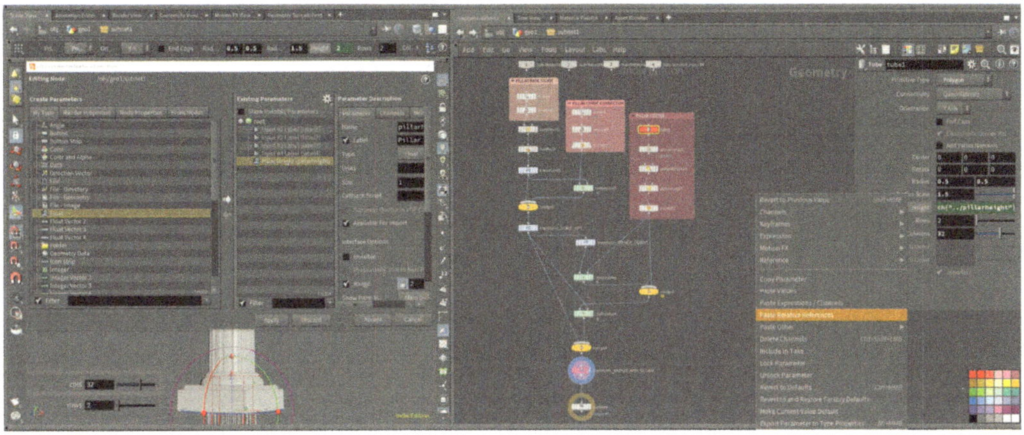

Figure 2.22 – Pasting relative references

I'm going to add one new **Transform** node before the output inside of the subnet. This *purple* **Transform** node, named **transform_RADIUS_AND_GLOBAL** will help us to control the extra parameters that we will be creating.

Although we did everything correctly, notice that the pillar height has changed and the pillar is much shorter now. This is because, instead of the original height of 8.5 that the pillar had, we linked the parameter that had the height value of 2. We can now easily change the pillar height without affecting the base and everything else will be kept aligned correctly. All you need to do is to go back outside of the subnet and adjust the pillar height back to `8.5` or any number you want the height to be.

Moreover, you can set this new height parameter to be the new default for the pillar if you right-click on the **Pillar Height** and choose **Make Current Value Default**, as shown in *Figure 2.23*:

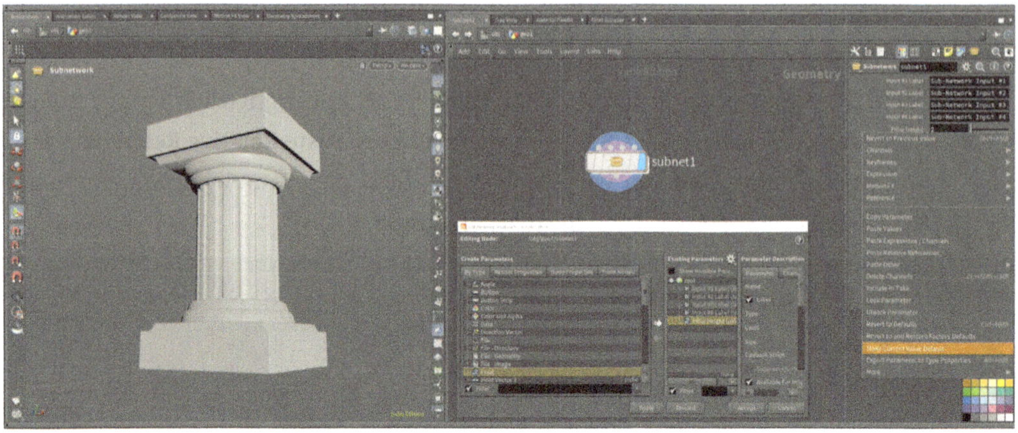

Figure 2.23 – Setting default parameter values

The **Edit Parameter** window needs to remain open during the parameter linking process. In *Figure 2.23*, I moved it outside of the capture area. Now, we can repeat the same steps and create a custom parameter for the **Base Height** that can be linked just to the **Y** component of the **Transform** node, which is called **transform_SCALE_UP**.

Also, you can create two other new global parameters for pillar radius and pillar uniform scale and link them to the new **transform_RADIUS_AND_GLOBAL** nodes scale in **X** and **Z** for the radius parameter and **Uniform Scale** parameter, respectively (see *Figure 2.24*).

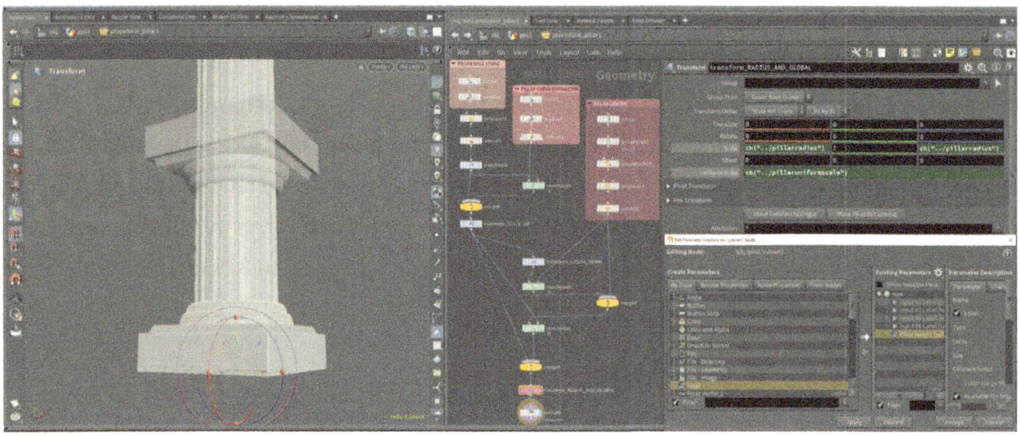

Figure 2.24 – Finalizing the pillar subnetwork

Even though all this took some time to build, you now have a lot of control and can create many pillar variations.

In the next steps, we will create procedural floor stairs and will instance the pillars onto the floor by utilizing copy tools.

Modeling using Copy node tools

Copy node tools are very efficient, are fun to use, and let you replicate pieces of geometry quickly and create instances of objects with variations.

In this section, we'll create floor stairs and a repeating roof base using the **Copy** and **Transform** node, one of the first and simplest in the **Copy** tool set:

1. Create a **Circle(Polygon)** node with **Orientation** set to **ZX plane**, **Uniform Scale** set to `12`, and **Divisions** set to `512`.
2. Create a **PolyExtrude** node and set the **Distance** parameter to `1`, this will be the height of each stair. On the **Extrusion** tab, check the **Output Back** setting to close the top surface of the stair.
3. Add a **Copy** and **Transform** node after the **PolyExtrude**. By default, this node will have the **Total Number** parameter set to **2**, which means that currently the cylindrical stair is copied into two objects sitting on top of each other. Set **Total Number** to 3—this parameter will let us adjust the amount of copies.
4. Now, to offset the copies from each other, we can change the **Transformation** parameters. You can make the stairs offset downwards if you adjust the **Translate Y** axis to either a positive or negative value. I am going to set **Translate 1** to `-1.01`. Now, you have three copies of exactly the same object, which are offset from each other by -1.01.
5. You can also make the stairs gradually grow in the **X**, **Z** scale if you start adjusting the **Scale** in the **X** and **Z** parameters. For example, if you set the **Scale** to increase, then each next copy is going to increase in scale, if you decrease the **Scale** from its original value, then each copy will decrease in scale.

Figure 2.25 shows the setup and node parameters as follows:

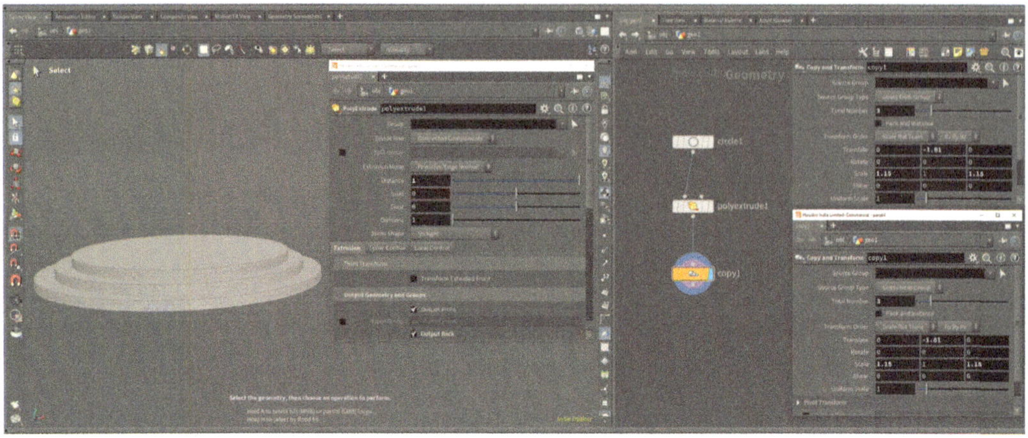

Figure 2.25 – Utilizing the copy and transform node

Now, let's use the **Copy to Points** node to copy the pillar around the top stair. Follow these steps to carry out this task:

1. Create a circle with the **Orientation** set to **ZX plane**, a **Radius** of `10`, and **Divisions** set to `8`. The number of divisions will define the number of pillars you will copy.
2. Create an **Add node** and check the option saying **Delete Geometry But Keep The Points**. This will blast off all the polygons and edges and will leave only points that you will use for copying.
3. Create a **Copy to Points** node and connect the points to the second input.
4. The first input of **Copy to Points** node needs to take in the geometry that will be copied. You can either use the *procedural pillar subnetwork asset* in that input or just use the final merged pillar with all the elements.

You should now have eight pillars copied equally on the points of the circle. If you merge the result of **copytopoints1** and **copy1**, you will have three stairs rising with eight ancient pillars located on the top floor, as shown in *Figure 2.26*:

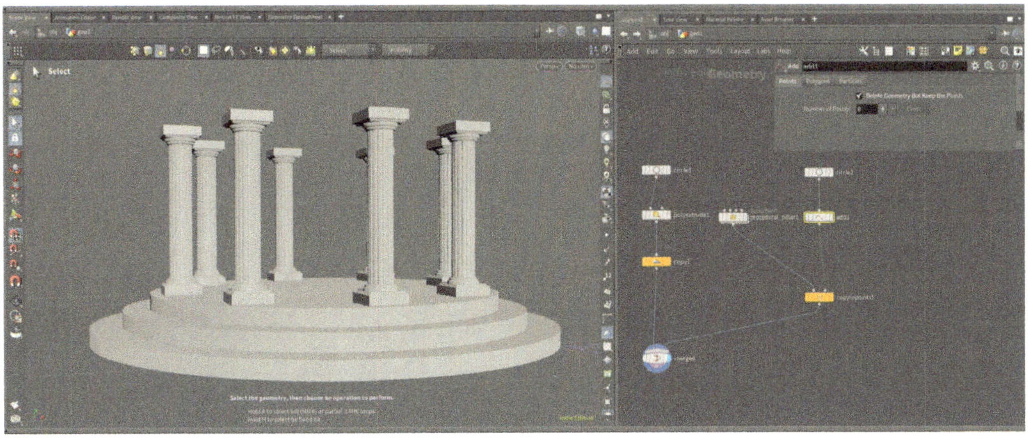

Figure 2.26 – Instancing geometry on points

The scene is slowly coming together.

Creating a correct orientation vector

Now, the only problem we have is that all the pillars are oriented the same way instead of being gradually oriented outward from the center. Unfortunately, this is not something fixable with a **Transform** node, rather with a global attribute that can tell the copy to points how to orient the pillars. Fortunately for us, if we create a normal attribute on points that will be pointing outward from the center, **Copy to Points** will use this and orient the pillars correctly.

To create the **Normal** attribute directed outwards from the center, we can use an **Attribute Wrangle** node. **Attribute Wrangle** lets you write snippets of code using Houdini's native VEX language, which is very fast and easy to use with lots of ready functions.

Let's create the correct orientation normal vector by following these steps:

1. Create the **Attribute Wrangle** node and place it after the **Add** node and before the **Copy to Points** node.
2. In the **VEXpression** box, write the following expression: `@N = (@P - getbbox_center(0));`.

Now, all the pillars will be oriented the correct way. Congratulations on writing your first line of code in Houdini!

You can also add some beveling and sharp normals to the stairs. In fact, this finalizing **Bevel** and **Normals** with a cusp angle of *less than 30* is recommended for every object that has sharp edges and a final polish step (see *Figure 2.27*).

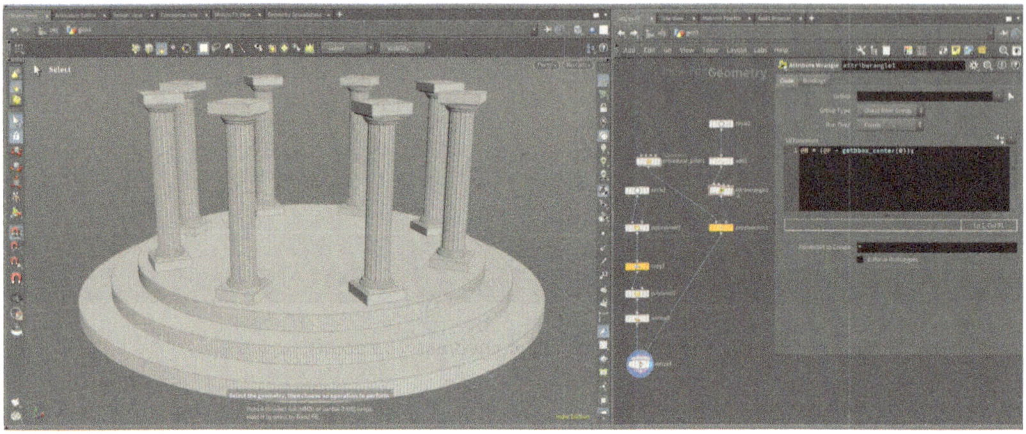

Figure 2.27 – Creating a correct orientation vector

In the next section, we'll learn how to create the roof base and roof dome.

Creating the roof base and roof dome

Now, by using the same copy and transform techniques we can create a roof base constructed on one thick cylinder and three thinner ones that are copied towards **Y** up with increasing **X** and **Z** scale. You can also come up with your own design for the roof base and have more or less copies. *Figure 2.28* shows what I created for the roof base:

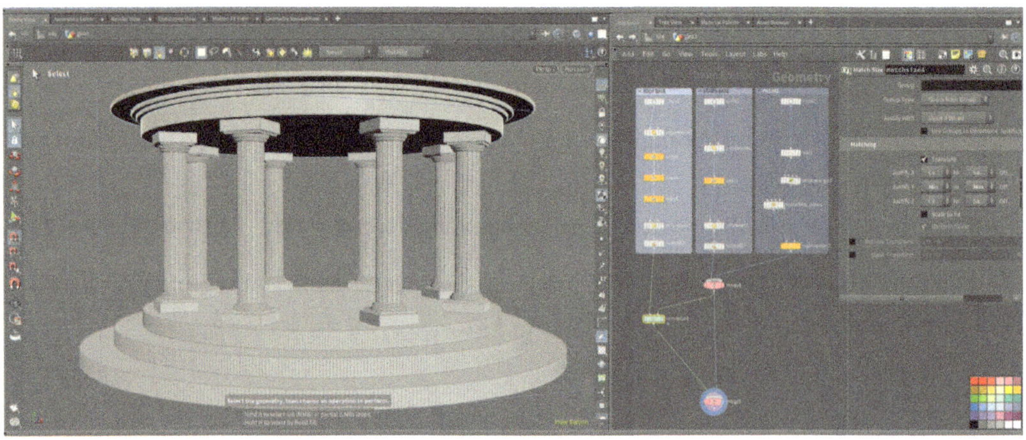

Figure 2.28 – Combining pillars with the base

Notice that I have also aligned the roof to the top of the pillars combined with the stairs and merged everything together. Our system is still very procedural, and you can now even adjust the pillar's height and scale and everything will update, so the procedural rotunda can be any height that we need.

I will make a couple of variations by changing the number of pillars, the pillars' heights, and the rooftop design so you can get some ideas, as shown in *Figure 2.29*:

Figure 2.29 – Rotunda variations

In the preceding screenshot, you can see the amounts of variations that you can get very fast and the flexibility of the procedural system that we are building!

The first variation on the left, which is *brown*, uses the default settings that we have been following so far; the *gray* variation in the middle has higher pillars and the base is scaled up; and the *blue* variation on the right has six pillars instead of eight, bigger pillars stairs and roof scale, and a modified roof base design.

Let's build the roof dome using mixed modeling techniques:

1. Create a **Sphere (Polygons)** and connect the output of the **Circle** node to the input of the **Sphere** node. This way, the sphere will inherit the dimensions of the circle radius and will give us a much closer look at the fine scale of the roof dome.
2. Add a **Subdivide** node after the **Sphere** and set the **Depth** parameter to 2. The **Subdivide** node allows us to take the input 3D mesh and more polygons smoothly. This is a very good procedural solution for getting a high-resolution smooth mesh from a low polygon geometry.

3. To turn this sphere into a dome, we are going to need the **Clip** node to cut away the bottom. **Clip** node will cut the geometry and delete all polygons, edges, and points that are above or below the clip plane based on the **Keep** parameter.
4. Another important parameter in the clip node is the **Direction**, which will define the axis along which the polygons will be preserved.
5. Since our sphere is located exactly at (**0,0,0**), the **Clip** node will delete everything that is below **0** on the **Y** axis because **Keep** is set to maintain everything above the **Plane** and the **Direction** parameter is set to 1 in **Y**.
6. The dome is pretty much ready; we only need to add some inner depth with the help of **PolyExtrude** node with the **Distance** parameter set to -1 and the **Output Back** option checked on to close the rooftop. You can additionally check **Front Group** and **Back Group** to create extra groups.
7. Finally, let's add a **Reverse** node to make the polygons orient the correct way.

Take a look at *Figure 2.30* for the roof dome extrusion parameters and placement:

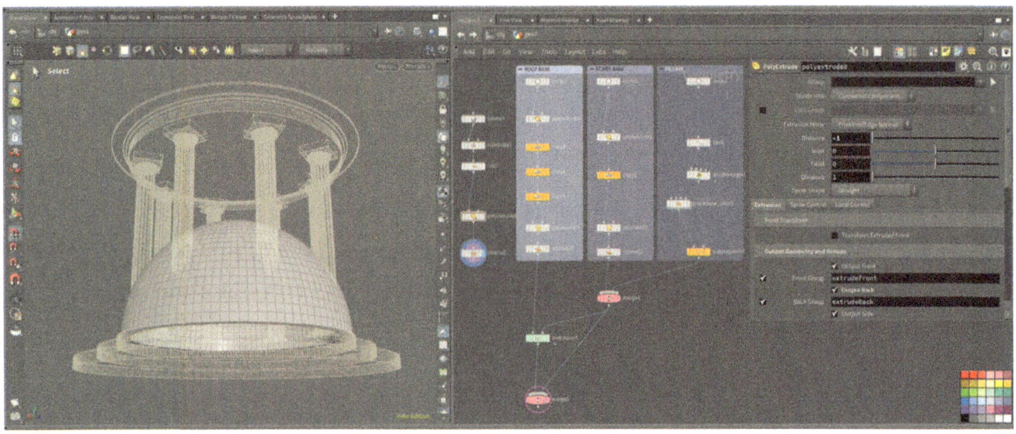

Figure 2.30 – Building the roof

For now, we are going to keep the dome at the center of the grid before we build all the details and extra modeling elements attached to it.

Adding finer details to the roof dome

For the next steps, we are going to add extra details to the roof dome by branching out from the main dome shape and reusing some of the nodes. We'll also create railing structures along the bottom of the dome and the top surface by following the next steps:

1. Branch out from the **Clip** node and add a **Group** node next to the **Poly extrude** (see *Figure 2.31*). We are going to group the open edges at the bottom of the dome that were produced as the result of clipping.
2. In the **Group Name** box, type edges to create a custom group name and set the **Group Type** to **Edges**.
3. Disable every group option except **Include by Edges**. Check the **Enable** and **Unshared Edges** checkboxes. This way, we can always group any edges that are open and don't have any geometry after them.

   Figure 2.31 shows the image with the group of unshared edges selected in *yellow* for your reference:

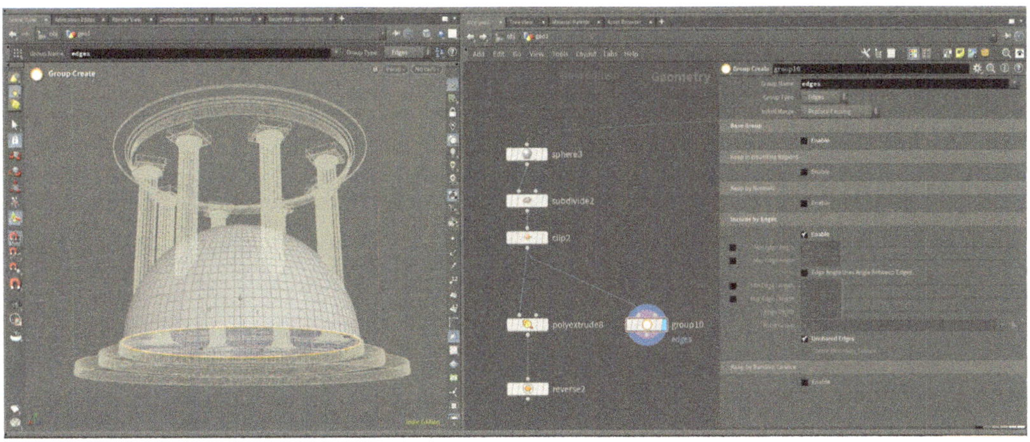

Figure 2.31 – Using groups for modeling

4. Now that we have created the group, it is very easy to isolate this unshared edge and convert it to a curve with the help of **Convert Line** node that has its group set to **Edges**.
5. You will notice that there are some leftover points on the top surface of the sphere that we can delete by turning on the **Remove unused points** checkbox on the **Convert Line** node.

6. As the last step, we are going to add a **PolyWire** node (see *Figure 2.32*) that will take any curve or line and make it into a 3D shape that will have depth and radius.

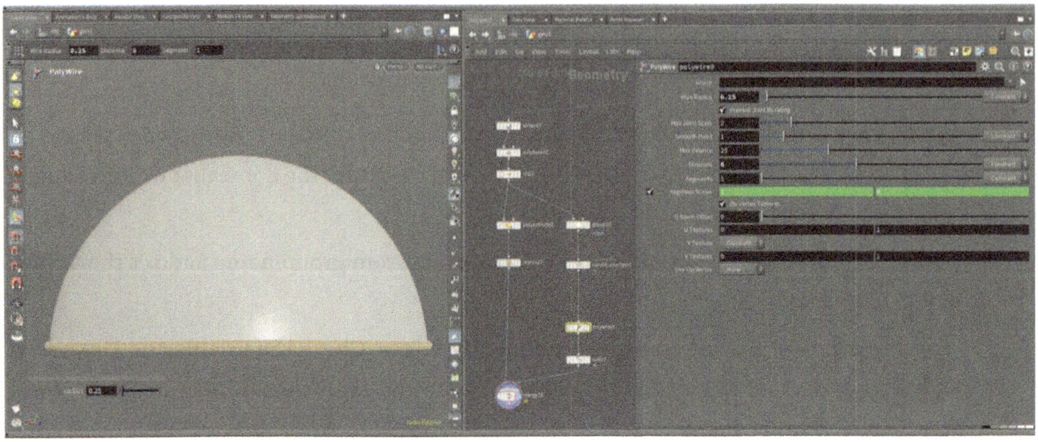

Figure 2.32 – Utilizing the PolyWire node

The **Wire Radius** parameter will be responsible for the thickness of the wire and **Divisions** and **Segments** settings can add more polygons and resolution to the output mesh.

Adding the side railings

Now, let's add the side railings that will go around the spherical shape:

1. Duplicate the initial dome sphere by holding *Alt*, clicking on the **Sphere** node, and dragging it to the side. This way, we will maintain the scale and dimensions for the original dome sphere and still have it linked to the base circle radius.
2. The only change we need to make in the newly copied **Sphere** node is in the **Connectivity**, which must be set to **Columns**.
3. You can also copy the **Subdivide** and **Clip** nodes the same way and connect them after the **Sphere** since these nodes will remain unchanged.

   The main reason we had to copy the **Sphere** is because procedurally isolating just the columns could be a bit tricky. Also, we would need to be able to adjust the amount of columns independently from the topology anyway.

4. Finally, let's add another **PolyWire** node after the **Clip** with a smaller **Wire Radius** and merge all the elements together, as shown in *Figure 2.33*:

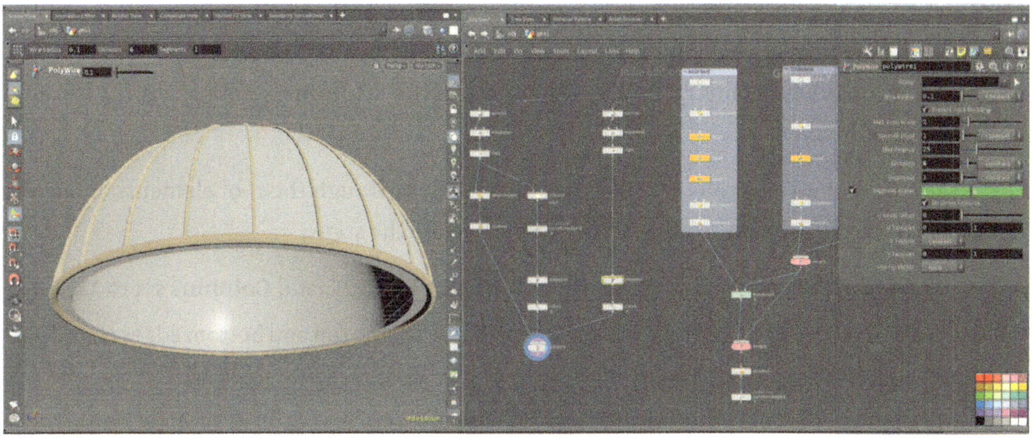

Figure 2.33 – Completing the roof

The rooftop dome is now complete and can be aligned with the top of the rooftop base. *Figure 2.34* shows the correct roof placement after the **Match Size** node was used for alignment, as well as the node network for the completed rotunda elements:

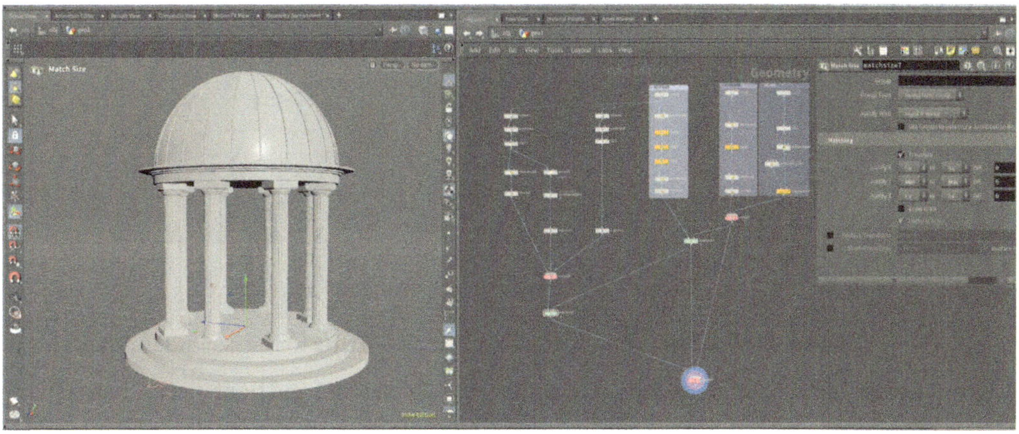

Figure 2.34 – Completed rotunda elements

This rotunda asset is pretty much complete. We can also additionally utilize Boolean modeling techniques to carve out a small indent on the floor and to create a hole in the roof base by subtracting one piece of geometry from another.

Using Boolean tools for extra detailing and cutting holes

Houdini comes with some very powerful **Boolean tools** that can be used to cut pieces from geometry based on other geometry, find a 3D intersection object from two objects going through each other, and much more.

Let's take a look at an example; we are going to cut holes through the roof elements and carve out a small piece of the floor to add extra details. Here are the steps:

1. Create a **Tube** with **Radius Scale** set to 8, **Height** set to 25, and **Columns** set to 128.
2. Add a combination of **PolyBevel** and **Normal** to make the top and bottom edges chamfered to give details during the cutout.
3. **Transform** the tube so it fully crosses through the roof and captures a little intersection with the top part of the stairs, as shown in *Figure 2.35*:

Figure 2.35 – Using the side view for alignment

4. Create two **Boolean Subtract** nodes and connect the **Tube** to the second input for both.
5. The first input of **Boolean Subtract** is going to take the roof and floor pieces that we want to cut out from.

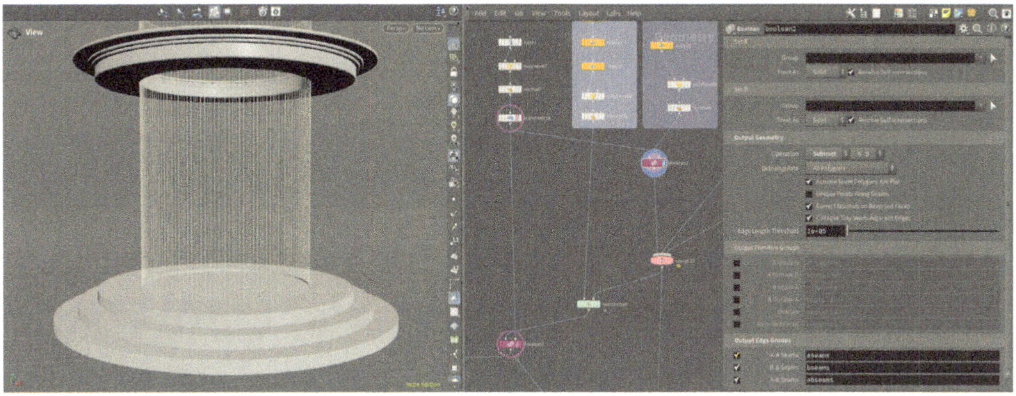

Figure 2.36 – Utilizing Boolean for extra details

This way, you can now use the Boolean techniques to carve out or add extra details based on the designs of the asset you are building.

You can also add an extra central altar bowl element, which we built with the curve tools earlier. You can use the transform node to scale it up to your liking and place it on top of the stairs surface.

In *Figure 2.37*, you can see how the central pedestal asset can be aligned on the rotunda floor.

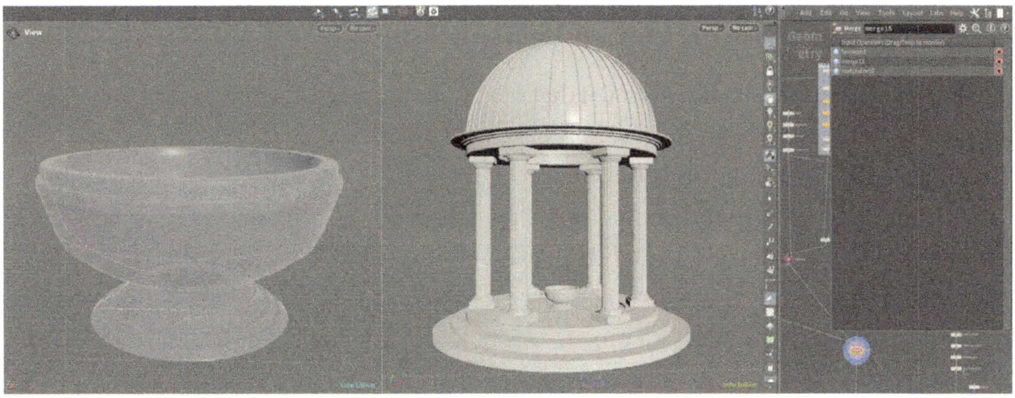

Figure 2.37 – Adding central pedestal inside rotunda

You can play with the number of copied pillars and roof side detail segments to achieve the desired look.

I have also added some details to the main stair floor and added some more objects to the rotunda by copying extra elements that we created with **Curve** and **Revolve** modeling.

Mainly, I have copied the torch bowl pedestals in between the pillars. Based on specific references, your creativity, and your imagination, you can build lots of variations of procedural ancient rotunda temples.

Figure 2.38 – Completed rotunda model

Save your Houdini file before jumping into the next steps!

We now have a completed rotunda model that can be placed in any environment or even on a big piece of a procedural rock that can be easily built with procedural noises using mountain nodes, or volume surface organic noise distortion.

Organic modeling using volume tools

Now, let's take a look at how we can build complex organic shapes, such as a small rock island to be used as a base for the rotunda temple.

Organic modeling with **Volume Data Blocks** (**VDBs**) tools in Houdini involves using volumetric data to create and sculpt organic shapes. VDBs are an efficient way to represent and manipulate volumes, commonly used for effects such as smoke, fire, and clouds, but they're also powerful for organic modeling.

The main benefit of volumes in creating organic shapes based on noise functions is that we don't need to worry about topology or polygons getting stretched or pinched in a bad way. **Volumetric pixels** (**voxels**) allow much more flexibility in resolution, more detail, and act pretty much like sculpting with clay.

In this section, we are going to explore how to convert any polygonal mesh into a VDB volumetric surface, and add procedural organic details based on complex noise functions.

VDBs represent volumetric data as a grid of voxels. When converting a 3D object into volume, voxels basically act as cubes stacked together that follow the shape of an object that becomes a volume primitive (see *Figure 2.39*).

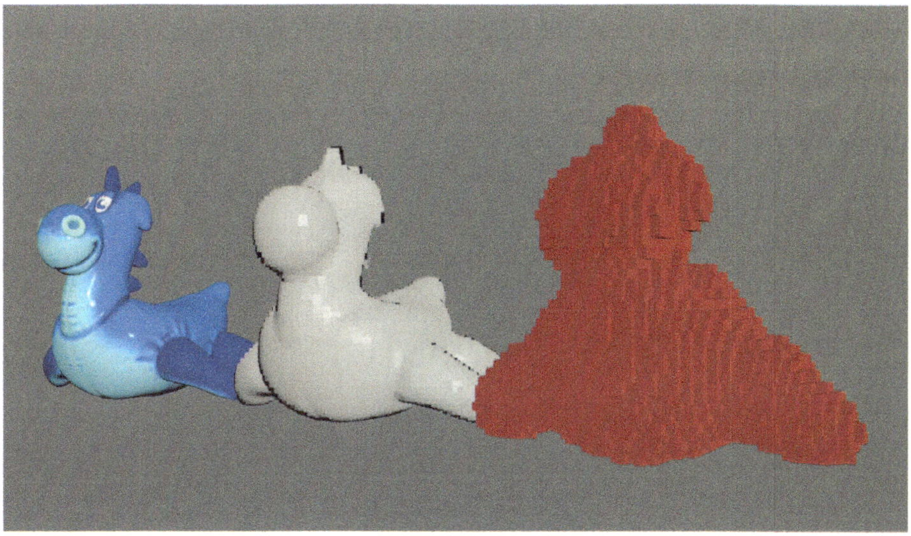

Figure 2.39 – VDB surfaces

Figure 2.39 shows a 3D polygonal object converted into a VDB volume surface, the *red* cubes represent the actual volumetric data that is created under the hood.

Each voxel stores information such as density, velocity, temperature, surface **Signed Distance Field** (**SDF**), or any other attribute relevant to the specific effect or model being created.

Follow these steps to create the base rock shape:

1. Create a tube with a **Radius** of `22.5` in *X*-axis and `30.5` in *Y*-axis, respectively, **Height** set to `20`, and **Columns** set to **64**.
2. Add a VDB from the **Polygons** node after the cylinder with a **Voxel Size** (volume resolution) of `0.25`.
3. Add a **VDB smooth SDF** node with **Operation** set to **Gaussian** and **Filter Voxel Radius** set to 4 to make the sharp cylinder into a smooth shape base for the rock.
4. Create a **Volume Noise SDF** node to start adding organic noise details to the volume.

Depending on the lots of parameters, mainly **General Displacement**, **Noise Value Amplitude**, and **Noise Pattern**, you can get an infinite amount of varying organic shapes from realistic hard solid rocks to soft alien structures.

I encourage you to experiment with different parameters and settings and refer to some of the examples provided in *Chapter 1* for the noise functions in the **mountain** node.

If you would like to follow and create the rock base design that I have created for the temple, refer to the settings provided in *Figure 2.40*:

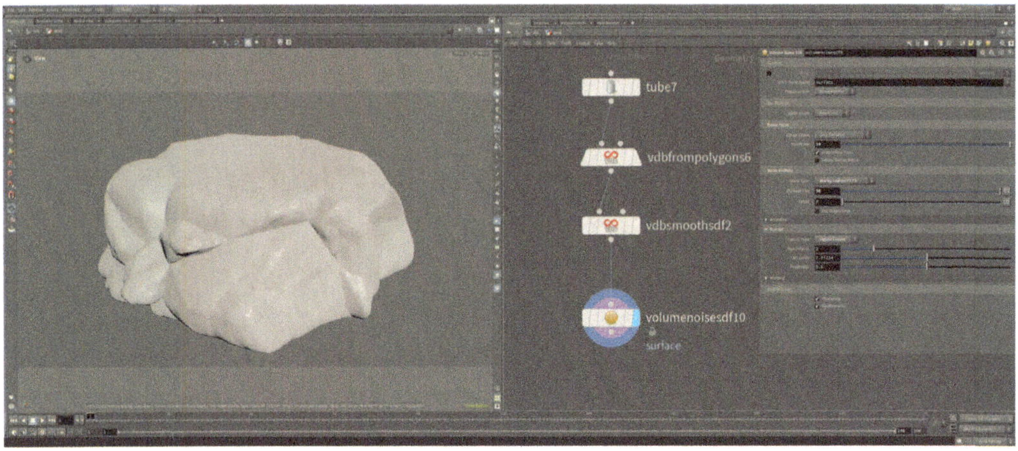

Figure 2.40 – Initial big shapes noise

This is the first layer of noise that is going to give us mostly big shapes defining the silhouette of the rock. One of the important settings is the noise is that the **Displacement** is set to **Using Vector** mode and excludes any displacement on the **Y** axis to keep the top of the rock mostly flat.

Increasing the voxel resolution and adding details

For the next steps, we are going to increase the voxel resolution and add finer details to layer up on the big shapes:

1. Create a **VDB Resample** node, set **Define Transform** to **Using Voxel Scale Only** mode, and adjust **Voxel Scale** to `0.75`. We are basically increasing the base voxel resolution by 25 percent.
2. Add another **Volume Noise SDF** node and follow the settings in *Figure 2.41*:

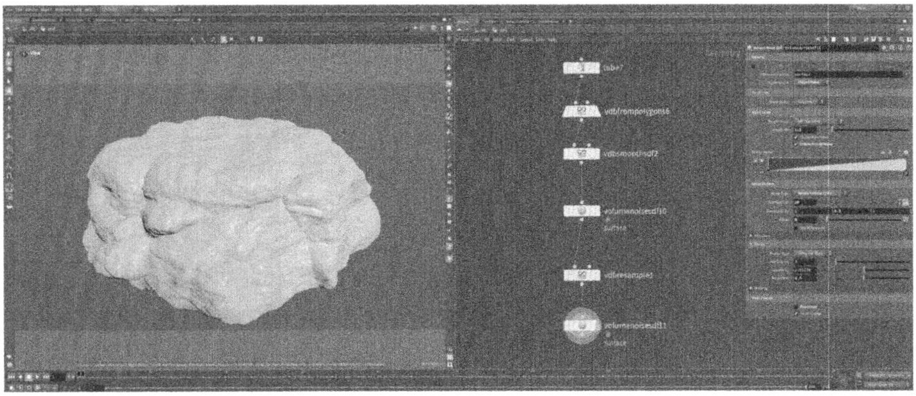

Figure 2.41 – Layering up the procedural noise details

Notice that, this time, I'm using the **Displacement** option as **Closest Point** since it is going to add noise details nicely and uniformly along the volume surface. Another important option is in the **Post-Process** tab, where I turned off the **Deactivate** checkbox.

The **Deactivate** option deletes all the extra expanded voxels needed during the noise displacement, which is useful if you are done with the volume modeling and want a clean optimized VDB. However, in this case, we are going to need these extra voxels to do one more operation.

We are going to create a flat box volume, add a small amount of noise to the sides, and subtract it from the top of the rock to flatten it organically:

1. Create a **Bound** node after **Volume Noise SDF**. This will make a flat box geometry that inherits the dimensions of the rock.
2. Add a **Transform** node with **Translate** on the **Y** axis set to `23.75`.
3. Convert the **Box** into a VDB by using the **VDB From Polygons** node with a voxel size of `0.15`.
4. Add a **Volume Noise SDF** node to create small surface details, as shown in *Figure 2.42*:

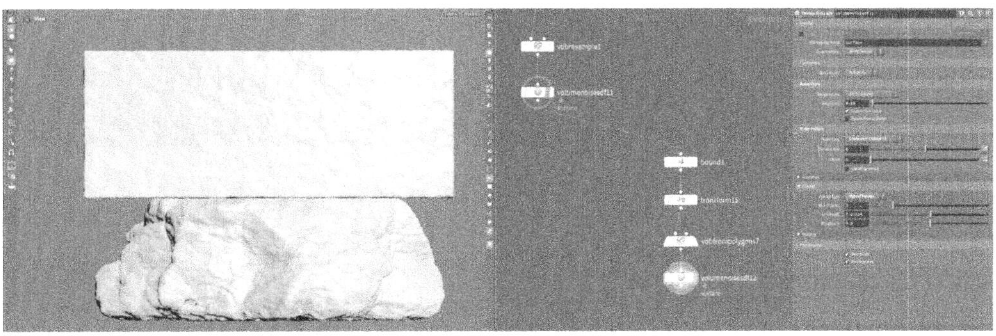

Figure 2.42 – Placing the flattening box

5. Create a **VDB Combine** node, connect the rock to the first input and the box to the second input, and set **Operation** to **SDF Difference**. This will subtract the flat, noised-up box—which we created in the above steps—from the top surface of the rock, and will create a natural flattened shape.
6. Add a **Convert VDB** node after the **VDB Combine** node and set it to **Polygons** to convert our final volume shape, as shown in *Figure 2.43*.

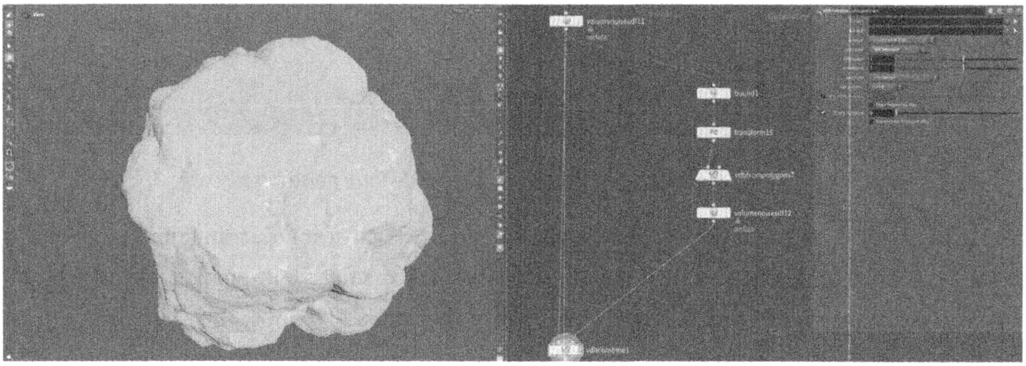

Figure 2.43 – Combining top and bottom

Additionally, you can use **SideFX Labs tools** to sharpen the rock shapes and color it based on geometry curvature.

Refer to *Figure 2.44* to follow the suggested settings for the sharpening and curvature:

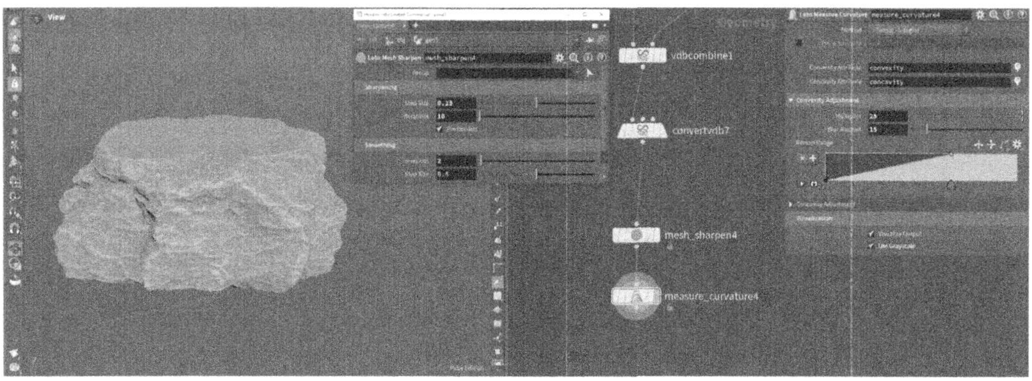

Figure 2.44 – Finalized procedural rock

We can now put the rotunda temple that we have created on top of the rock to have a complete scene, as shown in *Figure 2.45*:

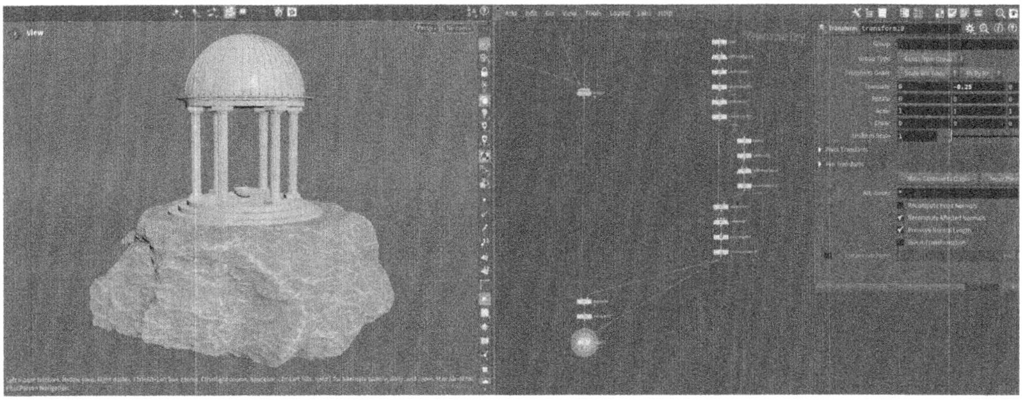

Figure 2.45 – Finalized procedural scene assets

Congratulations on creating your first procedural models in Houdini! In the next part, we will learn how to quickly render and present your model.

Rendering and presenting your model

Let's now take everything we have created and present our models in a nicely rendered way. For this section, I will be using **Houdini 20.5**, since it has some additional features that we can utilize for the rendering of the rotunda in an outdoor scenario.

We can follow these next steps to add some basic colors to the assets based on curvature that we can later use in the material:

1. Add a **Labs Measure Curvature** node after the transformed rotunda to create some value attributes for convex and concave areas of the model. You can use the settings provided in *Figure 2.46*.
2. Add a **Color** node after and set the **Color Type** to **Ramp from Attribute** to use the values of the curvature that can drive the color.
3. Set the **Attribute** to **convexity** and play with the range as well as the color points to get the desired color. You can also use the values I have provided in *Figure 2.46*.
4. Repeat the same set of steps for the rock geometry.

Refer to *Figure 2.46* to see the updated color by curvature on the rotunda model and the rock:

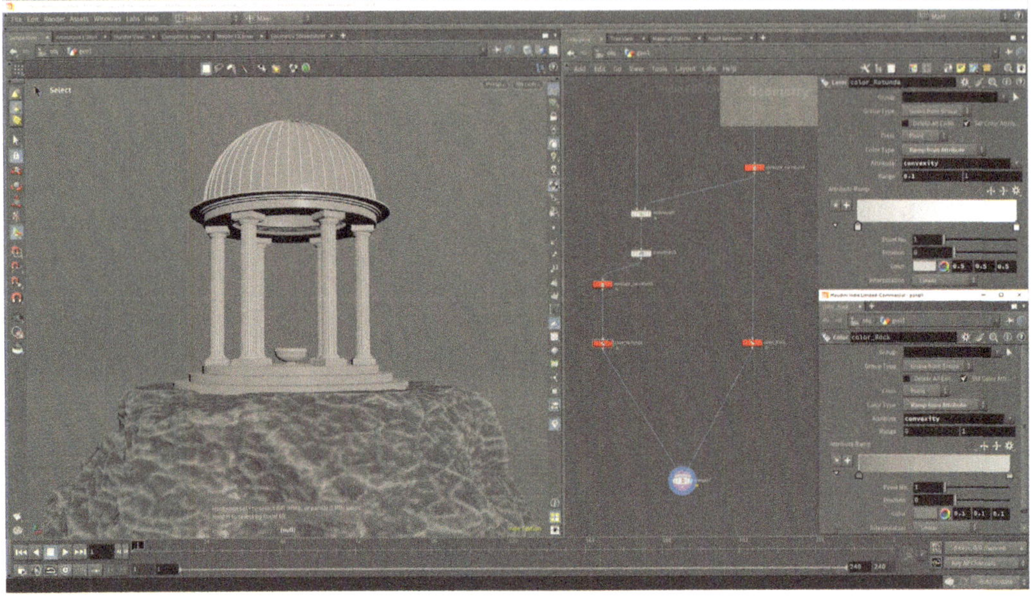

Figure 2.46 – Quick color based on curvature

Enhancing rock details with subdivision and noise

Notice that now the assets have interesting color values ranging from dark to light. This will help add a more interesting look during the rendering. We can enhance the details on the rock by subdividing the polygons and adding high-frequency noise representing the small details. Follow these steps to achieve this:

1. Add a **Subdivide** node after the **color_Rock**. This will divide the polygons and add more mesh resolution.
2. Add a **mountain** node and use the settings provided in *Figure 2.47* to achieve a high-frequency small detail noise.
3. Add two **Null** nodes: one for the rotunda output for rendering and the other for the rock. Name the **Null** nodes `OUT_RENDER_rotunda` and `OUT_RENDER_rock` respectively. We will bring these output nodes into the **stage** context for rendering.

Refer to *Figure 2.47* to see the extra details added to the rock for rendering:

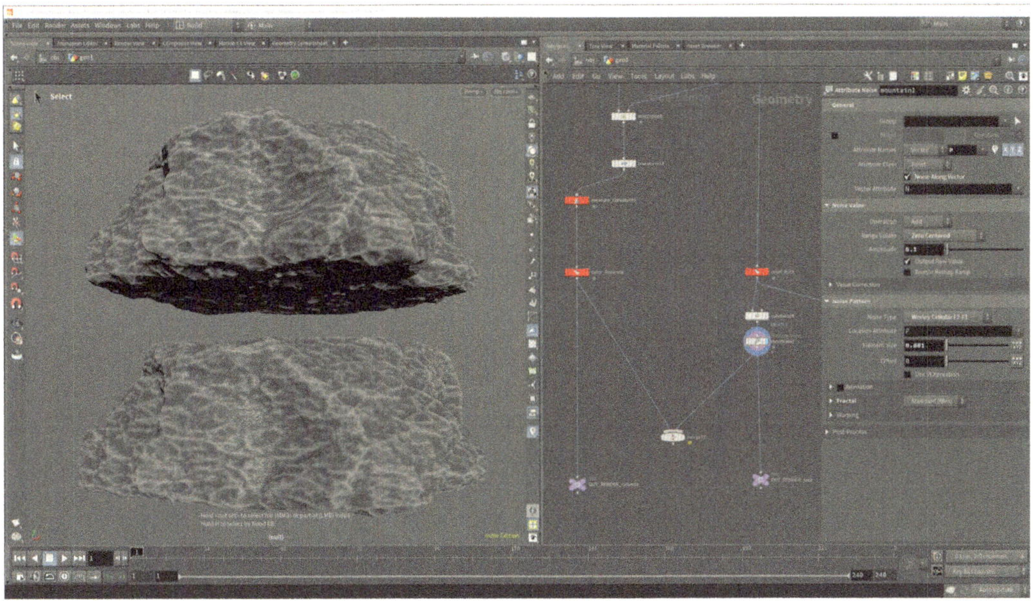

Figure 2.47 – Extra rock details

Importing the assets into Solaris (stage context)

Let's now bring everything into the **stage** context for lighting and rendering. The process is going to be very similar to the one used in *Chapter 1*. Press *Shift + W*, so you can keep using the tree view to easily access different contexts and sub levels and follow the next steps:

1. Switch to the **stage** context that is at the lower end of the tree view.
2. In the **stage** context, create two **SOP Import** nodes to bring in the respective outputs of the rotunda and the rock.
3. Name the **SOP Import** nodes as `sopimport_rotunda` and `sopimport_rock`, respectively.
4. Drag and drop the `OUT_RENDER_rock` and `OUT_RENDER_rotunda` outputs from the hierarchy tree view's **Geometry** level into the corresponding SOP paths of the corresponding **SOP Import** nodes.
5. Merge the **SOP Import** nodes to see both the rotunda and the rock.

Let's look at *Figure 2.48* to see the results:

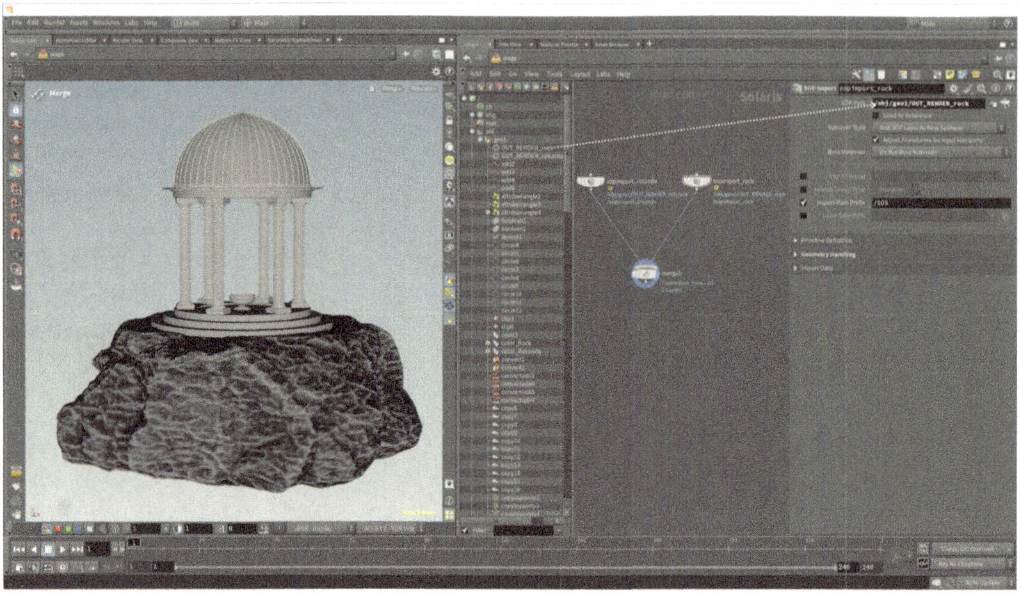

Figure 2.48 – Importing models into Solaris

Adding a camera and lighting

If everything is done correctly, you should see both the colored assets in the viewport.

Next, we will be adding a camera and lighting by following these steps:

1. Add a **Camera** node and set the parameters as shown in *Figure 2.49*.
2. Add a **karmaphysicalsky** node and set the parameters as visualized in *Figure 2.49*.
3. To achieve an interesting sky, set the **Sky Mode** to **Atmospheric**.

> Note
>
> The **Sky Mode** is only available in Houdini 20.5 or higher.

4. Adjust the **Atmosphere** parameters as shown in *Figure 2.50*, primarily setting the **Rayleigh's Scale** and **Mie Absorbtion Scale** to `0.0001`.
5. Do a quick render by changing the viewport top right mode from **Persp** to **KarmaXPU** or **KarmaCPU**.

Refer to *Figure 2.49* and *Figure 2.50* to see the outdoor sun lighting settings and results:

Figure 2.49 – Adding outdoor lighting

Figure 2.50 – Atmosphere settings

Applying simple materials

Our model already looks more interesting and realistic with the nice outdoor lighting and atmospheric sky. We can enhance this further by adding simple materials that will let us control some of the shading qualities, such as diffuse, specular, roughness and other parameters.

Let's quickly add simple materials by following these steps:

1. Add a **Quick Surface Material** node after the **karmaphysicalsky** and name it `quicksurfacematerial_rotunda`.
2. Adjust the material parameters as shown in *Figure 2.51* to make the surface qualities of the rotunda more realistic.
3. Add another **Quick Surface Material** node and name it `quicksurfacematerial_rock`.
4. Adjust the material parameters as shown in *Figure 2.51* to make the surface qualities of the rock more realistic.

Refer to *Figure 2.51* to see the material settings:

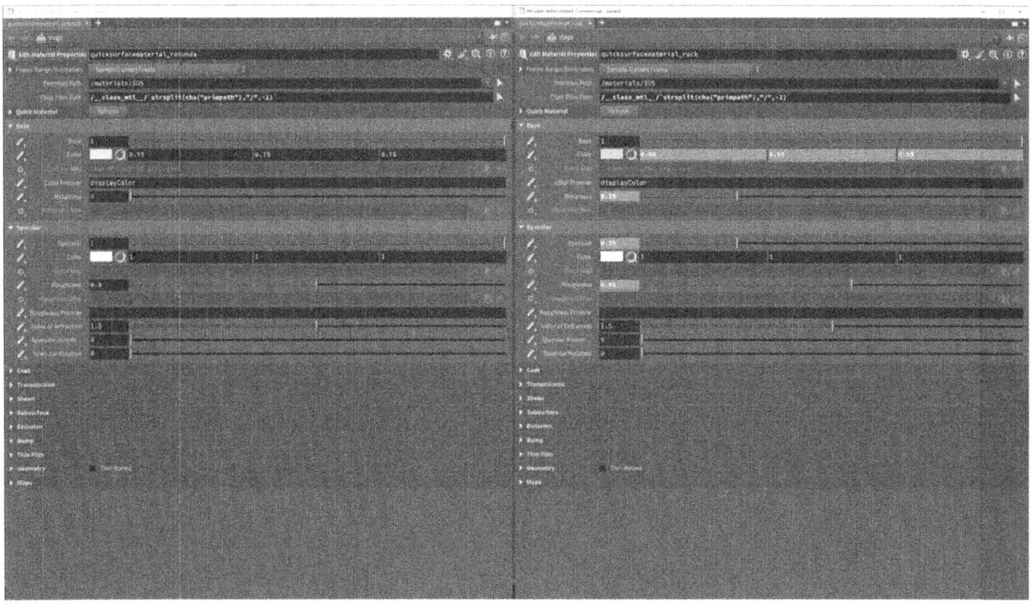

Figure 2.51 – Quick material settings

You can see that the rotunda material that is on the left of *Figure 2.51* has a brighter color, more specular, and less roughness to mimic the light stone surface qualities.

The rock material, on the right side, has a darker diffuse color multiplier, more metalness, less specular, and higher roughness, to mimic a dark mountain rock surface.

We are only scratching the surface of shading and materials here, and I encourage you to play with different **Quick Surface Material** settings to achieve different kinds of surfaces for your Houdini models.

Assigning materials with the Material Linker

These materials and surface settings will not make any difference to the scene unless we assign them to our models. For this, we will be utilizing the new **Material Linker** node.

The **Material Linker** is a new centralized interface for assigning, managing, and visualizing materials across your scene. It streamlines the process of linking materials to geometry by providing a node-based and spreadsheet-style view, allowing you to see what materials are applied, where, and how.

Material Linker includes access to built-in material catalogs and presets, such as Houdini's standard library and the **AMD MaterialX** collection. These templates allow you to quickly assign consistent, ready-to-use materials across scenes, streamlining *lookdev workflows* within **Solaris**. You can drag and drop materials from these catalogs directly onto geometry.

Let's follow these next steps to assign the materials to the imported models:

1. Add a **Material Linker** node after the **Quick Surface Material**.
2. Drag and drop the created materials from the materials side of the linker to the corresponding imported objects in the **Geometry Tree**. Follow *Figure 2.52* for guidance.
3. Enable the **Color Correction** panel on the bottom of the render view by clicking and holding the **eye** icon. Follow *Figure 2.52* for guidance.
4. Change the render view display colors to **ACES 1.0** for more realistic results.
5. Do a viewport test render with **Karma**.

Let's refer to *Figure 2.52* to see the **Material Linker** settings and the resulting render:

Figure 2.52 – Linking the materials and color correction

Rendering the final image

Now everything looks much more realistic, and we can control the material qualities at any time.

Finally, we can render our scene into a completed image by following these steps:

1. Add **Karma** through **TAB** search after the **Material Linker**.
2. **Karma** will come as two connected nodes: **karmarendersettings** and **usdrender_rop**.
3. In **karmarendersettings**, you can choose the render engine to be using either **CPU** or **CPU+GPU(XPU)**, depending on your machine configuration. **XPU** will be faster if you have a good graphics card.
4. You can also set many other render and quality parameters through **karmarendersettings**, however, since the scene is relatively simple, I am going to keep all the settings at default.
5. To create a completed render image, choose the **usdrender_rop** and make sure it is set to **Render Current Frame**, which should be the default option.
6. Click on the **Render to Mplay** button, and you will see a new rendering frame window appear with your 3D scene rendered into an image.

Let's refer to *Figure 2.53* to see the final result:

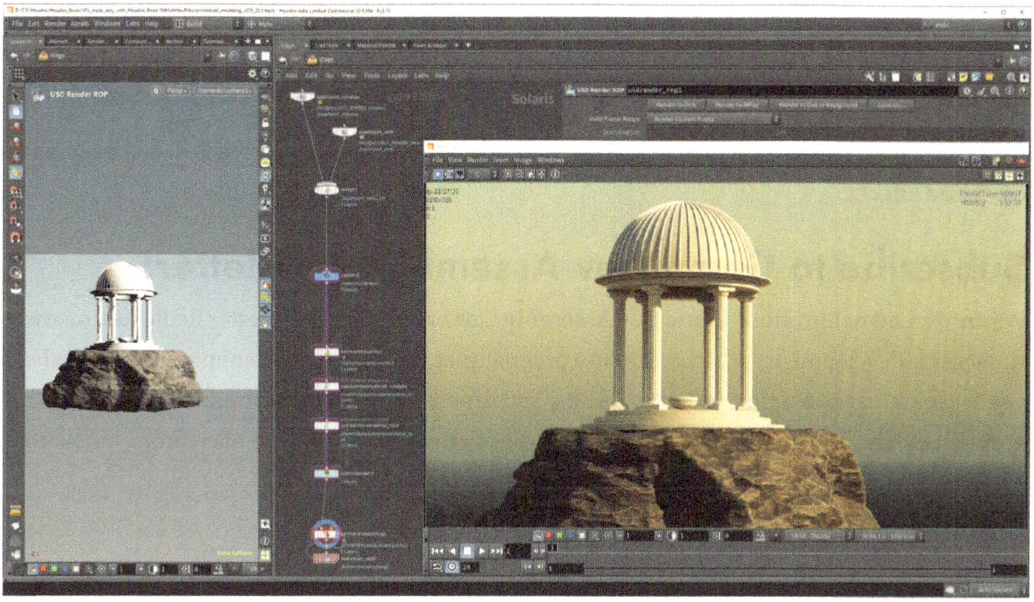

Figure 2.53 – Final rendered image

This wraps up the presentation and rendering of your procedural 3D models!

I encourage you to utilize these techniques with any other 3D asset you build in Houdini. Try using different light settings as well as different ready-to-use materials from the catalog.

Congratulations on completing this chapter! After following all the techniques and steps in this chapter, you should be able to create and present a procedural 3D model, based on custom reference, design, and your imagination.

Build, experiment, and most importantly, have fun with procedural modeling in Houdini!

Summary

Procedural modeling in Houdini combines powerful tools and techniques to create versatile and dynamic 3D models. By using custom draw tools, you can design unique forms with precision. The ability to utilize groups and selection sets enhances organization and control over specific parts of the model, while aligning 3D objects ensures accurate placement and consistency within scenes.

Creating procedural digital assets allows for reusable, customizable models, thereby streamlining the workflow. By utilizing the **Copy** node tools, you can achieve the efficient duplication of elements, while volume tools offer flexibility for organic modeling. This combination of flexibility, efficiency, and creativity defines Houdini's procedural modeling capabilities.

In the next chapter, we will dive into the world of simulations and explore how to create particle-based effects.

Part 2

Heart of Houdini: FX Simulations

Simulations are where Houdini truly comes alive, turning static geometry into dynamic, cinematic effects. In this part, you'll explore the core FX toolsets that power particles, smoke, fire, rigid bodies, and fluids. Starting with particles, you'll see how emitters, forces, and collisions combine to create natural motion before moving into Pyro FX to sculpt dramatic smoke and fire. From there, you'll learn how to fracture and simulate rigid objects, and then dive into the world of FLIP fluids to create believable liquid motion.

The part concludes with two guided case studies: disintegration and explosions. These examples bring together everything you've learned into complete, production-style effects.

By the end of this part, you'll understand how Houdini's simulation networks work and have the confidence to create striking, physics-driven effects of your own.

This part has the following chapters:

- *Chapter 3, Unleashing the Power of Particles*
- *Chapter 4, Igniting Pyro Effects*
- *Chapter 5, Breaking through Rigid Body Dynamics*
- *Chapter 6, Diving into Water FX*
- *Chapter 7, Effects Case Study: Disintegration FX*
- *Chapter 8, Effects Case Study: Explosion FX*

3

Unleashing the Power of Particles

Welcome to the exciting world of particle simulations in Houdini!

This chapter is designed to introduce you to the powerful tools and techniques that make Houdini a leader in the realm of particle simulations and visual effects. We will learn how to build efficient simulation emitters and particle sources, explore particle attributes and simulation parameters, and advance in simulation optimization, caching, lighting, and rendering.

Whether you are aiming to create rain, snow, sparks, or magical effects, understanding particle systems in Houdini will open a vast array of creative possibilities.

In this chapter, we will cover the following topics:

- Setting up the project
- Creating efficient emitters
- Diving into Dynamic Operator (DOP) and Particle Operator (POP) networks
- Combining forces and physical attributes
- Merging collision objects
- Particle caching and manipulation of attributes
- Shading and rendering particle effects

After completing this chapter, you will be comfortable creating versatile particle systems and effects. You will also have gained a solid understanding of key simulation principles that we will build upon in the next chapters.

In this chapter, we will be creating a versatile particle system inspired by the portal from the *Doctor Strange* (2022) movie. *Figure 3.1* shows an example of what this will look like:

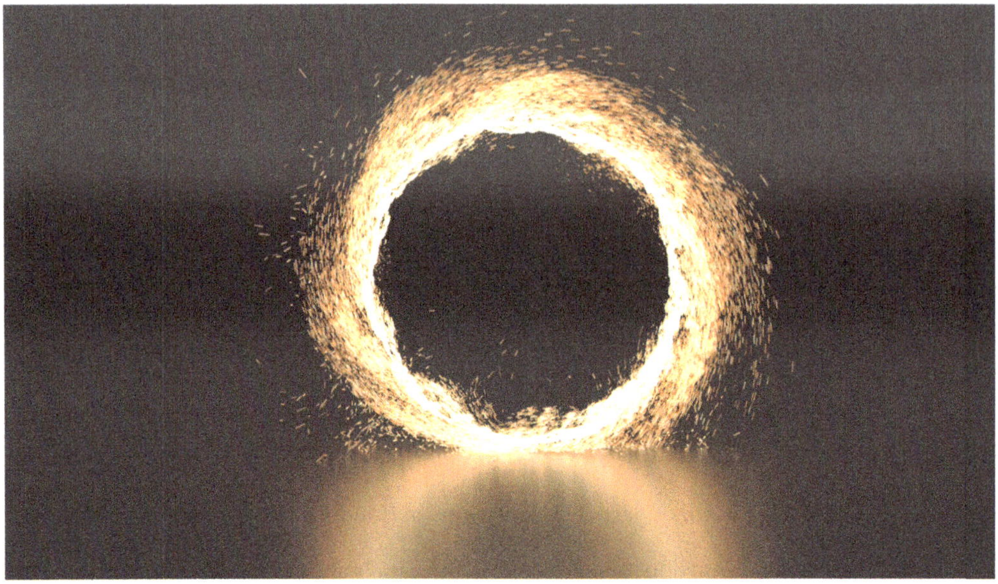

Figure 3.1 – Particle portal FX

Technical requirements

In this chapter, we will start writing and saving lots of simulation and rendering data to the hard drive on the disc, so it is a good idea to have at least 250 GB of hard drive space in your project directory.

You will have access to the Houdini file with the completed effect on the GitHub link at `https://github.com/PacktPublishing/VFX-Made-Easy-with-Houdini`.

To view the chapter images in better clarity, scan the provided QR code. It will direct you to a dedicated link where you can take a look at the images.

Setting up the project

Before we begin the project, let's follow these steps to set up the files:

1. Let us start by creating a new project and naming it `particle effects`.

> Tip
>
> I recommend creating separate folders for the projects of each chapter, so that everything related to each individual chapter is nicely organized.

2. Save the empty Houdini file to the project root directory by using the top window menu and clicking **File** | **Save as...**.
3. Name the file `particle_effects_v001`.
4. In this chapter, we will be completing certain checkpoints in the project. Every time we move into a new stage, I recommend incrementing the file version, so the next file that you save will be named `particle_effects_v002`.

Let's take a look at some of the important techniques for building an efficient emitter. The more time you spend on building a complex interesting emitter, the better your initial simulation result is going to be.

Creating efficient emitters

After setting up the project, let's follow the next steps to create our first particle emitter:

1. Press *Tab* and add an empty geometry container by adding a **Geometry** node.
2. Rename the newly created node from `geo1` to `particle_fx` and double-click on the node to dive inside.
3. Press *Tab* and create a **Circle (Polygons)** node that will serve as an initial shape of our emitter.

4. Adjust the **Circle** parameters, as shown in *Figure 3.2*:

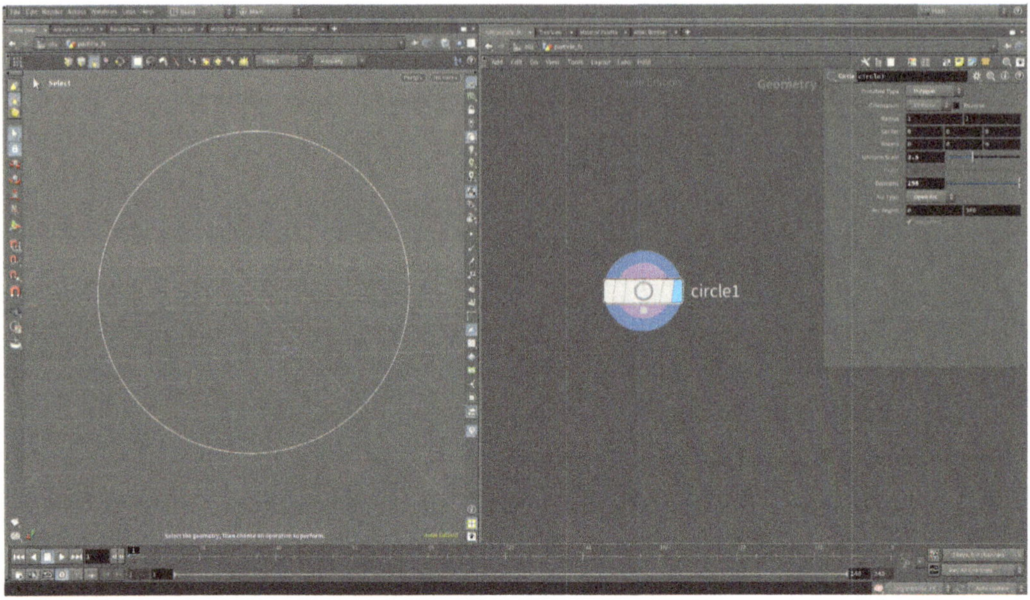

Figure 3.2 – Circle parameters

In *Figure 3.2*, the main reason why we changed **Arc Type** from **Closed Arc** to **Open Arc** is in the area for sourcing particles. **Closed Arc** would source particles from the entire polygonal surface, while **Open Arc** will make sure the particles are only sourced from the edges.

Adding layers of noise

For the next steps, we will be adding layers of noise to both the initial shape and the emission probability, which is the key to having an interesting particle source from the start:

1. Add a **mountain** node after **Circle** and uncheck the **Noise Along Vector** setting to distort the shape in all three dimensions.
2. Adjust **Element Size** to a value of `0.15` to make the shape distortion frequency higher and more detailed.
3. Check the **Animation** checkbox to make the noise dynamic and set **Pulse Duration** to `0.25` to make the noise animation faster.
4. We can additionally control how much noise will be distorting the edges by enabling the **Blend** checkbox and setting it to `0.5`. This will reduce the noise effect to 50%.

Refer to *Figure 3.3* while adjusting the noise settings:

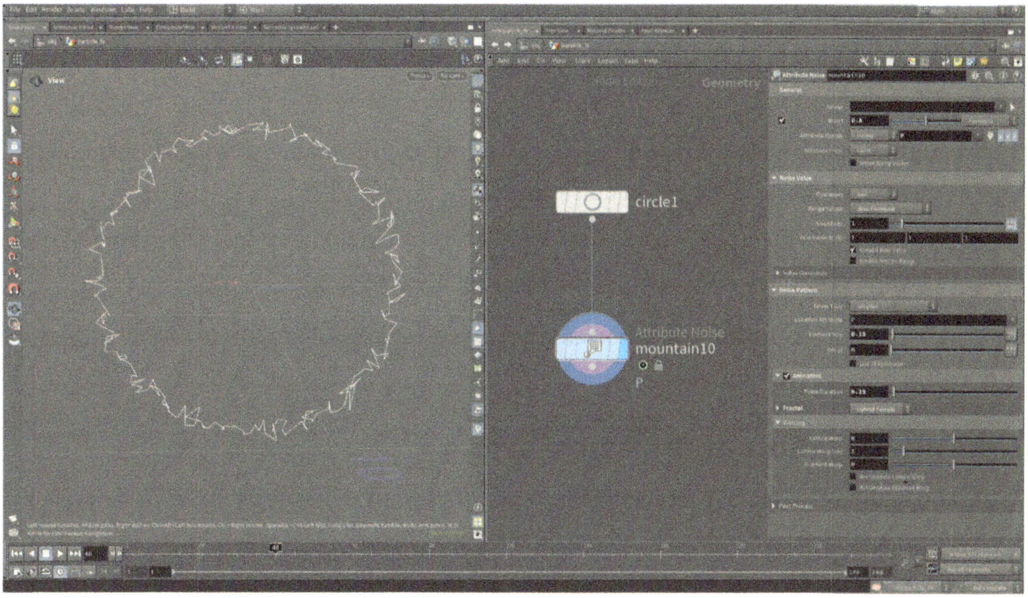

Figure 3.3 – Circle mountain noise settings

Quick tip: Need to see a high-resolution version of this image? Open this book in the next-gen Packt Reader or view it in the PDF/ePub copy.

The next-gen Packt Reader and a **free PDF/ePub copy** of this book are included with your purchase. Scan the QR code OR visit `packtpub.com/unlock`, then use the search bar to find this book by name. Double-check the edition shown to make sure you get the right one.

You can see that our shape is now much more distorted and broken up. In the next steps, we will be adding extra control over how much smoothness versus roughness we will need for a specific look. Since this portal is inspired by the type of portal in *Doctor Strange*, we will be smoothing it quite a bit:

1. Add a **Smooth** node after **mountain** and set its **Strength** parameter to `50`. This will smooth the overall shape of the rough noise areas.
2. Add a **Subdivide** node after **Smooth** and keep its default settings. This will add more resolution to the points and provide additional smoothing.

This should be a good base for the distorted emitter. Now we can also add varied source sections to break up the emitter even more.

Adding variation in emission areas

Another common technique that involves *noising up* the emitter is creating a custom attribute that will make the particles only be sourced from a specific area instead of being sourced from everywhere.

Imagine we have a noise pattern or specific data that contains a range of values from `0` to `1` mapped onto our emitter. If we use this data for sourcing in a specific way (that will be described once we enter the dynamics network), we can make the particles to be sourced for the areas that have a value of `1` or very close to `1`, while the areas that have a value of `0` will not get any chance to source particles.

Using this concept, we can create a custom attribute based on the noise values and name it `emit` (you can name it anything really; I picked `emit` since it makes sense for emission).

Follow these steps to create a custom attribute:

1. Add a node called **Attribute Noise** and connect it after the **Subdivide** node.
2. In the **Attribute Names** section, change the type from **Vector** to **Float** and type `emit` in the empty box.
3. Check the **Enable Remap Ramp** checkbox and adjust the ramp, as shown in *Figure 3.4*.
4. In the **Noise Pattern** rollout, adjust the **Element Size** parameter to `0.25`.

Refer to *Figure 3.4* to match the **Attribute Noise** node settings accordingly. I have also enabled the visualizer of this attribute in the viewport where the *purple* areas will not emit anything; *green* areas will have a medium emission chance; and *red* areas will have the highest emission chance:

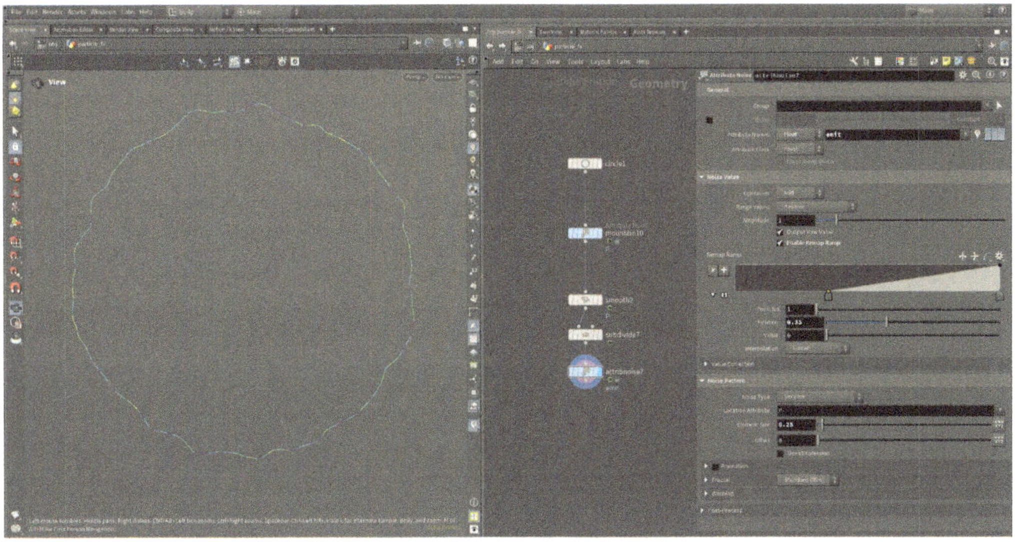

Figure 3.4 – Circle emit settings

After noising up the emitter, we can also create a reveal or build-up animation to make it even more interesting.

Animating emission parameters

For the next few steps, we will add some animated parameters to make our portal smoothly appear in a magical way. We will need two animations that will work together and will make sense for the portal reveal effect.

Let's look at the steps:

1. Create a **Carve** node and connect it after **Attribute Noise**. Notice how *25%* of the circle shape has disappeared in the viewport.
2. Set the **First U** parameter to 1 and then play with the *slider* by moving it right to left to see how the circle disappears and then reappears. We will be animating the **First U** parameter to ensure that we start with the circle being completely invisible, and then having it reappear in a clockwise rotation.
3. Use the timeline at the bottom of the Houdini window and go to frame **1**. With the **Carve** node's **First U** parameter set to 1, hold *Alt* on your keyboard and click on the **First U** box. You will notice that the box containing a value of 1 is now *green*, which means it has been keyframed.

4. In this step, we can decide how much time has to pass for the circle to be fully revealed back to its shape. I will give the animation 15 frames by setting my current frame to 15 in the timeline.
5. Let's keyframe the **First U** parameter back to a value of `0` by typing `0` instead of `1`, holding *Alt*, and clicking on the **First U** box.
6. Now, if you scrub the *animation timeline* back and forth between frames **1** and **15**, you will see the circle forming from a single point and two *green* keys appearing in the timeline.

Figure 3.5 shows the animated carve parameters and how the emitter should look when it builds up.

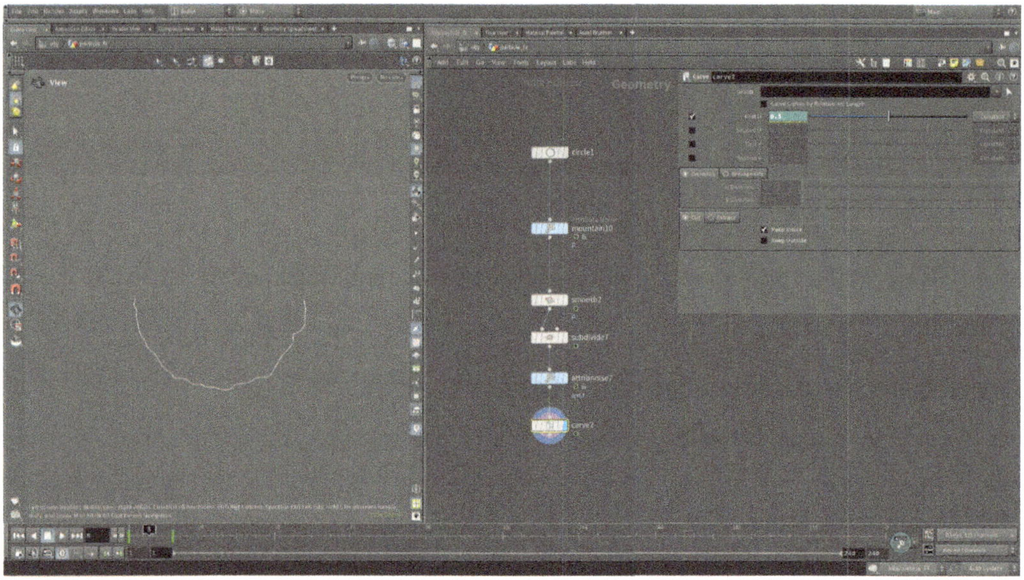

Figure 3.5 – Circle carve animation

Using the same logic, we can also animate the transformational scale-up of the circle to have a more complex motion of circle formation reveal and scale-up.

Let's look at the steps needed to execute this:

1. Add a **Transform** node after **Carve**.
2. Set your current frame to `1` on the animation timeline.
3. Set the **Uniform Scale** parameter to `0` in the **Transform** node.
4. Hold *Alt* and click on the value of **0** of the **Uniform Scale** parameter to set the first keyframe.

5. Set your current frame to 15 on the animation timeline.
6. Change the **Uniform Scale** value to 1 in the **Transform** node.
7. Hold *Alt* and click on the value of **1** to set the last keyframe.

After distorting the emitter, adding source area variation, and animating an interesting buildup, we will be moving on to creating initial velocity that will push the particles into interesting motion even before adding forces.

Adding initial velocity

The last step of creating efficient emitters will be adding initial velocity based on direction or noise, or calculated directly from object deformation. Houdini has a very versatile and useful node to perform this operation named **Point Velocity**:

1. Press *Tab*, type `Point Velocity`, and connect it after the **Transform** node.
2. In the first tab, named **Basic**, we can see some parameters, the first of which is **Initialization**. For this project, we will keep **Initialization** at its default value, that is, **Compute from Deformation**:
    - This first parameter is very important to look at and adjust to the specific velocity needs every time when working with **Point Velocity**. Depending on the default **Compute from Deformation** mode or any other mode, this can produce desirable or undesirable velocity results.
    - Every time that we would like to inherit the velocity based on the emitter's motion or deformation, it is recommended to keep **Initialization** at the default, which is **Compute from Deformation**. However, there could be many scenarios that we will cover in future chapters where we will need to change **Initialization** to another mode.

After creating different emission attributes, especially velocity, it is now necessary to be able to preview it in the viewport.

Previewing velocity attribute in the viewport

Houdini has many ways to preview and keep track of all the attributes that are being created on **Geometry**. One of the most visual and artist-friendly ways is by using the *node info flag* (which we discussed in *Chapter 1*) and then clicking on the attribute name.

Based on the knowledge from *Chapter 1*, you can put your mouse on any node. In our case, move the mouse to the **Point Velocity** node, and it will trigger all the flags to appear in a ring around the node. If you click on the flag that has **i** pictured, you will access node info.

The node info flag will give us all the information about our network system state, up to the very last node that was used to trigger the node information. In our case, we are mostly interested in previewing the velocity attribute that is defined as **v** in the node info box.

To make the velocity visible in the viewport, navigate your mouse on top of **v** inside the node info and click on the green **v** letter.

Figure 3.6 shows the preview of **Point Velocity**:

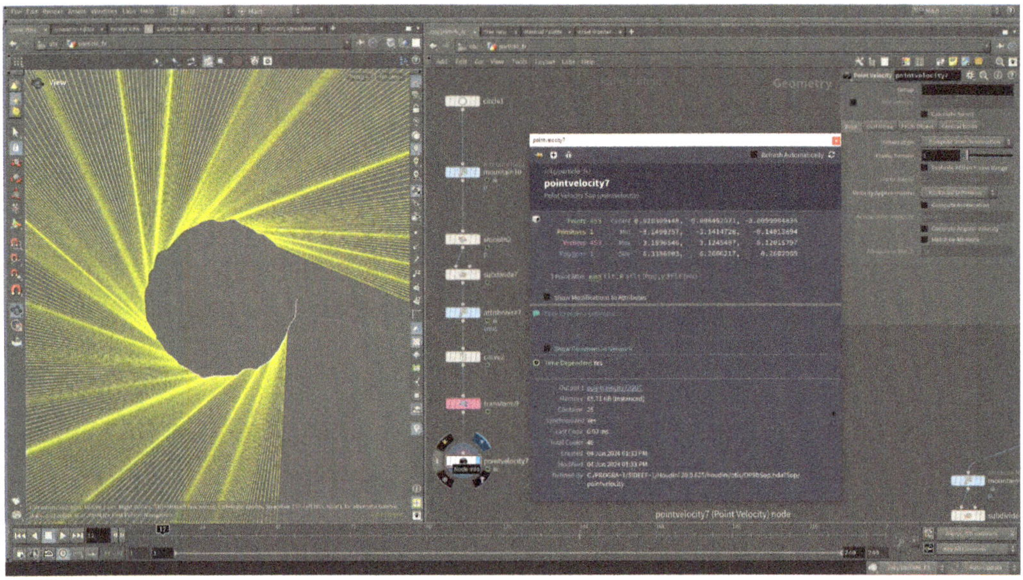

Figure 3.6 – Preview of Point Velocity

In the preceding screenshot, you can see many yellow lines coming out of the circle in an outward circular direction, which is, in fact, the velocity computed based on all the motion that the circle currently has.

After calculating the motion velocity vectors, it is now necessary to noise up the initially created velocity.

Adding noise to the initial velocity

Another common technique after creating an initial velocity based on the object's motion is adding extra noise to the velocity vectors.

There are many ways to distort, add, or multiply velocities by noise, ranging from custom-coded solutions to customizing vectors with visual programming nodes and using preset nodes to adjust vectors.

For this specific example, we will keep it simple and utilize the **Point Velocity** that already has the option to add extra animated noise in the **Curl Noise** tab. Now, let's look at the steps to execute this task:

1. Click on the **Curl Noise** tab and click on the **Add Curl Noise** checkbox.
2. Adjust the **Scale** parameter to `0.25` and **Swirl Size** to `0.25`, instructing the noise to add small gentle swirls to the original velocity.
3. Scrub the timeline further in time to frame **25**, for example, and notice how the velocity vectors have changed, resulting in nice random directions.

Refer to *Figure 3.7* to adjust the velocity noise parameters and see the resulting velocity vectors in the viewport:

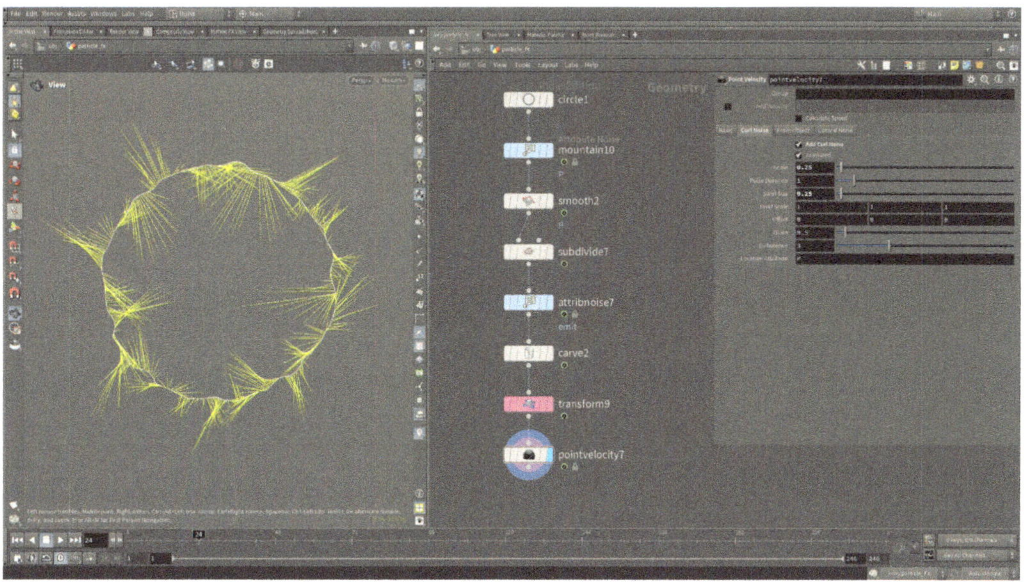

Figure 3.7 – Velocity curl noise

Congratulations on building your first efficient particle emitter in Houdini! Save your file and get ready to jump into the dynamics level!

Diving into Dynamics Operator (DOP) and Particle Operator (POP) networks

Dynamics Operators (**DOPs**) form a crucial part of Houdini's toolset, enabling artists to create complex simulations and dynamic effects with remarkable precision and control. DOPs are the backbone for simulating various physical phenomena, such as particles, rigid bodies, fluids, cloth, and more.

Particles, as a part of the dynamics environment, form specific toolsets and nodes called **Particle Operators** (**POPs**). In Houdini, POPs are integrated into DOPs to create complex and highly interactive simulations.

This integration allows particle systems to benefit from the dynamics environment provided by DOPs, enabling particles to interact with other dynamic objects and forces seamlessly.

In the example illustrated in the subsequent sections, I will build a particle system using POPs inside the dynamics network from scratch so you can understand what is happening under the hood of any particle simulation. After this, I will show you a very easy automated workflow.

DOP network

Let's create our first dynamics operators network and get familiar with the dynamics level:

1. First, create a DOP network. Follow these steps to execute this:
    1. Begin by pressing *Tab*, typing `dop network`, and placing the **dopnet1** node after **Point Velocity**.
    2. Notice that **dopnet1** has four inputs. Connect the output of **Point Velocity** to the *first* input of **dopnet1**.
    3. Double-click on the **dopnet1** node to dive inside. Alternatively, you can click on **dopnet1** and press *I* on the keyboard to dive in and press *u* to get back to the upper level.

2. Add core POPs for the particle system to become functional. This is done as follows:

    1. Create the three following nodes, one after another through the **TAB Menu**: **POP Source**, **POP Object**, and **POP Solver**.
    2. Connect the nodes; follow the instructions shown in *Figure 3.8*. Always keep the orange flag on the **output** node so the entire dynamics network is calculated properly.

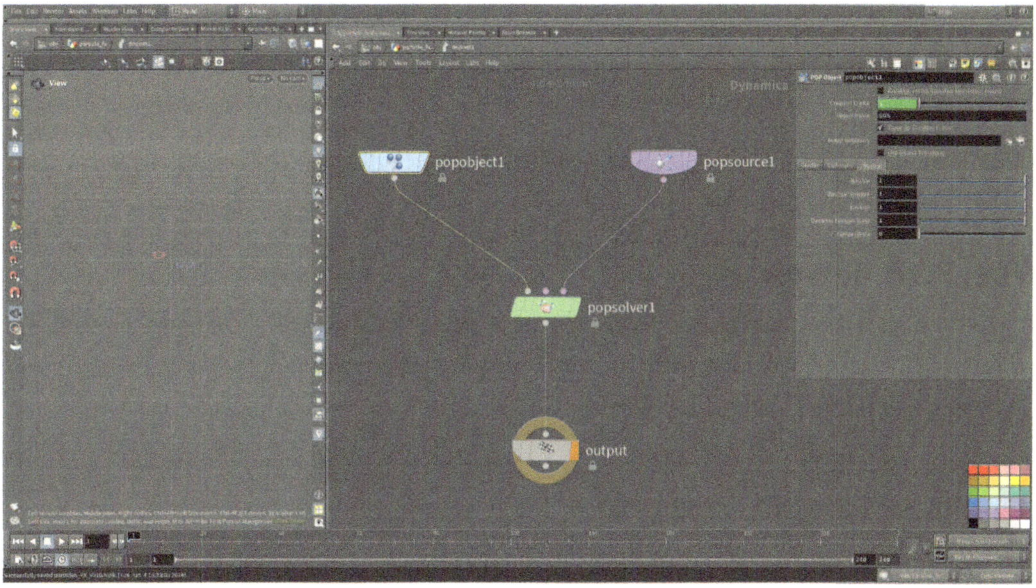

Figure 3.8 – Building a particle system from scratch

I have given the nodes different colors for illustrative purposes and will now give a brief explanation of their functions in a particle system:

- **POP Object**: It is a core node of a particle system that is specifically designed to represent particles within a dynamics simulation. It acts as a container for the particles and holds essential attributes and settings that define their behavior and interactions.
- **POP Source**: It is a core node of a particle system that is used to emit particles within a DOP network. This node specifies how and where particles are generated, what their initial attributes are, and how they enter the simulation.

- **POP Solver**: It is a core node of a particle system that is used to calculate the dynamics and behavior of particles within a particle system. It operates within the DOP network and is responsible for updating particle attributes over time based on the forces, interactions, and other rules defined in the simulation.

Without these three nodes, a particle system will not be able to exist and function, so they will need to be created and connected properly every time we need a simple particle simulation.

Now, it will be cumbersome to go ahead and create all the nodes and connect them every time you need a particle system, especially if you need to create more than one system.

Luckily, Houdini gives us a simple and fast solution that is called a POP network, which is ready to be dropped in and used.

The POP network

The **POP network** is a preset that has a DOP network with all the core POP nodes created and connected in the correct order, with the source settings designed to take the input geometry and start sourcing particles from its surface.

Let's go outside of the particle dynamics network that we have just built by pressing *u* on the keyboard and test out the POP network:

1. Press *Tab*, search `POP network node`, and place it after **Point Velocity** next to **dopnet1**.
2. Connect the output of **Point Velocity** to the *first input* of **popnet** and put the display flag on **popnet**.
3. Scrub the timeline ahead to frame **20** and notice that we now have lots of particles, and that yellow velocity vectors are still enabled (see *Figure 3.9*).
4. Also, notice how the timeline is now being colored blue in the frames that we have simulated, which is a very important indicator showing that the simulation is up to date and being stored in memory.

Let's turn off the velocity vectors' **v** visualizer the same way we turned it on: by hovering the mouse over the **Point Velocity** node, clicking on the node info **i** icon, and then clicking on **v** in the point attributes.

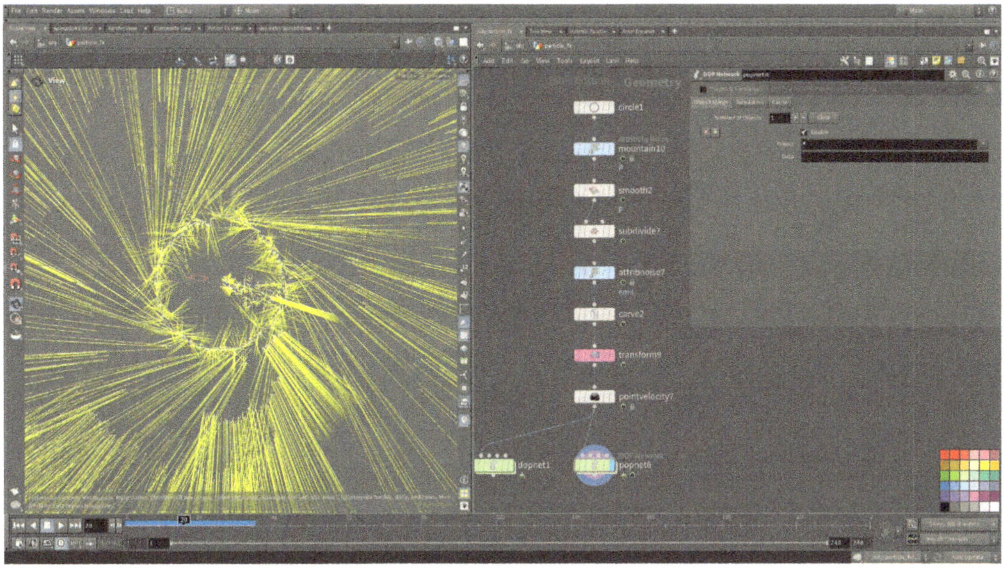

Figure 3.9 – POP network with velocity visualizer

Let's dive inside the POP network by selecting the **popnet** node and pressing *I* on the keyboard. Interestingly enough, we are going to see the same setup that we did manually, with one minor difference in an additional **Merge** node after **POP Source**, which is actually not needed and can be deleted, as shown in *Figure 3.10*:

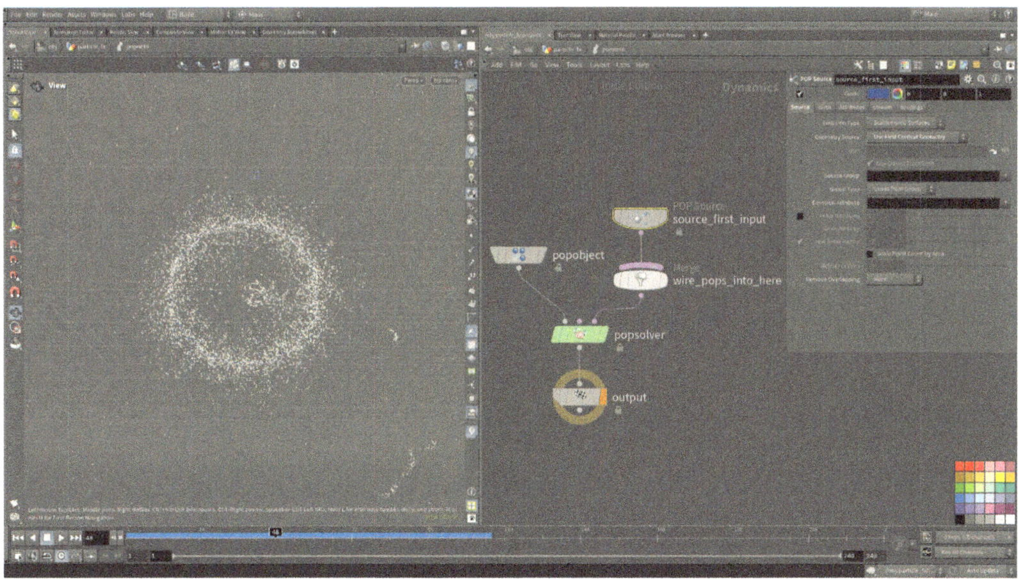

Figure 3.10 – Inside the POP network

Another minor and rather convenient difference of this preset is in the **POP Source** node that is named `source_first_input`. This is actually set to take any geometry connected to the first input of the POP network and scatter the particles to begin emission.

After connecting the emitter to the POP network and running a first test particle simulation, let's adjust the emission and particle source settings.

Adjusting the emission with custom attributes

Remember how we created a custom **emit** attribute based on the noise function (see the *Adding variation in emission areas* section)? Well, now is that exciting moment when we are going to use it to make our emission more interesting and random.

Here are the steps to accomplish that:

1. Select the **POP Source** node and use the **Source** tab's **Emission Attribute** box to type `emit`, the name of a custom attribute that we created earlier.

   Notice how the simulated frames in the timeline now changed from *blue* to *orange*, which means that we have changed a parameter, and our simulation is no longer up to date (see *Figure 3.11*)!

2. Scrub back to the first frame to clean the previous simulation data from the timeline and start a new simulation.

   Note that this step is very important and necessary every time we change a parameter or add new data to the particle simulation.

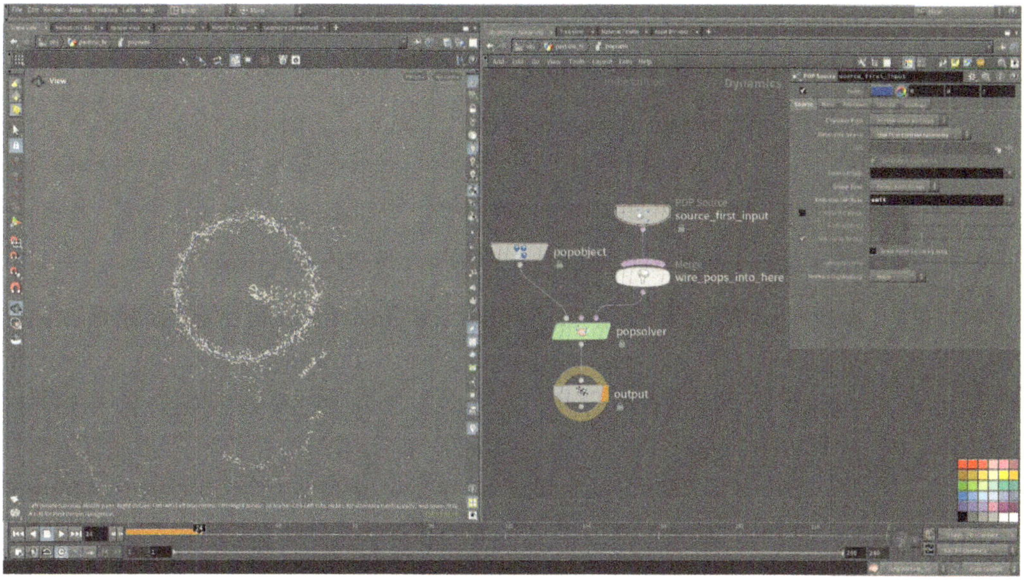

Figure 3.11 – Custom emission attribute

After setting and adjusting custom emission settings by attribute, let's take a look at the simulation settings.

Controlling particle simulation settings

Let's navigate to the next tab, which is called **Birth**, which controls how particles are added to the simulation and how long they will remain there. These settings determine the rate of particle emission, the conditions under which particles are created, and the initial states of these particles.

Here's a detailed explanation of the **POP Source** node's **Birth** settings and how they are used:

- **Emission**: Here are the key settings:
  - **Impulse Activation**: This toggle controls whether an impulse emission occurs, which is a burst of particles emitted at specific times. A value of `0` completely turns off particle emission, while a value of `1` turns emission on.
  - **Impulse Count (Birth Rate)**: This controls the number of particles emitted per frame/timestep during each impulse activation. This setting specifies how many particles are created during the burst.
  - **Constant Activation**: This toggle controls continuous particle emission over time. A value of `0` completely turns off particle emission, while a value of `1` turns emission on.

    - **Constant Birth Rate**: This is the rate at which particles are continuously emitted, specified as particles per second or the goal number of particles per second.

    To avoid any confusion and achieve the exact amount of particles that we entered in the **Count** box, I recommend setting all **Constant** parameters to `0` and using **Impulse Activation** and **Impulse Count** for particle emission.

- **Limit Emission Amount**: Let's look at the key settings in this group:
    - **Max Sim Points**: It will limit the total amount of particles to the number entered in the box. For example, if the number is set to `1000000`, then the number of particles in the simulation will increase until it reaches 1,000,000 and then be stopped from increasing.
    - **Max Points per Frame**: It will limit the maximum amount of particles emitted per frame to the number entered in the box.

    These emission limits are very useful to control how many particles are allowed in the particle system and prevent it from generating a huge number of points, which can give a lot of overhead on the CPU, RAM, and video memory, causing the Houdini session to crash.

- **Birth Groups and Seed**: Let's understand these as follows:
    - **Just Born Group**: It allows you to assign new particles to a specific group upon creation. This is useful for only applying subsequent operations to certain particles based on their group membership. It will also store which frame every burst of particles was created on.
    - **Seed**: It allows you to change the randomized initial scatter position of each particle in a burst. This is useful when creating different wedges of small particle amounts that can be combined into a larger simulation.
- **Life Expectancy**: It sets the average lifespan of particles. This value determines how long particles exist before they are removed from the simulation:
    - **Life Variance**: It adds randomness to the lifespan of particles, creating variation in how long particles live.
- **Jitter Birth Time**: It adds randomness to the birth time of particles, creating a more natural and less uniform emission. This is useful for avoiding a static look and making the particle emission appear more organic.

After learning about the parameters in the **Birth** tab, let's adjust them to get closer to the portal look that we need.

Adjusting birth and simulation settings for the portal

Refer to *Figure 3.12* and the **Birth** tab settings to achieve the desirable initial look of the portal:

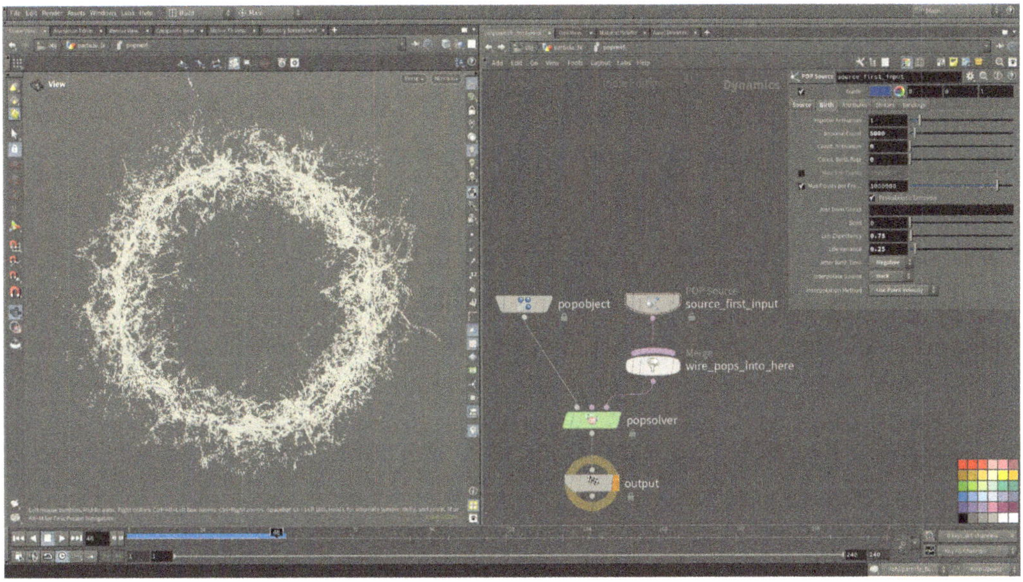

Figure 3.12 – Birth and Life settings

I will give a brief explanation of the steps that need adjustment:

1. Adjust **Impulse Count** to `5000`, which means that the particle system will be emitting 5,000 particles in every frame.
2. Set all the **Constant** settings to `0`, so we avoid using constant emission altogether.
3. Adjust **Life Expectancy** to `0.75`, which will significantly reduce the particle life and have them disappear from the simulation much more quickly. The value of `0.75` is in seconds, meaning that the particles will die in just under a second.
4. Set **Life Variance** to `0.25`, which is also in seconds. This will result in some random particles having a life of `0.75 + 0.25`, other random particles having a life of `0.75 - 0.25`, and the rest of the random particles having a life in between these ranges.
5. Adjust **Jitter Birth Time** to a **Negative** setting. This will result in the particles' births being randomly offset back in time by extending the source and fixing any potential stepping or emitter artifacts caused by fast motion or fast velocities.

6. Set **Interpolate Source** to **Back** and **Interpolation Method** to **Use Point Velocity**. This will blend the offset position and the current position of the emitter in a linear manner based on the trailed **Point Velocity**, and will result in smooth emission that will fix any clumping or stepping.

Moving forward, let's add some forces to have better control and guide the particles' motion.

Combining forces and physical attributes

Our portal simulation is slowly starting to take a nicer shape, and we are going to gain extra control over the motion and overall dynamics by adding forces to shape the simulation better.

If we analyze any reference to the *Doctor Strange*-inspired portal or most portals seen in movies or games, we will notice a very distinct circular motion component.

In other words, there is some kind of force that is making the particles orbit around a specific central axis. Let's use the repository of available POPs that are basically building blocks of different particle forces, attributes, and rules and recreate this circular motion.

Spinning with POP Axis Force

The next force that we are going to add will help to create a rotational force field and make the particles spin around a specified axis. Let's look at the steps in detail:

1. Press *Tab*, search for `POP axis force`, and connect it between **POP Source** and **Merge** nodes. You will need to connect the output of **POP Source** to the input of **POP Axis Force** and the output of **POP Axis Force** to the input of the **Merge** node (see *Figure 3.13*). Let's explore this in more detail:

    - Notice that we now have a *red* spherical shape with a *white* vertical line in the middle. The **POP Axis Force** node will affect the particles that are within the *red* sphere radius and will push them to orbit around the white axis.
    - The **Activation** parameter is for turning this force on or off, the same as particle birth activation.
    - The *red* **Guide** checkbox controls the visibility of the red spherical shape and the white axis in the viewport.
    - The parameters in the **Shape** tab will control the guide shape, size, and axis direction.
    - Clearly, all the particles are being sourced outside the red sphere, so the force currently has no effect.

2. Adjust the **Radius** and **Height** parameters by increasing the values to `10`, so all the emitting particles will be contained within the *red* shape.

   Now the particle motion has changed, and the particles are spinning around the white axis. It is not very visible at the moment since the particles are disappearing too soon.

   This axis, however, is not oriented in the way that we need for the portal. For the correct portal motion, we need to adjust the white axis to be perpendicular to the portal emitter and go through its center.

3. Adjust the **Axis** direction parameter by zeroing everything out and setting the direction in **Z axis**, which is the third input box, to `1`.

Now everything is moving accurately and the portal particles are correctly orbiting around the white axis.

If you want to disable the red spherical shape guide, you can uncheck the **Guide** checkbox on top of the **Node** settings.

We can further adjust how fast the particles spin and add extra force directions in the **Speed** tab.

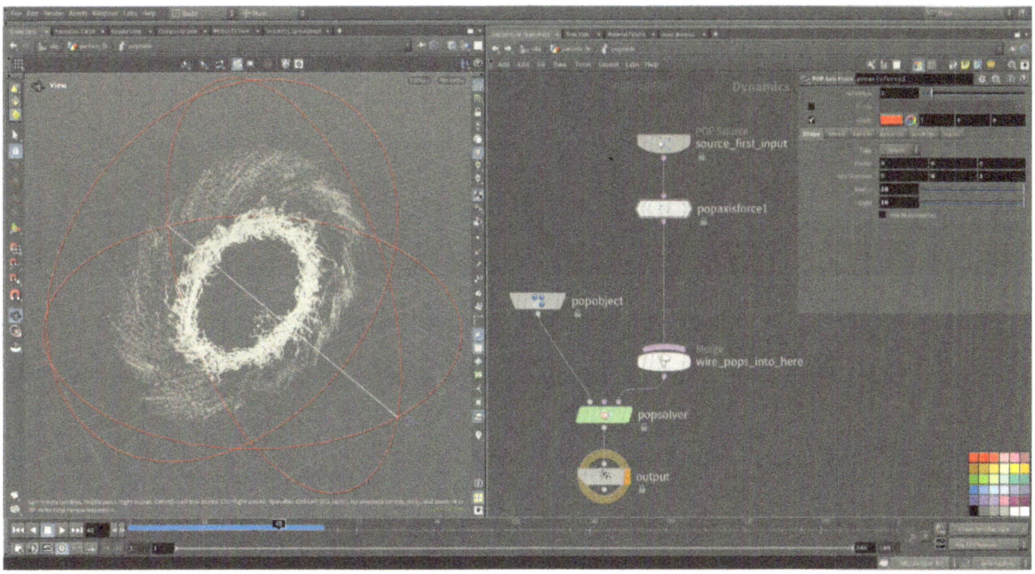

Figure 3.13 – POP Axis Force settings

Further, the **Speed** tab has three main forces for us to control the motion:

- **Orbit Speed**: It is used to control how fast the particles are spinning around the white axis
- **Lift Speed**: It is used to control how fast the particles will move along the white axis forward or backward depending on the value
- **Suction Speed**: It is used to control how quickly the particles will be attracted to the white axis equally depending on their position in 3D space

Let's adjust the **Orbit Speed** settings to make the spin faster and add some attraction to the center of the portal with **Suction Speed** (see *Figure 3.14*):

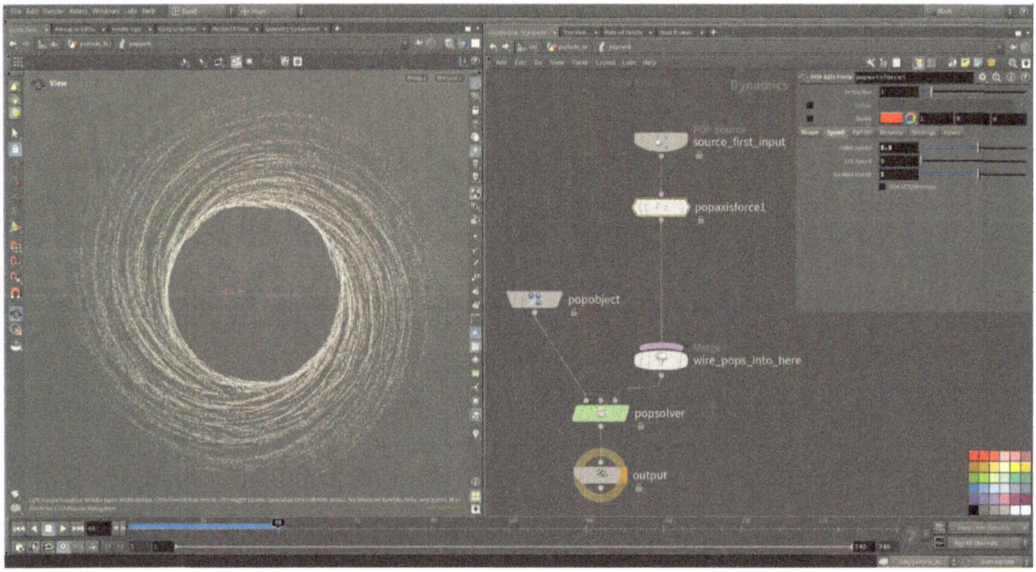

Figure 3.14 – POP Axis Force speed adjustment

After the rotational force, let's move on to adding some air noise turbulence to the motion of the particles.

Adding turbulent curl noise forces

Turbulent forces are important since they add extra variation and details, mimicking real-world wind turbulence, which happens due to different air densities.

Follow these steps to add turbulent curl noise forces:

1. Press *Tab*, search for `POP force`, and connect it after **POP Axis Force**. By itself, this force is not going to do anything until we enter a value for **Amplitude** in the **Noise** tab.

   POP Force also gives you the ability to add a directional wind force in the **Force** input boxes. However, for the purpose of this portal effect, we are not going to use it here.

   > Note
   >
   > Combining two or more forces can take some experimentation, and eventually, with experience, you will note that some forces have to overpower others to balance out and have any effect.

2. Set **Amplitude** in the **Noise** tab to a value of `30` for the force to compete and balance out **POP Axis Force**.

   Notice that we are still getting the spinning component, and it is now being broken down and varied nicely by the turbulent noise force.

   > Tip
   >
   > A good practice is to have two turbulent forces for better control and variation. Usually, one force will have a smaller swirl size and faster moving noise, and the second force will have larger slower swirls with a lower amplitude.

   Some of the main parameters that will define the look and motion of the turbulence are **Amplitude**, **Swirl Size**, **Pulse Length**, **Roughness**, **Turbulence**, and **Offset**. All the other parameters usually stay set to their default settings, unless there is a specific or abstract scenario.

Let's examine these options:

- **Swirl Size**: It will control the frequency or the element size of the noise pattern, as the element size setting in the mountain node does
- **Pulse Length**: It controls how fast the noise function changes over time, with values closer to `0` making it faster and values further from `0` making it slower
- **Turbulence**: This setting lets us add levels of complexity into the noise function and swirls
- **Offset**: It will change the position values of the noise function based on the values in 3D space

3. Adjust the rest of the **Noise** settings; refer to *Figure 3.15*.
4. Add a second **POP Force** with larger swirls and varying settings; refer to *Figure 3.15*:

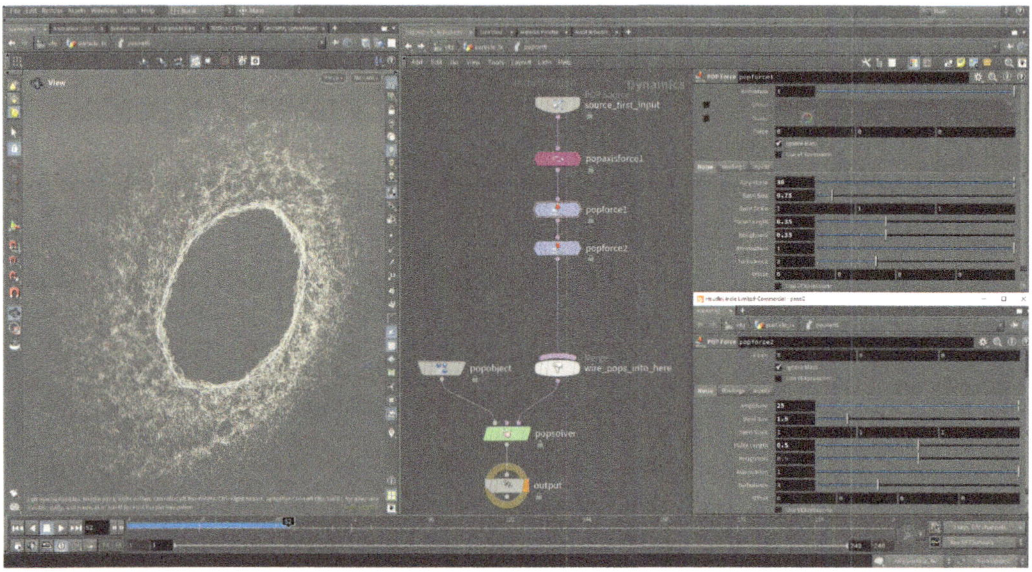

Figure 3.15 – POP Force

After adding the main guiding forces, let's move on to adding a specific force that will mimic air drag.

Introducing air resistance with POP Drag

Air resistance is another important concept in achieving realistic motion and effects. In other words, drag force will prevent the particles from accelerating infinitely and act as a deceleration force that will reduce the speed of particles over time:

1. Add a **POP Drag** node after **POP Force** and set the **Air Resistance** value to `0.5`. This force is very simple and abides by a simple rule: the higher the air resistance is, the faster the particle will come to a stop.
2. Turn off the **Ignore Mass** checkbox under **Air Resistance**. This action will be tied to the next node that I will introduce shortly. It will help us achieve randomized drag per particle and add further realism to the motion of our system.

Let's move on to adding some specific particle properties such as particle mass.

Unlocking particle properties and attributes

There is a very special node that will allow us to create or adjust specific particle properties, one of them being particle mass.

Let's look at the steps to do this:

1. Add a **POP Properties** node after **POP Drag** and enable the **Mass** checkbox.

   Now, each particle will have a **Mass** attribute of **1**. This is only a first step, however, since the actual goal is to make each particle have a random mass value that will fall within a certain range. This could be easily achieved by a few lines of code.

2. Check the **Use VEXpression** checkbox in **POP Properties** and you will see an empty box where we can input the code.
3. Type the following code into the empty box:

   ```
   mass *= fit01(rand(@id), 0.5, 1);
   ```

Let's break down the meaning of the above expression:

- This expression will use a unique particle ID to randomly multiply every particle's mass attribute by a range of values between `0.5` and `1`
- After this, the minimum value of mass will be `0.5`, the maximum will be `1`, and all the particles in between will get a random value from `0.5` to `1`

Quick tip: Enhance your coding experience with the **AI Code Explainer** and **Quick Copy** features. Open this book in the next-gen Packt Reader. Click the **Copy** button

(1) to quickly copy code into your coding environment, or click the **Explain** button

(2) to get the AI assistant to explain a block of code to you.

Copy (1) Explain (2)

```
function calculate(a, b) {
  return {sum: a + b};
};
```

The next-gen Packt Reader is included for free with the purchase of this book. Scan the QR code OR go to `packtpub.com/unlock`, then use the search bar to find this book by name. Double-check the edition shown to make sure you get the right one.

Check out *Figure 3.16* to see the POP property and expression settings:

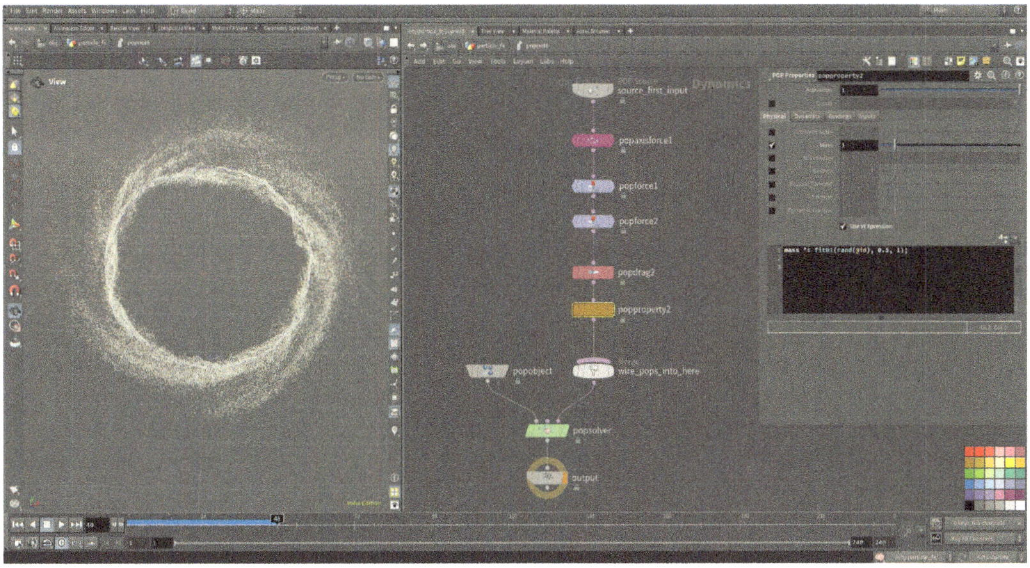

Figure 3.16 – POP property and expression settings

Next, we will move on to add a ground collision object for the portal.

Merging collision objects

There are several types of collision objects that can be merged with particle simulations. One type can be created internally inside the dynamics network and the others can be imported from other contexts, such as **obj** (SOP). **Colliders** can also be static or deforming and can use different methods that can be optimized before the simulation.

In this example, we will take a look at a simple ground collider that can be created right inside the dynamics network.

Follow these steps:

1. Press *Tab*, search for a `Ground Plane` node, and place it to the left of **POP Solver** without connecting to anything.

   We have reached a point where a very important concept of the dynamics network will be introduced. The order of all operations in the dynamics network is from left to right. In other words, nodes on the left affect nodes on the right, unlike in the **Geometry** level, where the order is from top to bottom.

This concept is *important*, especially for collisions, meaning that the collision object must be merged first from the left, and the result of the **POP Solver** containing particle data must be merged second from the right.

2. Create a **Merge** node. First, connect the ground plane from the left and then **POP Solver** node from the right.
3. Connect the **Merge** node to the **output** node so the entire system gets evaluated.

By referring to *Figure 3.17*, we can see how the ground collision works with the particles:

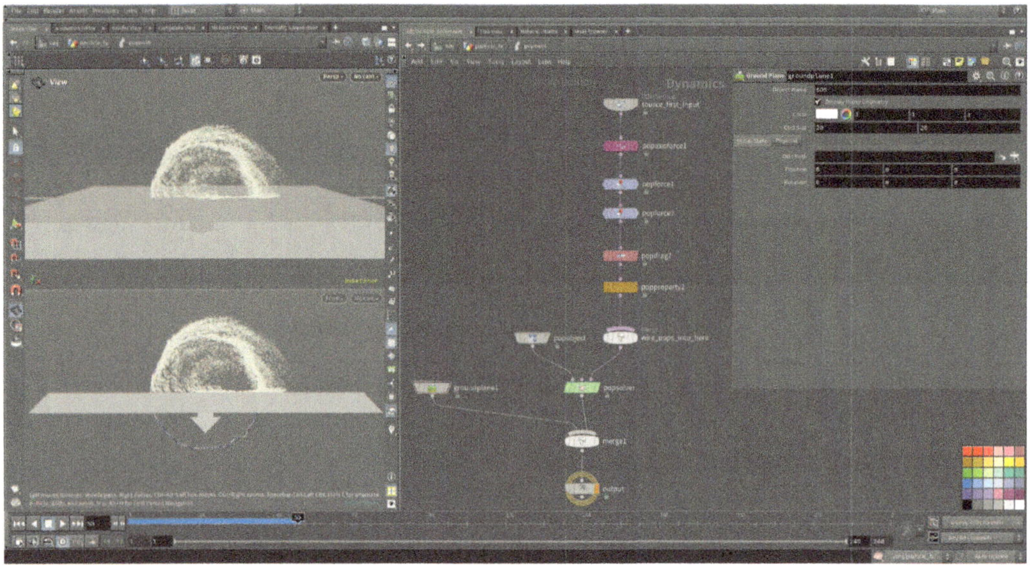

Figure 3.17 – Merging ground collider

The collider works. However, it is positioned right in the middle of the portal, causing it to only collide with the part above zero.

The easiest way to fix this would be to transform the ground plane in the *Y*-axis to a distance below the portal. Let's see the steps for fixing this:

1. Select **groundplane1** and use the **Initial State** tab to adjust the position on the *Y*-axis to `-3.75` units.

   Since our portal radius scale was set to `3.5` in the beginning, a transformation value of `-3.75` will be enough for the particles to be able to emit and collide with the ground nicely.

2. Click on the **Physical** tab of **groundplane1** and adjust the **Bounce** and **Friction** parameters to `0.25`; this will result in nice sparks-like collision behavior.

   Physical parameters can be modified on each of the colliders separately and on the particles themselves. Particle physical settings can be found in **POP Object**.

In *Figure 3.18*, we can see how the updated collision with the ground plane is going to look:

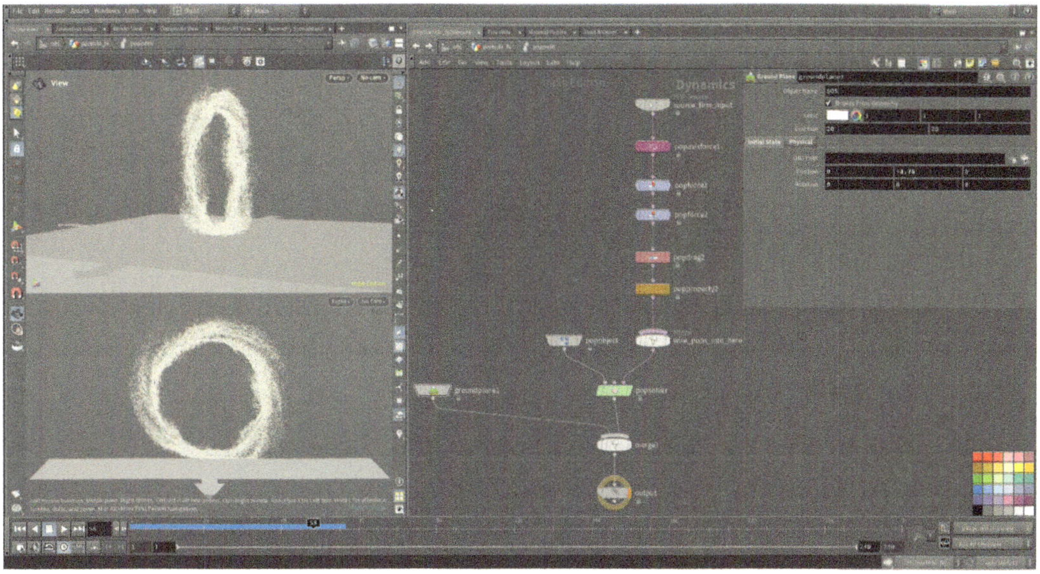

Figure 3.18 – Corrected collision

Congratulations on completing the dynamics simulation part of the portal effect! Save your file and prepare for post-simulation output.

Particle caching and manipulation of attributes

For the next steps, we will continue in the **Geometry** (SOP) context to cache simulation to the disc, create additional attributes, and prepare particles for rendering.

Let's look at the steps for bringing the particles back into the **Geometry** level from the dynamics level:

1. Press *u* on the keyboard to jump up to the **Geometry** (SOP) level and look at our simulation output (see *Figure 3.19*).

   As you've probably noticed, the POP network already has the result of the dynamics simulation merged into the **Geometry** level via the **Object Merge** tab.

   However, the default settings are bringing both the particles and the ground collider. We are not interested in the ground collider geometry for further actions, so we need to adjust **Object Merge** to only bring back particles.

2. Click on the **Object** box under the **Object Merge** tab, remove the * symbol, and type `popobject` instead.

   The * symbol means that everything will be brought up from the dynamics network to the SOP level, and the `popobject` command will force it to only bring the particle simulation data stored in **POP Object**.

Refer to *Figure 3.19* to see the object merge settings from the POP network:

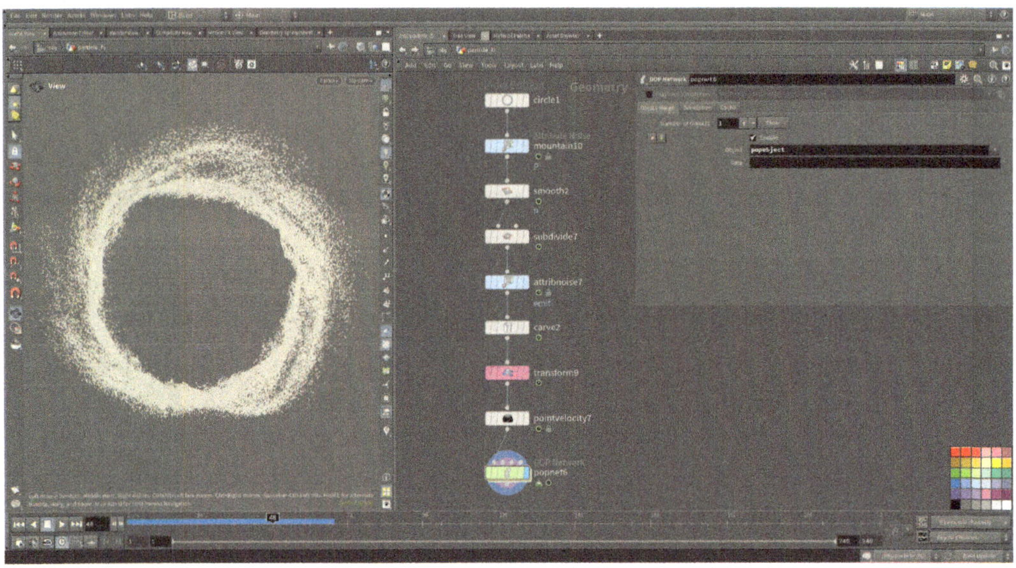

Figure 3.19 – Particles Object Merge

In the next section, we will explore how to optimize and output the particles after the simulation.

Optimizing simulation output and attributes

Particles usually come out from the context of the dynamics with lots of simulation data and attributes.

> Important note
>
> It is always good practice to delete unnecessary data and only keep what we will need for post-sim manipulation and rendering.

Now, let's look at the steps for previewing attribute data:

1. Create an **Attribute Delete** node and prepare to analyze the data stored on particles.

   You can easily check all the data stored on points by right-clicking on the **Attribute Delete** node and choosing **Spreadsheet...**.

   You will notice a huge list of all the attributes that come out of the simulation. Some of them can be used in the future, and some of them are no longer needed and just taking space and memory (see *Figure 3.20*).

2. Usually, the main attributes that we need for the post-simulation adjustment, caching, and rendering are the following:

   - **P**: Particle position in 3D space
   - **v**: Particle velocity
   - **age**: Particle age
   - **hittotal**: Particles that interacted with collision object
   - **id**: Unique particle identification number
   - **life**: Total life of a particle
   - **mass**: Particle mass property

Important note

Remember that Houdini is case-sensitive, so it is very important to type or enter the exact name of an attribute, respecting the use of lower or upper case.

In *Figure 3.20*, you can see all the attributes that we have on our particles:

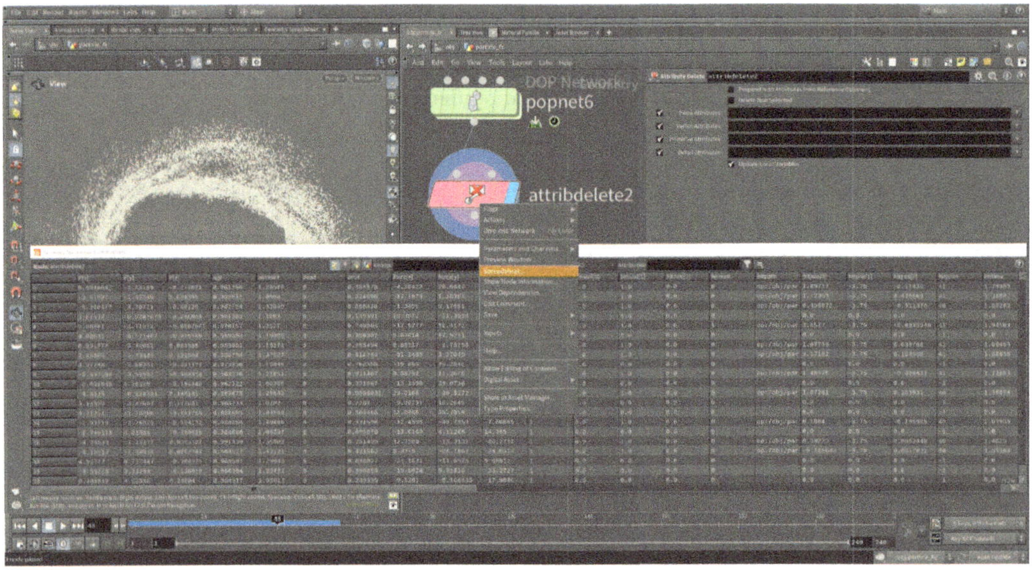

Figure 3.20 – Geometry spreadsheet

1. In the **Attribute Delete** node, enable the **Delete Non Selected** checkbox.

   By doing this, we can specify what attributes we want to keep, which will result in a much shorter list and will be way less time-consuming.

2. Type the following attributes into the **Point Attributes** box, using spaces in between to keep them separate: `P v age hittotal id life mass`.
3. Check the **Geometry** spreadsheet and notice that it now looks much lighter more and optimized.

Refer to *Figure 3.21* to see the updated attribute list after the **Attribute Delete** node:

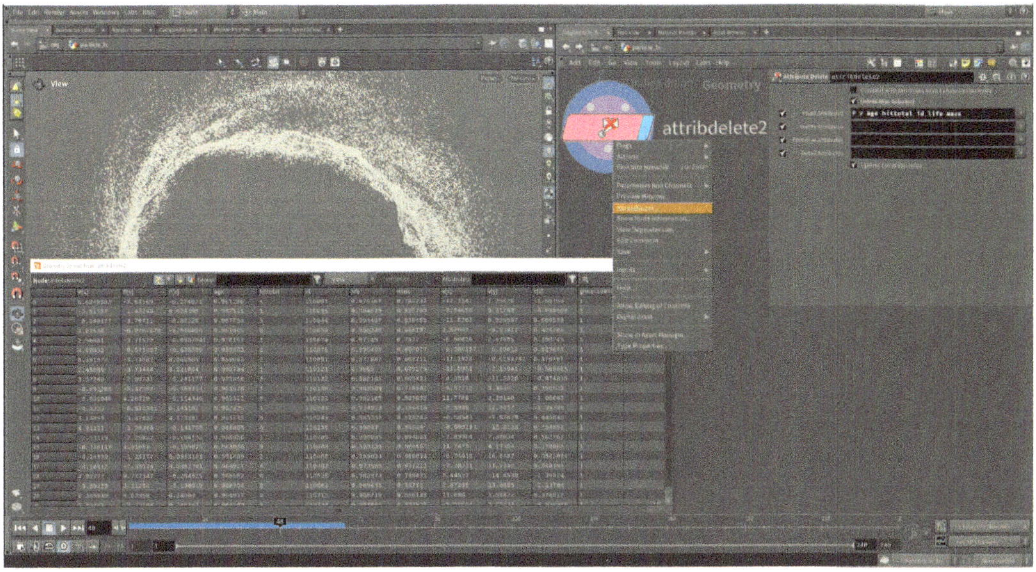

Figure 3.21 – Optimized particle attributes

Moving on, we'll now look at the process of saving particle simulations to the disc.

Caching geometry data to the disc

Geometry caching is a vital process in Houdini, especially when working with complex simulations or heavy geometries. It involves saving a computationally expensive or time-consuming operation to the disc, allowing you to reuse the precomputed data instead of recalculating it each time.

Geometry caching is the process of storing the result of a geometry operation or simulation to the disc. This process helps in the following ways:

- Reducing computation time by avoiding recalculations
- Managing large simulations by breaking them into manageable chunks
- Facilitating iterative workflows by saving different stages of the process

Now that we've explored the importance of caching, let's take a look at the actual node that will help us in this process.

Using the File Cache node

The **File Cache** node is designed to handle the storage and retrieval of cached geometry data. It offers a straightforward interface for writing and reading geometry caches.

Follow *Figure 3.22* to see the file cache settings and parameters:

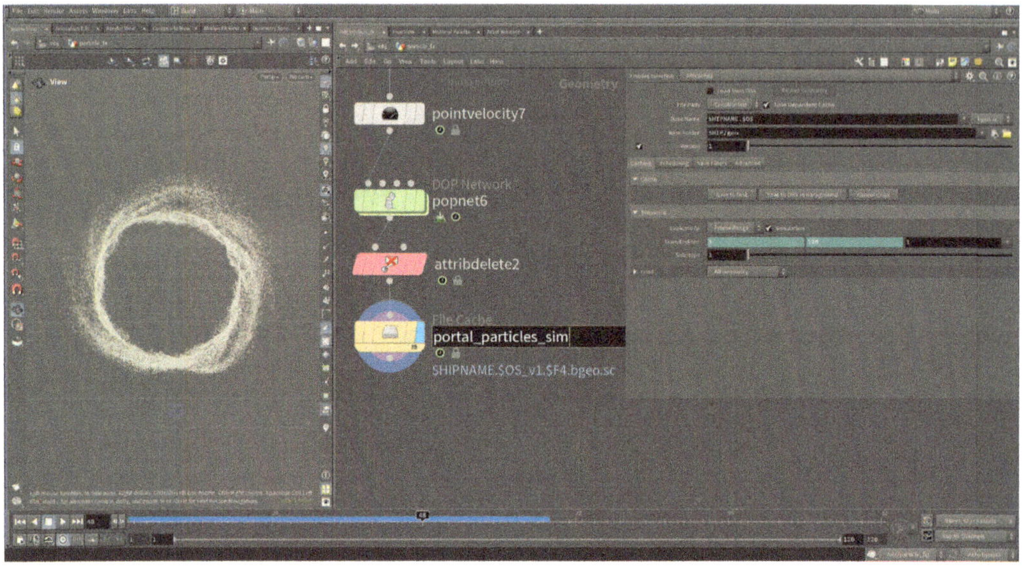

Figure 3.22 – File Cache

Now, let's move on to starting the caching process:

1. Press *Tab*, search for `file cache` node, and place it after the **Attribute Delete** node.

   Some of the most important parts of the file cache workflow include setting the cache name and frame range that will be saved. All the other properties will be created automatically and saved in the correct directory, especially if the Houdini Project was set from the beginning.

2. Click on the name next to the **File Cache** node to be able to edit it. Type `portal_particles_sim` instead of `filecache1`.

File Cache will use specific tokens to save everything correctly in the provided directory. **Base Name** will be equal to the name of your Houdini file and the name of the file cache. **Base Folder** is set to the geo folder, which is in the directory where your project is saved.

Important tip

If you are ever confused about where your cache will be saved, click on the **Advanced** tab and you will see the **Output File** path highlighted in blue.

Right underneath the **File Cache** node, you will see the following token written in blue letters: **$HIPNAME.$OS_v1.$F4.bgeo.sc**.

I will give a quick explanation of what this label means:

- **$HIPNAME**: This is the current name of your saved Houdini file, which was set to `particle_effects_v0xx` (x being the custom increment version that you are currently on).
- **.$OS_v1**: This is the name of the **File Cache** node, which is **portal_particles_sim**, as well as the version parameter the node is set to. By default, the file cache version is set to **1** from the beginning and you can increment it up to have different versions of simulations if you would like to compare them in the future.
- **.$F4**: It is the current frame number formatted as a four-digit padded integer, so if the first frame of the cache is **1**, it will be saved as **0001**.
- **.bgeo**: It is Houdini's native file format for saving geometry data.
- **.sc**: It is a suffix that indicates that the file is compressed using Houdini's internal compression algorithm, resulting in smaller file sizes while maintaining the integrity and detail of the geometry data.

As you can see, all the paths and names are conveniently stored in the tokens that are also called global variables, so all we need to worry about is doing the following:

1. Set a Houdini project directory from the beginning.
2. Save our file into the root of that project.
3. Name the file cache in a way that represents what are we caching.
4. Set a preferred version of the cache (it can also stay at the default, **1**, and override the old cache).
5. Set the frame range of our project timeline that will instantly be linked to the first and last frame of the file cache.
6. Click on **Save to Disc**.

We have all the steps ready except for the last few ones, which are setting the desired timeline frame range (*Step 5*) and saving the cache to the disc (*Step 6*).

Now let's move on to the final steps to execute caching to the disc:

1. Press *Alt* + *Shift* + *G* to bring up the **Global Animation Options** menu.
2. Leave the **Start** frame set to `1`. Change the end frame to `120` instead of `240`, press *Enter*, and click on the **Apply** button.

   Notice that both the timeline frame range and the frame range on the file cache are now set to from `1` to `120`.
3. Click on the **Save to Disc** button on the file cache to start the caching process.
4. Click on **Play** in the playback menu and observe the cached simulation from start to finish.

Congratulations on creating your first cache in Houdini! Incrementally save your file and get ready to prepare the particles for rendering.

Creating extra attributes for rendering

One important aspect that our portal is currently missing is the fiery spark-like colors that we can see in the *Doctor Strange* portals.

For the next steps, we will be creating a color attribute that will be dependent on a particle's age. It will be mapped to a custom color gradient that we can artistically control.

Let's look at the steps for doing this:

1. Add a **Color** node after **File Cache**.
2. Set **Color Type** to **Ramp from Attribute**.
3. Type age in the empty **Attribute** box.
4. Adjust the **Range** to capture particle age from `0` to `0.75`.
5. You can double-click on the existing color markers to modify them or click on an empty spot anywhere on the color ramp to create a new marker.

6. Set the color using *Figure 3.23* as your reference, representing a fiery gradient.

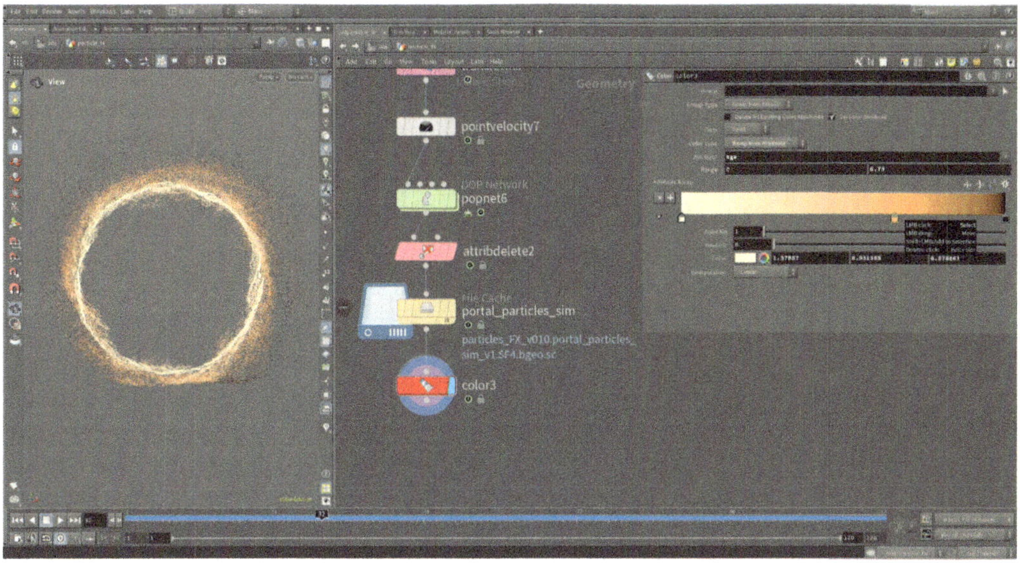

Figure 3.23 – Color by age

We can further adjust the color by making random particles brighter to add more variation and details:

1. Add an **Attribute Adjust Color** node after the **Color** node.
2. Set **Operation** to **Add**.
3. Set **Pattern Type** to **Random**.
4. In the **Random** tab, choose **Randomization by Custom Attribute**.

5. Adjust the color gradient to be similar to the colors provided in *Figure 3.24*:

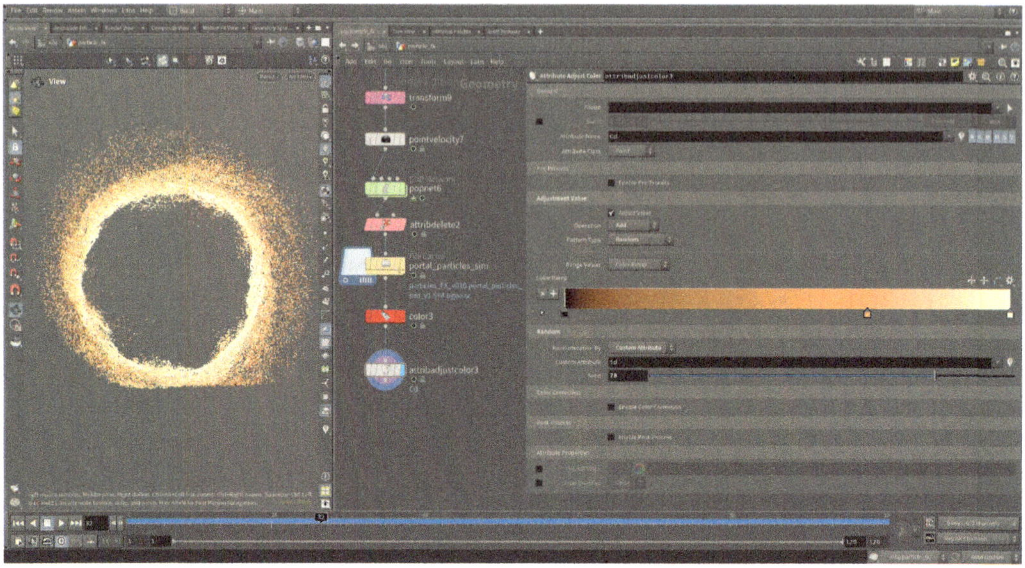

Figure 3.24 – Adjust color by randomization

For the last few steps before rendering, we will use the randomized mass attribute created in the simulation, map it to the particle scale, and multiply it by velocity such that the particles with higher mass will have a bigger scale and velocity and vice versa. Here's how:

1. Create an **Attribute Wrangle** node and connect it after **Attribute Adjust Color**.
2. In the **VEXspression** box, type the following code:

   ```
   @pscale = 1;
   ```

   With this first expression, we are creating a particle scale (**pscale**) attribute and giving it a default value of `1`.

3. Press *Enter* and write the following code on the second line:

   ```
   @pscale *= fit(@mass, 0.5, 1, 0.0025, 0.0125);
   ```

   This second expression takes the randomized mass attribute per particle that has a range of values from `0.5` to `1` and fits it to a new range that has values from `0.0025` to `0.0125`.

   This range is then multiplied by a default value of particle scale, making the smallest particle size equal to `1*0.0025` and the largest particle size equal to `1*0.0125`.

Let's adjust the **Point Velocity** values using another attribute wrangle:

1. Create a second attribute wrangle and connect it after the first.
2. In the **VEXpression** box, type the following code:

   ```
   @v *= fit(@pscale, 0.0025, 0.0125, 0.1, 0.5);
   ```

   This expression will take the existing velocity attribute per particle and multiply it by the particle scale attribute that has its range of values remapped to fit a new range of `0.1` to `0.5`.

As a result, we are reducing the maximum velocity by 50 percent, and the minimum velocity will only be 10 percent of its original value.

In other words, particles with the minimum value of mass will get a new velocity that will be equal to 10 percent of the original value, and the particles with the maximum value of mass will have their velocity reduced to 50 percent of the original value.

This step is not absolutely necessary. However, we often need to reduce the stretching of motion blur based on velocity vectors for a better-looking image.

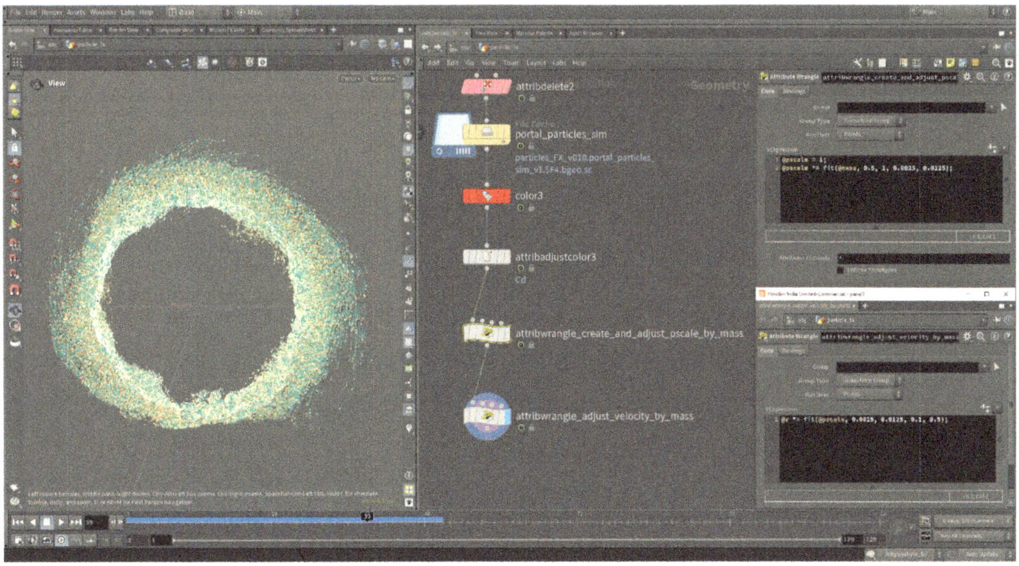

Figure 3.25 – Adjusting pscale and v

We are now ready to transition to the most exciting part, which is the lighting and rendering of the portal effect.

Before we get to the rendering stage, create a **Null** node and name it `OUT_Portal_FX_for_rendering`. The reason why we write `OUT` in capital letters is that Houdini's operator chooser will put all the nodes that have upper case names at the top of the selection list, so by using all-capitals, we can find them more easily when importing to other contexts or levels.

After caching the simulation, you can preview the result in the viewport or create a flipbook. An important option to enable while previewing the simulation in the viewport is real-time playback, so the viewport plays everything at a defined 24 frames per second.

To enable real-time playback, you can open global animation options by entering *Alt* + *Shift* + *G* and checking the **Realtime Playback** checkbox under the **Playback** section.

Increment save your file and get ready to jump into the **Solaris** context for rendering.

Shading and rendering particle effects

In this final part, we will look into importing the result of our particle simulation into the **stage/ Solaris** environment for lighting and rendering, as well as setting up basic materials for particles and creating a simple environment for the particles to render in.

Based on the knowledge from *Chapter 1*, you should know how to switch to the **stage** context via the tree view, which is accessible by pressing *Shift* + *W*, so I will move on to setting up the **Solaris** scene right away.

Setting up Solaris for quick render tests

Here are the steps you need to follow to set up **Solaris**:

1. Switch to the **stage** context and create an **SOP Import** node.
2. Link the path to the **OUT_Portal_FX_for_rendering Null** node into the **SOP Path** box.
3. Create a camera looking straight into the portal opening.
4. Create a dome light and set its intensity to `0.25`.
5. Press *D* to open the display options and set the background color option to **Dark**.
6. Change **Perspective** to **Karma CPU** or **Karma XPU** and do a quick render test.

Refer to *Figure 3.26* to see the initial **Solaris** and render test setup:

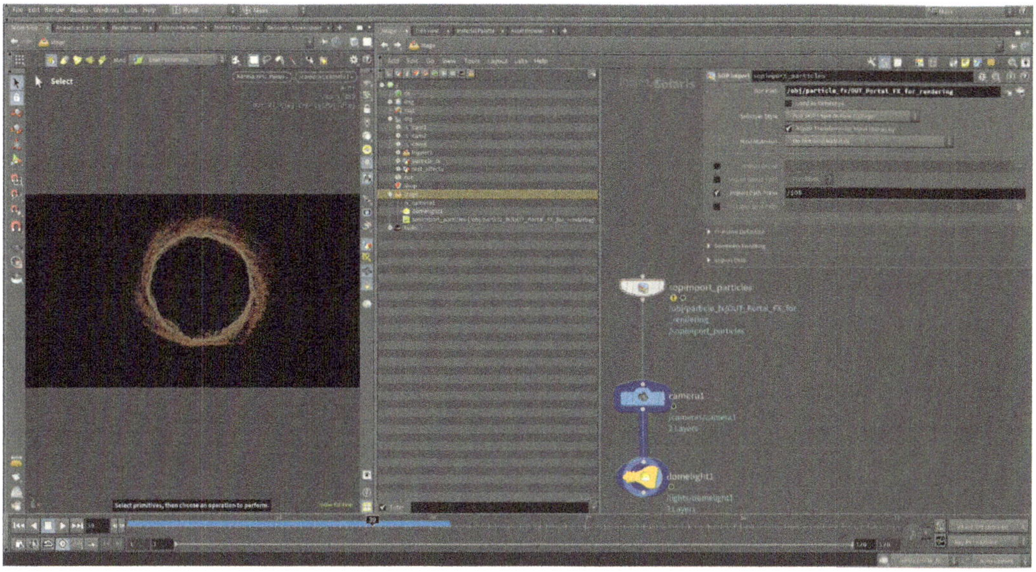

Figure 3.26 – Solaris and quick render test

After the initial render test, let's move on to creating shaders and materials.

Shading and adding materials

Looking at our first test render, we can notice that most things work as expected. However, there are still many things we will need to add and fix.

Currently, the portal looks very dull and dark instead of being bright and emitting fiery light. We are also missing a ground plane to catch reflections or an environment for the portal to live in.

Finally, we will need to add motion blur based on the velocity attribute of the particles for a realistic film look.

Follow the next steps to start adding materials to the scene:

1. Create a **Material Library** node and connect it after the dome light.
2. Double-click on **Material Library** to dive into the material creation environment.
3. Press *Tab* and search for `Karma Material Builder`.
4. Click on the material name and rename it `karmamaterial_particles`.
5. Double-click on **Karma Material Builder** to get inside the shader building environment.
6. Press *Tab* and search for the `MtlX Geometry Color` node.

7. Connect the **MtlX Geometry Color** node to both **base_color** and **emission color**.
8. Set the **Specular** parameter on the material to `0`.
9. Set **Emission** to `1.5`.

Refer to *Figure 3.27* for the values and to follow along with these steps:

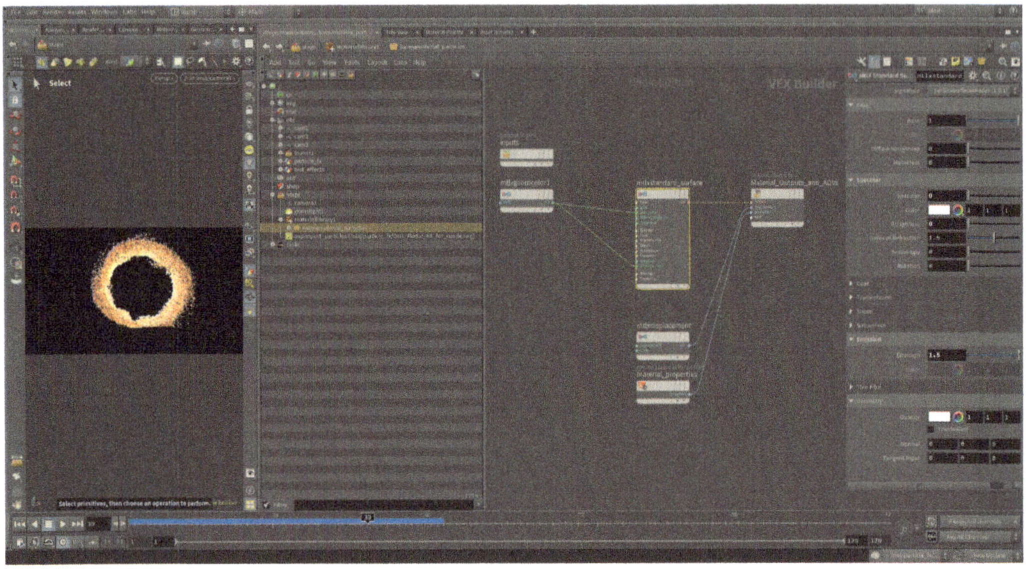

Figure 3.27 – Building emissive material

All the steps we just performed basically created a simple material builder and imported the particle color attribute with the help of the **MtlX Geometry Color** node, which we are plugging into the base color of the particle material. We are also making it emissive with the same color.

Assigning materials

The material that we have created is ready to go. However, it is not going to work on particles in the render until we assign it properly. Let's look at how we can do this:

1. Press *u* on your keyboard two times to go back up to the **Solaris** level.
2. Press *Tab*, create a **Material Linker** node, and connect it after the material library.

   In the UI of **Material Linker**, you will see all the created existing materials in the scene located in the **Material List** box. On the very right of the **Material Linker** node is **Geometry Tree**, which has a list of all objects in the **Solaris** scene.

The process of assigning material to a corresponding object is very simple: you have to drag the required material from **Material List** and drop it onto the corresponding geometry in **Geometry Tree**.

3. Click and hold on **karmamaterial_particles** and drag it onto **sopimport_particles**.
4. Create a quick Karma render test.

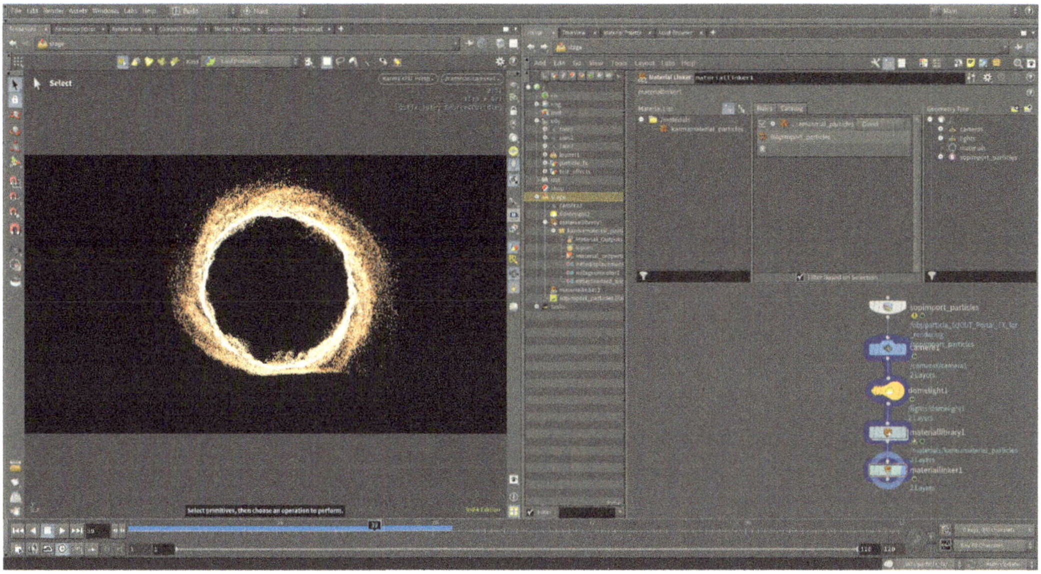

Figure 3.28 – Assign material to particles

Everything is slowly coming together, and now, our portal particles are looking nice and bright. I encourage you to create a simple ground or cylinder with curved edges and an open top for a quick environment around the portal to catch reflections.

The simple object can be created in the **Geometry** context and linked to **Solaris** the same way as particles using a separate **sopimport** node and then merged using a **Merge** node with SOP import that brings in the particles.

Another quick way would be to create a simple reflection catcher by executing the following steps:

1. Create a grid node in **Solaris**.
2. Set **Transform Uniform Scale** to `100`.
3. In the **Transform** settings, set **Translate** in *Y*-axis to `-3.75` for the grid to be below the portal.

4. In the **Transform** settings, set **Rotate** in *X*-axis to `30` or more depending on the camera angle.
5. Create a **Merge** node and connect both the **sopimport** particles and **grid1** to the merge inputs.

This simple ground could also use a simple **karmamaterial** with a dark color and can be assigned through the same material linker:

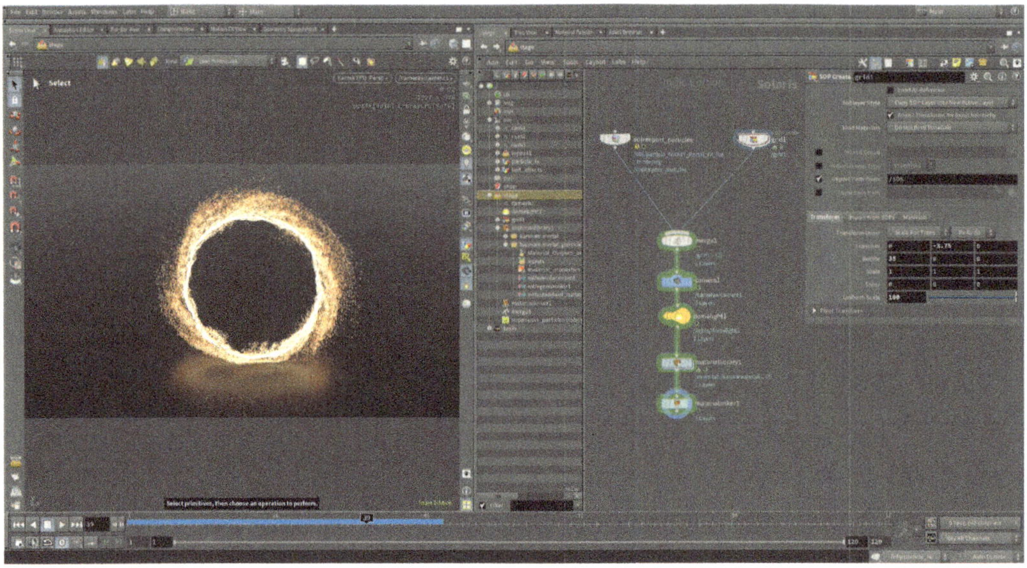

Figure 3.29 – Simple ground for reflections

Now, we'll move on to begin adjusting the final image render settings with the help of **Karma** nodes.

Inspecting the Karma render settings

For the final steps, let's create Karma rendering nodes and start the rendering process:

1. Press *Tab*, search for `karma`, and select the result. As a result, the `karma` command will give us two connected nodes: one for render settings and another for image output.
2. Connect **materiallinker1** to the first input of **karmarendersettings**.
3. In **karmarendersettings**, click on the **Camera Effects** tab.
4. Set the **Velocity Blur** setting to **Velocity Blur**.

5. In **Rendering Engine**, you can use either **CPU Engine** or **XPU Engine** depending on your hardware:
    - If you're using **CPU Engine**, set **Primary Samples** to a minimum of 16; higher samples will result in a cleaner render
    - Alternatively, if you're using **XPU Engine**, set **Primary Samples** to a minimum of 256; higher samples will result in a cleaner render
6. You can set the final render resolution in the **Resolution** setting input.
7. Do a test render in the viewport.

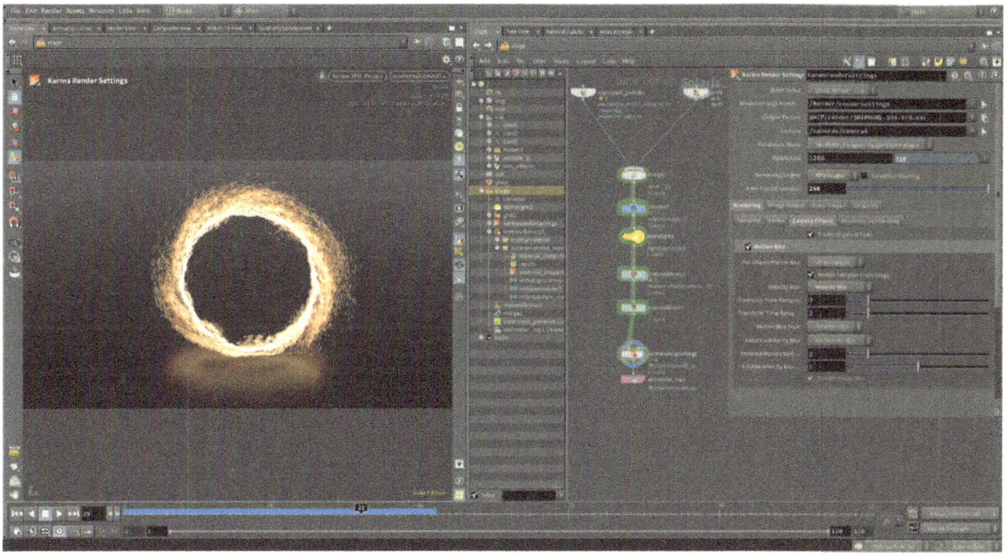

Figure 3.30 – Karma render settings

After adjusting the render settings, it's now time to set up the process of saving images to the disc.

Rendering images to the disc

After we have done enough test renders and made sure that everything is working properly in different frames, we are now ready to render our first image sequence to disc.

Let's look at the steps to do this:

1. Click on **usdrender_rop1**.
2. Set the **Valid Frame Range** setting to **Render Specific Frame Range**.

   Since we have our project and timeline frame range set already, everything is going to work by default and our images are going to be saved to the `render` folder of the project directory as an `.exr` sequence.

3. Click on **Render to Disc** and receive my congratulations!

Refer to *Figure 3.31* to see the render output settings:

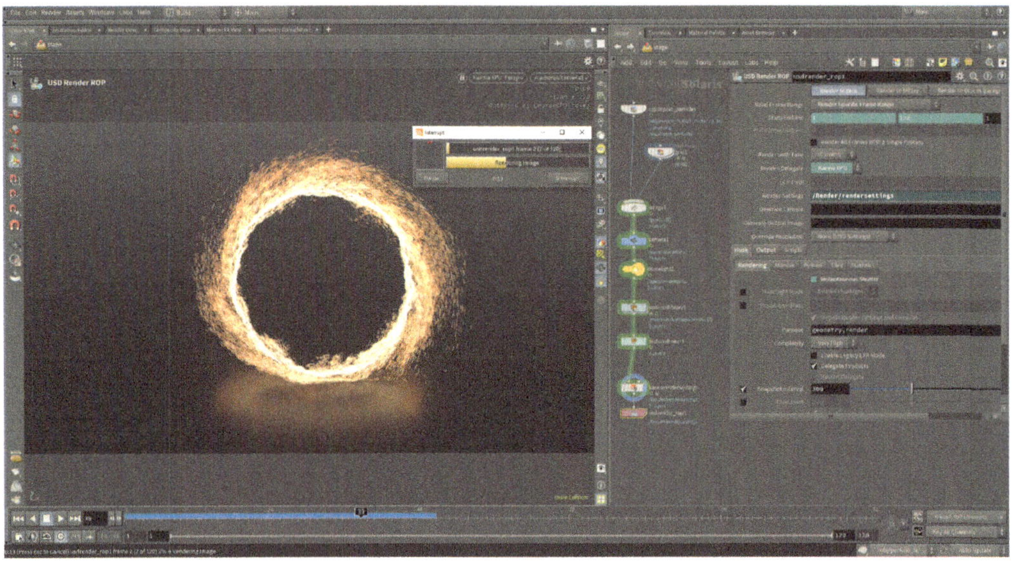

Figure 3.31 – Rendering to the disc

After completing all the preceding steps, our renders will be saved into an image sequence in the `render` folder of our project.

Congratulations on completing your first rendered particle simulation!

Summary

As we conclude this chapter on the fundamentals of particles in Houdini, you should now have a solid understanding of the basic concepts and tools available for creating and manipulating particle systems. We explored the POP network, delved into the intricacies of DOPs, and examined the pivotal role of **POP Solver** in driving particle behaviors. With a grasp on using nodes such as **POP Source** and **POP Drag**, and understanding parameters such as **Birth** settings and velocity, you are well-equipped to start experimenting with particle effects.

Particles are a cornerstone of many visual effects, enabling the creation of everything from dust and smoke to magical effects and complex simulations. The knowledge gained here sets a strong foundation for more advanced topics, such as fluid simulations, rigid body dynamics, and custom particle behaviors using **VEX**.

As you move forward, continue to explore the extensive capabilities of Houdini's particle system. Experiment with different nodes, tweak parameters, and push the boundaries of what particles can do. In the upcoming chapters, we will delve deeper into advanced particle techniques and explore how to integrate particles seamlessly with other aspects of Houdini's robust toolset.

Remember, mastering particles in Houdini requires both creative experimentation and technical proficiency. So, keep iterating, keep learning, and most importantly, have fun bringing your imaginative particle effects to life.

In the next chapter, we will utilize the knowledge that we gained about creating efficient emitters and simulations and apply it to pyro simulations for creating smoke and fire.

Subscribe to Game Dev Assembly Newsletter!

We are excited to introduce **Game Dev Assembly**, our brand-new newsletter dedicated to everything game development. Whether you're a programmer, designer, artist, animator, or studio lead, you'll get exclusive insights, industry trends, and expert tips to help you build better games and grow your skills. Sign up today and become part of a growing community of creators, innovators, and game changers.

`https://packt.link/gamedev-newsletter`

Scan the QR code to join instantly!

Unlock this book's exclusive benefits now

UNLOCK NOW

Scan this QR code or go to `packtpub.com/unlock`, then search for this book by name. Ensure it's the correct edition.

Note: Keep your purchase invoice ready before you start.

4

Igniting Pyro Effects

In this chapter, we will explore Houdini's powerful pyro effects tools and learn how to create our first smoke and fire simulation!

We will start with fundamental concepts and tools, guiding you through the basics of setting up and manipulating smoke and fire simulations. From there, you'll learn how to fine-tune parameters and integrate these effects seamlessly into your projects, equipping you with the skills to produce visually stunning and dynamic results.

Here are the main topics that we will cover in this chapter:

- Volumes, VDBs, and Pyro FX workflow theory
- Importing a custom 3D asset
- Creating a universal geometry source for smoke and fire
- Converting geo into a pyro source and adding core pyro simulation attributes
- Creating pyro volumetric fields from attributes
- Learning the new **Pyro Solver** workflows and simulation settings
- Sculpting smoke and flames with pyro forces and parameters
- Preparing the pyro simulation for output and caching
- Lighting and rendering a realistic fire with smoke

After completing this chapter, you will have a solid understanding of how to build pyro smoke and pyro fire simulations and how to apply this fundamental knowledge to building more complex pyro simulations.

Figure 4.1 shows an example of the pyro effect that we will be creating in this chapter:

Figure 4.1 – Smoke and fire effect created and rendered in Houdini

Technical requirements

As you can see in *Figure 4.1*, I have rendered a 3D model of fire and smoke with some stones that looks like a campfire pit. This model was downloaded from an online resource named **Sketchfab** by 3D artist Meerschaum Digital; here is a link to where you can obtain it:

`https://sketchfab.com/3d-models/fire-pit-game-ready-2k-pbr-9490039432e94536b05ac5bd3406ed61`

All the workflows that I am going to show for this project can be applied to any 3D model of your choice, so feel free to either proceed with the same asset from Sketchfab or use anything that you have created yourself.

You will have access to the Houdini file with the completed effect on the GitHub link at `https://github.com/PacktPublishing/VFX-Made-Easy-with-Houdini`.

To view the chapter images in better clarity, scan the provided QR code. It will direct you to a dedicated link where you can take a look at the images.

Before importing the 3D asset and starting on our first pyro project, let's learn about some important workflows for pyro effects and pyro dynamics theory in general.

Volumes, VDBs, and Pyro FX workflow theory

In Houdini, **volumes** and **Volumetric Data Blocks (VDBs)** are fundamental data types used extensively in Pyro FX simulations to represent smoke, fire, and other gaseous effects. Understanding their roles and differences is crucial for effectively creating and manipulating volumetric effects like Pyro FX.

Let's understand these concepts in greater depth in the subsequent sections.

Standard volumes

In this section, we will discuss some key features of volumes in Houdini.

Standard volumes in Houdini are grid-based data structures that store information across a 3D space, such as **density**, **temperature**, **velocity** (or **v**), and **burn**, which are essential for fluid and Pyro FX simulations. These volumes are essentially 3D arrays of voxels (volume elements), where each voxel contains specific data.

For example, in smoke simulations, a density volume defines how thick or opaque the smoke is at each voxel location.

In Pyro FX, standard volumes are used to define the key attributes of smoke and fire, such as the following:

- **Density**: Controls the opacity and appearance of smoke
- **Temperature**: Influences how smoke rises and affects fire behavior
- **Burn**: Dictates how the fire burns and generates smoke
- **v**: Governs the initial velocity of the fluid, driving the dynamic behavior of smoke and flames

These volumes are constantly updated during the simulation as the solver calculates how the fluids evolve over time.

The names of initial volumes that are being mapped into the pyro simulation source volumes often match; however, the matching name is used purely as a part of the standard workflow.

For example, during sourcing, **density** and **temperature** are mapped to the simulation volumes with the same name; however, the **burn** and **v** volumes will be mapped to flame and vel, respectively, as defined by the **Pyro Solver**.

Ultimately, you can name your source volumes in any descriptive way, but they have to be mapped correctly to **density**, **temperature**, **flame**, and **vel** inside of **Pyro Solver Sourcing** tab.

Volumetric Data Blocks (VDBs)

VDBs are an optimized type of volume developed by DreamWorks Animation, widely supported in Houdini. They store sparse volumetric data more efficiently than standard volumes, using a tree structure that only retains data where necessary, minimizing memory usage.

Unlike *standard volumes*, VDBs do not allocate memory for empty space (where the values are 0), making them particularly efficient for large-scale simulations with vast empty regions.

Advantages of using VDBs in Pyro FX

Here are the key benefits of using VDBs in Pyro FX:

- **Efficiency**: VDBs are significantly faster and consume less memory, which is crucial when working with high-resolution simulations or large domains.
- **Faster operations**: VDB operations like smoothing, reshaping, and converting are generally quicker compared to standard volumes, making them ideal for iterating complex effects.
- **Flexibility**: VDBs can store multiple types of data (float and vector) in the same data block, allowing complex interactions between various fields (**density**, **velocity**, etc.).

Conversion between volumes and VDBs

Houdini allows easy conversion between standard volumes and VDBs using nodes like **Convert VDB** and **Volume Rasterize**. Converting to VDBs is common in Pyro FX to optimize performance, especially when caching or exporting simulations.

Relation of volumes and VDBs to Pyro FX in Houdini

Let's see how volumes and VDBs serve as the building blocks of Pyro FX:

- **Simulation data representation**: In Pyro FX, both standard volumes and VDBs are used to represent the simulation data, but VDBs are often preferred due to their efficiency. During the simulation, fields like **density**, **temperature**, and **velocity** are represented as volumes that define how the smoke and fire behave and appear.
- **Caching and storage**: When storing pyro simulations, VDBs are preferred due to their reduced file size and faster read/write times. This makes iterating on simulations less cumbersome and more efficient, as the cached VDB data takes up less space and loads quickly.

SOP-based Pyro FX workflow in Houdini

Houdini versions after 17 have a new **SOP-based pyro workflow** that streamlines and accelerates the process of creating **Pyro FX** (as pyro tools and features are officially known in Houdini).

The SOP-based Pyro FX workflow in Houdini provides an artist-friendly approach to creating smoke and fire effects directly within the SOP (Surface Operators) context, bypassing the more complex DOP (Dynamics Operators) network traditionally used for simulations.

This workflow leverages Houdini's powerful **Pyro Solver** to simulate realistic smoke, fire, and explosions while offering a more intuitive and accessible node-based setup.

In the sections that follow, we'll look at the key steps in the SOP-based Pyro FX workflow.

Setting up the source

The first step in the SOP-based Pyro FX workflow is to define the **source geometry** from which smoke or fire will be emitted. This can be any SOP geometry, such as a sphere, a box, a custom imported 3D asset, or custom animated shapes.

Next, the **Pyro Source** and **Volume Rasterize Attributes** nodes are used to convert the geometry into the necessary fields (**density**, **temperature**, and **burn**) required by the **Pyro Solver**.

Pyro Source creates all the required attributes on the geometry points. **Volume Rasterize Attributes** prepares the geometry as a volume suitable for simulation, defining where the smoke or fire originates and its initial properties.

After converting source attributes into volumetric fields, the next step is connecting the SOP-based **Pyro Solver**, which will do all the internal calculations using the laws of fluid dynamics, math, and complex data manipulations to return a dynamic gaseous volume that will behave like smoke, fire or explosion.

Utilizing the Pyro Solver (SOP)

The **Pyro Solver** (SOP) is the core of the simulation process. It handles the simulation of fire, smoke, and other gaseous effects by evolving fields like **density**, **temperature**, **velocity**, **burn**, and other internal fields over time.

You can use this solver right in the **Geometry** level of **obj** context, as this node integrates directly into the Surface Operators (SOP) network, allowing for fast feedback and easy access to simulation parameters without switching contexts.

Shaping and refinement

The next step is to use **Shaping** controls to refine the look of the smoke or fire, such as adding noise, sharpening the flames, or enhancing the motion to create more visually appealing results.

Then, we apply additional forces like wind or custom vector fields to influence the direction and shape of the smoke or fire, giving you greater artistic control over the effect.

Visualization and rendering prep

You can easily access the built-in visualization options right on the **Pyro Solver** (SOP) that allow you to preview the simulation directly in the viewport, adjusting the color and opacity of the smoke and fire to assess the effect's look.

After simulation, use the **Convert VDB** node to convert the simulation fields (**density**, **temperature**, etc.) into VDBs for efficient rendering and storage.

Caching simulation data

Once you are satisfied with the simulation, cache the data using the **File Cache** node. This step saves the simulated volumes to disk, allowing faster playback and more efficient iteration during the rendering phase.

Lighting and shading

Next, we set up appropriate lighting to enhance the visual appearance of the smoke and fire. Pyro effects respond well to dynamic lighting setups that emphasize the volume's depth and detail.

Use Houdini's dedicated **Pyro Shader** to control the appearance of the rendered smoke and fire. The shader allows you to adjust the color, transparency, emission, and scattering properties, enabling you to achieve realistic or stylized looks.

Rendering

Finally, we render the simulation using Houdini's built-in renderers like **Mantra** or **Karma**, or export the data to third-party render engines. We wrap it up with fine-tuning render settings to capture the subtle details of smoke density and fire glow, enhancing the overall realism.

Moving on, we will start our first Pyro FX project by importing the 3D asset of a fire pit.

Importing a custom 3D asset

Before we get to the steps of importing a 3D asset into Houdini, please go ahead and open an empty Houdini file. Create a new project and name it `intro_to_pyro_effects`.

Now, let's start by bringing in a campfire pit 3D model into Houdini:

1. Press *Tab*, type `file` in the search bar, and place the **File** node in the **obj** context.
2. Double-click on the newly created **File** node to get into the **Geometry** level.

   The **File** node can bring in static or animated 3D assets as well as a 3D geometry cache via a file path link.

Figure 4.2 demonstrates the steps to bring in the 3D asset:

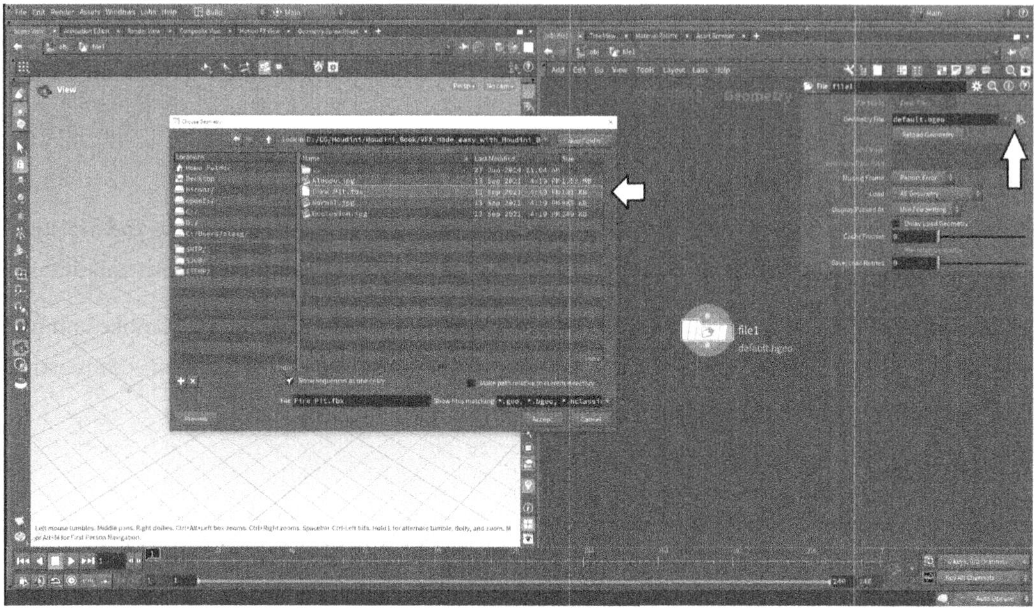

Figure 4.2 – Opening the file path for a 3D asset

1. Click on the icon pointed to by the large *white* arrow in the preceding figure to open the floating file chooser.
2. Choose the 3D asset fire pit, pointed to by the smaller *white* arrow in *Figure 4.2*, and click **Accept**.

You should now see that the default file box has disappeared, and the fire pit stones 3D asset appears in the viewport.

One important thing to note is often, when you bring in 3D assets that were built outside of Houdini, their scale can be too big because those assets were built using *centimeters* as their metric system.

Houdini uses meters as its default measuring units, so if the asset was built in another software package and is, for example, 100 centimeters, then it will come into Houdini as a huge 3D model equaling 100 meters.

We can easily fix this by adding a **Transform** node and scaling the 3D asset down. A general rule is to set the scale to 0.01 of the original size; however, you can set it to a slightly bigger value depending on your project scale and needs.

For this pyro fire project, I have set the scale to be `0.0175`.

Follow these steps to set the correct scale of the fire pit asset in your Houdini scene:

1. Press *Tab*, search for the **Transform** node, and connect it after the **File** node.
2. Set the uniform scale to `0.0175` in the **Transform** node.
3. Press *Spacebar* + *H* to zoom focus on the 3D asset.

Refer to *Figure 4.3* to see the **Transform** settings and 3D asset:

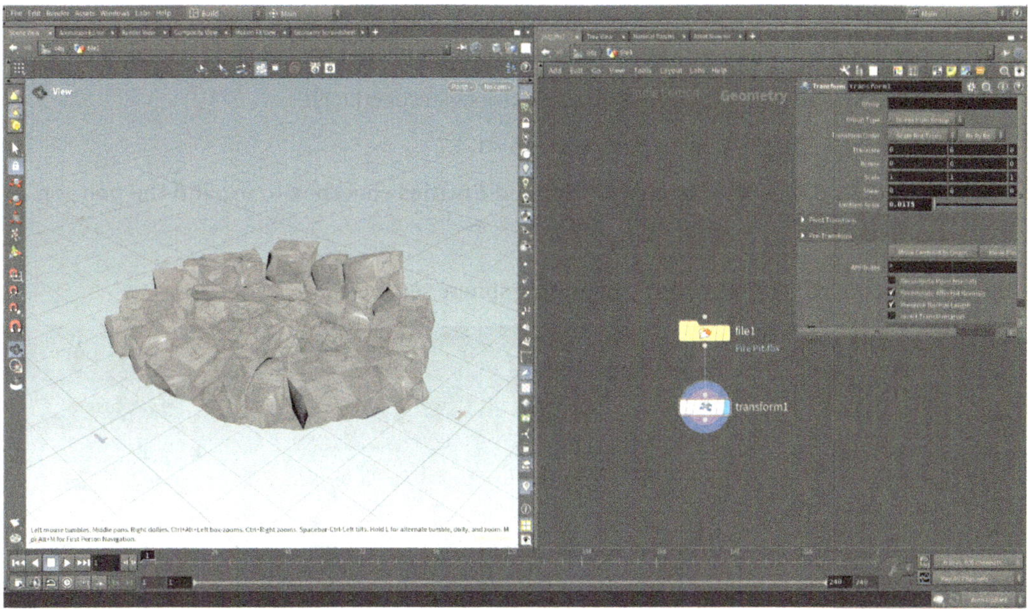

Figure 4.3 – 3D asset correct transformation

For the next steps, we are going to procedurally select the area inside the fire pit and start creating our pyro source from it.

Creating a universal geometry source for smoke and fire

Let's follow these steps to make a custom geometry that can be used to emit pyro:

1. Press *Tab*, search for a **Group** node, and place it after the **Transform** node.
2. In the first box, called **Group Name**, type `pyro_source_grp`. This will be the custom name of our polygons group.
3. Turn off the **Enable** checkbox in the **Base Group** rollout that is currently grouping all the polygons.
4. Turn on the **Enable** checkbox in the **Keep in Bounding Regions** rollout and you will see that there is a virtual bounding box that is now grouping polygons inside it.
5. Change **Bounding Type** to **Bounding Sphere**, to have a more organic selection area.
6. Set the **Size** parameter to `0.65` in all three axes respectively.
7. Set the **Y** axis of the **Center** parameter to `-0.15`.
8. Turn on the **Include Partially Contained Entities** checkbox to expand the polygon selection.

Refer to *Figure 4.4* to see the group by bounding sphere settings:

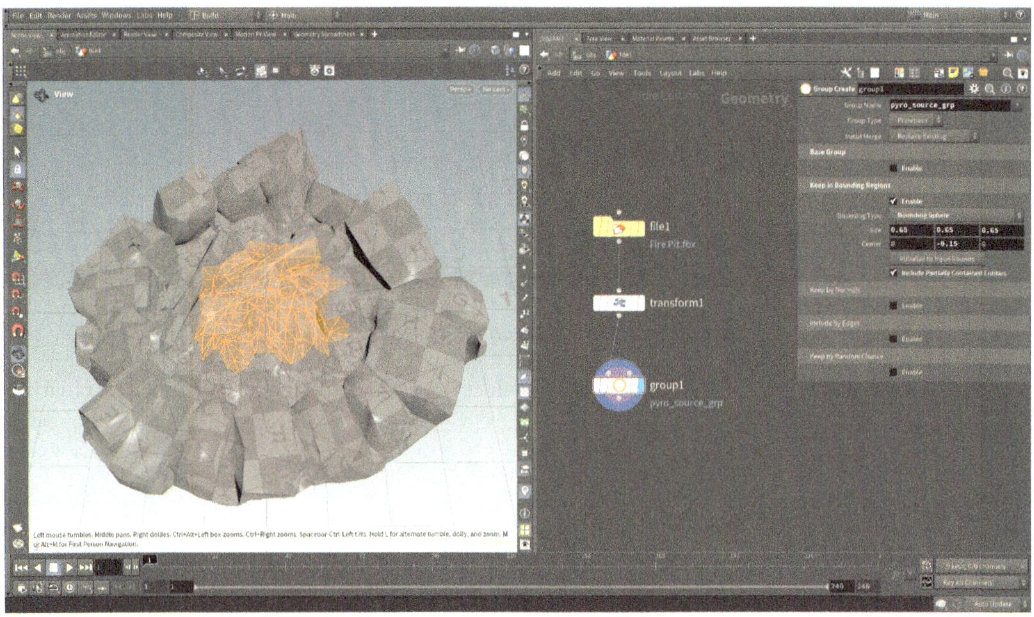

Figure 4.4 – Group by bounding sphere

After creating the group, we need to isolate the grouped polygons from the fire pit asset:

1. Press *Tab*, search for `blast node`, and place it after the **Group** node.
2. In the **Group** box of the **Blast** node, type the name of our polygons group: `pyro_source_grp`.
3. Enable the **Delete Non-Selected** checkbox to keep the source polygons instead of deleting them.

Moving on, we will convert the selected polygons into pyro source points and create some important attributes required for any pyro simulation.

Converting geo into a pyro source and adding core pyro simulation attributes

The **Pyro Source** node in Houdini is used to define the initial conditions for smoke and fire simulations. It specifies where and how the smoke or fire will start, by allowing you to choose from various source types like geometry or particles.

You can adjust key attributes such as temperature, density, and emission rates to control the behavior of the simulation. The node serves as the starting point for your Pyro FX setup, working in conjunction with the **Pyro Solver** to create and animate realistic fire and smoke effects.

Continue with these steps to turn our geometry into pyro source points:

1. Press *Tab*, search for `pyro source node`, and place it after the **Blast** node.
2. Click on **Initialize** and choose **Source Smoke** from the drop-down menu. This will create two fundamental attributes needed for any smoke simulation: **Density** and **Temperature**.
3. Click on **Initialize** again and this time choose **Source Burn** from the drop-down menu. This will add a third fundamental attribute that will be responsible for the ignition of the fire.
4. Set the **Mode** parameter to **Surface Scatter**. This will add uniformly scattered points covering the object and replacing the polygons.
5. Set the **Particle Separation** parameter to `0.005`.

Figure 4.5 provides an overview of the **Pyro Source** settings and parameters:

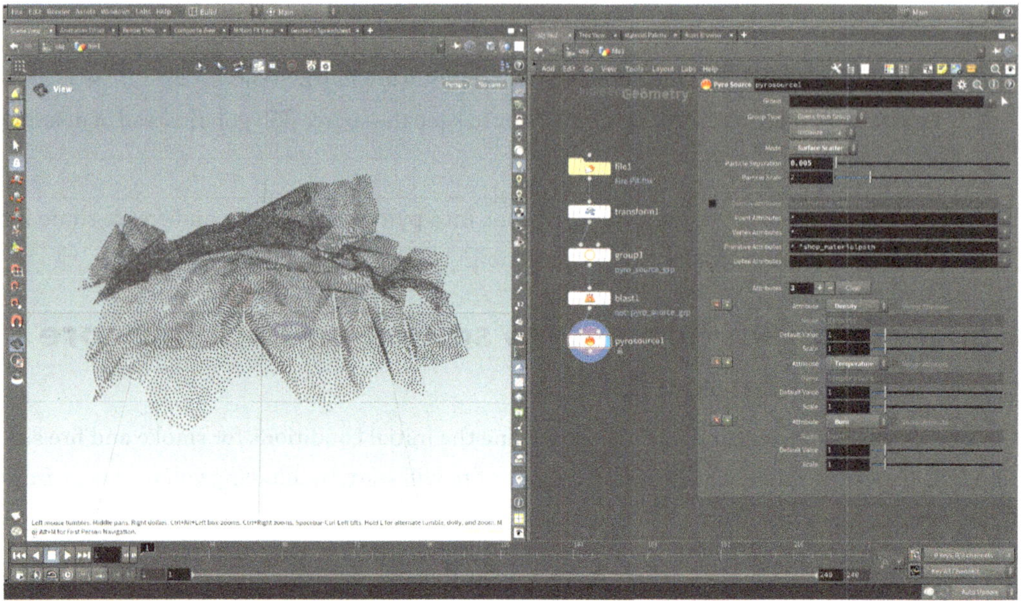

Figure 4.5 – Pyro source points

Quick tip: Need to see a high-resolution version of this image? Open this book in the next-gen Packt Reader or view it in the PDF/ePub copy.

The next-gen Packt Reader and a **free PDF/ePub copy** of this book are included with your purchase. Scan the QR code OR visit `packtpub.com/unlock`, then use the search bar to find this book by name. Double-check the edition shown to make sure you get the right one.

In the next section, we will add some variation to the source with the help of noises to make the emission more interesting from the start.

Noising up the pyro source

For the next steps, we are going to add some noise to the emitter as a usual workflow to make it more interesting and varied:

1. Press *Tab*, search for the **mountain** node, and place it after the **Pyro Source** node.
2. In the **General** rollout, turn off the **Noise Along Vector** parameter to just distort the points in 3D space.
3. Use the **Noise Value** rollout and set **Amplitude** to `0.025`.
4. Use the **Noise Pattern** rollout to change **Element Size** to `0.05`. Notice how the points became more clumped and look more organic and fluid-like.
5. Turn on the **Animation** checkbox to have the noise pulsing procedurally.

Figure 4.6 shows the **mountain** node settings and parameters:

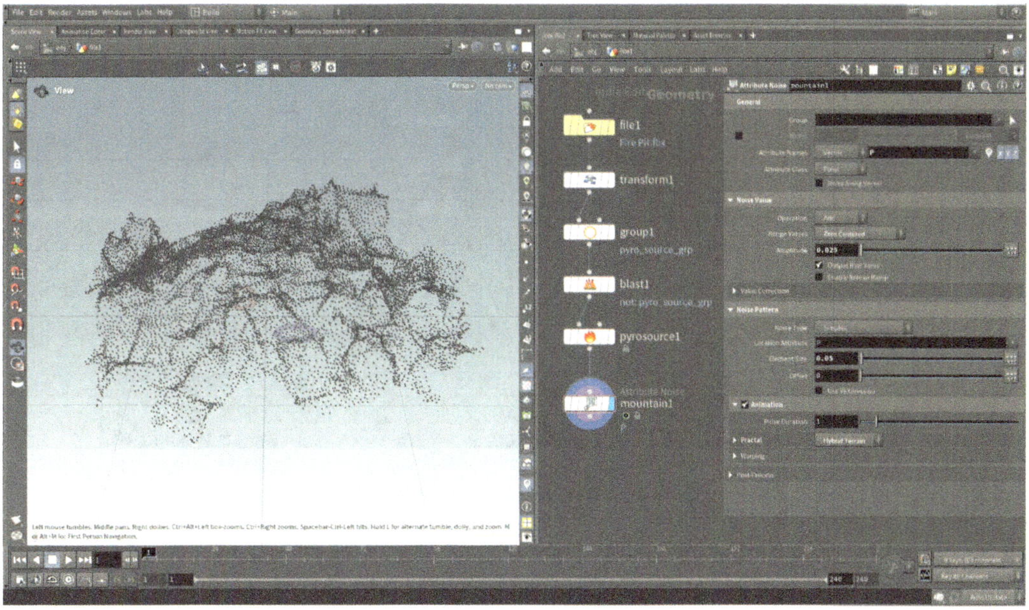

Figure 4.6 – Noising up pyro source points

Now, let's create additional noise on the **burn** attribute, so the ignition areas will be sparse, random, and more realistic:

1. Press *Tab*, search for the **Attribute Adjust Float** node, and place it after the **mountain** node. Since the **burn** attribute is a float and one-dimensional, we can adjust its values with the **Attribute Adjust Float** node.

2. In the **General** rollout, change **Attribute Name** from **pscale** to **burn**.
3. Use the **Adjustment Value** rollout to modify the **Operation** and **Pattern Type** parameters.
4. Set **Operation** to **Multiply** and **Pattern Type** to **Noise**.
5. Adjust **Remap Ramp** by moving the left end of the ramp to the middle.
6. Use the **Noise Pattern** rollout to set **Element Size** to `0.1`.
7. Turn on the **Animate Noise** checkbox and set **Pulse Duration** to `0.5`, so the noise animates faster.

Refer to *Figure 4.7* to see the **Attribute Adjust Float** settings and parameters:

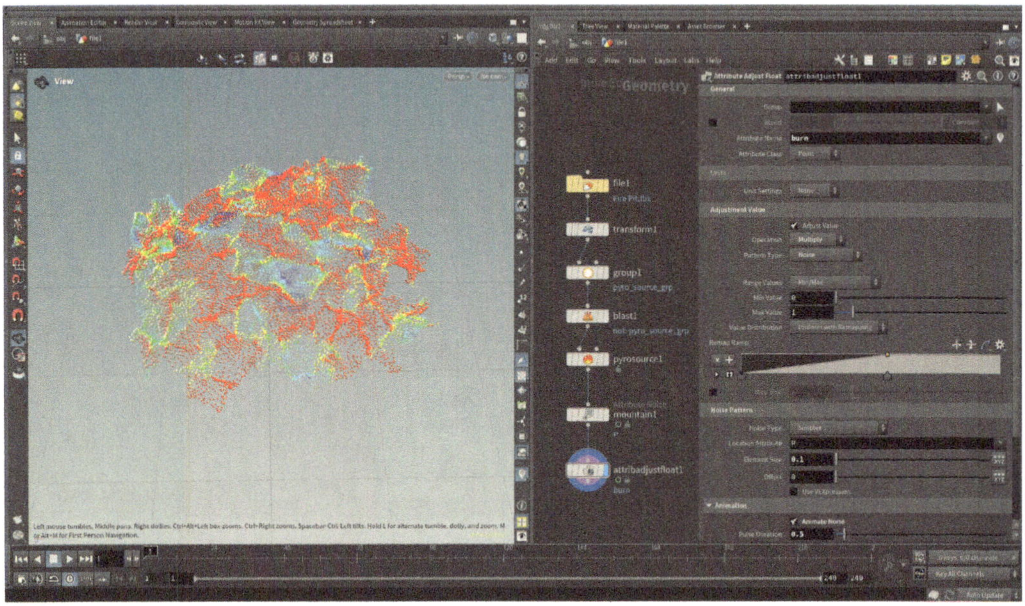

Figure 4.7 – Noising up pyro source points

In the preceding screenshot, I have turned on the visualization of the **burn** attribute in the viewport temporarily. The *red* areas of the points will have a high burn chance, and the *bluish-purple* areas will have a lower chance of ignition.

As the last step, we will add a node to create some interesting initial velocity just in case we need it:

1. Add a **Point Velocity** node after the **Attribute Adjust Float** node.
2. In the **Curl Noise** tab, enable the **Curl Noise** checkbox and set **Scale** and **Swirl Size** to `0.5`.

Having an initial velocity attribute is always good for breaking up the smooth smoke shapes in the beginning; however, if we find that initial velocity works for smoke but doesn't work for fire, we can always turn off the velocity injection in the **Pyro Solver**.

Moving on, let's now convert all our pyro point source attributes into rasterized volumes for simulation.

Creating pyro volumetric fields from attributes

Before continuing, I recommend setting the viewport background to dark gray or another dark color to see the volumetric data better (see *Chapter 1* for a refresher on how to adjust the background color).

To begin the conversion of point attributes into volumetric fields, follow these steps:

1. Press *Tab*, look for `volume rasterize attributes`, and place it after the **Attribute Adjust** node.
2. In the **Attributes** box, we will need to type the names of the attributes that we want to convert, separating them with a space. Type these names into the **Attributes** box: `burn density temperature v`.

   By doing this, we specify the exact attributes that will be converted to volumetric fields for pyro simulation. Notice that now, instead of source points, we have a blurry white cloud contained in a red box.

3. Set the visible volumes to **burn** to only see the noised-up burn field source. This is exactly what the volumetric source looks like and it will be able to emit smoke and fire after we connect it to the **Pyro Solver**.
4. Set **Voxel Size** to `0.01` temporarily; we will adjust this value later.
5. Set **Particle Scale** to `0.75` to make the source area thinner.
6. In the **Coverage** rollout, remove **density** from **Coverage Attribute** to have the source fully inject all the fields into the simulation.

Figure 4.8 demonstrates the **Volume Rasterize** settings and parameters:

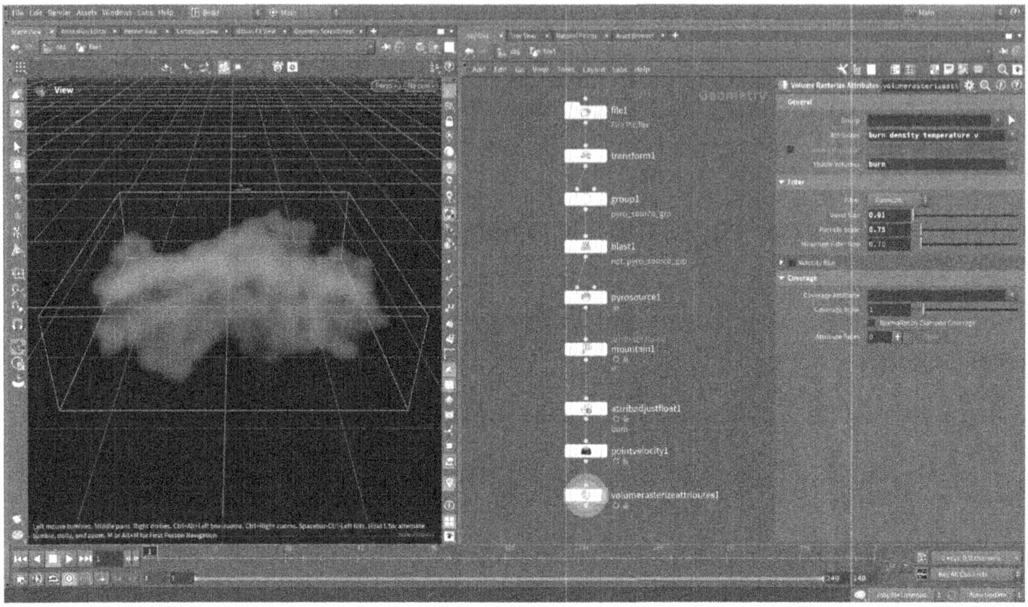

Figure 4.8 – Volume Rasterize pyro source

In the preceding screenshot, the two main parameters in **Volume Rasterize** are **Voxel Size** and **Particle Scale**. Let's understand these in more detail:

- **Voxel Size**: This is responsible for the volumetric resolution of the pyro source volume. This resolution works based on the voxel size; the *smaller* the **Voxel Size** parameter, the *more* resolution a volume will get.
- **Particle Scale**: This will define the diameter of a volumetric cloud that will be covering each particle of the incoming source. The *bigger* the **Particle Scale** parameter, the *thicker* and *bulgier* the pyro source will get. The **Particle Scale** parameter can vary depending on the scene scale and the amount of source points that we convert to a volume. For this scene, the value that worked for my fire example was a particle scale of `0.75`.

Feel free to experiment with this value, where you get a thicker fire with a **Particle Scale** close to 1 and a thinner fire with a **Particle Scale** closer to `0`.

Important note

A general rule for the voxel resolution is to have the voxel size on the pyro source be the same as the voxel size on the **Pyro Solver**. Therefore, we will link these two parameters after we add the **Pyro Solver** in the next steps.

Let's move on to adding the heart of pyro simulation, the **Pyro Solver**, and testing our first simulation.

Learning the new Pyro Solver workflows and simulation settings

We will next be focusing on the new **Pyro Solver** node, which has all the necessary settings to create and modify any pyro simulation.

Pyro Solver has lots of tabs and settings and can be a little overwhelming in the beginning. Don't worry, though; I will direct our focus only to the tabs and settings needed for this introductory smoke and fire effect.

We will mainly focus on the **Setup** tab for simulation resolution settings, the **Sourcing** tab to adjust our source inputs, the **Fields** tab to adjust the life expectancy of smoke and fire, and the **Shape** tab to add forces and interesting motion to the simulation.

Adjusting the initial simulation setup settings

Before starting the simulation and pressing play on the animation timeline, let's set the initial parameters for a simple smoke simulation:

1. Press *Tab*, search for `pyro solver`, and add it after the volume rasterize node.
2. In the **Setup** tab and the **General** rollout, set **Voxel Size** to `0.01` (same as **Voxel Size** under the **Volume Rasterize** attributes).
3. In the **Simulation** tab, set **Max Substeps** to 2, in order to have a better quality simulation, especially in fast-moving areas.
4. Set **Advection-Reflection** to **Single-Project**, to enable energy preservation and to have more details in the simulation.

I have merged the result of the pyro sim with the pit asset to have a better representation of the effect. Refer to *Figure 4.9* for the initial simulation settings:

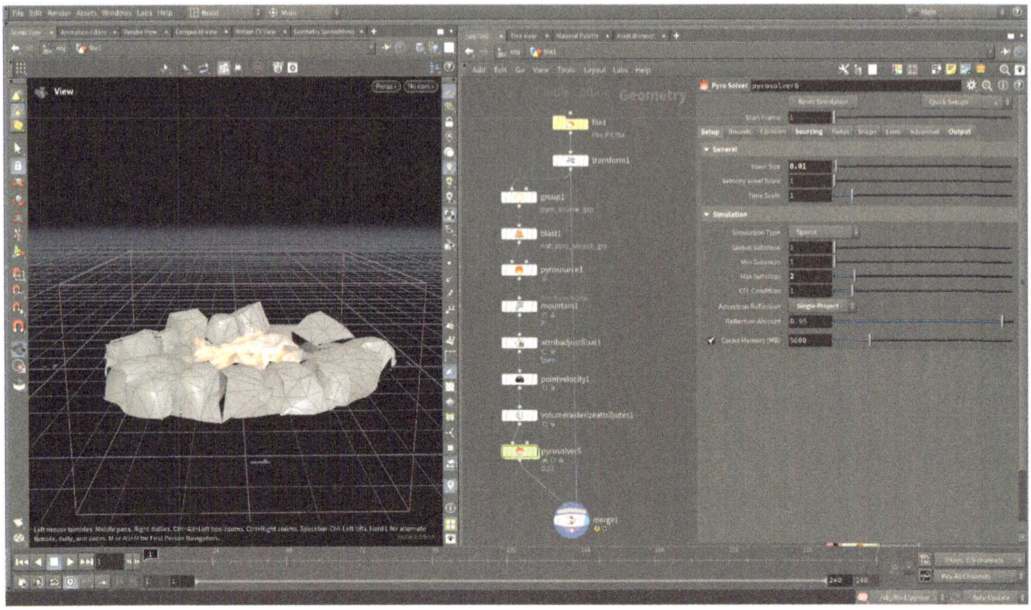

Figure 4.9 – Pyro initial setup

In the viewport, we can see a bright yellow glowing volume that will ignite into a fire; however, for now, I would like to show you how to simulate just smoke without fire.

This can be simply done by setting the burn volumetric field scale to `0`. Without **burn**, **density** and **temperature** will create a basic smoke rising simulation and the initial velocity will add interesting details to the smoke.

Adjusting the sourcing parameters

All of the sourcing parameters for smoke, fire, temperatures, and velocities can be controlled in the **Sourcing** tab:

1. In the **Pyro Solver**, click on the **Sourcing** tab and notice where all the source volumetric fields are being connected to.
2. In the **Sourcing** tab, under the **Sourcing Volumes** rollout, set the **Source Scale** parameter of **Source 3: flame** to `0`. This way, we turned off the **burn** field being added to flames and no fire will be generated as a result.

3. Set the **Source Scale** parameter of **Source 2: temperature** to `0.05`. We are significantly reducing the temperature of the smoke so it will rise very slowly and nicely.
4. Finally, let's add more density to the initial smoke source by setting the source scale in the **Source 1: density** parameter to `10`.

Play the simulation in the viewport till frame **48** and you will see some nice, dense smoke rising from the pit.

See *Figure 4.10* for the **Sourcing** tab settings and parameters, as well as the smoke in the viewport:

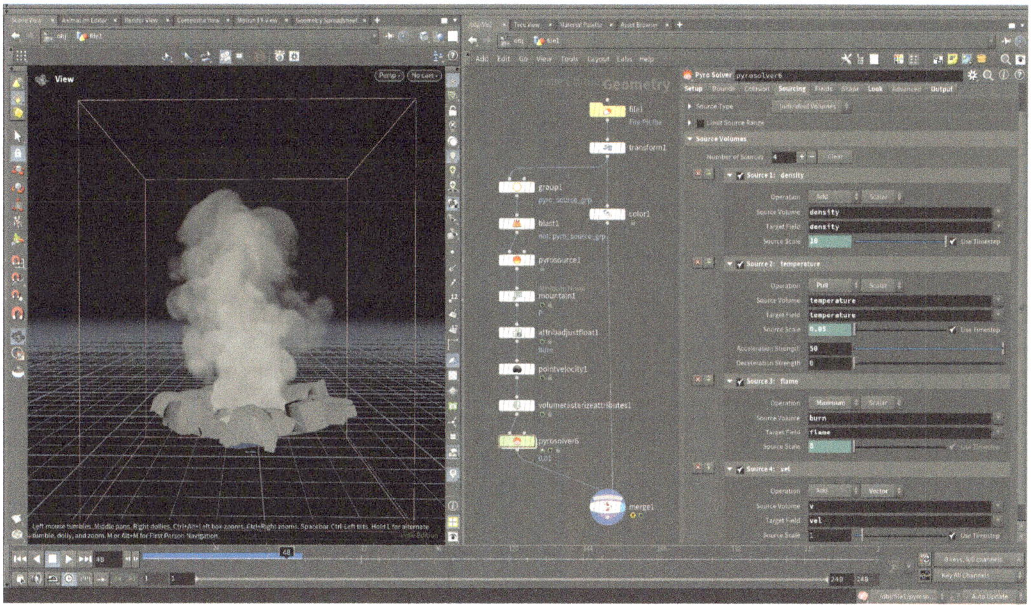

Figure 4.10 – Pyro initial setup

We can adjust the smoke simulation further by switching to the **Fields** tab and modifying smoke dissipation:

1. Go to the **Fields** tab and change the dissipation values under the **Density** rollout.
2. Change **Dissipation** from `0.1` to `0.2` and the smoke will lose 20 percent of its density over time, resulting in a shorter life of the smoke. Play the simulation and make a flipbook, if necessary, to see the dissipation and the motion.

3. Change **Dissipation** from `0.2` to `0.05` and the smoke will lose only 5 percent of its density value over time, resulting in a much longer life and thicker smoke. Play the simulation and make a flipbook, if necessary, to see the dissipation and the motion.
4. You can also turn on the **Speed** checkbox, which will calculate the magnitude of the velocity in the pyro simulation and store it in the **Speed** field, which can be used as a control field to apply forces to only fast- or slow-moving areas.
5. Additionally, you can preview any fields or force shapes by using the **Guides** rollout on top of the **Fields** and **Shape** tabs. Every guide will have a range mapped to a color, where *red areas* describe the maximum of the range and *purple areas* describe the minimum values in the range.

Figure 4.11 demonstrates the faster-dissipating smoke and the slower-dissipating smoke, as well as field guides:

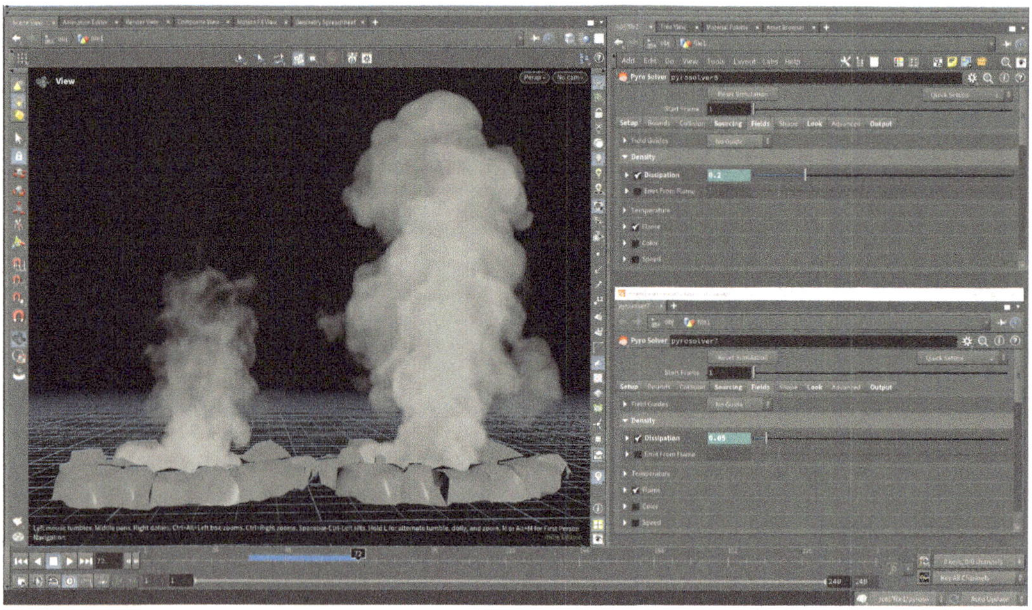

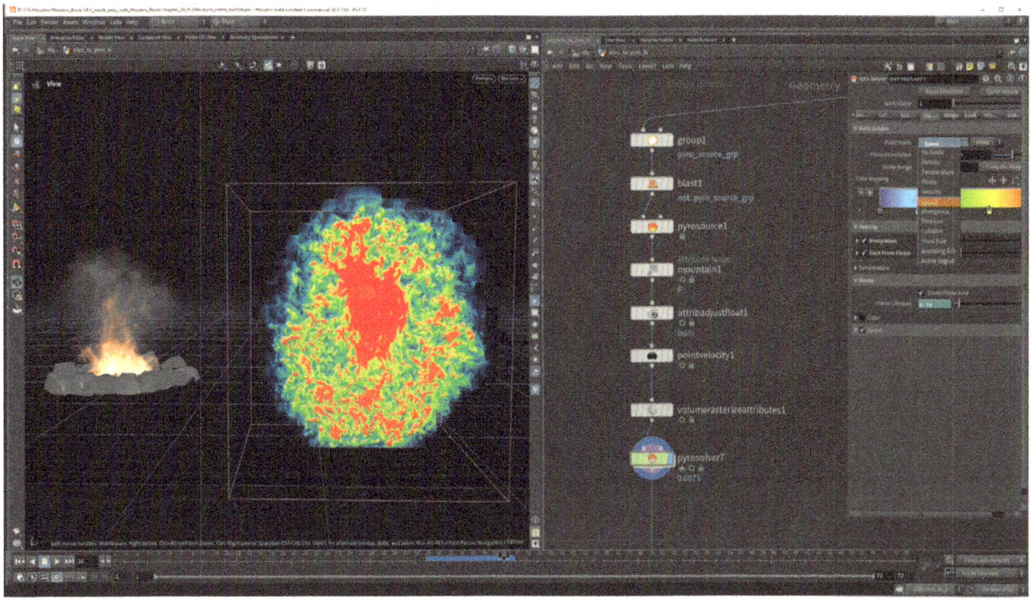

Figure 4.11 – Smoke dissipation (top) and field guides (bottom)

Since we can visualize and explore the simulation forces on bigger smoke volumes much better, we will proceed with the slower-dissipating smoke that has a dissipation value of `0.05`.

Adding air disturbance to the smoke

Moving on, we can add more details to the smoke with the help of **air disturbance**, which is a noise-based force that mimics differences in the air flow and densities and breaks up the smooth, round edges of the pyro simulation.

Before adding disturbance, we can activate the calculation of the fast and slow areas of the pyro simulation, which will be saved in a speed field. Having a **speed field** will help us achieve a much more interesting and variable disturbance in fast and slow areas of the smoke simulation.

Follow these steps to calculate smoke speed and add disturbance:

1. While in the **Fields** tab, click on the **Speed** checkbox to activate the calculation of the speed field.
2. Switch to the **Shape** tab, click on the **Disturbance** checkbox, and open the **Disturbance** rollout.
3. Set the **Disturbance** value to 5, to increase the overall force.
4. Set the base block size to `0.075` to make the air noise pattern smaller, so it will maintain the big shapes and will just distort the smoke edges.

5. Turn on the **Use Control Field** checkbox, for the force to automatically dilate the disturbance by pyro speed.
6. Compare how the smoke looks with and without disturbance force. Smoke affected by disturbance will have more swirls and edge details and will look more realistic than smoke without disturbance, which will look smooth and more cartoony.

Refer to *Figure 4.12* to see the comparison of the pyro sim with disturbance on the right and without disturbance on the left, as well as the **Disturbance** settings.

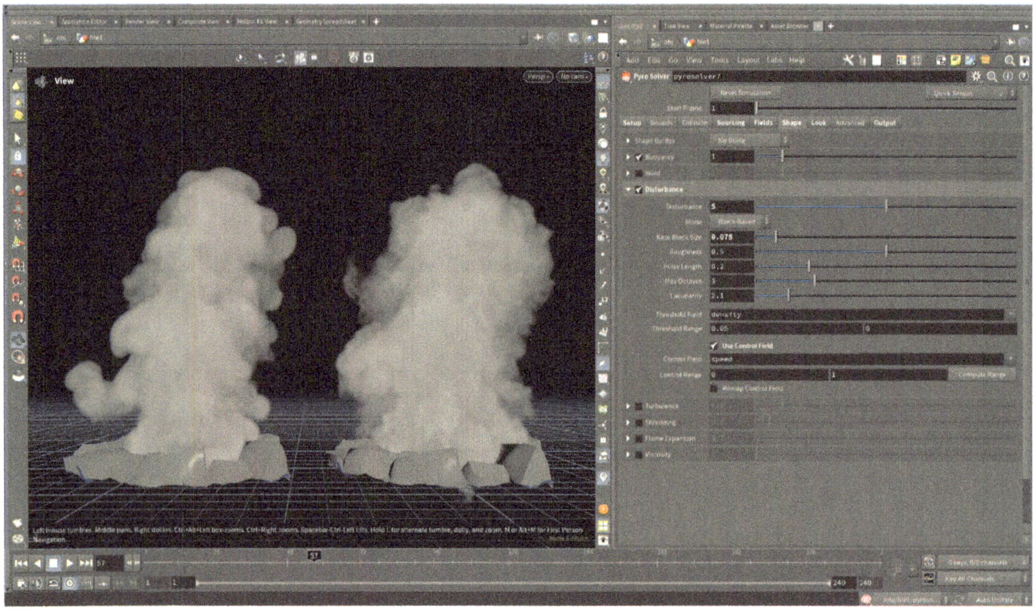

Figure 4.12 – Smoke disturbance

You can see that we have two almost identical simulations, with the only difference being in the air disturbance. This force adds lots of realistic details to the smoke on the right.

We have covered some of the most important basic techniques in creating interesting smoke simulations. By following the workflows shown, you can create a variety of smoke simulations, from wispy smoke with low density and higher dissipation to dense pyroclastic smoke with lots of density and low dissipation.

Additionally, you can play and experiment with extra forces in the **Shape** tab, such as **Wind** and **Turbulence**, which should be easy to experiment with since they resemble lots of similar qualities of noises and POP Force.

Moving on, we will be adding fire to our existing pyro simulation by adjusting the **Source**, **Fields**, and **Shape** tabs once again.

Adding burn and fire to the pyro simulation

Thanks to the procedural nature of Houdini and our pyro setup, it will be very easy to turn our billowy smoke simulation into a campfire by just adjusting a few parameters in the **Pyro Solver**.

Follow these steps to add fire to the simulation:

1. In the **Pyro Solver** node, go to the **Sourcing** tab and set the **Source Scale** of **Source 1: density**, **Source 2: temperature,** and **Source 3: flame** to a value of `1`. This way, we have set the density to a lower value of 1, increased the temperature, and added a burn source to the simulation.
2. Staying in the **Sourcing** tab, go to **Source 4: vel** and set the **Source Scale** parameter to `0`. We rarely need an initial velocity for the fire, since the main motion will be pushing the flames up because of the high temperature.

Refer to *Figure 4.13* to see how adjusting the source parameters and adding the burn and fire will look like:

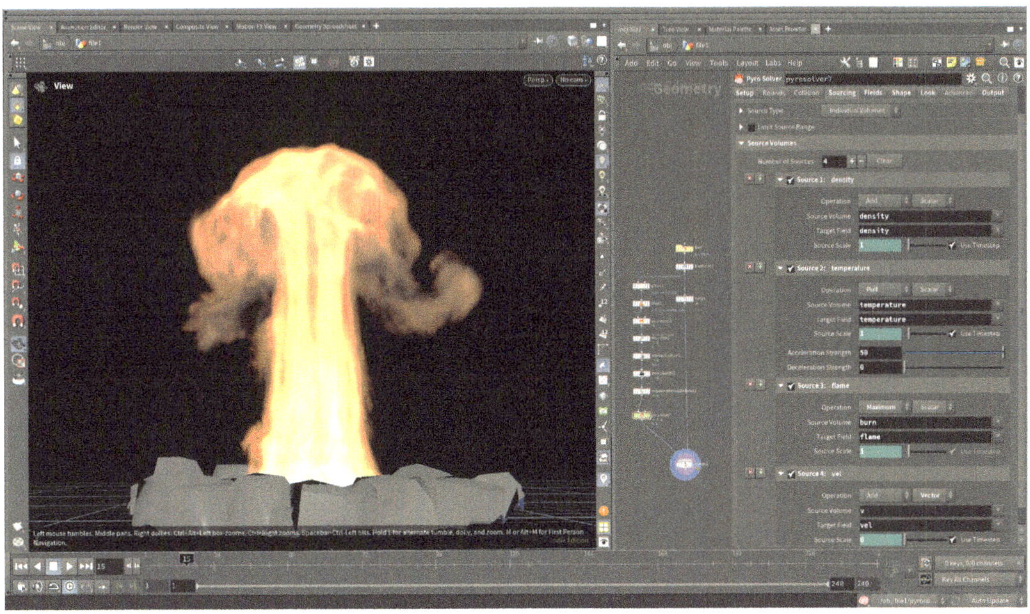

Figure 4.13 – Adding burn and flames

If we play the simulation till at least frame **15**, we will see something resembling a fast-moving flame burst or a fireball, which has a fiery look but is far off from the small campfire that we are aiming for. This fast motion upward is happening because the high temperature is pushing the pyro volume up with high energy and causing the mushroom head shape.

In the next steps, we will adjust the fields for smoke and fire and tweak more parameters in the **Shape** tab to achieve nice flame licks and shapes. Switch to the **Fields** tab and follow these steps:

1. Turn on the **Emit from Flame** checkbox to make the flames emit smoke as they cool down.
2. Turn on the **Flame** checkbox and expand the **Flame** rollout.
3. Change **Flame Lifespan** from **2** to `0.75`. This will cause a shorter life for the fire.

See *Figure 4.14* for the simulation result and the **Fields** tab settings:

Figure 4.14 – Adjusting fire fields

Play the simulation till frame **30** and notice that we are now much closer to the campfire look. The only thing that we still need to adjust is the height of the flames and the intensified distortion of the fire licks.

Moving on, we will reduce the flame height and will add extra details to the flames.

Sculpting smoke and flames with pyro forces and parameters

Switch to the **Shape** tab and follow these steps:

1. Let's reduce **Buoyancy** from **1** to `0.1`. **Buoyancy** acts as a temperature multiplier, therefore by adjusting the **Buoyancy**, we are now injecting 10 times less temperature and the flames will not rise as high.
2. Let's increase the **Disturbance** force to `15` and increase **Base Block Size** to `0.1`. Since we introduced flames, there should be a much higher air disturbance to have a more aggressive breakup in the smoke and fire.
3. Let's enable the **Shredding** checkbox. Set the **Shredding** force to `5` and set the **Base Block Size** of Shredding to a value of `0.1`. **Shredding** will mainly affect the flames, causing the squashed noisy fire shapes in the bottom and stretched fire licks at the top of the flame.

Follow *Figure 4.15* to see the final fire shape and the **Shape** tab parameters:

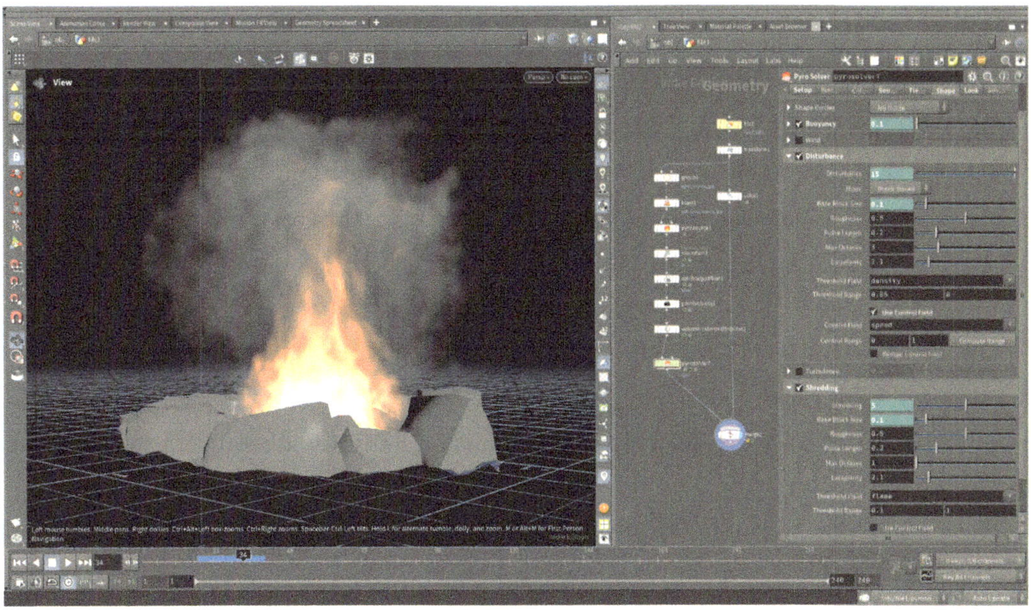

Figure 4.15 – Adjusting the fire shape

Play the simulation till at least frame **30** to see the updated flames that are more detailed, shorter, and much closer to the realistic campfire.

Moving on, we will set the final sim resolution, optimize the simulation output, and prepare for caching the pyro simulation to disc.

Preparing the pyro simulation for output and caching

Pyro output and **caching** are crucial for efficiently managing and rendering complex fire and smoke simulations. Once you've set up your pyro effects, caching allows you to save the simulation data to disk, which prevents the need to recalculate the simulation each time you make adjustments or render the scene. This process involves writing out the simulation frames to cache files, which can significantly speed up playback and rendering times.

By leveraging Houdini's built-in caching tools, you can ensure a smoother workflow, enabling quicker iterations and more reliable results for your pyro effects.

Follow these steps for the simulation output:

1. Click on the **Volume Rasterize Attributes** node and increase the resolution by changing **Voxel Size** from **0.01** to `0.0075`.
2. Click on the **Pyro Solver** node, then go to the **Setup** tab and set **Voxel Size** also to `0.0075`, which is going to be a final high resolution for our fire pyro sim.
3. Click on the **Output** tab of the **Pyro Solver** and look at the **Post-Process** rollout.
4. Turn on the **Convert to VDB** and **Use 16bit Float** checkboxes to optimize the simulation data.
5. Press *Tab* and put a **File Cache** node after the **Pyro Solver**.
6. Set the **File cache** node name to `pyro _fire _sim`.
7. Press *Alt* + *Shift* + *G* to open the global animation settings and set the frame range from `1` to `72`.
8. In the **Cache** rollout of the **File Cache** node, click on the **Save to Disk in Background** button to start saving the pyro simulation to disc.

Refer to *Figure 4.16* to see the pyro optimization and the **File Cache** settings:

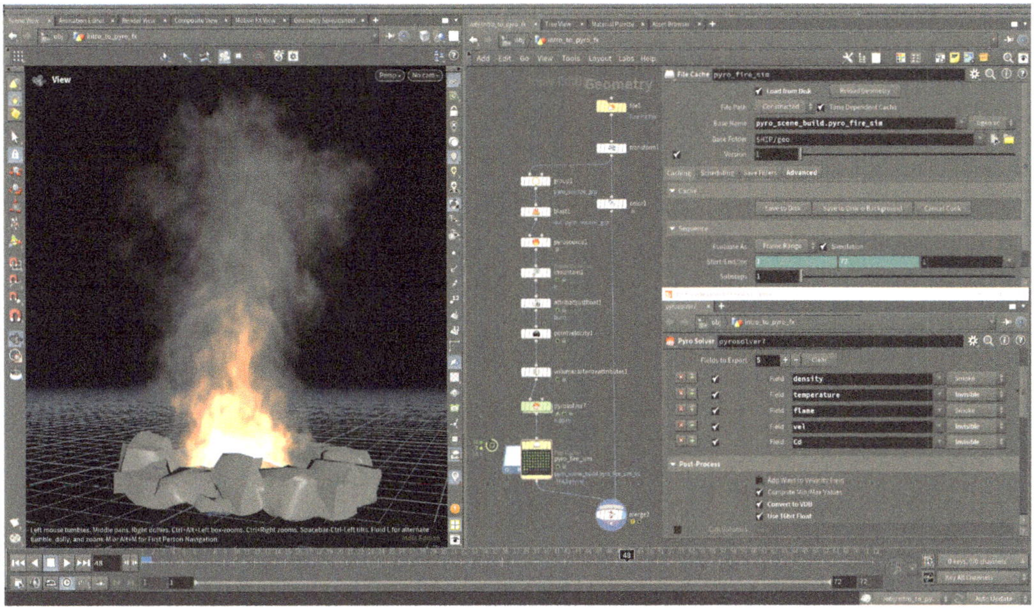

Figure 4.16 – Pyro simulation output

Now, let's create some **Null Output** nodes that will be easy to link from **obj** to **stage** context. This **Null** node is created purely as a checkpoint that will indicate a transition to rendering visually in the network view:

1. Connect the first **Null** after the **File Cache** and name it `OUT_fire_render`.
2. Connect the second **Null** after the **Transform** node that scales down the pit asset and name it `OUT_firepit_render`.

Moving on, we will look at how we can light and render our fire and pit assets in **Solaris**.

Lighting and rendering a realistic fire with smoke

We'll begin by switching to a **stage** context for rendering and bringing our simulated fire with smoke as well as the firepit into **Solaris**.

Follow these steps:

1. Press *Tab*, find `sop import` node, place it in the network view, and name it `sim_pyro`.
2. For **SOP Path**, link the **fire null out** node path into the empty box as usual.

3. Create a second **SOP Import** node, place it next to the first one, and name it `geo_firepit`.
4. Create a **Merge** node and connect both **SOP Import** nodes to the **Merge** input.

Figure 4.17 shows the **SOP Import** nodes and the **Merge** node:

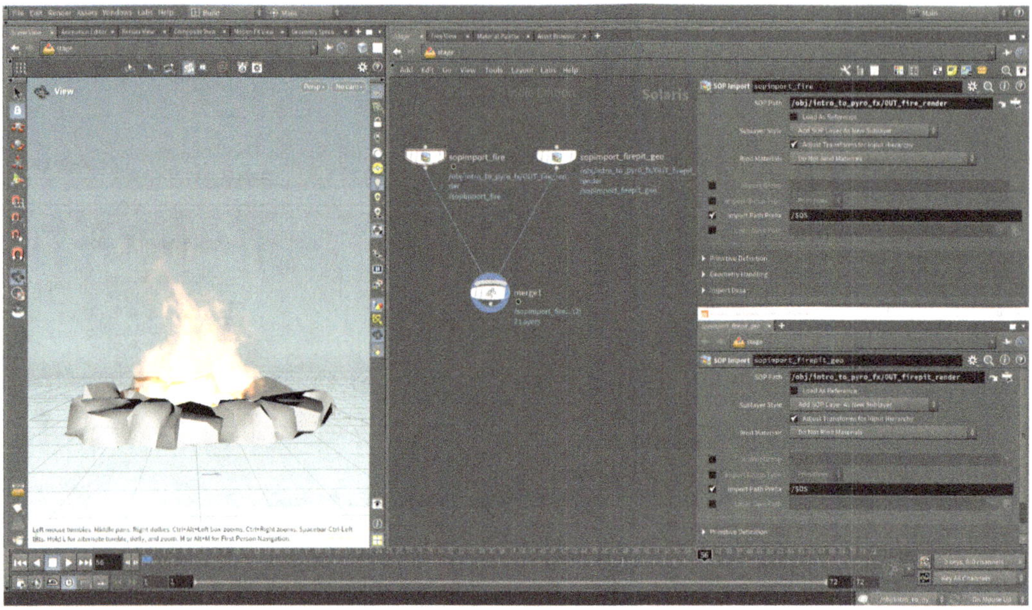

Figure 4.17 – Importing the pyro sim and pit asset

For the next steps, we are going to add materials for the pyro and firepit, add a basic environment light, and start doing render tests.

Change the viewport background to dark and continue with these steps:

1. Press *Tab*, look for the **Material Library** node, and place it after the **Merge** node.
2. Double-click on the **Material Library** node to dive inside.
3. Press *Tab*, look for `karma pyro fire material`, and place it in the network.
4. Double-click to dive inside and adjust the fire material parameters.
5. Inside **Karma Pyro Fire Material**, click on the **kma_pyroshader1** node, which is the main shader with fire material properties.
6. In **kma_pyroshader1**, go to the **Bindings** tab and change **Intensity Volume** to **Flame** instead of **Temperature**. The **Flame** field that comes out of the pyro simulation is much sharper and more detailed and will be much better for fire intensity than **Temperature**.

See *Figure 4.18* for the pyro shader parameters:

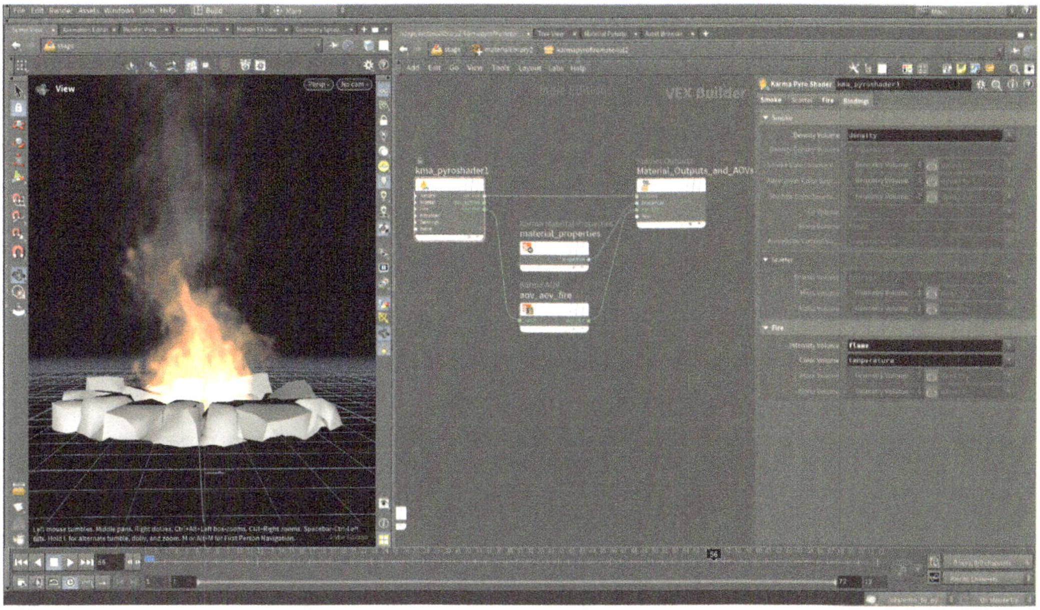

Figure 4.18 – Adjusting the karma pyro shader

For the next steps, we will use the **Fire** tab and the **Smoke** tab of **kma_pyroshader1** to set the desired look for the fire and smoke.

Setting up the look of the fire

I will set specific values that worked well for this scale of fire and interaction with the pit asset. Feel free to experiment with other values and do render tests, since this will be the best way to learn and advance.

Follow these steps for setting up the look of the fire:

1. In **kma_pyroshader1**, switch to the **Fire** tab.
2. In the **Intensity** rollout, set **Intensity Scale** to `100`, to make the flames much more emissive and brighter.

Note

Intensity Scale will need to be different depending on whether you're using the **Karma CPU** or the **Karma XPU** render engines. The **Karma CPU** usually needs much less intensity than **Karma XPU**.

3. Adjust **Source Range**, **Fire Intensity Ramp**, and **Color | Source Range** (see *Figure 4.19*). In order to emphasize the details in the flames, I tweaked **Fire Intensity Ramp** in an increasingly zig-zag way and had low points in the end.
4. Bringing the **Source Range** values closer to `0` also will help in capturing the hottest areas of the flames and making them pop in the render.

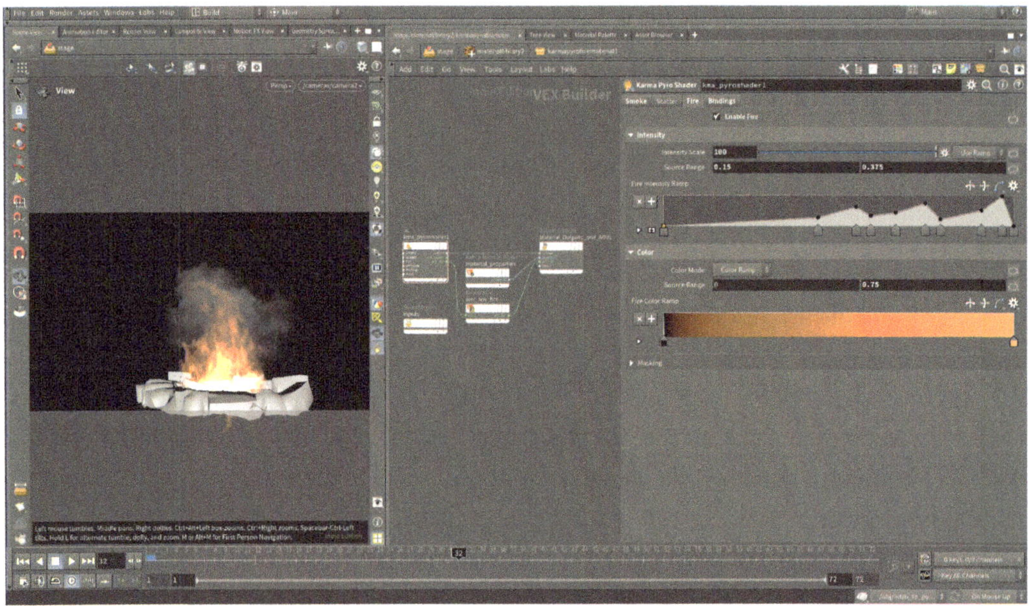

Figure 4.19 – Tweaking fire shading parameters

Let's now switch to the **Smoke** tab and adjust the shading of the smoke. If you would like to render just the fire without smoke, you can always turn off the **Enable Smoke** checkbox.

I have increased the density scale to 5 and adjusted the smoke color to be a little brighter, as can be seen in *Figure 4.20*:

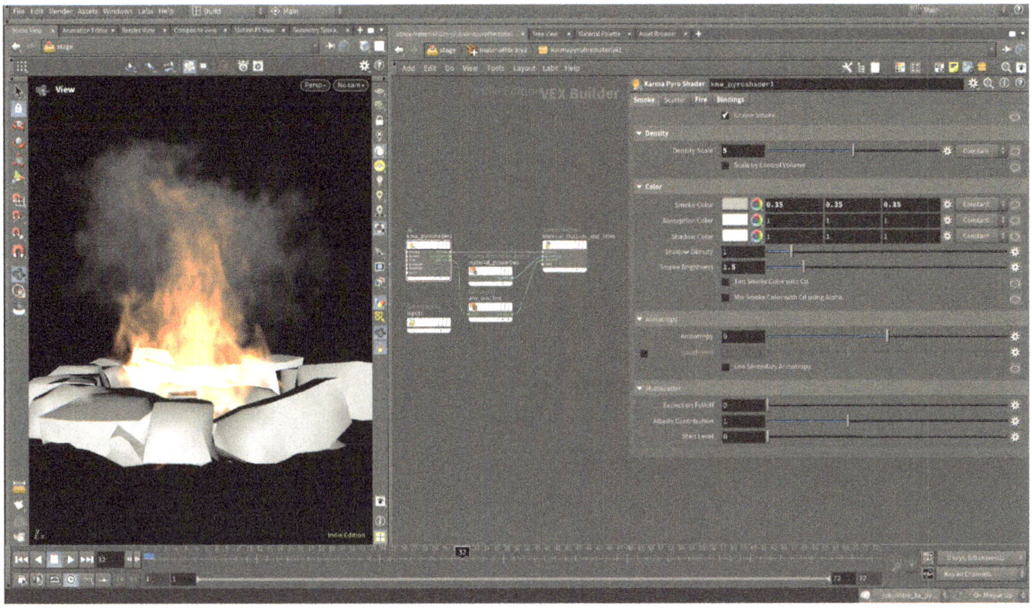

Figure 4.20 – Tweaking the smoke shading parameters

Additionally, we can control how much light emission the flames will have right in the fire material. This controller is located in the **Material Properties** node and is called **Light Source Diffuse**. For this specific scene, I have increased the **Light Source Diffuse** parameter from **10** to 25 to have the fire emit more light.

Now, let's assign the fire and smoke material to our pyro simulation:

1. Press the *U* key two times to go up to the **Solaris** scene level.
2. Press *Tab*, look for the **Material Linker** node, and place it after the **Material Library**.
3. Click on the **Material Linker** node and you should see the pyro fire material on the left and scene objects on the right of the **Rules** tab.
4. Drag and drop **karmapyrofirematerial** to the **sim_pyro** object to assign the material to the fire.
5. Frame the viewport so you can see both the fire and the pit and do a test render by changing the **Persp** at the top of the viewport to **Karma XPU**.
6. Additionally, I have added a **Transform** node after the **Merge** node to be able to rotate the fire and the pit to a more interesting angle.

Refer to *Figure 4.21* to see the test render and the **Material Linker** parameters:

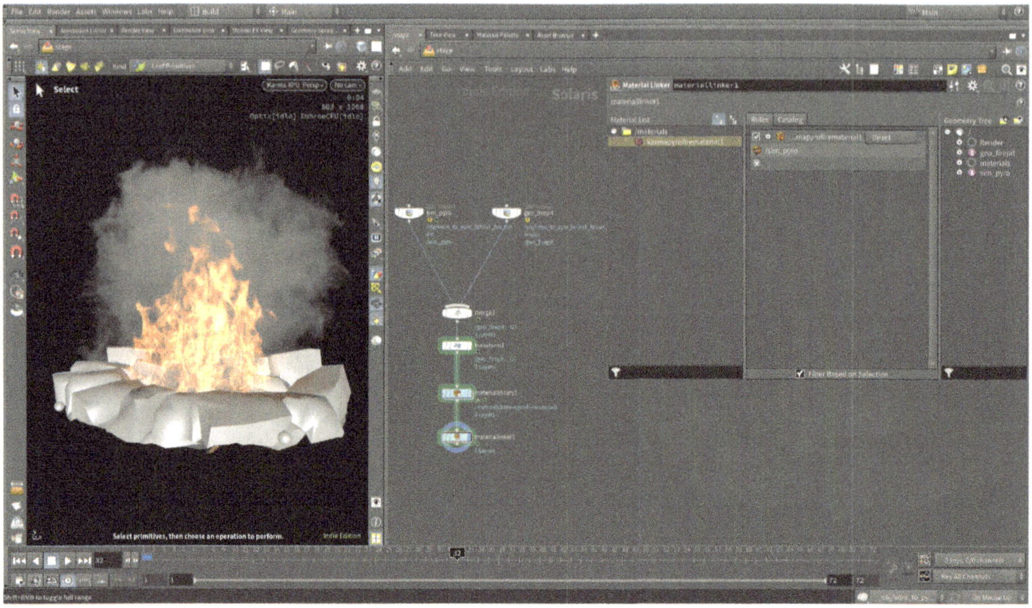

Figure 4.21 – Assigning the material to the pyro shader

The material is looking great and emphasizing all the details that we have created in the fire and smoke!

However, the lighting is still not quite working because whenever there are no physical light nodes in the **Solaris** scene, it will default to the headlight option.

In the next section, we'll look at how we can set up the lighting.

Setting up the lighting

Let's create a simple dome light resembling a night blue sky:

1. Press *Tab*, search for `dome light`, and add it after the **Material Linker** node.
2. Set **Color** to light sky blue and the light **Intensity** to `0.025`.
3. Create a simple camera from the viewport that has a nice framing of smoke, fire, and pit stones.
4. Finally, do a quick test render.

See *Figure 4.22* for the results and light parameters:

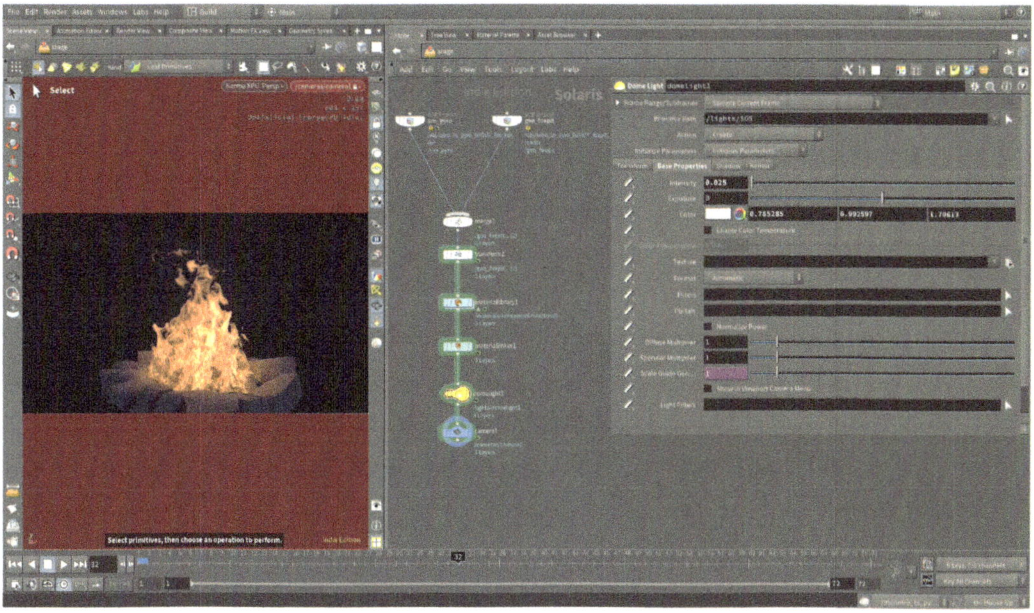

Figure 4.22 – Adding a skylight and a camera

Our scene is getting closer to the final look; there are just a few things that we will need to add and modify. As we can see, the smoke is no longer visible because of the dark lighting and the stones are missing the texture details.

For the next steps, we are going to quickly add a material to the stones and enable volume scattering in the render parameters to brighten up the smoke with the light of fire.

Let's follow these steps to create the stone pit material and link the textures:

1. Jump back into the **Material Library** and add a **Karma Material Builder** node.
2. Dive inside the **Karma Material Builder** node and click on the **mtlxstandard_surface** node.
3. Expand the **Base** rollout and the **Geometry** rollout on the **mtlxstandard_surface** node and look for the **Base Color** and **Normal** inputs.
4. We will bring in the corresponding textures from the `firepit asset` folder on our hard drive and connect them to **Base Color** and **Normal** for extra bump details.
5. Add an **mtlx pbr texture set** node and connect the **Base Color** and **Normal** output to the corresponding inputs in the material.

6. Go to the **Bump** tab, and in the **Height Map** box, link the path to the normal texture on your hard drive. You can also click on the **file chooser** icon and select the normal map from the file browser.

   We are going to use a normal map that ships with the fire pit asset to add more details to the rock's surface.

7. You can use **Bump Style** in either **Height** or **Normal**; depending on the lighting, each style will have its advantages. For this scenario, I found that using the **Normal** map with the **Height** style worked better.
8. Go to the **Textures** tab and link the **Albedo texture** to the **Base Color** box.
9. You can also adjust the **Specular Roughness** parameter in the **mtlx standard surface** node to adjust how blurry and glossy the reflection of the rock will be.
10. Go up to the **Solaris** level and use the **Material Linker** to assign the stones shader to **geo_firepit**.
11. Do a test render and get ready to move to the final stage.

Refer to *Figure 4.23* to see the texture assignment parameters and material network:

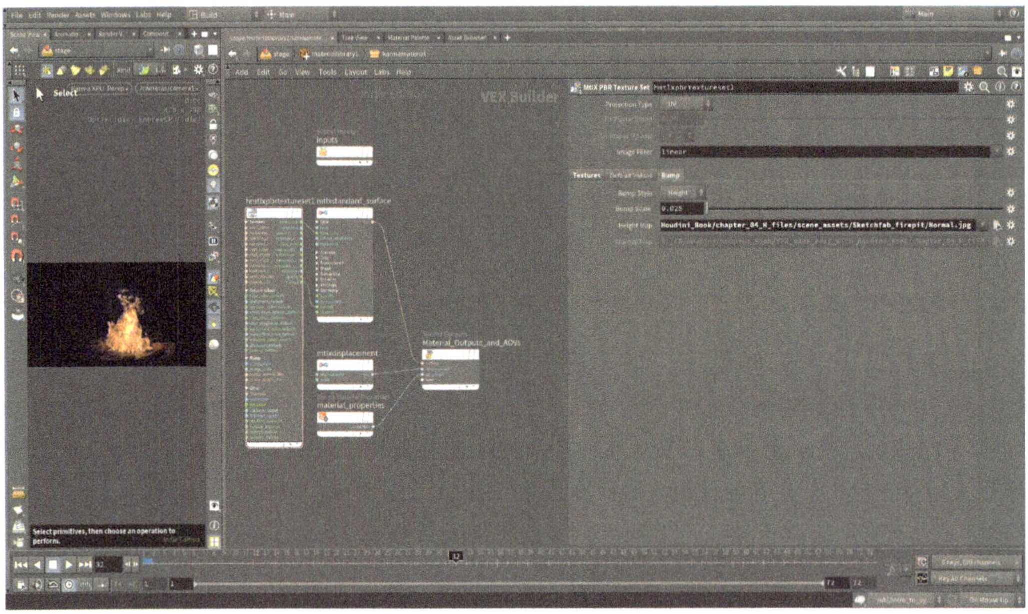

Figure 4.23 – Adding textures to the stone pits

Let's move on to the final adjustment of rendering parameters and setting up render output.

Adjusting the render settings

Let's follow these steps to set up the rendering parameters:

1. Press *Tab*, search for `karma node`, and place the result after the **Camera** node.
2. Change **Rendering Engine** to **XPU Engine** for faster GPU-accelerated rendering.
3. Keep the path-traced samples at 128. For higher quality, you can set them to 256.
4. In the **Rendering** tab, go to the **Limits** tab and change **Volume Limit** from **0** to 1. This will add extra bounces of light in the smoke and will make it visible with a nice light scattering.
5. Go to the **Camera Effects** tab and turn on **Velocity Blur** to achieve a realistic motion blur effect from the fire.

Refer to *Figure 4.24* to see the final pyro render result and render settings:

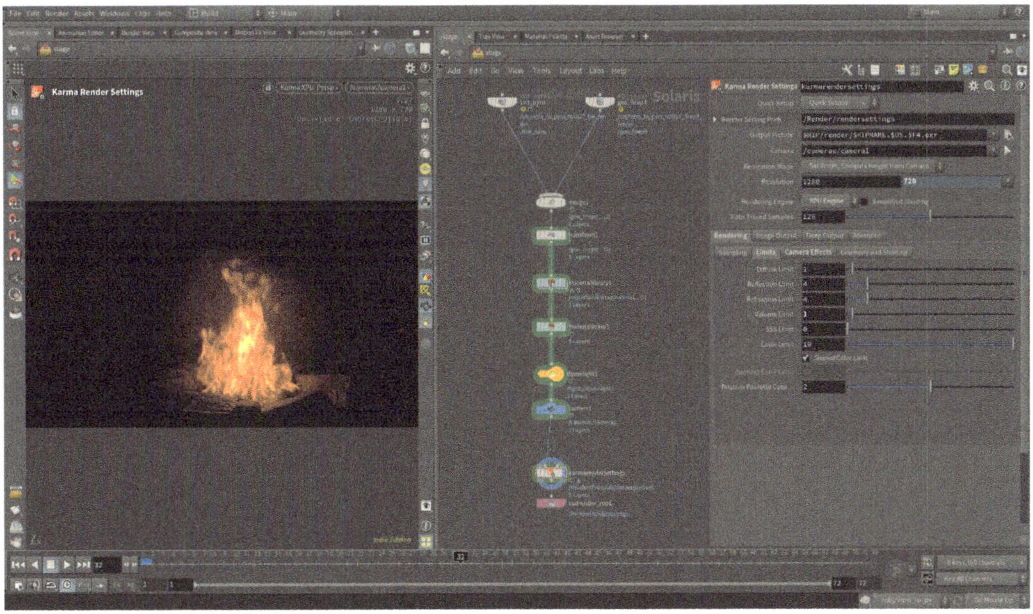

Figure 4.24 – Adjusting the pyro render settings

Congratulations on creating your first pyro effect in Houdini! You can take this further and render an image sequence of the full fire effect the same way as we did with the particles in *Chapter 3*.

Summary

As we wrap up this introduction to Pyro FX in Houdini, let's summarize everything that we have learned.

We learned new ways and workflows for creating efficient emitters specifically for pyro simulations. Next, we explored basic **Pyro Solver** simulation settings and parameters.

Then, we utilized the built-in forces and source field manipulations to create smoke and fire effects. Finally, we learned how to efficiently cache pyro simulation data to disc, as well as how to render the cache into a final realistic image.

This knowledge will be fundamental in building bigger and more complex pyro simulations.

In the next chapter, you will learn the basics of fracturing geometry and destruction methods.

5

Breaking through Rigid Body Dynamics

Rigid body simulations are a cornerstone of visual effects, enabling the realistic portrayal of objects interacting, colliding, and breaking apart.

In Houdini, powerful dynamics tools allow artists to create intricate and believable rigid body effects, from simple collisions to complex destruction scenes. This chapter introduces you to the fundamental concepts and techniques for crafting rigid body simulations in Houdini, setting the stage for more advanced applications.

Here are the main topics that we will cover in this chapter:

- Preparing 3D geometry for fracturing and rigid body simulation
- Exploring the **Rigid Body Dynamics (RBD) Material Fracture** node
- Adjusting RBD attributes before the simulation
- Creating more advanced multi-material fractures and simulations
- RBD simulation caching and output

By mastering the techniques covered in this chapter, you will be well equipped to create realistic and compelling rigid body simulations in Houdini. Whether you're simulating a simple stack of blocks or an elaborate demolition scene, the principles and practices you learn here will form the foundation of your work in RBD.

Figure 5.1 shows an example of the rigid body effect that we will be creating in this chapter:

Figure 5.1 – Rigid body simulation in Houdini

Technical requirements

I will be using some downloaded 3D assets that you can access for free from **Poly Haven** and **Sketchfab**:

- **Models**: `https://polyhaven.com/models`
- **Cat statue**: `https://polyhaven.com/a/concrete_cat_statue`
- **Wooden table**: `https://polyhaven.com/a/wooden_table_02`
- **Wine glass**: `https://sketchfab.com/3d-models/wine-glass-480cfc5b09ce4a1bb6b262e3686077c7`

All the workflows that I am going to show you for this project can be applied to any 3D model of your choice, so feel free to either proceed with the assets from Poly Haven and Sketchfab or use anything that you have created yourself.

You will have access to the Houdini file with the completed effect on the GitHub link at `https://github.com/PacktPublishing/VFX-Made-Easy-with-Houdini`.

To view the chapter images in better clarity, scan the provided QR code. It will direct you to a dedicated link where you can take a look at the images.

Setting up the project

Before we get to the steps of importing a 3D asset into Houdini, please go ahead and open an empty Houdini file, create a new project, and name it `intro_RBD effects`.

After creating the project, import the `concrete_cat_statue` file downloaded from Poly Haven, using the same workflow we used in *Chapter 4*, utilizing the **File** node.

Refer to *Figure 5.2* to see the initial setup and imported asset:

Figure 5.2 – 3D asset correct transformation

Moving on, we will start the preparation process for fracturing and RBD simulation for the concrete type of material.

Preparing 3D geometry for fracturing and rigid body simulation

Before starting any fracturing process or rigid body simulation, I usually recommend inspecting the 3D geometry to check for the following occurrences that can cause problems in the fracturing or simulation process:

- **Check whether there are any open holes in the mesh that is about to be fractured**: If there are any open holes, most of the fracturing methods will either fail or will not operate correctly, resulting in badly fractured geometry. Fracturing algorithms are designed to operate on an entirely enclosed mesh without any open polygon holes.

  In case your imported 3D asset has visible open holes, you can easily fix this with the help of the **PolyFill** node.

- **Check whether there are any intersecting, overlapping polygons or separated thin single-sided surfaces in the 3D geometry**: In case any of the preceding is present in your 3D geometry, the fracturing algorithm can also fail or produce a corrupt fragment that will also break the simulation.

  Most of the time, you can fix the issues with the bad mesh either with the help of the **Clean** node or by adding Boolean **Surface Operators** (**SOP**) with the operation set to union.

  Additionally, you can clean up the geometry by converting the geometry into a VDB surface volume and then converting it back to polygons, which will result in clean, watertight blended mesh.

- **Check whether the 3D geometry is either too big or too small relative to Houdini scene scale units**: In case the imported 3D geometry scale is too big or too small, it can lead to either a very slow fracturing process or to fracturing and simulation artifacts and instabilities. The scale problem could be easily fixed by adding the **Transform** node and multiplying the scale up or down based on the relative Houdini scale units.

  As a general rule, keeping the objects for small-scale simulations within `0.5` to 2 meters scale, and keeping objects for big-scale simulations within `25` to `100` meters, will operate well and be realistic for both the fracturing and simulation process.

Now, keeping all the preceding information in mind and looking at the concrete cat 3D model, I didn't find any packed geometry, open holes, or bad, intersecting and overlapping polygons. However, the scale of the asset is too big compared to what a concrete statue like this would be in the real world.

Currently, when looking at the node info as can be seen in *Figure 5.2*, we can see that the concrete statue dimensions are roughly *15 x 28 x 25* meters, which is roughly 10 times bigger than what this kind of structure would be in the real world.

Let's follow these steps to adjust the scale of the concrete cat statue for better performance:

1. Add a **Transform** node after the **File** node.
2. Set the **Uniform Scale** parameter to `0.175`.

Figure 5.3 shows the scaled-down asset and **Transform** node settings:

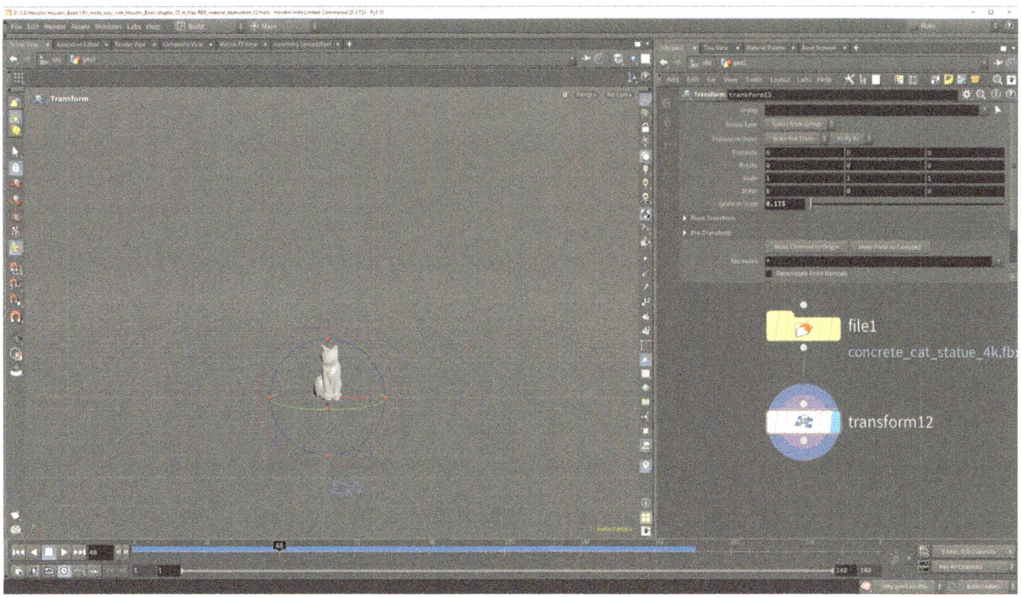

Figure 5.3 – 3D asset correct transformation

Now, we will move on to beginning the fracturing process on the 3D asset in the next section.

Exploring the Rigid Body Dynamics (RBD) Material Fracture node

Let's follow these steps to utilize the new **RBD Material Fracture** workflow:

1. Press *Tab*, search for the `RBD material fracture` node, and place it after the **Transform** node.
2. Add **RBD Exploded View** and connect all the outputs of the previous into inputs, to preview the generated fragments.

Figure 5.4 shows the fractured asset as well as the **RBD Material Fracture** settings:

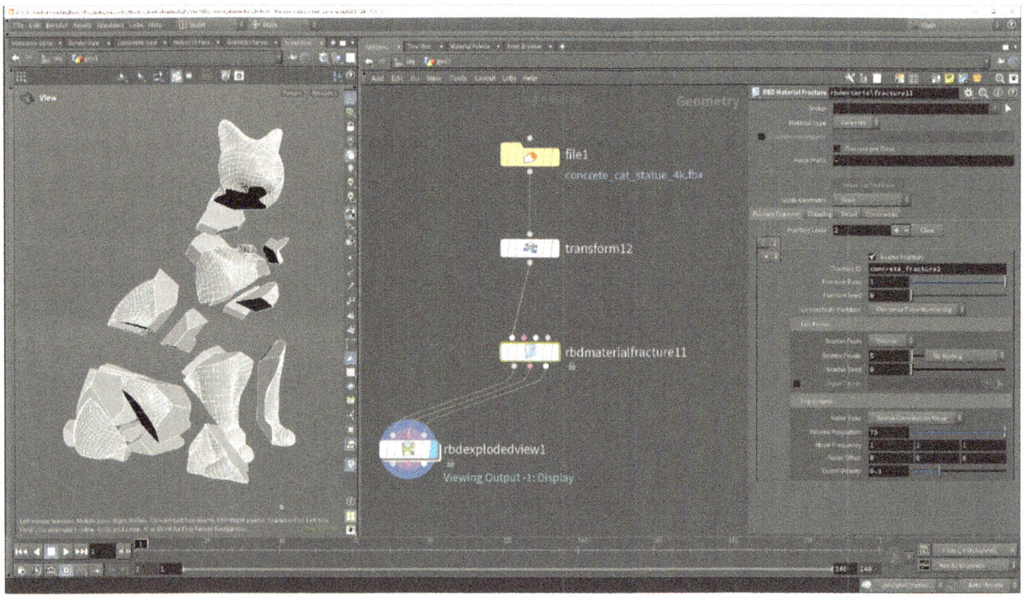

Figure 5.4 – Initial fracture

RBD Material Fracture is a very versatile node with lots of settings and parameters. It might look overwhelming at the beginning; however, I will direct your focus through some of the main parameters.

Refer to *Figure 5.5* for some of the main parameters that we need to focus on, highlighted in *green*:

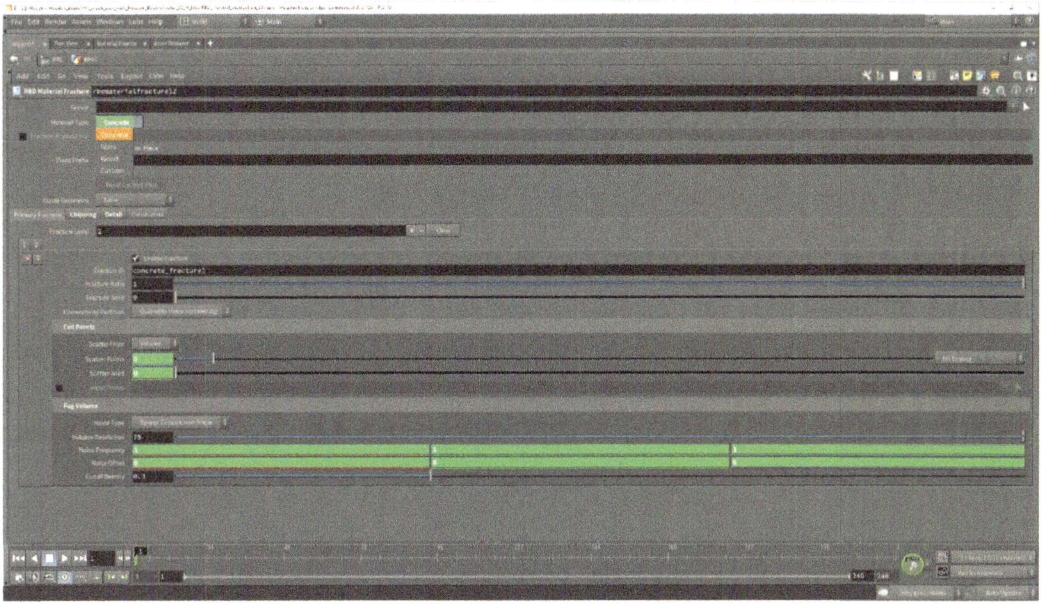

Figure 5.5 – RBD material fracture settings

The first option that we usually must choose and set correctly is the **Material Type** settings. You can choose from some of the most common materials used in rigid body simulations, which are concrete, wood, and glass.

Choosing the right type of material is important since each of the types has unique fracture settings for achieving a realistic result. For this example, since we will be using the concrete cat statue and our main 3D object for simulation, we will choose the material type to be **Concrete**.

Adding a unique fracture namespace

It is also important to set a unique fracture namespace parameter, especially when having multiple RBD objects interacting in the simulation. **Fracture Namespace** is a unique identifier for the set of fragments of each object. If you are creating an effect with only one RBD object and type of material, you can avoid **Fracture Namespace**.

However, if you are creating a simulation where you have two or more objects in the same or different material type, the fragment names can get duplicated, and this will result in an incorrect simulation with artifacts and dynamics errors. This is because the RBD solver will get confused when dealing with fragments that have the same name.

To avoid any issues in advance, let's enable the **Fracture Namespace** checkbox that is right under the **Material Type** setting, and give it a descriptive name: `Concrete`.

Exploring primary fracture settings

Next, we will focus on the tabs that are located under **Guide Geometry**, starting with the **Primary Fracture** tab. Under the hood, the **RBD Material Fracture** node generates a VDB fog volume and scatters points inside the volume. Each point acts as a seed for a Voronoi cell, dividing the geometry into distinct regions. The **Voronoi method** creates natural, irregular fragments, perfect for simulating realistic breakage patterns.

Under the **Cell Points** rollout, you can see that, by default, we have five scattered points that have generated a certain amount of randomly cut fragments. The more scattered points you are going to add, the more fragments are going to be generated. What is even cooler is that you can also add fracture levels and further fracture the fragments from the first level of fracture.

By default, **RBD Material Fracture** gives you two fracture levels from the start, and each of these levels has a separate control for scattered points. You can adjust the amount of fracture levels by using the + and – buttons near the **Fracture Level** box.

Usually, two levels of fracture are enough, since there are more options to add extra details and sub-fragments after the primary fracture.

The main settings that we are going to use to control the look and number of fragments in **Primary Fracture** are the **Scatter Points** amount in both fracture levels and the volume noise settings located under the **Fog Volume** rollout, which will define the density areas of scattered points.

Let's follow the next steps to adjust the fracture parameters for the concrete cat stature:

1. Select the **RBD Material Fracture** node and click on the first level tab of **Primary Fracture**.
2. In the **Cell Points** rollout, set the scatter points to 25.
3. Adjust the noise offset in the **Y** axis to `50` in the **Fog Volume** rollout.

Figure 5.6 shows the **Primary Fracture** settings of fracture level one:

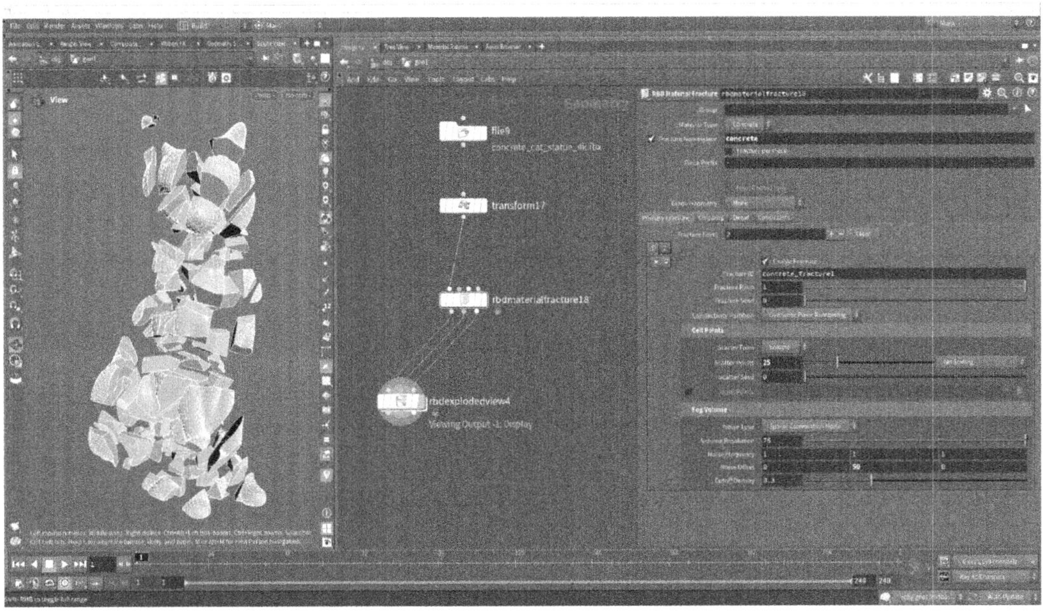

Figure 5.6 – Primary fracture level one settings

You can see that we have way more fragments now and we are going to add even more fragments with a second fracture level by following the next steps:

1. Click on tab number **2** under **Primary Fracture** to open parameters for the second fracture level.
2. Under **Cell Points**, set the **Scatter Points** setting to `30`.
3. Set the **Noise Offset** setting to the same amount of `50` in the **Y** axis as in the first fracture level.

Refer to *Figure 5.7* to see the result of two fracture levels and fracture settings:

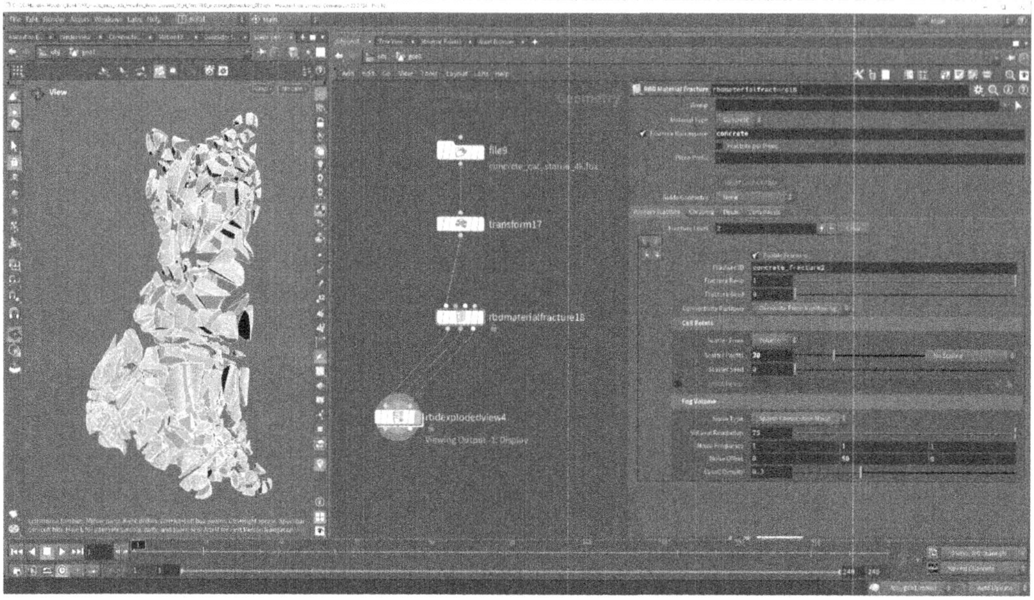

Figure 5.7 – Second level of primary fracture

> **Quick tip**: Need to see a high-resolution version of this image? Open this book in the next-gen Packt Reader or view it in the PDF/ePub copy.
>
> **The next-gen Packt Reader** and a **free PDF/ePub copy** of this book are included with your purchase. Scan the QR code OR visit `packtpub.com/unlock`, then use the search bar to find this book by name. Double-check the edition shown to make sure you get the right one.

This amount of fragments will work very nicely with the concrete crumbling effect that we will simulate. Having a high number of fragments contributes to making the simulation more detailed, however, it is usually not enough to achieve maximum realism.

Some of the other common techniques would be adding *chipping into much smaller fragments* and *edge details to the fractured pieces*. These two techniques help in adding more variation in fragment sizes, as well as adding extra details to the flat areas from the fracture cutting process.

All we need to do is to go to the **Chipping** tab, check the **Enable Chipping** checkbox, and then go to the **Detail** tab and enable the **Edge Detail** checkbox. We can further adjust the **Chipping** and **Edge Detail** settings by referring to *Figure 5.8*:

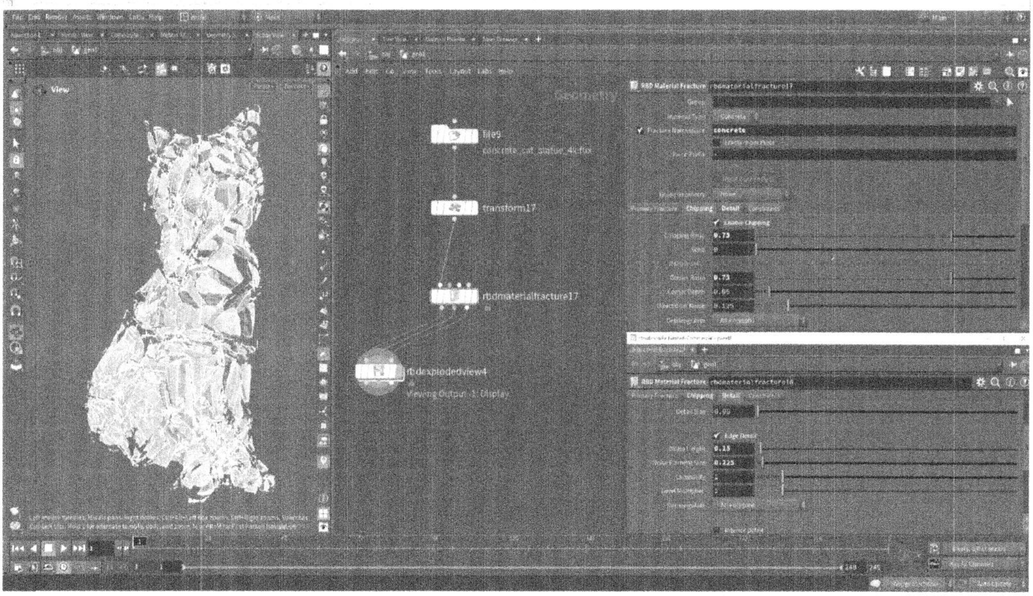

Figure 5.8 – Fracture chipping and edge details

Moving on, we'll learn how to adjust the rigid body constraints in the next section.

Adjusting initial constraint settings

Now, with this amount of fractures and details, we are ready to adjust the last RBD material fracture setting, which is in the **Constraints** tab.

In Houdini's RBD simulations, **constraints** are essential for controlling how fractured pieces behave and interact. Constraints appear as thin white lines connecting the fragments together. One of the most common, basic, and simple constraint types is a **glue constraint**, which is used to hold fractured pieces together in RBD simulations until a certain force threshold is exceeded. It's commonly used for simulating materials, such as concrete or glass that should stay intact until impacted by sufficient force.

Usually, I reduce the initial **Glue Constraint** amount in **RBD Material Fracture** to give the objects a higher chance of breaking apart. Let's adjust the **Primary Strength** and **Chipping Glue Strength** settings, as shown in *Figure 5.9*:

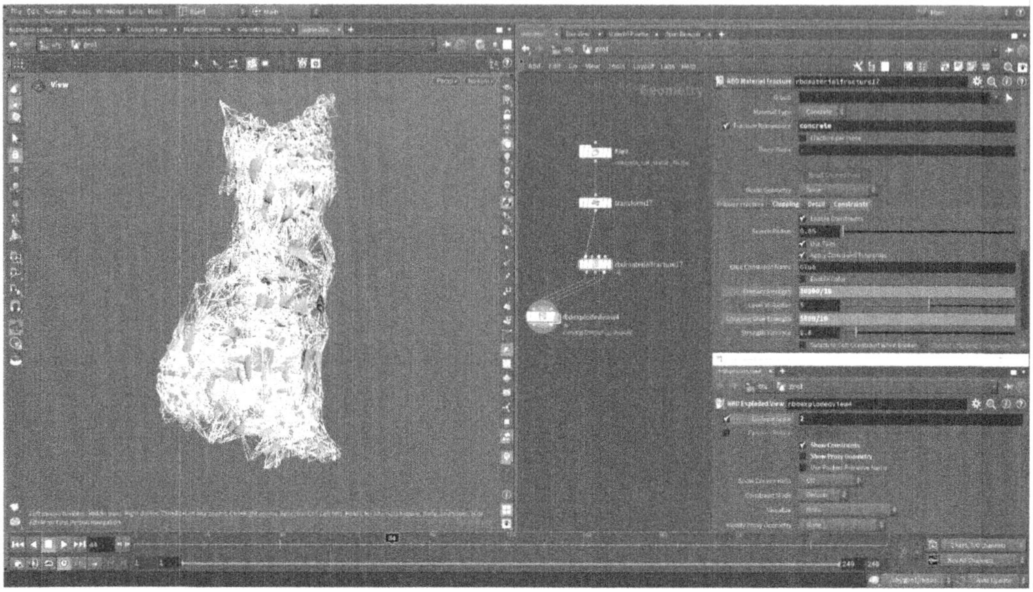

Figure 5.9 – Fracture chipping and edge details

Let's move on to adding pre-simulation transformations, groups, and other attributes.

Adding pre-simulation transformations, groups, and other attributes

The **RBD Material Fracture** node has three outputs:

- The *first output* gives access to high-resolution geometry with all the edge details
- The *middle output* provides constraint lines geometry
- The *last output* offers proxy geometry that is simplified for the simulation

Usually, after fracturing the imported 3D geometry, the next step would be transforming it into a pre-simulation state; for example, we can create a test simulation of the cat statue falling down from a distance and breaking into pieces.

Another important step would be adding a group to the fractured fragments, so we can access them easily later.

All these operations will need to happen on the packed state of RBD fragments and constraints since we want to affect all three outputs of the RBD material fracture. This could be easily done with the **RBD Pack** node, which will pack and combine all three outputs into one.

Let's follow these steps to RBD pack the outputs and transform and create groups:

1. Add an **RBD Pack** node and connect the three outputs from **RBD Material Fracture** to the respective three inputs of **RBD Pack.**
2. Add a **Transform** node and translate the fractured cat up in **Y** to `2.5` units above the ground.
3. Additionally, you can add a small rotation of `-30` in the **Z** axis to get a more interesting result.
4. Create a **Group** node and name it `concrete_cat`.

Refer to *Figure 5.10* to see the updated cat position and node network:

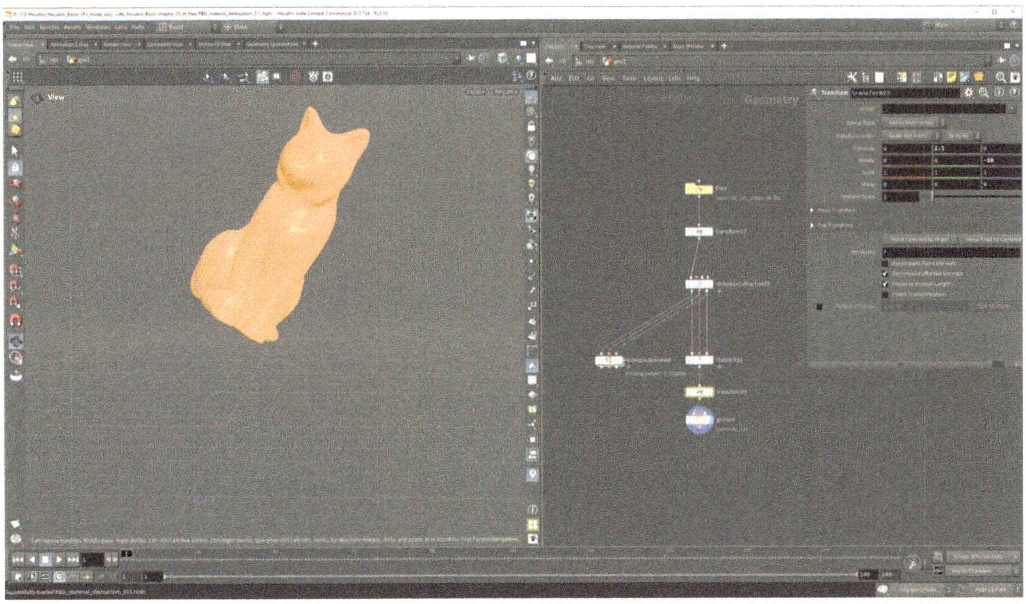

Figure 5.10 – Pre-simulation transform

Now we move on to adding rigid body properties before the simulation.

Adjusting RBD attributes before the simulation

The last step before the RBD simulation is adding important rigid body attributes and turning RBD fragments into packed primitives.

Before we can add these properties, we need to RBD unpack merged outputs for high-resolution geometry, constraints, and proxy geometry so that we can connect all three to the simulation inputs.

Continue with these steps to prepare the fragments for the simulation:

1. Add an **RBD Unpack** node after the **Group** node to get access to the three outputs.
2. Press *Tab*, search for `RBD configure node`, and place it after the **RBD Unpack** node.
3. Connect the outputs of the **RBD Unpack** node to the inputs of the **RBD Configure** node.
4. In the **RBD Configure Physical Attributes** rollout, set all to **Concrete** to achieve the realistic mass, friction, and density of the concrete material for the simulation.

RBD Configure is a very powerful node that does a lot of things under the hood for you. Most importantly, it converts the RBD fragments to packed primitives, which is the most optimized data type for rigid body simulation.

This node also handles all the transfers of attributes on fragments to packed primitives as well as gives us access to modify any rigid body state-specific attributes, such as active, animated, deforming, and many others.

You can also set unique material physical properties whenever simulating multiple different material types based on their groups. We will add these properties later in a more complex example in this chapter.

Adding an RBD Bullet Solver

The SOP **RBD Bullet Solver** in Houdini is a dynamics simulation tool that utilizes the Bullet physics engine to create realistic RBD simulations. It allows artists to create complex simulations of objects interacting with each other and their environment, including collisions, friction, and gravity. The solver is applied at the SOP level, enabling a procedural and non-destructive workflow.

Let's finally add an **RBD Bullet Solver** node after the **RBD Configure** node and enable **Ground Plane** in **Ground Collision** on the **Collision** tab.

After this, press play on the timeline and observe the concrete cat statue falling down, colliding with the ground, and breaking into the fragments that we fractured. We can also see how important it is to have a **Glue Constraint** to hold the remaining statue pieces together.

The reason why only the fragments at the base and the side of the statue were broken is that during the impact with the ground, a certain impact threshold for the **Glue Constraint** was reached and the fragments were allowed to get detached.

Glue constraints are used to bond RBD objects together, creating connections that can break under certain conditions, and simulating real-life fracture behaviors. Glue constraints hold pieces together until a set force threshold is reached, at which point they break, allowing the pieces to separate and behave independently.

The strength of the **Glue Constraint** can be adjusted directly in the RBD material fracture's **Constraints** tab by tweaking the **Primary Strength** parameter.

Follow *Figure 5.11* to see the **RBD Bullet Solver** and concrete cat broken into pieces:

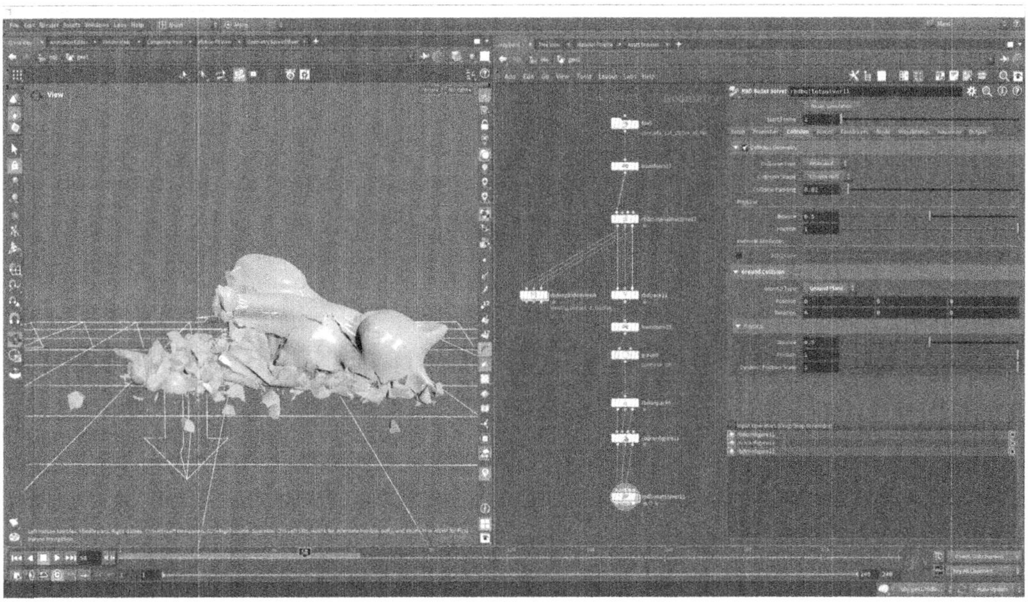

Figure 5.11 – First RBD simulation of a concrete cat breaking into pieces

The **RBD Bullet Solver** has several tabs and sections that provide settings for specific rigid body simulation types and destruction scenarios. It can look like a lot and too complicated. However, for the beginner-level RBD effects, we only need to focus on three main tabs:

- **Setup**: This is for adjusting the time scale, speed, and quality of the simulation. The quality of the RBD simulation can be improved by increasing the number of **Bullet Substeps** and **Constraint Substeps**. In the case of fast-moving objects or colliders, it would be a good idea to slowly increase the substeps by a factor of 10. However, the default amount of 10 substeps is usually enough for simple simulations.

- **Collision**: To configure collision objects, such as ground planes or any additional colliders. In the case of a moving collider, I would recommend setting the collision type to **Deforming**. Additionally, you can adjust the **Collision Padding** setting to achieve a higher quality collision representation by decreasing the padding amount. The collision padding can also be adjusted separately for the fractured pieces in the **Properties** tab.
- **Forces**: To modify or add simple forces, such as gravity and drag. Additionally, you can double-click on the **RBD Bullet Solver** and add **POP Particle Forces** into the **PRESOLVE** output to affect and guide the broken fragments in a specific way.

For a more detailed overview of settings and parameters, you can click on the **question** icon (**Click for Help**) in the top-right corner of any node's parameters pane and it will open a quick help window with detailed explanations.

We have already set individually all of the other important settings for the constraints and simulation attributes in the RBD nodes before the **RBD Solver**.

Moving on, we will create a more complex destruction scene with four interacting materials.

Creating more advanced multi-material fractures and simulations

For our next multi-material RBD example, let's import the *wooden table* from Poly Haven and the *wine glass* from Sketchfab (see the *Technical requirements* section) with the help of two separate **File** nodes.

After importing the assets, let's follow these steps to prepare the geometry for fracturing:

1. Add a **Transform** node after the file that imports the glass and set the **Uniform Scale** value to `0.75`.
2. Add a **Transform** node after the file that imports the table asset and set the **Uniform Scale** value to `0.1`.
3. Add an **Exploded View** node after the **Table Transform** node to inspect the asset and see whether it has any visible openings or holes.

Refer to *Figure 5.12* to see the updated node network:

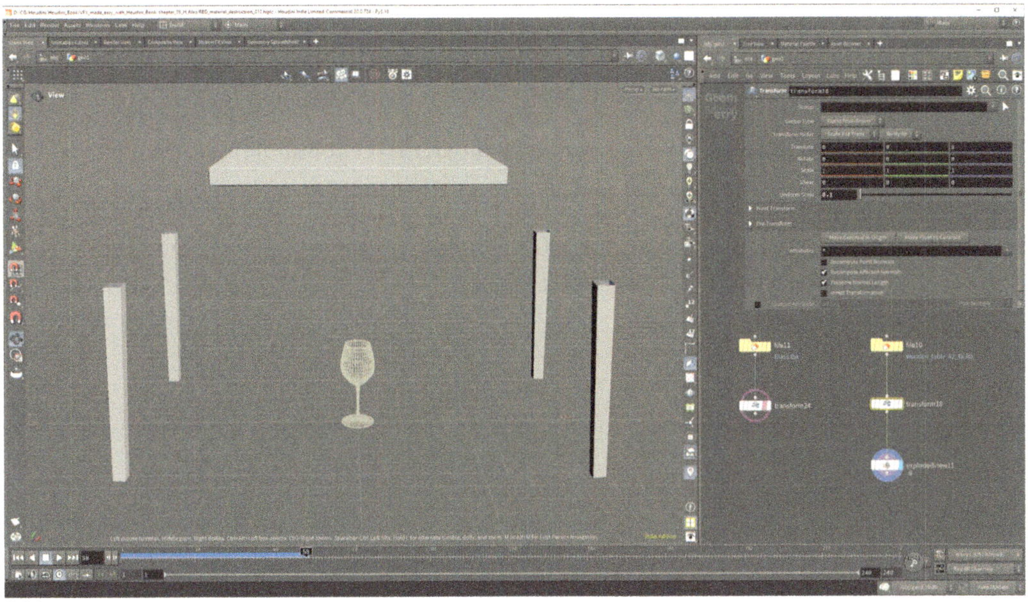

Figure 5.12 – Inspecting the table asset for open holes

The **Exploded View** node pushes the non-connected elements and polygons of a 3D geometry apart, letting you see any potential problems. This node is very similar to the RBD Exploded View, which has more options, especially for inspecting the fractured fragment pieces.

As we can see, the table legs have an opening on the top that will cause issues in the fracturing process.

In the next steps, we will fix the opening and start a fracturing process for a wood type of material that is very similar to concrete but has its own parameters and cutting patterns:

1. Add a **PolyFill** node after the **Transform** node and set the **Fill** mode to **Single Polygon**.
2. Add a **Connectivity** node that will assign a unique class attribute for each piece of the table, which we can use for unique fracture directions and patterns.

3. Add an **RBD Material Fracture** node, set the **Material Type** setting to **Wood** and **Fracture Namespace** to `wood`.
4. We can fracture each piece of the table individually by turning on the **Fracture Per Piece** option and setting the **Piece** attribute to **Class**.

Fracturing wood has lots of different settings and parameter combinations. The best way to understand what each of the parameters does is to test them one by one and try different values.

For the best results, I recommend turning off **Enable Cluster** in the **Cluster** tab, testing grain parameters while having the **Cut** tab off, and then testing the cut parameters while having the grain off.

Also, for a more detailed overview of all the settings and what they do, you can hover the mouse over any parameter and hold it there for a second and a small description prompt will appear on top.

Additionally, you can click on the **question mark** icon on the **RBD Material Fracture** node, and it will open a **Help** document describing every setting of the node.

Since there is no magic recipe of parameters for each material fracturing, it will take some time and experimentation for you to find the right values for each type of material and 3D object.

Important note

As a general rule, it is important to have a variation of small, medium, and big fractures for the best results.

Wood material fracturing methods

For the next steps, I am going to provide a screenshot of the **RBD Material Fracture** parameters that worked best for fracturing this specific table asset.

Refer to *Figure 5.13* to see the parameters for the **Grain** wood fragmentation with the **Cut** option turned off:

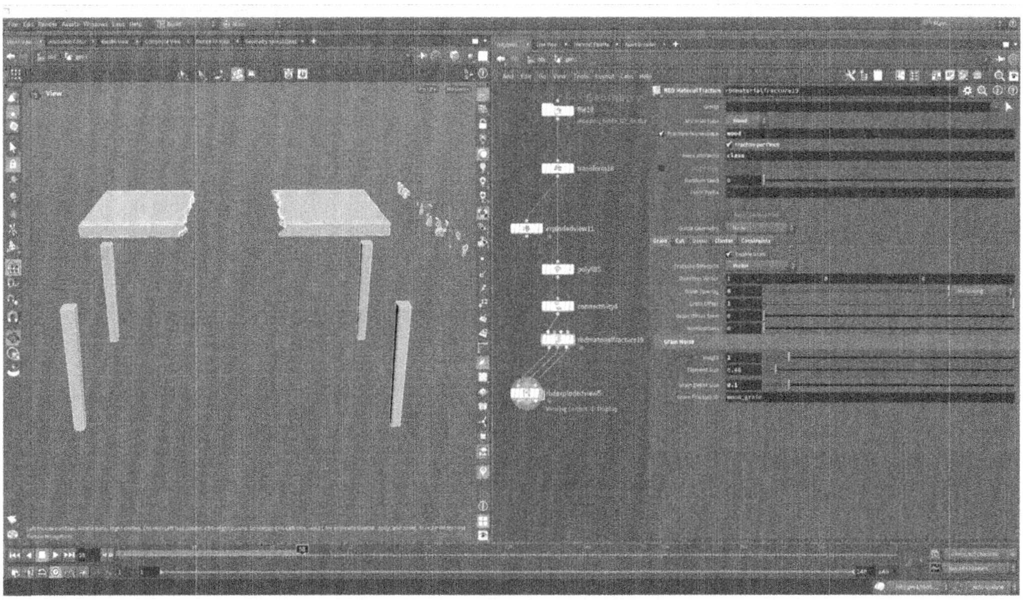

Figure 5.13 – Wood grain fragmentation with cuts turned off

Refer to *Figure 5.14* to see just the cuts fragmentation with the grain turned off:

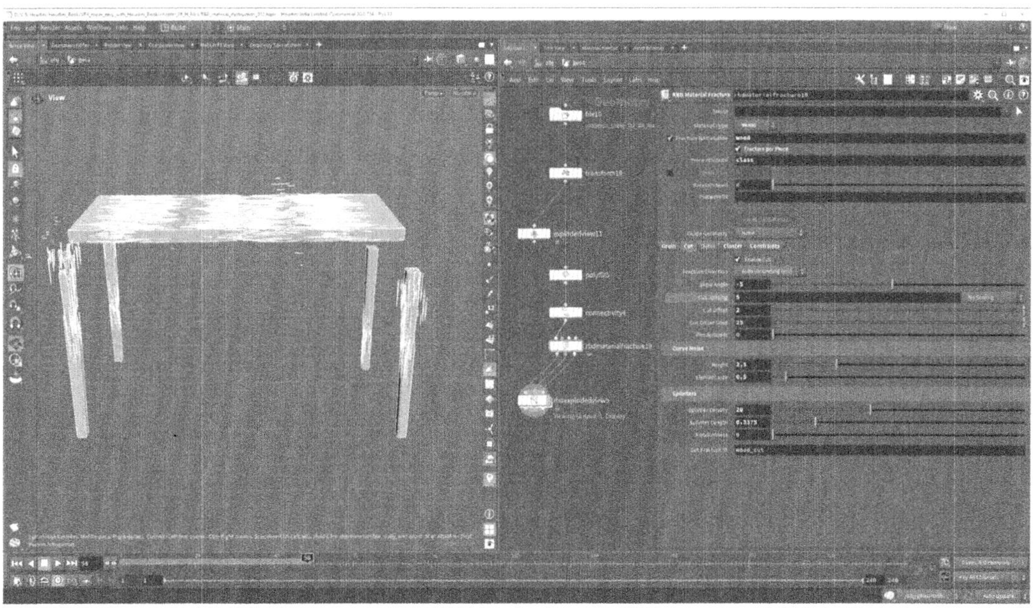

Figure 5.14 – Wood cut fragmentation with grain turned off

Now, look at *Figure 5.15* to see both the **Grain** and **Cut** fracturing combined as well as the wood constraint settings:

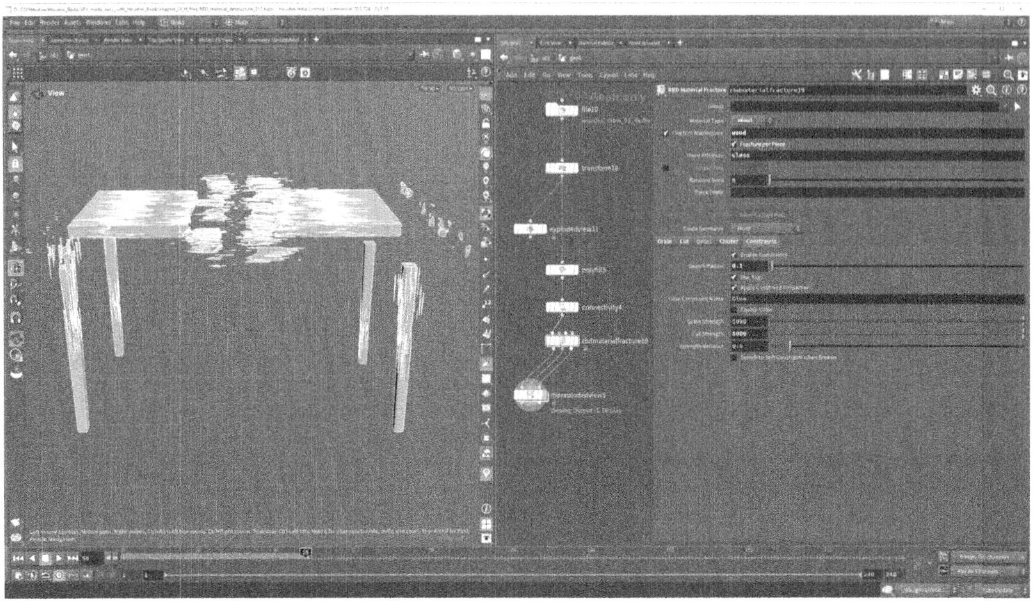

Figure 5.15 – Wood grain and cut combined with constraint settings

After creating the fractures, select the **RBD Exploded View** node and check the **Show Constraints** checkbox. In *Figure 5.16*, we can see that there are not enough constraints gluing the table legs to the tabletop, hence making the table unstable and very easy to break without any force:

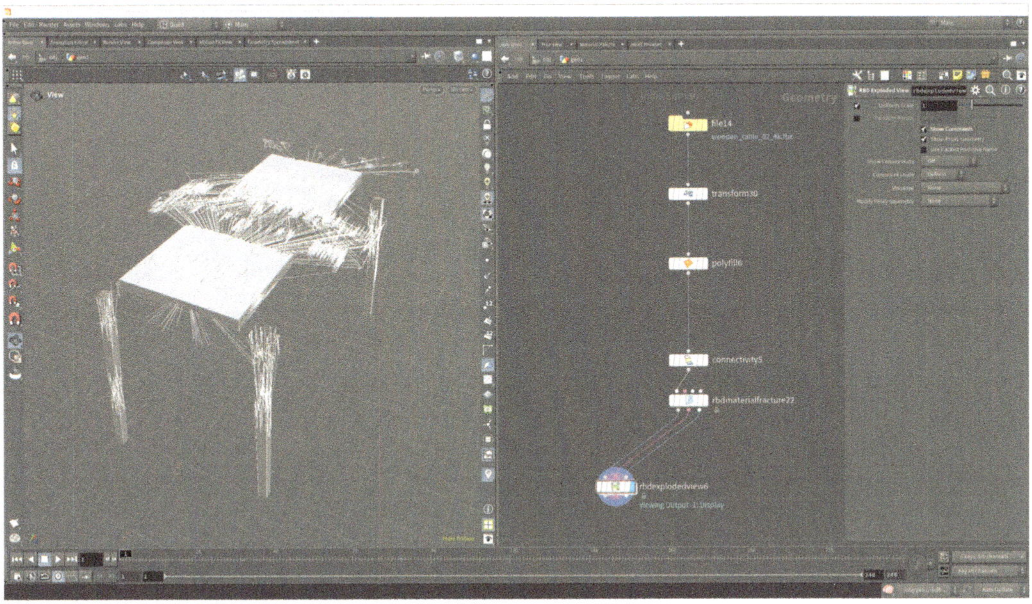

Figure 5.16 – Table constraints and stability

In the next steps, we will add more stability to the table constraints.

Creating additional constraints with extra properties

To add more stability to the table structure, we can create additional constraints with the help of the **RBD Constraints from Rules** and **RBD Constraint Properties** nodes. Let's follow the next steps to add extra constraints and finalize the fracturing setup:

1. Add an **RBD Constraints from Rules** node after the **RBD Material Fracture** node.
2. In the parameters, increase **Search Radius** to 1 and **Max Connections** to 2.
3. Add the **RBD Constraint Properties** node after and set **Glue Strength** to `100000`.
4. Add another **RBD Exploded View** node with the **Show Constraints** checkbox to inspect the newly created constraints.
5. Add an **RBD Pack** node to combine the wood fragment inputs into one.
6. Add a **Group** node and set the group name to `wood`.

Refer to *Figure 5.17* to see the newly created constraints and node network:

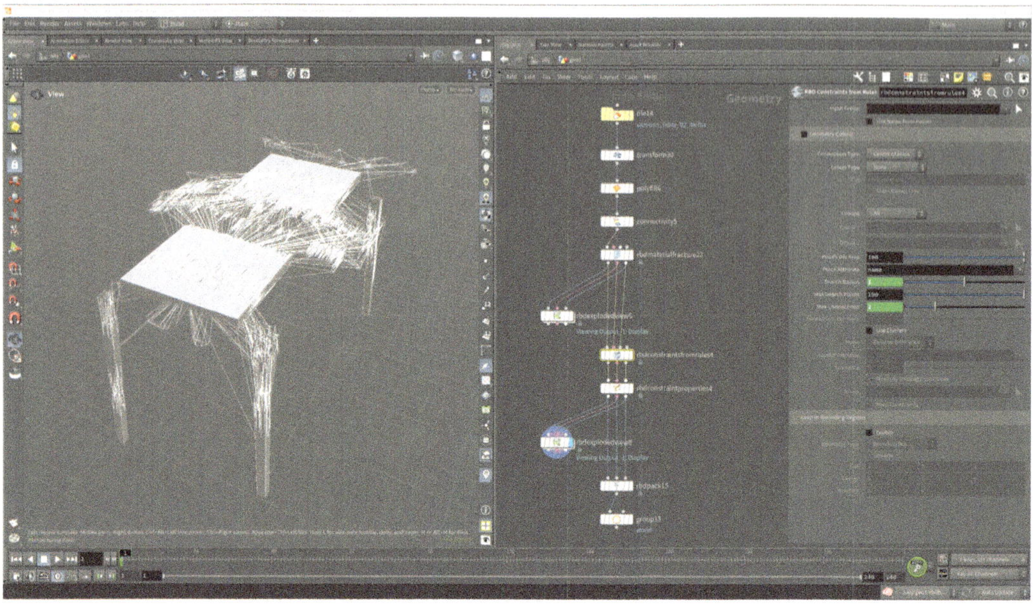

Figure 5.17 – Extra table constraint connectors

Notice that all the legs are now connected to the tabletop surface and there are also extra connectors in between fragments. This will make the structure more stable.

Now, we will move on to fracturing the 3D wine glass asset that we imported earlier.

Shattering the glass material

Let's now take the 3D wine glass asset and look at the fragmentation settings for the glass material by following the next steps:

1. Select the **Transform** node after the file importing the wine glass.
2. Add a **Subdivide** node after the **Transform** node to make the glass surface smoother.
3. Add **RBD Material Fracture** after the **Subdivide** node.
4. Set **Material Type** to **Glass** and **Curved Glass**.
5. In the **Impact Points** tab, set **Scatter Points** to `2` to have a minimum of two points of radial shatter.
6. Go to the **Cracks** tab and set **Radial Crack Number** to `15`.
7. In the **Concentric Crack** rollout, increase the minimum width to `0.25`.
8. Switch to the **Chipping** tab and turn on **Enable Chipping**.

9. Increase **Corner Ratio** to `0.75` to get more broken chips on the corners of the fracture.
10. Go to the **Constraints** tab and set **Radial**, **Concentric**, and **Chipping Strengths** respectively to these decreased values of `2000`, `8000`, and `1000`.

These settings that we have set are not arbitrary, but rather the values that I found during my experimentation with fractures and test simulations. I encourage you to also test out different settings for the glass and see how the simulation will change based on different values.

For the next steps, we are going to RBD pack the glass fracture inputs and transform them to be placed on top of the table by following the next steps:

1. Add an **RBD Pack** node after the **Glass RBD Material Fracture** node.
2. Add a **Match Size** node and connect the **RBD Pack** node to the first input and the table connectivity output to the second input.
3. Set the **Justify Y** parameter from center in both to **Min** to **Max** to align the bottom of the glass to the top of the table.
4. Add a **Transform** node and set the **Translate** parameters to these values in **X**, **Y**, and **Z**, respectively: `-4`, `0.0005`, and 2.

Refer to *Figure 5.18* to see the **Match Size** and **Transform** settings as well as the node network:

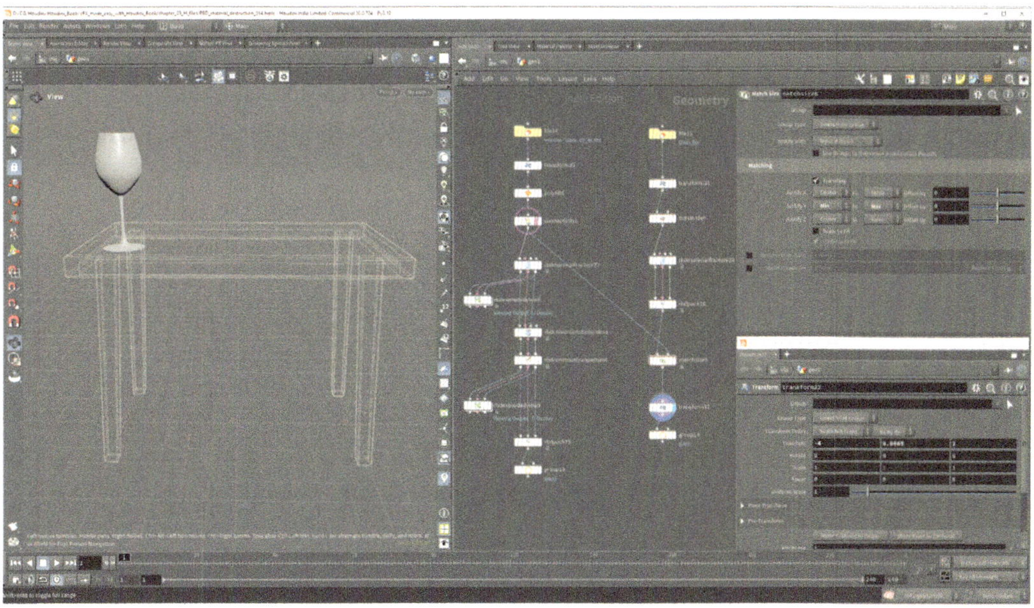

Figure 5.18 – Glass aligned with the table

We'll now move on to adding a metallic ball collider to break the table and the glass.

Adding a metallic wrecking ball for destruction

We can easily add a sphere lifted above the table and the glass. Given the sphere's metal qualities for density and mass, it will fall under the force of gravity, causing a destruction effect upon impact with the table.

Let's follow the next steps to add a wrecking sphere:

1. Create a sphere; set **Type** to **Polygon**, **Radius** to `1.5` in all axes, and **Frequency** to 16.
2. Add an **RBD Pack** node and connect the sphere only to the first and the third input to be able to merge it with the wood and glass-packed RBD objects correctly.
3. Add a **Transform** node and lift the sphere to 18 units in the **Y** axis.
4. Add a **Group** node and name it `metal`.

Our wrecking ball is ready; now, let's merge it with the fractured wood table and the glass.

Merging multiple RBD objects and setting multi-material properties

Let's merge all the groups of RBD objects and add an **RBD Unpack** node to get access to high-resolution geometry, constraints, and proxy simulation geometry.

Add an **RBD Configure** node after the **RBD Unpack** and prepare to assign different material properties to different groups of RBD objects. I have colored the nodes for better visualization.

Follow *Figure 5.19* to see the node network and result of merged RBD objects:

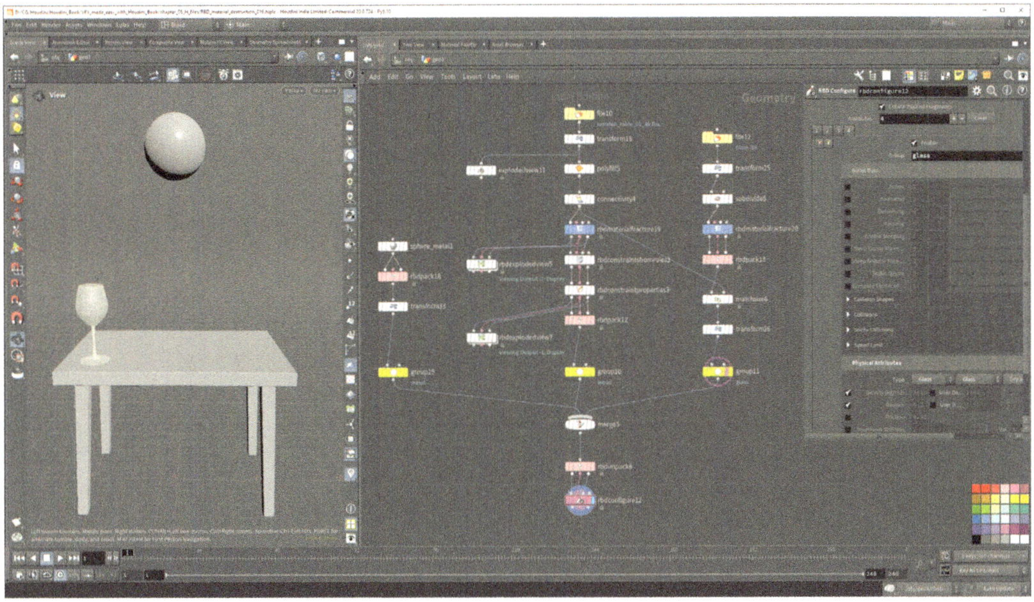

Figure 5.19 – Glass aligned with the table

For the next steps, we will need to create a numbered tab for each material group to be able to set unique RBD material properties and attributes.

The number of tabs must match the number of RBD materials that you have. In our example, we have wood, glass, and metal, so we will need to create at least three tabs. You can also additionally create an extra tab for the concrete cat statue if you would like to add it to the simulation.

> Important note
>
> For everything to work correctly, it is very important that the actual RBD group name matches the group name that you type in the **RBD Configure** node.

You can create a new tab by clicking on the + button near the **Attributes** box.

Follow *Figure 5.20* to see the **RBD Configure** node and **Material** tab settings for wood, glass, metal, and concrete:

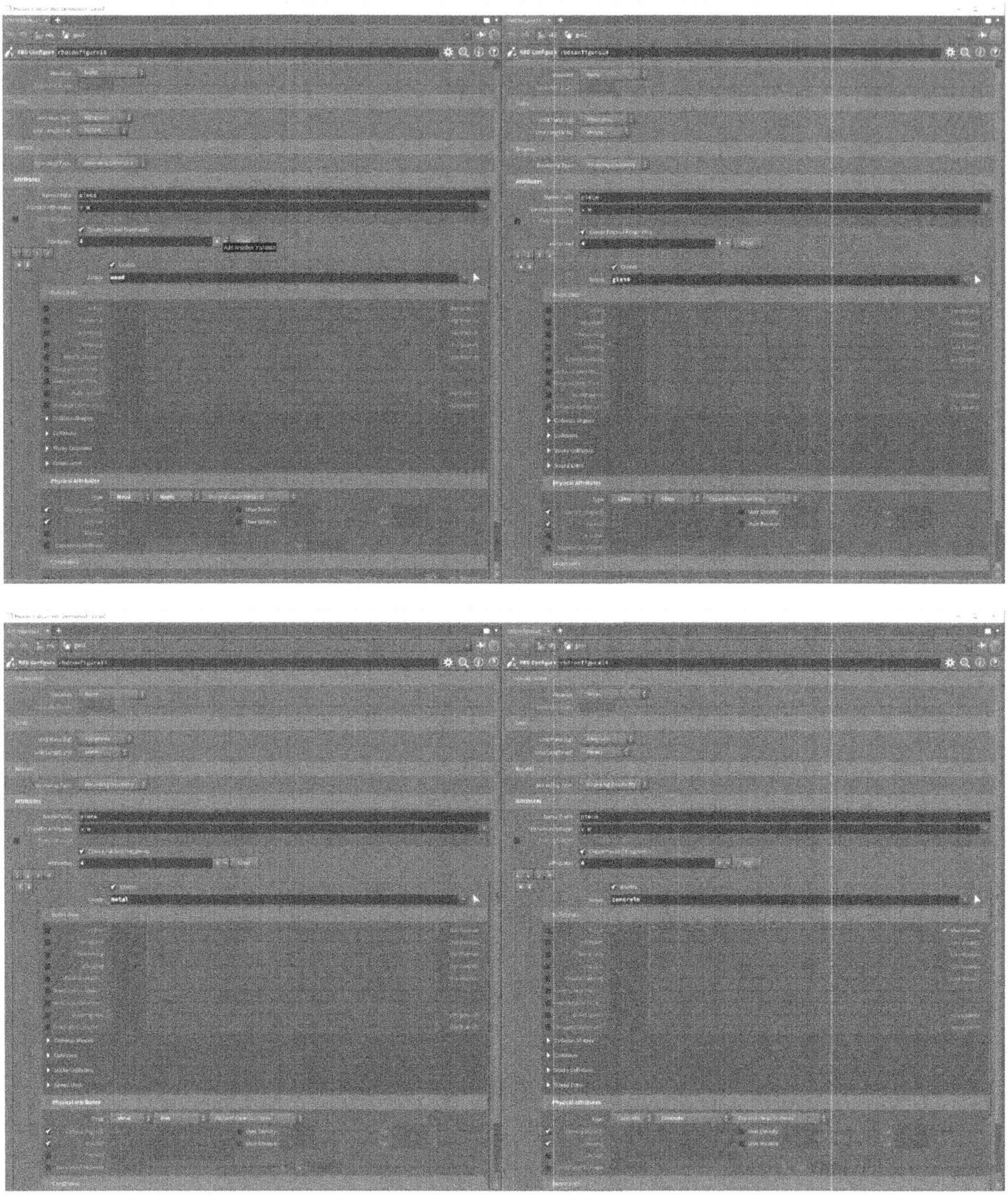

Figure 5.20 – RBD Configure multi-material settings for wood, glass, metal, and concrete

Finally, let's add the **RBD Bullet Solver** and take a look at some of the simulation parameters that you can experiment with:

- **Time Scale** in the **Simulation** tab can help you achieve a slower or faster simulation and you can even animate the time to go from a normal value of `1` to a lower value to create a slow-motion effect.
- **Bullet Substeps** and **Constraint Substeps** will help you increase the resolution and quality of the simulation by increasing the values. It is recommended to start from `10` substeps for both. If you have very fast motion or need to reinforce the constraints, you can increase the value to higher numbers in iterations of `10`.
- Inside the **Collision** and **Properties** tabs, you can adjust the physical parameters of RBD fragments and collision objects. Those physical parameters will act as multipliers over the properties set in the **RBD Configure** node.
- Finally, inside the **Forces** tab, you can add drag force and adjust the gravity force if needed.

Refer to *Figure 5.21* to see the result of a multi-material RBD simulation:

Figure 5.21 – RBD multi-material simulation

Let's move on to output and caching the simulation results.

RBD simulation caching and output

As with any simulation in Houdini, we will need to cache the RBD simulation to disk for the best results and further output. You can use the **File Cache** node workflow, which we have been using for particles and pyro simulations in the previous chapters.

Additionally, after caching to disk, you can unpack the result of the simulation and split it into different outputs by material group to bring it into **Solaris** and apply the textures that come with the asset.

Refer to *Figure 5.22* to see the result of the RBD caching and output:

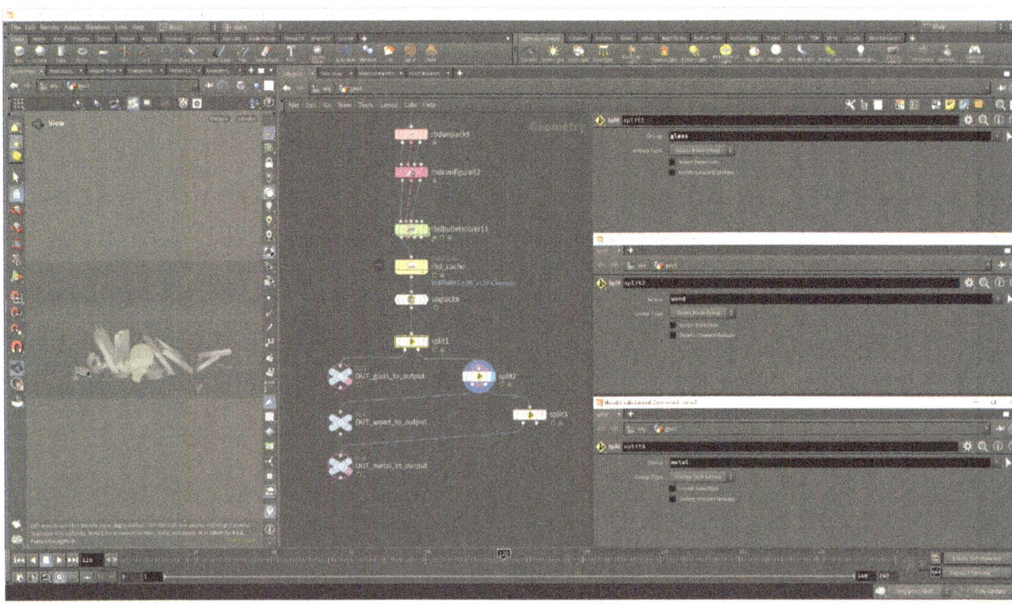

Figure 5.22 – RBD caching and output

I encourage you to take this project further and render it into a final image sequence. Use all the knowledge from the previous chapters on creating cameras and light materials and rendering with the **Karma** engine. Refer to the project file in the book's GitHub repository (see the *Technical requirements* section) to review the complete sequence and explore the setup in detail.

Summary

In conclusion, this chapter has equipped you with the skills to create sophisticated RBD simulations in Houdini. We covered the intricacies of RBD fracturing, demonstrating how to break objects realistically.

You learned to adjust constraints, allowing for precise control over interactions and movement. Setting RBD attributes enabled customization and fine-tuning of simulations, enhancing realism.

By utilizing the **RBD Solver**, you gain the ability to manage complex simulations efficiently. With these techniques, you're now prepared to create dynamic, visually compelling effects, pushing the boundaries of your projects in visual effects and animation.

In the next chapter, we will learn how to utilize particles and volume dynamics to create fluid effects.

Subscribe to Game Dev Assembly Newsletter!

We are excited to introduce **Game Dev Assembly**, our brand-new newsletter dedicated to everything game development. Whether you're a programmer, designer, artist, animator, or studio lead, you'll get exclusive insights, industry trends, and expert tips to help you build better games and grow your skills. Sign up today and become part of a growing community of creators, innovators, and game changers.

`https://packt.link/gamedev-newsletter`

Scan the QR code to join instantly!

6

Diving into Water FX

In this chapter, we will delve into the fascinating world of FLIP fluids in Houdini, which serves as a powerful tool for simulating realistic liquid behaviors in 3D environments.

Fluid Implicit Particle (**FLIP**) fluids combine the best of both particle and volume grid-based methods, allowing for the creation of stunning visual effects with a high degree of control and flexibility. We'll explore the fundamental concepts behind FLIP fluids, including their unique characteristics, workflows, and essential parameters, equipping you with the knowledge to create dynamic and visually captivating fluid simulations.

Here are the main topics that we will cover in this chapter:

- FLIP fluid dynamics explained
- FLIP fluid sourcing methods
- Guiding the motion of FLIP fluids
- FLIP fluid optimization and caching
- Liquid meshing workflows
- Liquid mesh lighting and rendering

By learning the techniques covered in this chapter, you will be well-equipped to create realistic and compelling water simulations in Houdini. Whether you're a beginner or looking to refine your skills, this introduction will set the stage for mastering fluid dynamics in Houdini.

Figure 6.1 shows an example of the water simulation that we will create with FLIP fluids.

Figure 6.1 – Water simulation in Houdini

Let's look at how the **FLIP Solver** works under the hood.

Technical requirements

This chapter will cover the new SOP-based FLIP fluid nodes and tools, which were first introduced in Houdini 19.5 and will not be found in earlier versions of Houdini. For best results and compatibility, use **Houdini version 20 and above** when following the content of this chapter.

You will have access to the Houdini file with the completed effect on the GitHub link at `https://github.com/PacktPublishing/VFX-Made-Easy-with-Houdini`.

To view the chapter images in better clarity, scan the provided QR code. It will direct you to a dedicated link where you can take a look at the images.

FLIP fluid dynamics explained

FLIP Solver is a hybrid approach to fluid simulations, blending particle-based and volume grid-based solvers. Let's break down the main components and building blocks of this method:

- **Particle-based**: Particles track the movement and velocity of the fluid, giving flexibility and detail in representing complex motions such as splashes and waves
- **Volume grid-based**: A voxel (grid) system is used for solving fluid dynamics equations, such as pressure and velocity, ensuring stability and physically accurate behavior

Under the hood, a FLIP simulation is represented by the following steps:

1. **Particle advection**: A FLIP simulation starts as a defined number of particles that move based on initial velocity or forces such as gravity, simulation of the overall motion of the fluid. **Advection** refers to the process of transporting a substance or quantity through a medium by the movement of a fluid.
2. **Velocity transfer to voxel grid**: After advection, particle velocities are transferred to a grid, which breaks the simulation space into voxels. This step allows the solver to use the **Navier-Stokes physics equations** on a grid to calculate physical behaviors such as pressure and velocity changes.
3. **Voxel grid-based simulation**: During this step, the **FLIP Solver** then solves one of the main fluid dynamics equations on the grid such as **Pressure Solve**. By solving the pressure, FLIP adjusts velocities to account for pressure forces, ensuring that the fluid doesn't compress (since liquids are incompressible).
4. **Velocity transfer back to particles**: After the grid-based operations, the updated velocities are transferred back from the grid to the particles. This step ensures that the particles move according to the pressure-corrected and stable velocity field.

Overall, **FLIP Solver** combines the strengths of both particles (for details and motion) and volume grids (for accurate fluid dynamics) to simulate realistic fluid behaviors. One of the downsides of the **FLIP Solver** is that the simulation can only live in a container with a limited size. The container can be quite large, however, and can dynamically resize its volume grid fields preventing intense calculation and large memory usage.

Moving on, we will explore the most common sourcing methods for FLIP fluids.

FLIP fluids sourcing methods

During the next steps, we will learn how to efficiently source and simulate FLIP fluids.

Let's dive into Houdini for further steps:

1. Create a new project with the name `Intro to FLIP fluids`.
2. Add a geometry container in the network view with a descriptive name of `intro_to_flip`.
3. Inside the geometry container, create a `flipcontainer` node via the **TAB Menu**.

Here, the **FLIP Container SOP node** represents the core of the fluid simulation where the particles are generated, stored, and managed during the FLIP fluid simulation. It provides the volume and environment in which the fluid simulation takes place and sets up various attributes required for the behavior of the fluid particles.

The **FLIP Container SOP** node is a part of a new SOP-based solvers workflow, designed to improve the flexibility and performance of fluid simulations using the **FLIP Solver**.

SOP-based FLIP nodes

These were first introduced in Houdini 19.5 and were designed to streamline the setup process and introduce new features to make fluid simulations more intuitive and optimized.

During this chapter, we will also explore some of the other important common SOP-based FLIP nodes to create your first liquid simulation in Houdini:

- **FLIP Source** for sourcing fluids from objects
- **FLIP Collide** for adding collisions to the simulation
- **FLIP Solver** for computing the actual fluid simulation

Now, let's look at some of the settings that come with the **FLIP Container** (`flipcontainer`) node by referring to *Figure 6.2*:

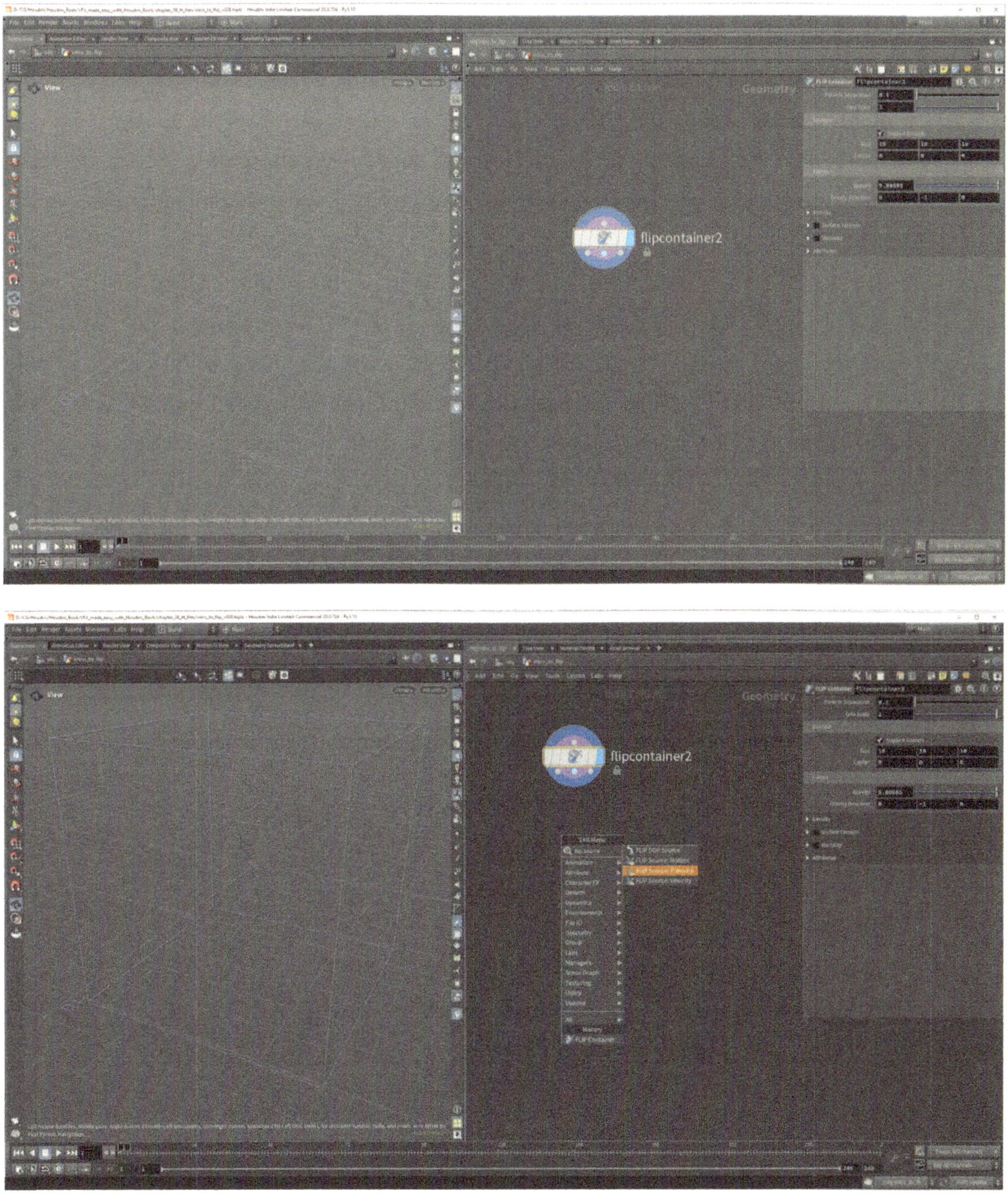

Figure 6.2 – FLIP Container settings (top) and FLIP Source (bottom)

Here is an explanation of some of the most important parts of the `flipcontainer` node:

- **Particle Separation**: This is set to a value of **0.1** by default, which is usually a good starting value for medium-size fluid simulations. This parameter controls the spacing between particles, directly impacting the resolution and detail of the simulation. A lower **Particle Separation** value results in more particles and higher detail, but also increases computational cost.
- **Grid Scale**: This is set to a value of **2** by default, meaning the simulation grid cells are twice the size of the particle separation. This parameter in the **FLIP Container** node controls the resolution of the grid relative to the particle separation in a FLIP simulation. **Grid Scale** directly affects how detailed the pressure solve and collision detection in a fluid simulation will be and plays a critical role in balancing simulation quality with performance.
- **Domain Size**: This is the *purple* box in the viewport that is set to be **10** x **10** x **10** by default. This setting defines the spatial bounds of the fluid simulation. Essentially, it specifies the physical region in 3D space within which the FLIP simulation takes place, setting the limits for where particles and the simulation grid exist and operate. **Domain Size** helps to control the volume of the fluid simulation, ensuring it stays within a defined area and improving computational efficiency by restricting the simulation calculations to a relevant region.

All the settings, as mentioned earlier, will define the resolution and size of a fluid simulation that we will be creating in the next steps:

1. Adjust the **Particle Separation** parameter from **0.1** to `0.025` to be able to source a higher-resolution particle field.
2. Adjust the **Grid Scale** value from **2** to `1.75` to increase the voxel resolution of the pressure solve and fluid collision detection.
3. Adjust **Domain Size** to `15 x 15 x 1515x15x15` and set the **Center** parameter in the **Y** axis to `5`, to have a bigger fluid container.
4. Add a **FLIP Source: Pressure** node using the **TAB Menu** for sourcing initial fluid particles with initial pressure from an object.
5. Connect the three outputs of a **FLIP Container** node to the first three inputs of the **FLIP Source** node.
6. Create a sphere with a radius of `0.15` on the **X** and **Z** axis, and `0.35` on the **Y** axis, to have it stretched in the vertical axis.
7. Set the **Primitive** type to **polygon** and the **Frequency** parameter to `4`, to have more resolution for the distortion we will apply in the next step.

8. Add a **Point Jitter** node and set the **Axis Scales** in X and Z to `0`, so the emitter will only become noised up in the vertical axis.
9. In the **Point Jitter** node, type `$F` in the **Seed** parameter to have the jitter evolving every frame.
10. Add a **Point Velocity** node between the sphere and **FLIP Source** to inject an initial velocity into the simulation.
11. In the **Point Velocity** node, add a velocity of `5` in the **Y** axis and add a **Curl Noise**-based velocity with a **Scale** value of `5`, **Pulse Duration** of `0.1`, and **Swirl Size** of `0.1`.
12. Connect the output of **Point Velocity** to the last input of the **FLIP Source** to use as a particle field source geometry.
13. Add a **FLIP Solver** after the **FLIP Source** to combine all the elements into a fluid simulation.
14. Connect the three outputs of **FLIP Source** to the three inputs of **FLIP Solver**.
15. In the **FLIP Solver**, switch to **Collision** tab and Set the **Ground** parameter to **Ground Plane** to have the fluid colliding with the ground.
16. Play the simulation until frame **20** to see the result.

Refer to *Figure 6.3* to see how the nodes need to be connected and the **FLIP Solver** settings for your first fluid simulation resembling water splashing upward:

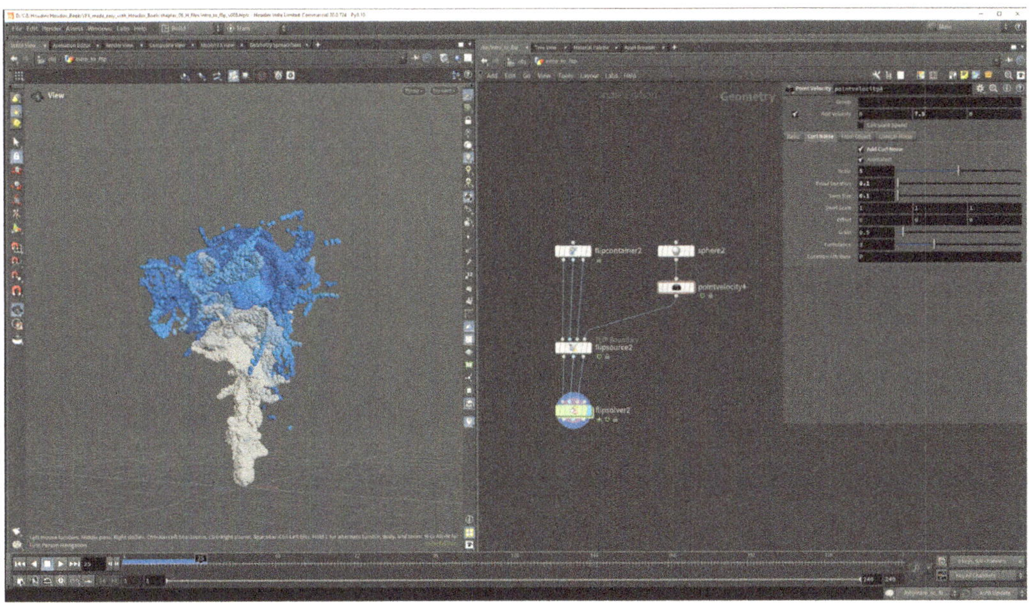

Figure 6.3 – Initial FLIP liquid simulation

Congratulations on creating your first splashing liquid simulation in Houdini! Over the course of these 16 steps we implemented, Houdini and **FLIP Solver** handled a lot of things under the hood, so let's break down the main events.

After we adjusted **FLIP Container** and updated the simulation resolution, the **FLIP Source: Pressure** node took the created sphere, with its initial velocity vectors stored on the polygons, and internally converted the sphere into a VDB voxel grid. **FLIP Solver** will then use this VDB to scatter the initial fluid particles inside the volume of the sphere.

The resolution of this voxel grid is directly tied to the resolution of the **FLIP Container** particle separation multiplied by **Grid Scale**. The **FLIP Source** node also converted the point velocity **v** attribute into a volume velocity field called **vel** so **FLIP Solver** can operate correctly on source velocities.

The **FLIP Source** node, also known as **FLIP Boundary**, is a highly versatile node that can be used to perform various operations, such as creating fluid sources based on just initial velocity or initial velocity combined with initial pressure. This node can also be used in **Sink** mode to remove particles from the simulation.

The other important parameter of **FLIP Source** is the **Activation** setting. When set to a value higher than 0, it will act as a continuous source of fluid and velocity in the simulation. However, you can achieve interesting effects by limiting the activation to certain frames by using expressions involving `$F < "number"` or `$F > "number"`. This would mean to keep sourcing only until the current frame is either smaller or greater than the custom number value.

Additionally, it is worth highlighting the three outputs and inputs that we will use frequently with SOP-based FLIP nodes. These three channels are designed to pass through the following types of data:

- Source data passing through the first channel
- Fluid container data passing through the second channel
- Collision data passing through the third channel

Based on all the data generated from the **FLIP Container** and **FLIP Source** nodes, **FLIP Solver** calculates the liquid simulation based on the steps described in the *FLIP fluid dynamics explained* section.

Let's save this file, as we will continue to work with this setup for further examples in this chapter.

Now, let's move on and explore how we can guide the motion of FLIP fluids.

Guiding the motion of FLIP fluids

By default, a fluid simulation is not going to have any interesting motion, shapes, or splashes until you start introducing extra components that will direct the fluid into a more complex motion. Therefore, we will explore different workflows to guide the fluid simulation.

Some of the most common and simple ways of guiding the motion of FLIP fluids are using the following:

- Initial or continuous velocities
- Particle-based forces
- Static or dynamic colliders
- Manipulating **FLIP Solver** settings
- Adding fluid-specific attributes, such as surface tension and viscosity

Let's continue working on the FLIP setup and experiment with some forces, attributes, and parameters.

Adding particle-based forces

We have already seen how the initial and continuous **Point Velocity** node can affect the simulation by pushing the liquid up from the start. For the next steps, we are going to introduce custom particle forces:

1. Continue with the Initial FLIP simulation setup that we have created.
2. Set the sphere **radius** to `0.15` across all axes.
3. Disconnect the **Point Velocity** and **Point Jitter** nodes after the source sphere.
4. Add a **Transform** node after the source sphere and set the **Y Translate** position to `5 units`.
5. In the same **Transform** node, increase the **Uniform Scale** to `1.25`.
6. Select the **FLIP Source** node and set the **Activation** to the `$F<2` expression, which will only allow the solver to source for two frames.
7. Select **FLIP Container** and set **Particle Separation** to `0.0125` to have a higher resolution for the tests (see *Figure 6.4*).
8. Select the **FLIP Container** node and set the default gravity to `0` in **Forces** as we will be creating a custom force.

Figure 6.4 shows the **FLIP Container** adjustment settings:

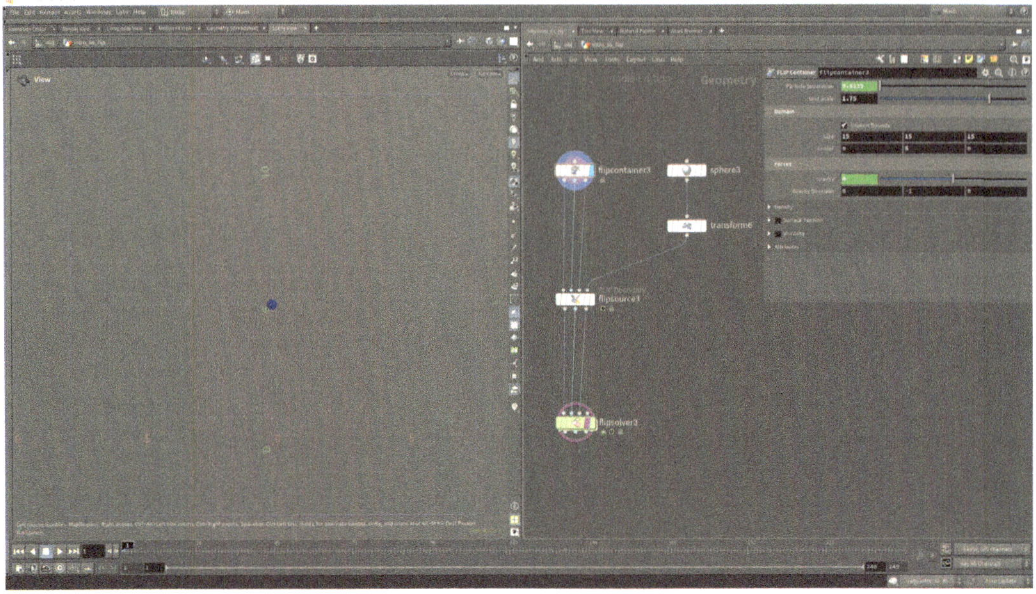

Figure 6.4 – Adjusting FLIP Container settings

For the next steps, we will dive into the **FLIP Solver** to add custom forces:

1. Double-click on **FLIP Solver** to get to a lower level where you can add custom forces and velocity fields.
2. Create a **POP Force** node and set the **Force** parameter in **Y** to `-0.98` to introduce a custom small-scale gravity force (see *Figure 6.5*).
3. Add a **POP Drag** node after **POP Force**, set the air resistance value to `0.1`, and connect the result to the **Force** output.

Figure 6.5 shows the settings for adding a **POP Force** node with custom gravity and air resistance with **POP Drag**:

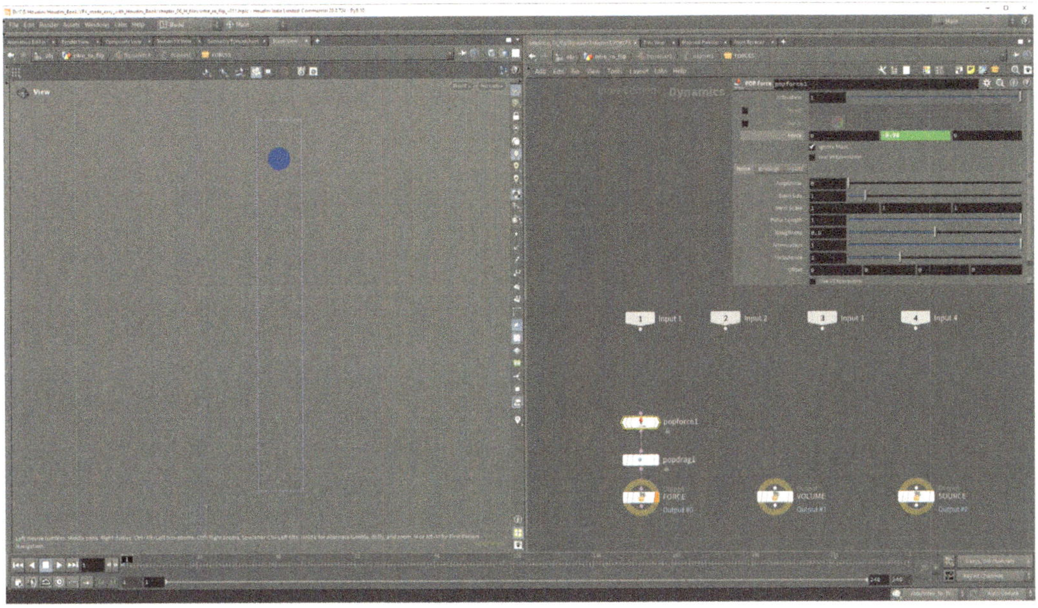

Figure 6.5 – Adding particle-based forces

You have probably noticed familiar nodes called **POP Force** and **POP Drag**, which we used in *Chapter 3* to drive particle simulations. Since FLIP uses particles to simulate fluid, we can use all the POP nodes and forces to direct the simulation in a specific way. This adds a lot of flexibility and control to FLIP simulations.

Also, in *Figure 6.5*, you can see that there are three main outputs inside **FLIP Solver**:

- **FORCE**: This is for adding and controlling FLIP with particle-based POP forces
- **VOLUME**: This is for adding and controlling FLIP with volume-based velocity fields
- **SOURCE**: This is for sourcing in additional fields and volumes mainly for advanced simulations

One important thing when working with internal **FLIP Solver** nodes is that we have to go back to the upper **Geometry** level to be able to see the simulation result. Press the *u* shortcut to go to an upper level and play the simulation, which will look like a falling water droplet, as shown in *Figure 6.6*:

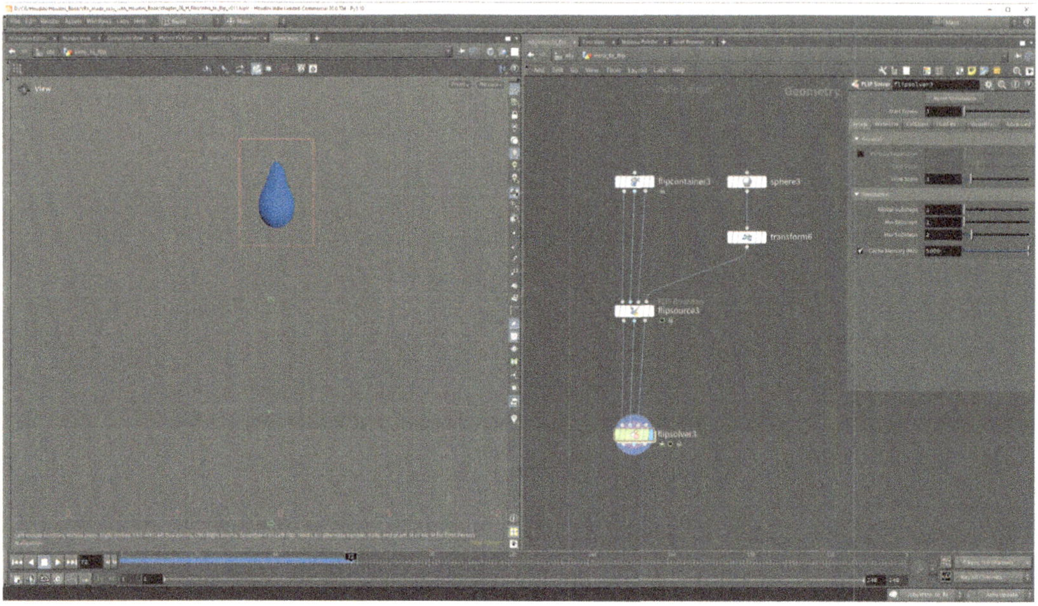

Figure 6.6 – Water droplet simulation

In the next section, we will introduce a collision object for the droplet to interact with.

Adding collision objects

Let's follow these steps to add a collision geometry into the FLIP simulation:

1. Create a sphere with a radius of `1`, which will act as a collision object.
2. Add a **Transform** node and translate the sphere by `2.25 units` up in the **Y** axis to move closer to the droplet.
3. Add a **FLIP Collide** node and connect it between the **FLIP Source** and **FLIP Solver** nodes with the respective first three inputs.

4. Connect the transformed sphere to the fourth input of **FLIP Collide**, as shown in *Figure 6.7*.
5. Play the simulation to see the result.

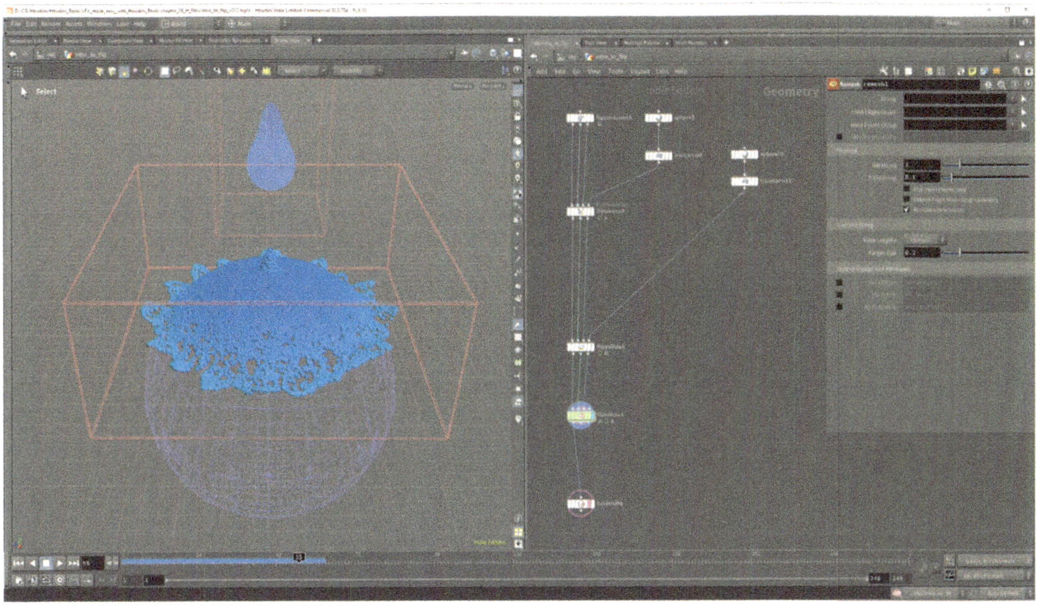

Figure 6.7 – Added sphere collider

We can now see the water droplet is colliding and splashing over the sphere. Now, with the introduction of collision geometry, we can explore more features and attributes both on **FLIP Container** and **FLIP Solver**. Let's follow the next steps to make the simulation more interesting:

1. Add a **Remesh** node after the transformed collider sphere to triangulate the topology and add more polygon resolution.
2. Add a **mountain** node after the **Remesh** node to make the sphere look like a small piece of rock.
3. Run the test simulation till frame **60**, as shown in *Figure 6.8*.

In *Figure 6.8*, we can notice that the splash became much more interesting without even changing any forces or simulation settings. This is an example of how important it is to have a detailed and complex-looking collider for more dynamic water details.

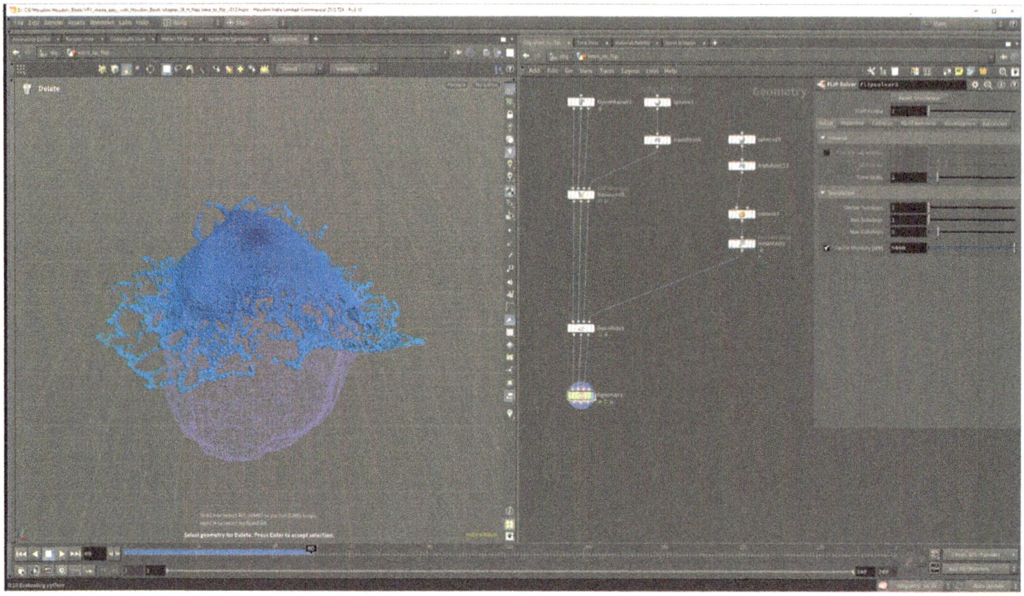

Figure 6.8 – Adding collider complexity

Now, let's explore some of the settings on **FLIP Solver** to be able to gain even more control over the liquid simulation.

Exploring FLIP Solver simulation settings

FLIP Solver has many settings and parameters varying from very simple to advanced ones. In this chapter, we will focus on the simple settings, which will allow us to quickly change and adjust the behavior of the liquid simulation.

Here are the settings we need to focus on in this chapter:

- **Time Scale** in the **Setup** tab can speed up the simulation if the value is set above 1. Alternatively, it can slow down the simulation if the value is set below 1. It can be tweaked and animated to achieve a slow-motion fluid effect or make the fluid move much faster than normal speed.

- **Particle Collisions** in the **Collision** tab can be set between a more accurate and slower method with **Particle**, and a less accurate but faster method with **Move Outside Collision**. The difference in quality will be mostly visible when the collider moving and deforming; otherwise, for faster simulation time, it is recommended to set the mode to **Move Outside Collision**.
- **Velocity Transfer** in the **Fluid Behavior** tab has two modes for smaller-scale swirly fluids that will be using the **Affine Particle in a Cell (APIC)** method or the splashy FLIP method for larger-scale turbulent water. This setting is one of the most impactful and can drastically change the look of the fluid simulation.

Look at *Figure 6.9* to see the main difference in the **Velocity Transfer** method, where the smoother and more swirly *APIC method* is on the *left* and the more splashy *FLIP method* is on the *right*:

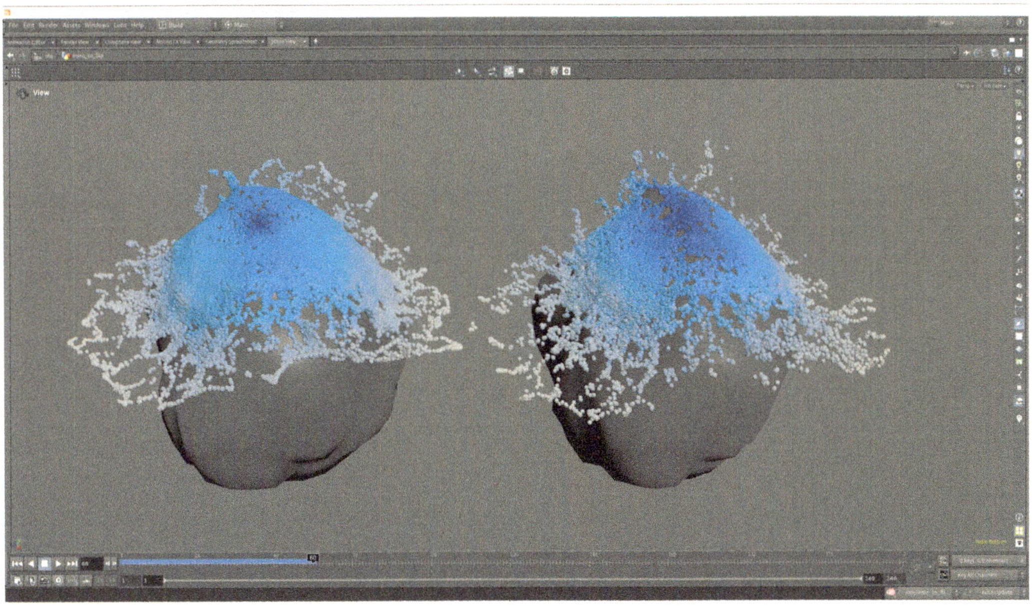

Figure 6.9 – Difference between the APIC method (left) and FLIP method (right)

For this project, we will continue to use the swirly velocity transfer, since the liquid scale that we are simulating is small and APIC will give us the best results for this kind of look.

In the next section, we will explore how fluid-specific attributes such as **surface tension** and **viscosity** can change the look and behavior of FLIP fluid simulation.

Adding fluid-specific simulation attributes

All the extra fluid attributes that we need can be located and created on the **FLIP Container** node. Let's follow the next steps to add surface tension to the water simulation:

1. Select **FLIP Container** and turn the **Surface Tension** checkbox on.
2. Unroll the **Surface Tension** parameters and set the **Surface Tension** value to 2 and **Blur Radius** to `0.001`, since the default values are set too high and will cause very chaotic results.
3. Play the fluid simulation till frame **60** to see the result.

Referring to *Figure 6.10*, notice that surface tension added much more clumping and ripples to the surface of the fluid simulation. This will increase the realism, especially during the rendering of the small-scale liquid with a refractive material.

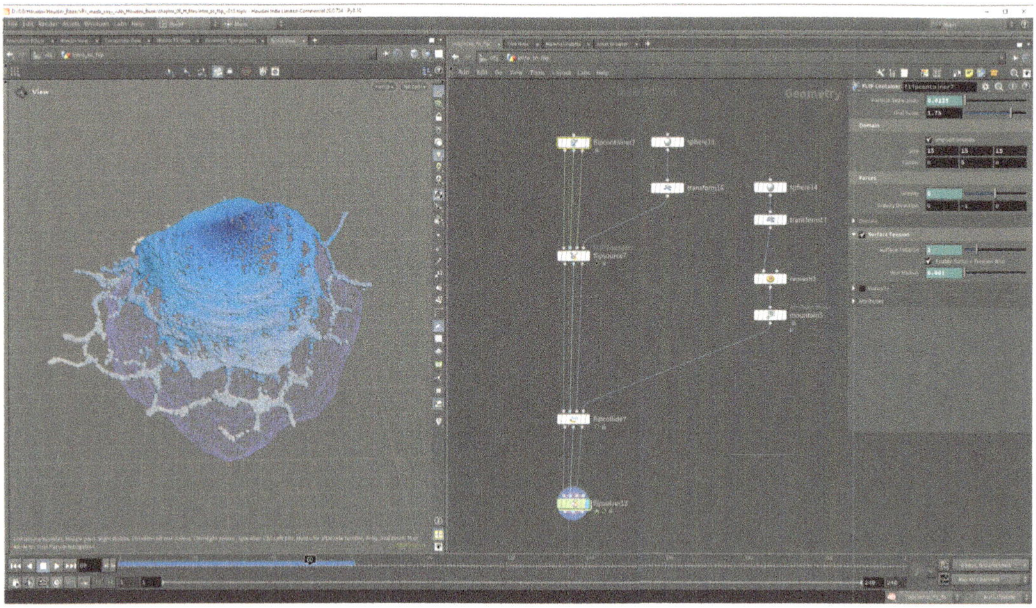

Figure 6.10 – Adding surface tension

Let's now follow the next steps to make the liquid sticky and viscous:

1. Select **FLIP Container** and turn on the **Viscosity** checkbox, to add the **Viscosity** attribute.
2. Set the **Viscosity** value to 1 to mimic medium viscous liquid.
3. Reduce the **Surface Tension** value from **2** to 1 to have a smoother fluid.
4. Play the simulation for a longer range of frame **120**, to see the viscosity progression.

Referring to *Figure 6.11*, we can now see a completely different liquid behavior. Liquid moves much slower and sticks to the surface by generating interesting blobs and drops:

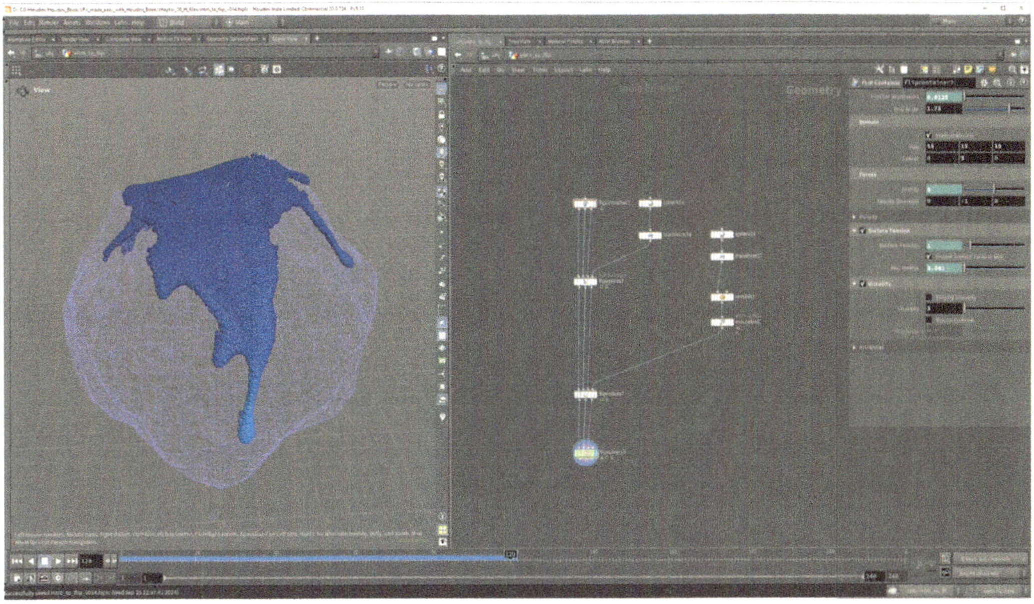

Figure 6.11 – Adding viscosity

The **Viscosity** attribute is mainly used to simulate thick liquids such as honey, liquid chocolate, and other viscous liquids.

Next, we will combine all the elements that we were testing into a completed project.

Simulating a big splash on the character

First, we will create a new **FLIP Container** node with animated surface tension.

Let's follow these steps to create a new **FLIP Container** node:

1. Create a new **FLIP Container** node and set **Particle Separation** to `0.01`.
2. In the **Domain** parameter, set the center in the **Y** axis to `3.5` to lift the domain.
3. Turn on **Surface Tension** and set the value to `0.01`.
4. Set your current frame to `10`, hold *Alt*, and click on the **Surface Tension** value to set a keyframe.
5. Scrub to frame **20** on the *timeline*, set **Surface Tension** to `5`, hold *Alt*, and click on the value to set a second keyframe.
6. Set the **Surface Tension Blur Radius** value to `0.001`.

Next, we'll add a new fluid source geometry with high velocity. I will provide the exact values that gave me the desired result; however, I highly encourage you to experiment with the provided settings and parameters and observe different simulation results. Even the smallest change in any of the provided parameters will result in different behavior, so experimentation is the best way to learn.

Adding a high-velocity source

Follow these steps to add a new high-velocity source:

1. Create a sphere with **Radius** values set to `0.25`, `0.15`, and `0.25`.
2. Set the sphere primitive type to **Polygon** and the **Frequency** parameter to `32`, to add more details to the sphere.
3. Add a **mountain** node after the sphere to make the source more detailed.
4. In the **mountain** node, set the **Noise** value to `0.05`, **Element Size** to `0.1`, and the **Offset** parameter to `$F/2`, to have a fast-pulsing noise.
5. Set the **Fractal** parameter to **None** to have a smoother noise.
6. Add a **Point Velocity** node after the **mountain** node, to create initial velocity.
7. Enable the **Add Velocity** checkbox and set the **Velocity** value in **Y** to `6.25`, to have a high upward velocity.
8. In the **Basic** tab of **Point Velocity**, set **Initialization** to **Keep Incoming**, to avoid calculating velocity from the fast-pulsing sphere geometry.
9. Go to the **Curl Noise** tab and enable the **Curl Noise** checkbox.
10. Set **Curl Noise Scale** to `0.25`, **Swirl Size** to `10`, and **Turbulence** to `2`, to add variation to directional velocity.
11. Add a **Transform** node to manipulate the emitter's position relative to the collider.
12. In the **Translate** parameter of the **Transform** node, set **Y** to `0.15` and **Z** to `1.5`.
13. Add a slight rotation to the emitter by setting the **Rotate** parameter in **X** to `-30`.
14. Add a **FLIP Source: Pressure** node after **FLIP Container** and connect the container to the first three inputs.
15. Connect the geometry source to the fourth input.
16. In **FLIP Source**, set **Activation** to `$F<5`, to only emit for the first 5 frames.
17. In the **Pressure** tab, decrease the **Pressure** value to `0.1` for a less turbulent water splash.

Moving on, let's add the character collider geometry. Houdini ships with many cool test 3D models for simulation and your personal projects, from animated to static characters. For this example, I am going to use one of my favorite test geometries, which is called *rubber toy Flippy*.

Adding a character collider

Let's follow these steps to add a character collider:

1. Search for `rubber toy` in the **TAB Menu** to add it to the scene.
2. Set **Uniform Scale** on the rubber toy to `1.5` to make Flippy bigger for a bigger splash.
3. Add a **Peak** node after the rubber toy and set **Distance** to `0.005`; this will ensure that the particles will collide with a slightly bulged-up geometry and will have a nice offset from the surface during meshing and rendering.
4. Add a **Transform** node after the rubber toy to manipulate it in 3D space.
5. Set the **Translate** value to `0.85` in **Y** to lift the rubber toy above the ground zero and emitter level.
6. Add a **FLIP Collide** node and connect the **FLIP Source** node to the first three inputs.
7. Connect the rubber toy geometry to the fourth input of **FLIP Collide**.

Finally, we are going to add a **FLIP Solver** node and adjust some of the simulation parameters for more interesting results.

Adding and setting up the FLIP Solver node

Follow the next set of steps to add and set the **FLIP Solver** node for the simulation:

1. Add a **FLIP Solver** node after the **FLIP Collide** node.
2. In the **Setup** tab of **FLIP Solver**, set the time scale to `0.75` for a slow-motion effect.
3. Go to the **Collision** tab and set **Particle Collisions** to the **Move Outside Collision** mode for a faster simulation.
4. In the **Collision** tab, set the **Ground** parameter to **Ground Plane** to add simple ground collisions.
5. Go inside **FLIP Solver** and create a **POP Drag** force with **Air Resistance** set to `0.25` to have the splash decelerate faster over time.
6. Connect **POP Drag** to the **FORCE** output and go back to the upper level of **FLIP Solver**.

7. Go to **Fluid Behavior** and turn on the **Enforce Particle Separation** checkbox. This setting is primarily used for small-scale, high-surface tension simulations, ensuring extra details and more evenly spaced out particles for smoother meshing.
8. Run the simulation till frame **24** and compare the results.

Refer to *Figure 6.12* to see the simulation result and node network:

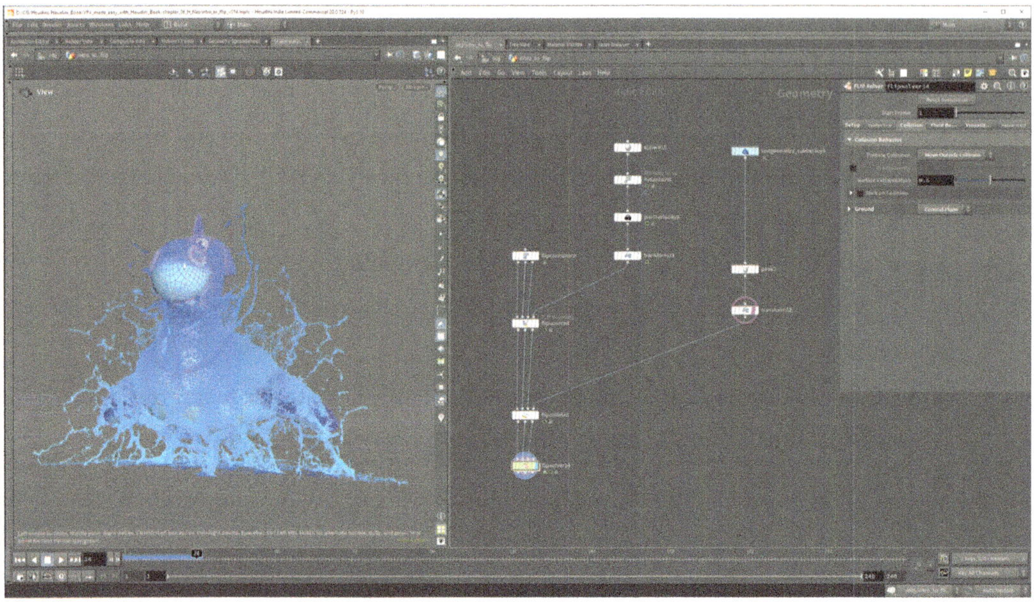

Figure 6.12 – Flippy splash simulation

Before we move to the next steps, feel free to experiment with different parameters, mainly **Surface Tension**, **Emitter Noise** and **Velocity**, **Velocity Transfer**, and even adding **Viscosity** and the other FLIP settings that we explored in this chapter. After getting the desired FLIP simulation, we will be optimizing, caching, and meshing out FLIP particles before rendering.

FLIP fluid optimization and caching

The result of FLIP simulation usually contains a lot of data both on particles and volumes, which can be quite heavy and expensive on disk space and loading times. Therefore, it is important to always optimize and compress the simulation data in a similar way as we did with particles and pyro simulations.

One of the easiest and fastest ways to optimize and compress FLIP simulation data is the **Fluid Compress node**. This node in Houdini plays a vital role in managing and optimizing particle data within FLIP simulations. Compressing, packing, and selectively handling particle attributes reduces memory usage, enhances performance, and streamlines the fluid simulation process.

Let's follow the next steps to integrate the **Fluid Compress** node into our water splash effect:

1. Look for the **Fluid Compress** node via the **TAB Menu** and place it after **FLIP Solver**.
2. Connect the three outputs of **FLIP Solver** to the three respective inputs of **Fluid Compress**.
3. Set the display flag on **Fluid Compress** to preview the result.

Figure 6.13 shows the compressed fluid data:

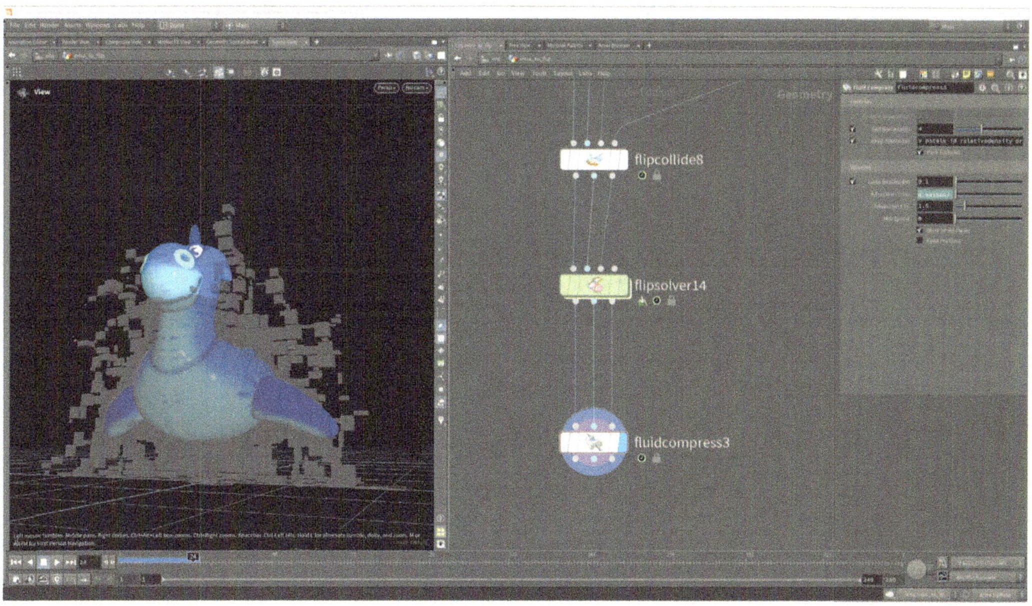

Figure 6.13 – Optimizing FLIP simulation

If we preview the fluid attributes and data before and after compression, we will see that now the simulation has packed hundreds of thousands of FLIP particles into just over a thousand packed points containing all that compressed particle data.

We can also see that all the volumes were converted to a more optimized VDB volume data type, thereby reducing the voxel amounts from millions to just thousands.

Our particle fluid viewport representation has also changed into small, packed box containers storing the particle data and attributes.

By converting particles into a packed representation, the node significantly reduces the memory footprint of the simulation. Packed particles are stored in a more compact format that retains essential attributes such as **Position** and **Velocity** while discarding or simplifying less important data.

The **Fluid Compress** node works well with the new SOP-based FLIP pipeline by automatically connecting the **Particle Separation** parameter and **Fluid Container** settings.

Figure 6.14 shows a comparison between the non-compressed data on the left and the compressed data on the right:

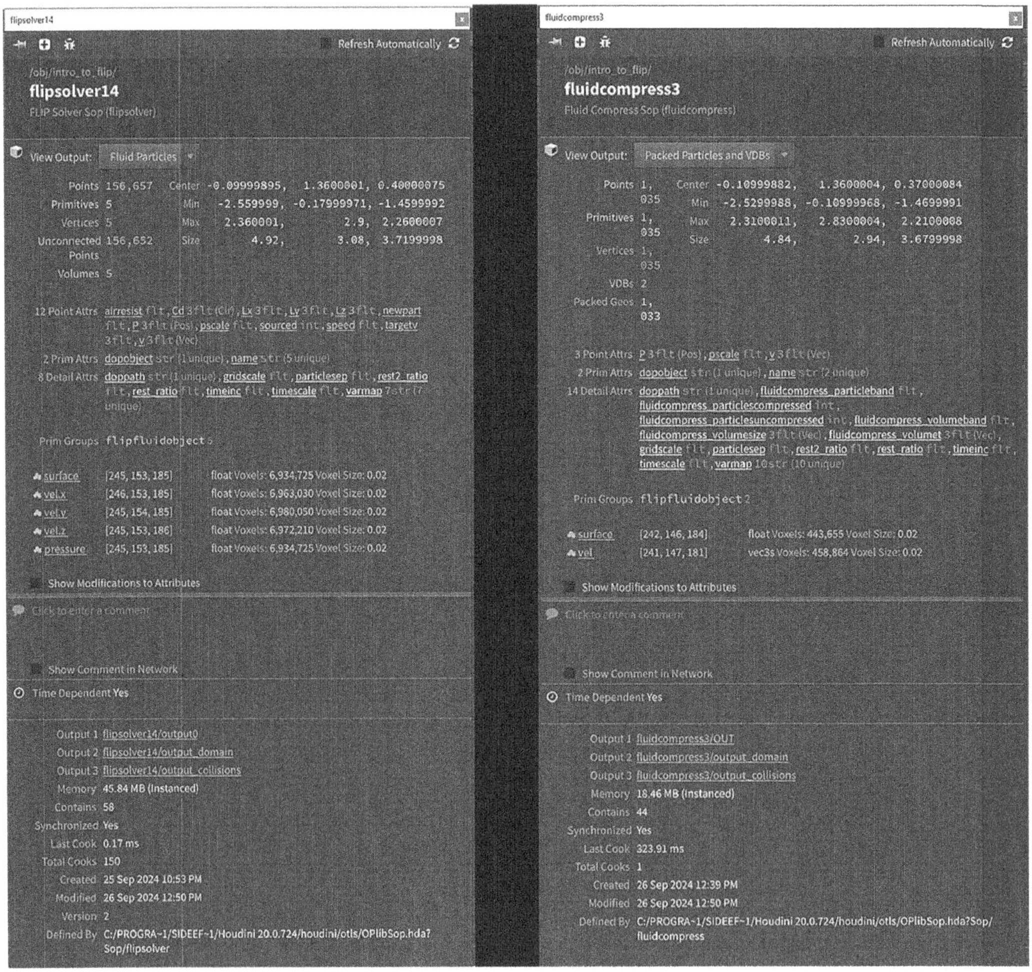

Figure 6.14 – Fluid Compress comparison

After compressing the fluid, we can use the first output of the **Fluid Compress** node, containing the compressed simulation data, and connect it to our trusty **File Cache** node, which we have been using for caching all types of geometry since *Chapter 1*.

Let's follow these steps to add **File Cache** to our simulation:

1. Add a **File Cache** node after the **Fluid Compress** node and connect the first output of the **Fluid Compress** node to the input of the **File Cache** node.
2. Rename the **File Cache** node to `flip_splash_sim_compressed` to keep it descriptive.
3. Set the **Base Name** box parameter of **File Cache** to `$OS`, allowing the cached frames to inherit the node name.
4. Set your timeline to **48** frames via the **Global Animation** settings (*Alt* + *Shift* + *G*).
5. Save your file before caching and then click the **Save to Disk in Background** button on **File Cache**.

Figure 6.15 shows the input for the **File Cache** settings:

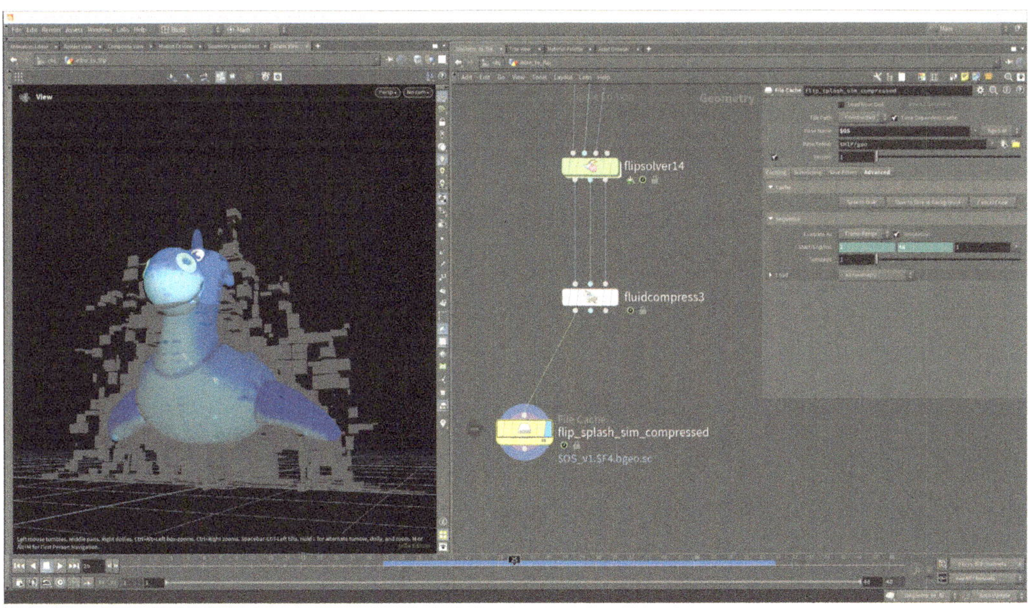

Figure 6.15 – File caching the fluid simulation

Moving on, we learn how to convert FLIP fluid particles into a render-ready liquid mesh.

Liquid meshing workflows

Liquid meshing in Houdini refers to the process of converting the particle-based representation of fluids, typically generated by a **FLIP Solver**, into a smooth, continuous surface suitable for rendering.

Meshing is an essential step in fluid simulation workflows, as the raw particle data cannot be directly rendered in a realistic way. The meshing process involves creating a polygonal surface that accurately represents the fluid's shape, including details such as splashes, ripples, and other small-scale features.

Understanding the concepts and workflow of liquid meshing

Let's break down the key concepts and workflow of liquid meshing in Houdini.

Particle data to mesh conversion

FLIP simulations generate fluid behavior using particles that represent fluid motion. However, particles alone do not create a solid-looking fluid; they need to be converted into a surface mesh that can be rendered.

The meshing process smooths out the particle positions and creates a cohesive surface that looks like liquid rather than a collection of individual points.

Primary node – Particle Fluid Surface

The **Particle Fluid Surface** node is the primary tool used for liquid meshing in Houdini. This node takes the particle data from the FLIP simulation and generates a polygonal surface based on various parameters.

It uses techniques such as **voxelization** (turning particle data into a grid of values) and surface reconstruction algorithms to create a smooth and detailed surface mesh.

Key parameters of Particle Fluid Surface

The key parameters worth considering are as follows:

- **Particle Separation**: This controls the resolution of the surface mesh relative to the particle distribution. Lower values result in a higher-resolution mesh with more detail, capturing small features such as thin splashes, but at the cost of higher computational effort.
- **Voxel Scale**: This sets the size of the grid cells used for surface reconstruction. Lower values provide finer detail but require more memory and processing time.

- **Smoothing and Filtering**: Houdini provides options to smooth the mesh to reduce noise and artifacts. Filters can be applied to refine the mesh's appearance, making the surface look more natural and less jittery.

Surface Smoothing and noise reduction

The meshing process often involves additional smoothing steps to eliminate jagged edges and reduce noise, especially in high-energy areas such as splashes or turbulent fluid.

Surface Smoothing can be controlled to preserve sharp details while eliminating unwanted noise, which is essential for achieving realistic fluid surfaces.

Attribute transfer

During meshing, important particle attributes such as velocity, color, and custom can be transferred to the mesh, allowing for more detailed rendering effects such as motion blur and shading.

Mesh optimization

Houdini's meshing tools provide settings to decimate or reduce the polygon count of the mesh where detail is not needed, optimizing the mesh for rendering. This helps maintain visual quality while reducing render times and memory usage.

Handling thin sheets and drops

Special settings in the meshing process allow for better handling of thin fluid sheets, droplets, and splashes. These adjustments ensure that small-scale features are preserved and accurately represented in the final mesh.

Techniques, such as curvature-based adjustments, help maintain thin areas without them breaking apart or disappearing during meshing.

Blending and refining the mesh

The meshing workflow includes blending options to merge separate fluid bodies or refine the interface between fluid and other objects, enhancing visual coherence and ensuring that the fluid interacts correctly with its environment.

Exporting and rendering

The final step involves preparing the mesh for rendering. Houdini allows exporting the meshed fluid as a standard polygonal object that can be used in render engines such as Karma, Mantra, Redshift, or third-party applications.

Additional refinements, such as adding displacement maps or shaders, can further enhance the visual fidelity of the fluid in the rendering stage.

Converting Packed Particle Data into a Polygonal Mesh

Now, with a better understanding of the meshing workflow process, let's switch from theory to practice while converting our packed particle data into a polygonal mesh by following the next steps:

1. Add a **Particle Fluid Surface** node after **File Cache**.
2. Connect the **File Cache** output to the first input of the **Particle Fluid Surface** node.
3. Connect the second and third outputs of the **Fluid Compress** node into the respective second and third inputs of **Particle Fluid Surface**.
4. Set the display flag on **Particle Fluid Surface** to preview the result.

Figure 6.16 shows the meshing result:

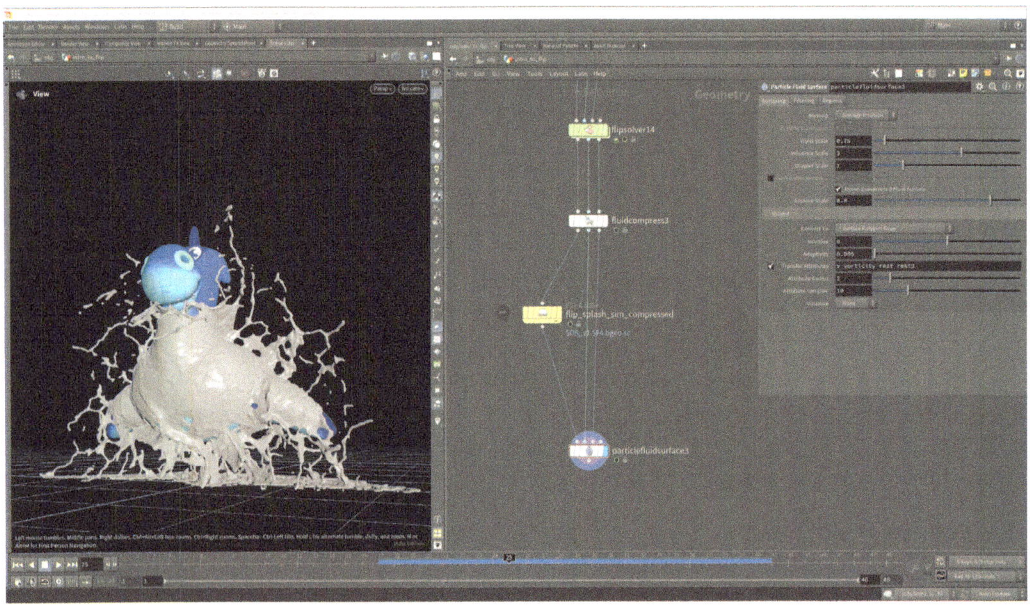

Figure 6.16 – Initial liquid meshing

Since our liquid simulation is relatively simple, we don't need to tweak many settings to get a good-looking mesh. Also, because of the great integration of SOP-based FLIP fluid tools, the simulation parameter will be automatically correctly linked to the mesh particle separation, and this will be one less parameter for us to tweak and worry about.

Workflow tips and tricks

In this section, I will share some workflow tips and tricks on the most important parameters that define the look of small to medium-sized liquid simulation meshes:

- **Choosing the meshing method in the surfacing tab**: There are currently two meshing presets in the **Particle Fluid Surface** node:
    - The **Average Position** method gives a much more connected and smooth mesh that works well for small-scale liquids. The main parameter that will set the mesh look is **Influence Scale**, which will give a more droplet-like disconnected mesh with lower values and a smooth continuous mesh with higher values. The **Droplet Scale** parameter can act as a multiplier on the thickness of the mesh.
    - The **Spherical** method gives a much more noisy and disconnected mesh full of droplets and high-frequency details. This method works best for bigger-scale fluid simulations, due to its faster calculations and preservation of turbulent surface details. This method is also much better to use with liquids that have underwater bubbles coming directly from FLIP simulation with the help of air incompressibility.
- **Mesh filtering and smoothing options**: There are multiple ways to make the liquid mesh more connected and smoother while preserving the detailed areas untouched with the help of masks and attributes:
    - **Dilate**, **Smooth**, and **Erode** is a combination of filters frequently used together, mainly on the mesh generated with the **Spherical** method, to smooth very noisy areas and have a more connected and continuous mesh surface. Under the hood, these are VDB operations that will reshape and smooth the surface **Signed Distance Field (SDF)** before converting it into polygons.
    - The **Final Smooth** operation can use heavier filters, such as **Gaussian**, to achieve a very smooth mesh, mainly for viscous liquid simulations.

Figures 6.17, *6.18*, and *6.19* show the compared results of the **Average Position** method mesh, the **Spherical** method generated mesh, and the **Spherical** method mesh with filters applied:

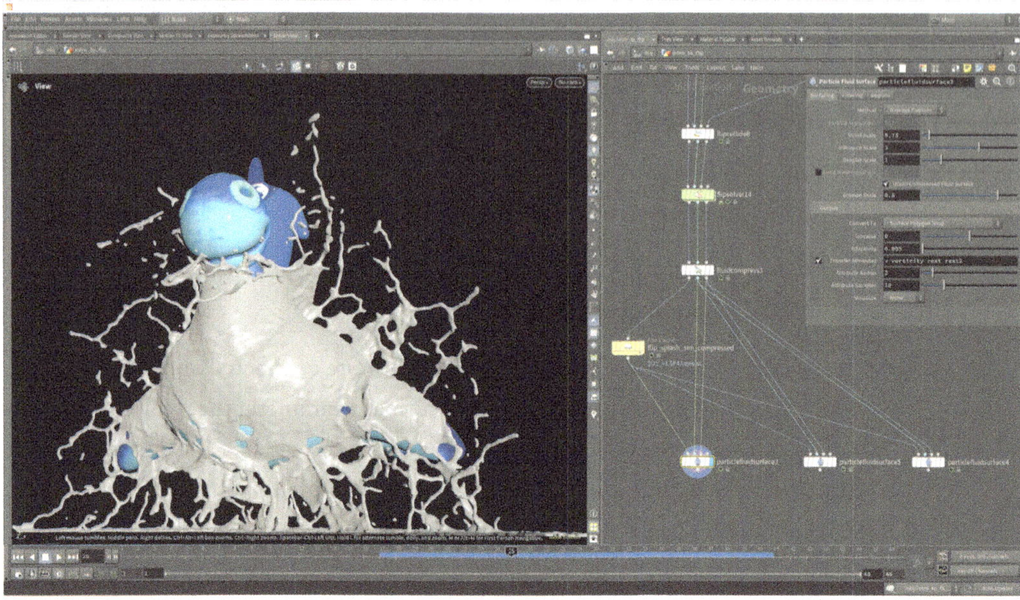

Figure 6.17 – Average Position meshing

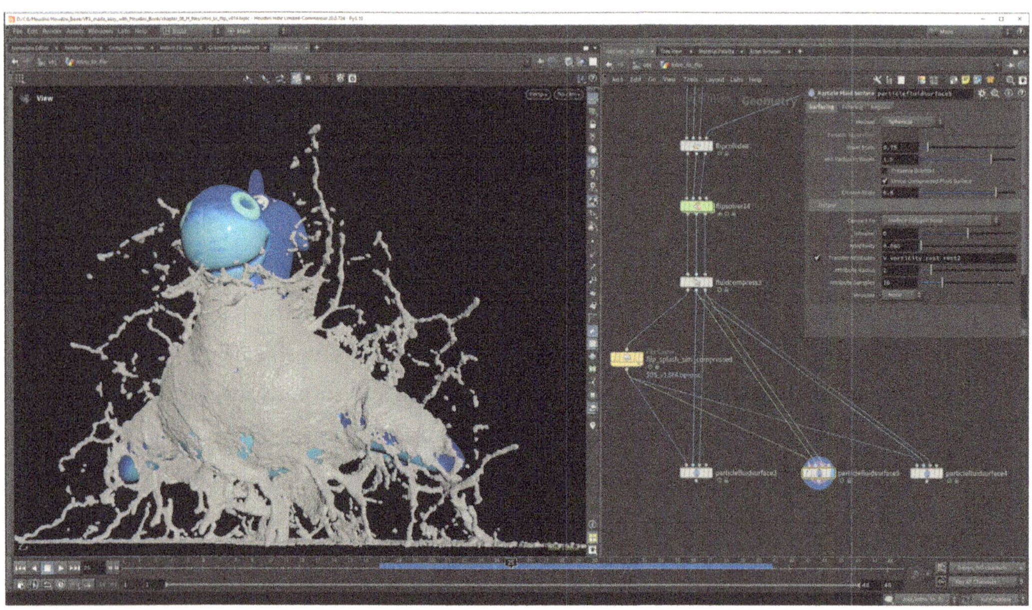

Figure 6.18 – Spherical meshing

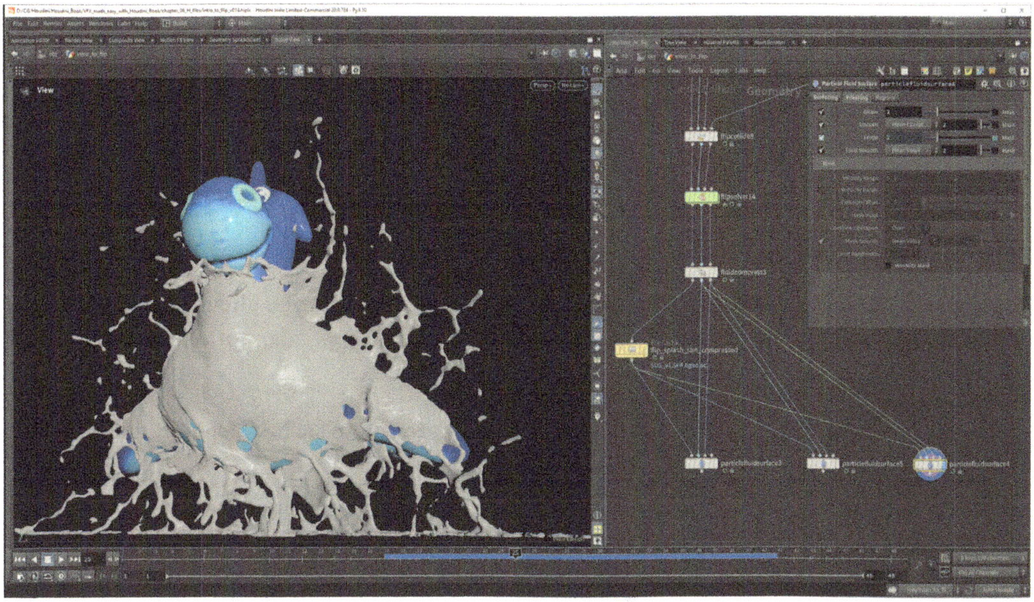

Figure 6.19 – Spherical with Smooth filters meshing

Based on the examples, the **Average Position** method clearly gives better results by striking the balance between the detail level and the smoothness of the mesh. Therefore, we will proceed with this method.

Applying the Average Position method

Let's adjust some of the settings on the **Average Position** method-based mesh for even better results by following the next steps:

1. On the **Particle Fluid Surface** node, set **Method** to **Average Position**.
2. Set the **Voxel Scale** parameter value to `0.575` to make the mesh more detailed.
3. Set **Influence Scale** to `2` to achieve more droplets from splash areas.
4. Turn on **Limit Refinement** and set it to a `1` iteration to make calculations faster.
5. In the **Output** rollout, set **Visualizer** to **Velocity**, with **Maximum Velocity Range** set to `3.5` to get the mesh colored with an aqua color gradient.

After refining the mesh, the final step before rendering would be caching the result to disk, so we don't have to recalculate the meshing every frame during the rendering process. Follow these steps for saving the meshed sequence to disk:

1. Create a **File Cache** node after the mesh.
2. Name the **File Cache** node `liquid_mesh`.
3. Set **Base Name** to `$OS`.
4. In the **Sequence** rollout, turn off **Simulation**. Assuming that you already have cached the FLIP fluid simulation, mesh caching can be sped up by allowing multiple cores to process a number of frames in a batch at the same time.
5. Save your file and click on **Save to Disk in Background** to cache the liquid mesh to disk.

Refer to *Figure 6.20* to see the final mesh result:

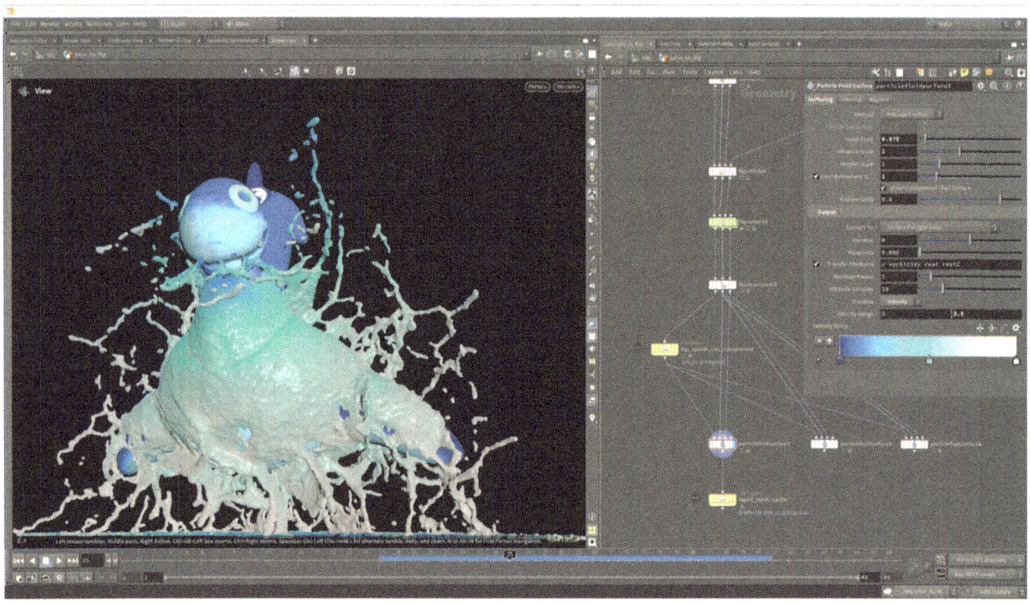

Figure 6.20 – Final liquid mesh

In the last section, we'll learn how to import the liquid mesh and rubber toy into **Solaris** for lighting and rendering.

Liquid mesh lighting and rendering

Let's prepare the cached liquid mesh and Flippy character for rendering in **Solaris** by following the next steps:

1. Create a **Null** node after the liquid mesh and name it `OUT_render_water_splash_mesh` so it will appear at the top of the list of 3D objects in the **obj** context. This **Null** node is created purely as a checkpoint that will indicate a transition to rendering visually in the network view.
2. Create a **Null** node after the transform connected to the rubber toy and name it `OUT_render_splash_character`.
3. Switch to the **stage** context to get access to **Solaris** rendering nodes.
4. Add an **SOP Import** node for the liquid mesh and name it `water`.
5. Add an **SOP Import** node for the rubber toy and name it `rubbertoy`.
6. Connect the path to the respective **Null** nodes in the **SOP Path** box of each respective **SOP Import** node (see *Chapter 4* for detailed information on how we bring 3D objects from SOPs to **Solaris**).
7. Merge both **SOP Import** nodes together to see the result in the viewport.

Figure 6.21 demonstrates the result of bringing the 3D objects into **Solaris**:

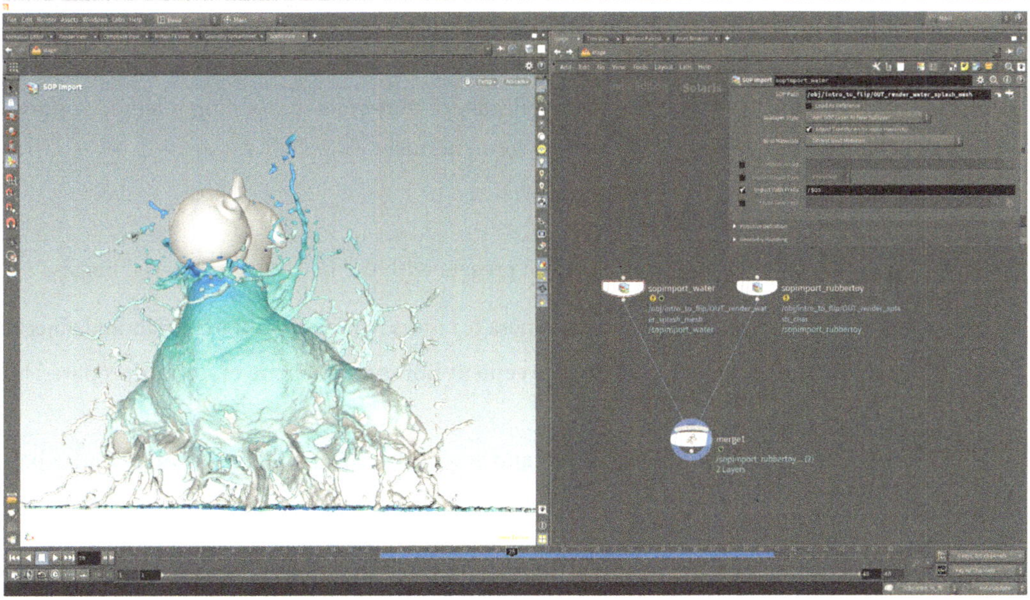

Figure 6.21 – Importing scene assets to Solaris

For the next steps, let's create a quick outdoor lighting with the **Karma Physical Sky** node and **Camera** from **View** after framing the assets in a desired angle. For more detailed instructions, see *Chapter 4* for lights and camera creation. You can also try the settings that I have for the lights and the camera position by referring to *Figure 6.22*:

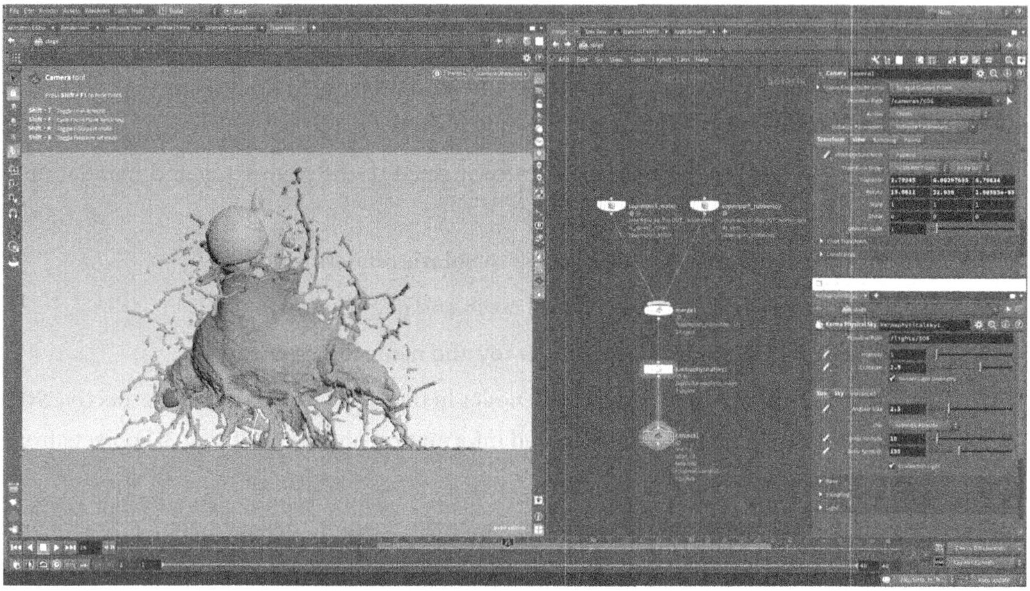

Figure 6.22 – Creating lights and camera

The main part of creating a realistic water render will be the actual refractive water material. It is amazing that Houdini 20 ships with a large library of materials resembling realistic surfaces that speed up the look development workflow tremendously.

Creating material presets

Let's follow the next steps for creating material presets with the help of the material library:

1. Add a **Material Linker** node after the camera to access parameters for materials and objects.
2. Click on the **Catalog** tab to see the convenient library of realistic materials prepared by Houdini.
3. Use the search bar in the **Catalog** tab and type `water`. You will see a water shader ball appear.
4. Drag and drop the water shader ball to the nearest left panel under **Material List**.

5. Use the search bar again and type `plastic`. You will see the water shader disappear and, instead, you now have a library of plastic materials.
6. Select the **PlasticBlue** shader ball, and drag and drop it onto **Material List** where the water material is.

Figure 6.23 shows the **Material Linker** settings:

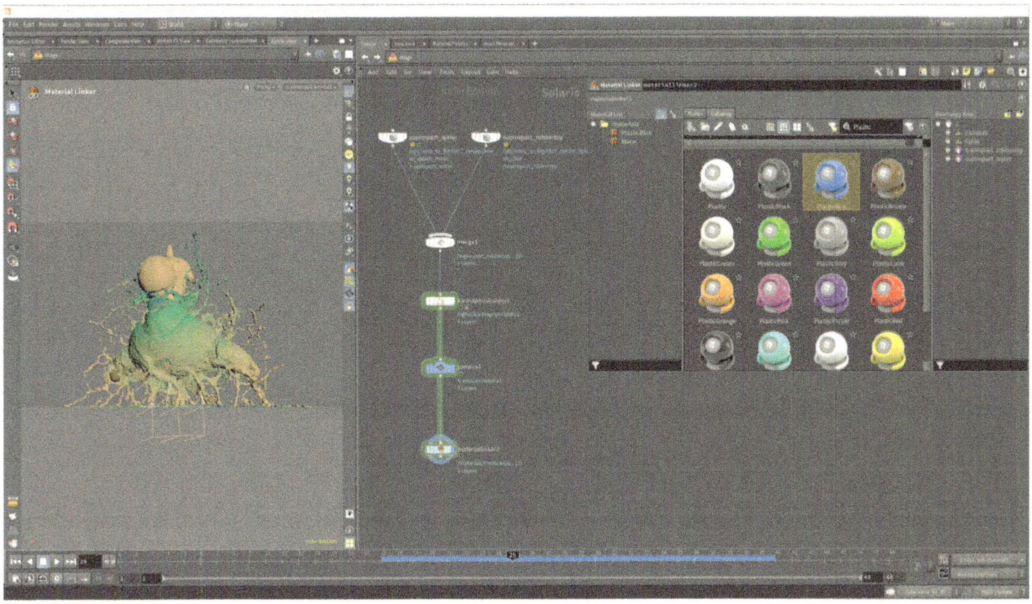

Figure 6.23 – Material Linker

Now, let's assign these materials to the liquid mesh and our character. You can either use the **Assign Material** method that we have used in previous chapters, or you can use **Material Linker** and the *drag and drop* method. Let's follow the next steps to assign the materials with **Material Linker**:

1. Click on the water in **Material List** and make sure that you can see the scene objects in the **Geometry Tree** panel on the right of **Materials Catalog**. If you don't see the scene objects, click on the + icon under **Geometry Tree** to expand the tree.
2. Drag and drop the water shader from **Material List** to **sopimport_water** in the **Geometry Tree**.
3. Drag and drop the *blue* plastic from **Material List** to **sopimport_rubbertoy**.
4. Set the display flag on **Material Linker** and do a viewport test render with either **Karma CPU** or **Karma XPU** to check the result.

Figure 6.24 shows the result of the applied materials:

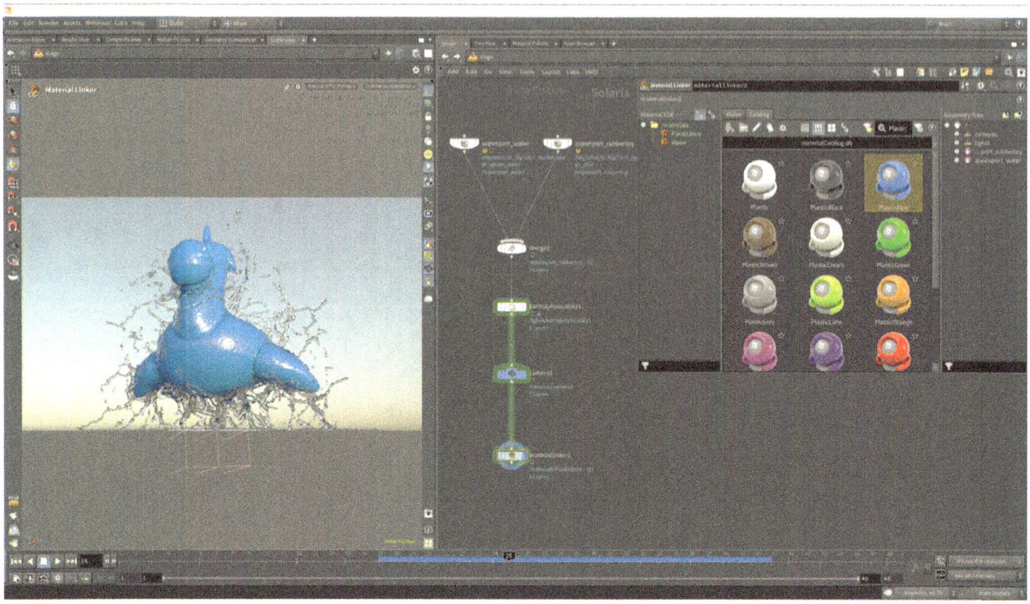

Figure 6.24 – Applied materials

Now that we have the materials working, I encourage you to test other materials in the library for creative exploration and fun! I am going to proceed with the realistic water surface material.

In the next section, finally, we will add the Karma render node and adjust the rendering parameters to achieve even more realism in the liquid rendering.

Tweaking Karma render settings to achieve more realism

Let's follow the next steps to have better control over the render quality:

1. Search for `Karma` in the **TAB Menu** and select only the option named **Karma**. This will place two nodes in your **Solaris** network: the **karmarendersettings** node and **usdrender_rop** to save the rendered sequence to disk.
2. Use **Karma XPU** with a **Path Traced Samples** value of 128 or **Karma CPU** with a **Path Traced Samples** value of at least 16 for a cleaner render result.
3. In the **Karma Render Settings** node, click on the **Rendering** tab and then click on the **Limits** tab.

4. Increase the **Reflection** and **Refraction** limits to 8 to have more light bounce within the water surface, therefore making it brighter and shinier.
5. Increase **SSS Limit** to 1 as when we use caustics for water self-shadowing, this extra bounce will help keep the water surface brighter on contact points.
6. Click on the **Camera Effects** tab and set the **Velocity Blur** option to **Velocity Blur** to achieve a realistic motion blur based on the velocity vectors of the water splash.
7. Click on the **Geometry and Shading** tab and enable **Caustics** for water self-shadowing and more realistic render in the areas where the liquid mesh contacts with the character.
8. Go to the **Image Output** tab, click on **Filters**, and use an available **Denoiser** filter for a cleaner render result.
9. Select **usdrender_rop** and change **Valid Frame Range** to a specific frame range.
10. Save your file and click on **Render to Disk in Background** to start rendering the effect to an image sequence.

Figure 6.25 demonstrates the final fluid simulation rendered result:

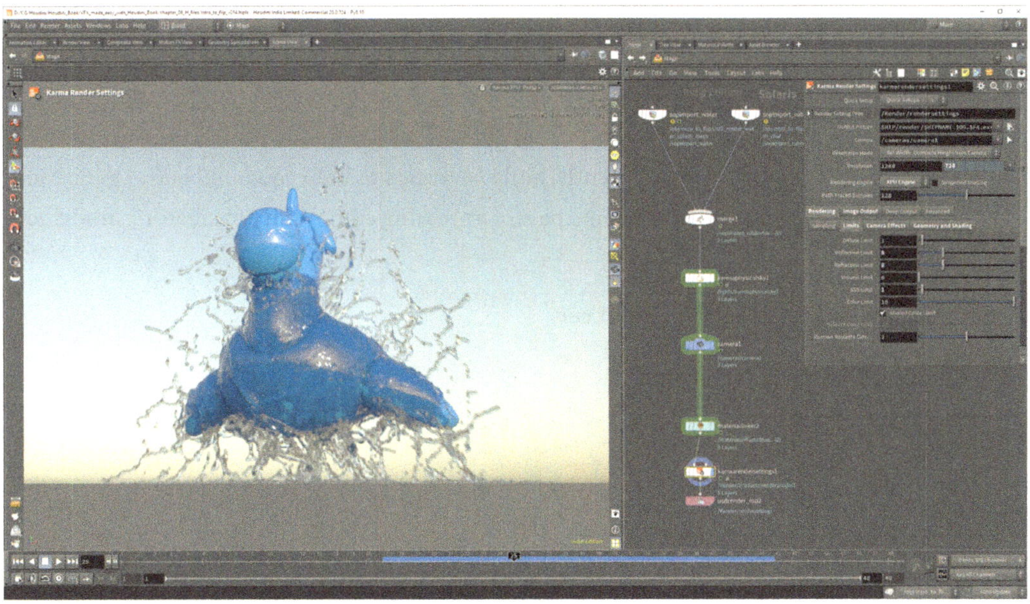

Figure 6.25 – Final render

Congratulations on creating your first complete water simulation in Houdini!

Summary

In conclusion, this chapter introduced the basics of FLIP fluids in Houdini, highlighting their effectiveness in simulating realistic liquid effects through a hybrid particle and grid-based approach.

Overall, we have only scratched the surface of simulating liquids and water effects, with the small-scale fluids examples and exercises.

Large-scale fluid simulations, such as big bodies of liquid, rivers, oceans, involve a lot of computational resources, multiple high-resolution layers, additional solvers, and advanced skills that need a lot more time and practice.

In this chapter we covered key tools such as SOP-based FLIP nodes, emitter and simulation settings, and workflows for fluid collisions, meshing, and rendering, providing a solid foundation for creating dynamic fluid simulations.

In the next chapter, we will use the knowledge gained in the previous chapters, specifically in *Chapter 3*, to create a case study of a particle disintegration effect.

7

Effects Case Study: Disintegration FX

In this chapter, we will learn an easy and efficient way of creating the disintegration effect in Houdini. There are many different ways to produce this popular effect, from creating a simple material opacity dissolve to developing custom erosion and growth solvers. Throughout my experience, I have tried different methods and refined the solution to be a relatively easy and flexible setup that can produce highly detailed disintegration.

The purpose of this chapter is to show you how to think as an effects artist and approach a complex effect in a creative and simple way, leaving room for exploration and experimentation.

We will utilize the knowledge from *Chapter 3* about particle simulations and combine it with procedural tools and techniques learned in the previous chapters.

Here are the main topics that we will cover in this chapter:

- Effect breakdown and workflow plan
- Preparing the geometry for disintegration
- Integrating easy methods for geometry erosion
- Adding attributes for disintegration source
- Sourcing dissolving particles and adjusting simulation
- Adding extra procedural layers
- Disintegration effect lighting and rendering

By the end of this chapter, you will be equipped with different SOP-level geometry manipulation, particle simulation, and rendering workflows that will help you to create an interesting-looking disintegration effect.

Figure 7.1 shows the disintegration effect that we will be creating:

Figure 7.1 – Disintegration in Houdini

Technical requirements

As you will notice in *Figure 7.1*, I have rendered the disintegration particles with a marble head 3D model. This model was downloaded from **Poly Haven**. Here's the link to the page where you can obtain it: `https://polyhaven.com/a/marble_bust_01`.

All the workflows that I am going to show for this project can be applied to any 3D model of your choice, so feel free to either proceed with the asset from Poly Haven or use anything that you have created yourself.

I will also utilize an HDRI map downloaded from Poly Haven for the environment light and background: `https://polyhaven.com/a/kloppenheim_02`.

You will have access to the Houdini file with the completed effect on the GitHub link at `https://github.com/PacktPublishing/VFX-Made-Easy-with-Houdini`.

To view the chapter images in better clarity, scan the provided QR code. It will direct you to a dedicated link where you can take a look at the images.

Now, let's break down the effect and analyze how we can achieve an easy disintegration workflow.

Effect breakdown and workflow plan

In a **particle disintegration effect**, the object begins to erode from a designated start point or multiple start points that are expanding through a disintegration edge. As the edge progresses across the surface, it also emits particles or small fragments of the disintegrating object.

This erosion effect often uses a *mask* or *noise field* to control the edge's movement, ensuring a dynamic breakdown that appears natural and random. As the edge moves, it releases particles, which inherit color and motion from the object's surface, creating a dissolving appearance. These particles may then be influenced by turbulence or wind forces for added realism, while their size or opacity fades over time to complete the effect.

Here's a list of the simple steps that are involved in the creation of the effect:

1. Prepare a 3D object for the effect.
2. Create erosion start point (or points).
3. Animate a dynamic mask that will start from the origin point and will progress until it covers the entire object.
4. Use the animated mask to erode the areas of the geometry that have the mask coverage.
5. Decouple the mask edge and use it to source dissolving particles or fragments.
6. Adjust the emitted particles to fade in time after they leave the object's surface.
7. Combine all the elements and render the complete effect.

Moving on, we will use the preceding breakdown and steps as our guide while creating the effect.

Preparing the geometry for disintegration

Before starting on the disintegration, we will need to import and prepare the 3D asset for the effect.

Let's dive into Houdini to execute the steps:

1. Create a new project and name it `particle_disintegration`.
2. In the network view, create an empty geometry container and name it `disintegration_fx`.
3. Inside the geometry container, create a **File** node via the **TAB Menu**.
4. In the **Geometry File** box of the **File** node, you can add the path to the downloaded model in the same way as we did in the previous chapters.
5. Let's add a **Transform** node to scale the object down to `0.1` units in the **Uniform Scale**. (The 3D model would be imported at a very large scale as usual; therefore, we need to scale it down respecting Houdini's metric units.)

For a more detailed explanation, refer to the *Importing a custom 3D asset* section in *Chapter 4*, where the metric units difference between Houdini and other software packages is explained.

Refer to *Figure 7.2* to see the imported asset and its scale in relation to Houdini's units:

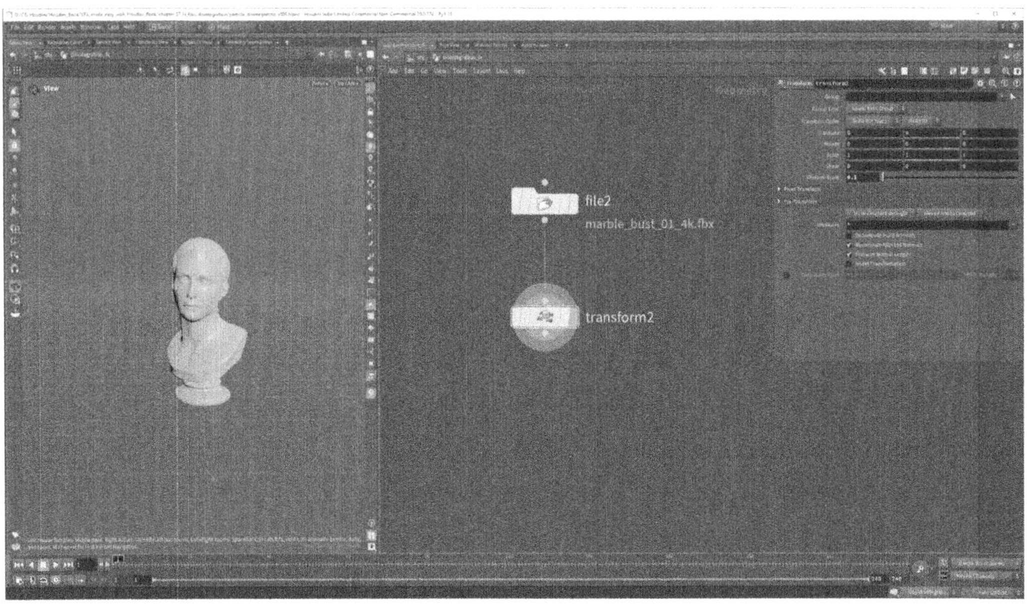

Figure 7.2 – Importing the 3D geometry for the effect

For the next steps, we are going to increase the mesh resolution to be able to capture and process more details from the **Color**, **Mask**, and **Noise** attributes that we will use for the effect:

1. Add a **Subdivide** node after the **Transform**, and set the **Algorithm** to **OpenSubdiv Loop**, which will increase the polygon amount and convert quads to triangles for better performance and details.
2. Change the **Depth** parameter in the **Subdivide** node to 2 for more polygon subdivisions.
3. Add an **Attribute from Map** node to use the marble texture that ships with the asset as the **Color** attribute.
4. Choose the path to the marble diffuse texture called `marble_bust_01_dif_4k.jpg` in the **Texture Map** box.

We will need the dissolving particles to inherit the colors of the marble texture that we will use during shading and rendering. Therefore, if we apply this texture through the **Attribute from Map** node, the values of the texture will be stored in the **Cd** attribute and particles will be able to inherit the color values and blend with the mesh in a much more realistic way.

Refer to *Figure 7.3* to see the result of the texture applied as the **Cd** attribute:

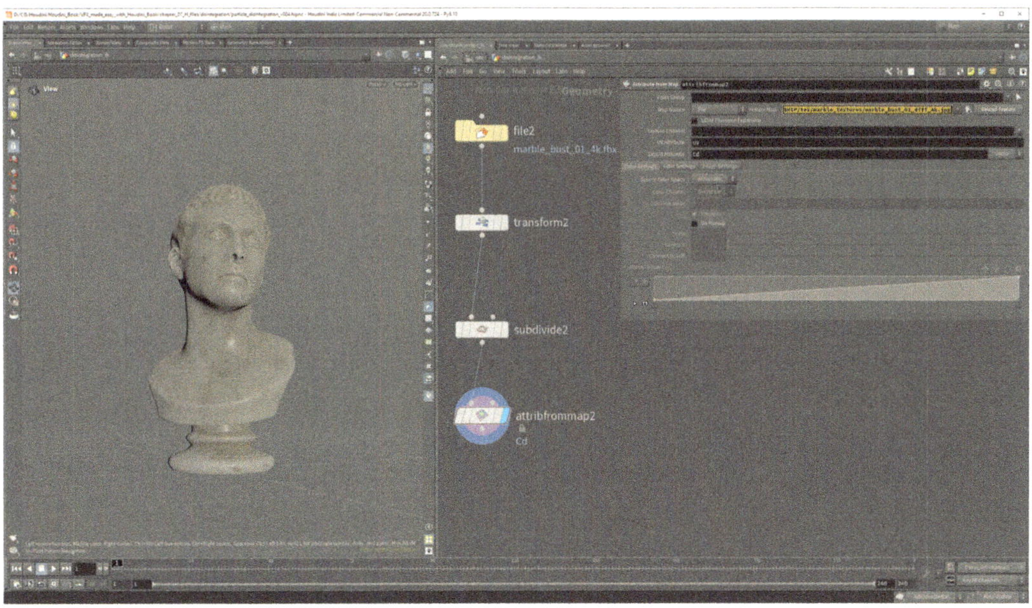

Figure 7.3 – Applying texture as a color attribute

For the next steps, we will create a procedural mask that can be animated and distorted with noise in the next section.

Integrating easy methods for geometry erosion

There are many different ways of creating a **dynamic dissolve** or **erosion mask**, from custom-built infection solvers to a complete coded solution in VEX. I will show you a highly customizable and flexible method of creating a dissolve mask that utilizes Houdini's relatively new mask nodes.

Let's follow the next steps to create a disintegration mask:

1. Create a **Mask from Geometry** node and connect the output of **Attribute from Map** to the first input of **Mask from Geometry**.
2. In the **Mask from Geometry** node, set the **Reference Group Type** to **Points**. We need to proceed with the **Points** type because according to our dissolve plan, we will need an origin point or multiple points for the erosion to start from.
3. Create an **Add** node and click on + to create a single point located at (0,0,0) in 3D space (see *Figure 7.4*).

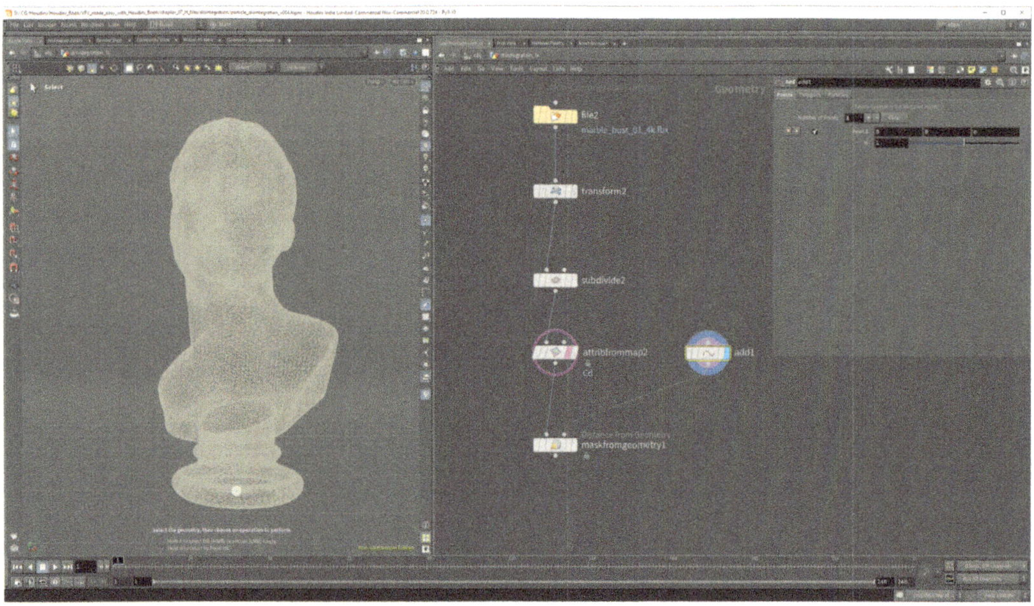

Figure 7.4 – Mask start reference point

4. Connect the output of the **Add** node to the second input of the **Mask from Geometry** node.
5. Set the **Mask Radius** to 5 in the **Mask from Geometry** node to increase the distance calculation from the reference point.

6. Put the **Display Flag** on the **Mask from Geometry** node and preview the **Mask** attribute by clicking on the name **mask** with the help of the **Node Info** flag (see *Chapter 1* for the **Node Info** flag and *Chapter 3* for the **Preview** attributes).
7. Bring the **Remap Ramp** ends closer to the center to achieve a sharper edge of the mask (see *Figure 7.5*).

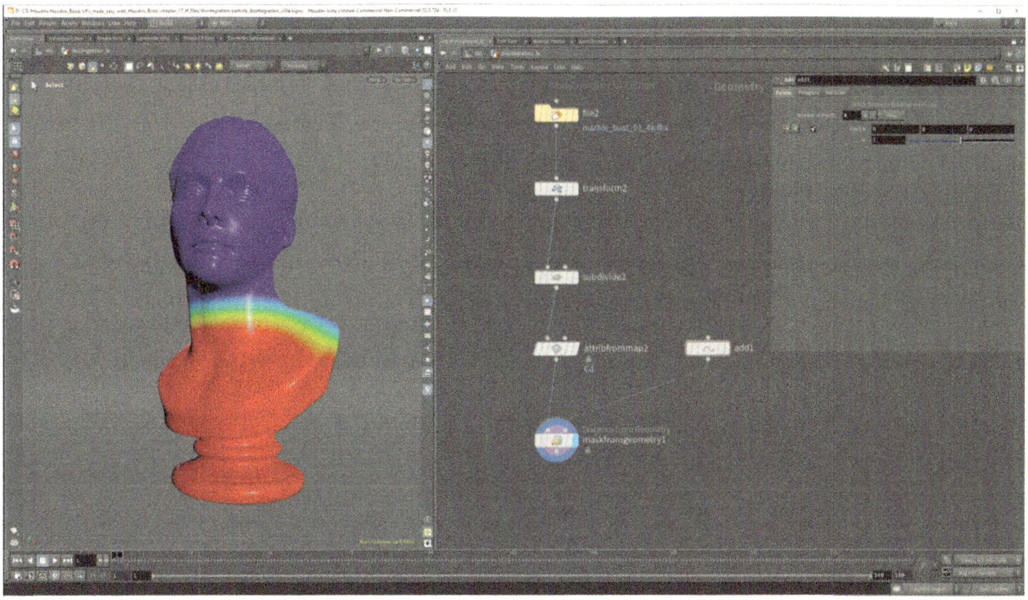

Figure 7.5 – Mask preview

Based on the color values that we see:

- **Red** means that the mask value is at 100%, or a full value of 1.
- **Purple** means that the mask value is 0.
- Other colors represent all the values in between.

The closer the ends of the **Remap Ramp** are to the center and each other, the sharper the mask edge is going to be.

Animating the disintegration mask

If you start playing with the **Radius** slider in **Mask from Geometry**, you will notice that we can control the growth and shrinking of the mask over the 3D object.

Let's set the animation keyframe for the **Radius** parameter to `0` at frame **1**, then switch to frame **144** while updating the **Radius** parameter keyframe to a higher value of **12**, for example. You will get a dynamic mask animating from **0** to **12** covering an entire object over **144** frames.

Using this logic, we can control the speed and coverage of the mask growth over time with two simple keyframes.

An important thing to keep in mind during this workflow is the initial distance of the origin point to the 3D object. Currently, the origin point sits right at the bottom of the 3D object; therefore, the starting mask distance is set to `0`. However, if the origin point is located further from the surface of the 3D object, the starting mask value can be higher than 0.

If you want to use a proven method for the origin point to always sit on the surface of the 3D object, then you can create that initial point by using a **Scatter** node on the object geometry with one or more points instead of adding a disconnected point in 3D space with an **Add** node.

Refer to *Figure 7.6* to see the workflow of using scattered points as the mask origin:

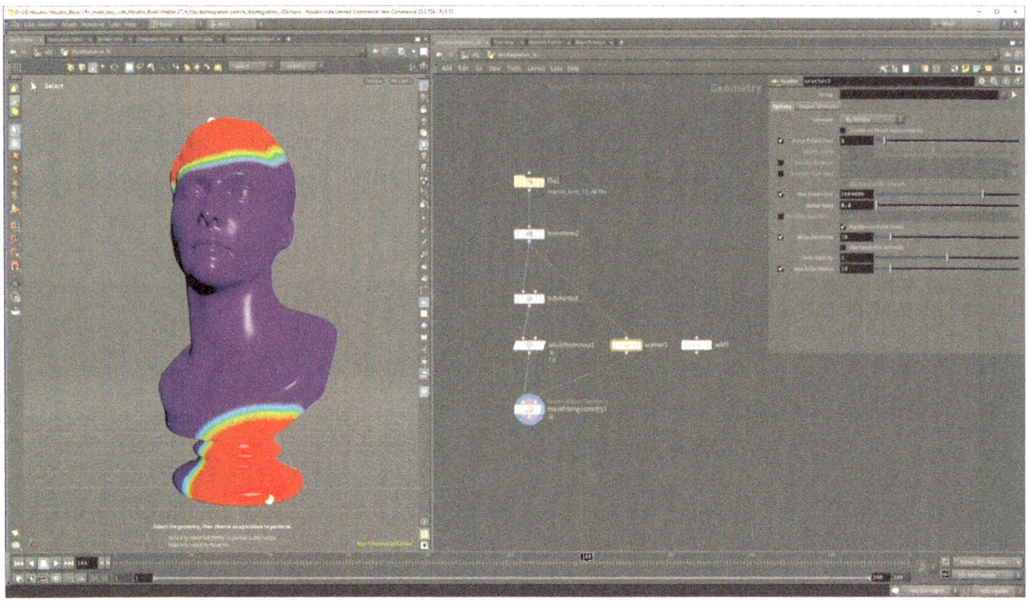

Figure 7.6 – Multiple scattered mask origin points

Let's continue with the **Scatter** node and animate the mask by following these steps:

1. Add a **Scatter** node after the **Transform** node to set random origin points.
2. In the **Scatter** node, set the **Force Total Count** parameter to `1` to source the mask origin only from one point.
3. Adjust the **Global Seed** value to `0.9`, which will set the origin point at the top of the object's head.
4. Scrub to frame **1** on the animation timeline to set the first keyframe.
5. In the **Mask from Geometry** node, set the **Radius** parameter to `0` and use *Alt + left mouse button* on the **Radius** parameter to animate the parameter.
6. Scrub to frame **144** and set the radius parameter to **12**.
7. Use *Alt + left mouse button* on the **Radius** parameter to set the second keyframe.
8. Scrub between frames **1** and **144** to see how the mask animates and covers the entire object.

Refer to *Figure 7.7* to see the animated mask result:

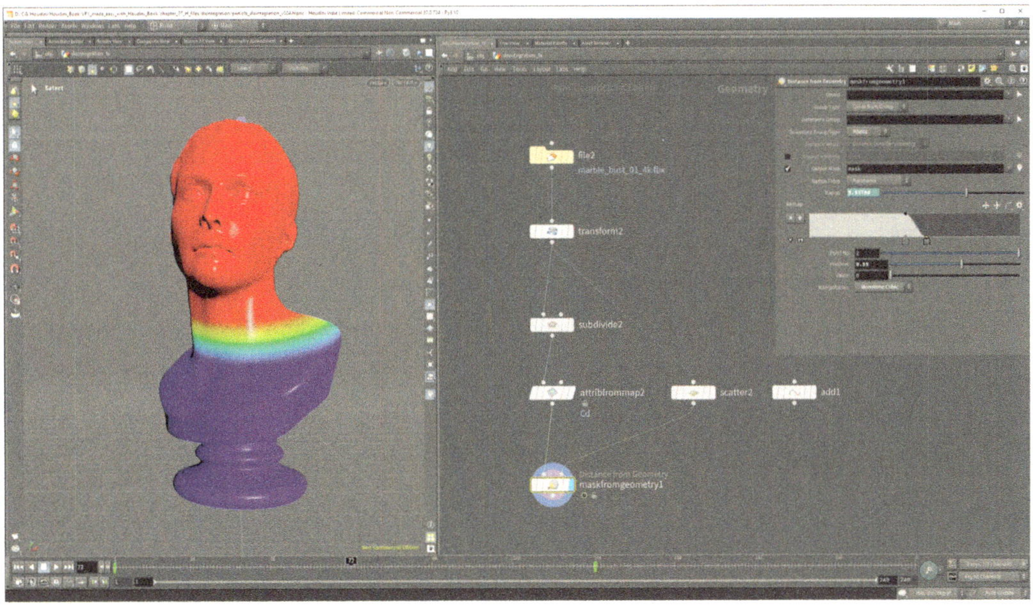

Figure 7.7 – Animated mask attribute

Moving on, we will make the mask more detailed and noise up the edges.

Adding more details to the mask

We have successfully created an animated dynamic mask, which works and can be used to be applied to the disintegration effect right away. However, we can achieve much nicer erosion and emission details by distorting the mask edge with noises.

The fastest and easiest way of distorting the edge of the mask is to use the noised-up geometry before sampling the mask from a reference origin point.

However, we will not be able to use the noised-up marble statue later for anything else. Therefore, we will need to find a way of storing the original position of the polygons before adding distortion, and then after we sample the mask on the distorted geo, we can bring back the original polygon positions while maintaining the noised-up mask edge.

Let's implement this technique by following these steps:

1. Add a **Rest** node after the **Attribute from Map** node and before the **Mask from Geometry** node. This **Rest** node is set to store the **Rest** option by default, which in other words means that it will store the object's original position into a vector rest attribute.
2. Add a **mountain** node right after the **Rest** node to add position-based noise to the marble statue.
3. Turn off the **Noise Along Vector** parameter in the **mountain** node to achieve a 3D distorting noise, rather than displacing along the normal vector.
4. Set the **Element Size** to `0.5` to have a smaller distortion pattern. Additionally, you can select the **Animation** checkbox if you want the noise to evolve over time.
5. Add another **Rest** node after the **Mask from Geometry** node. We will use this node to restore the original non-distorted marble statue.
6. In the **Rest** node, set the **Mode to Extract Rest** to restore the original position.
7. Add the **Normal** node after the **Rest** node to fix the distorted surface normals.

Refer to *Figure 7.8* to see the distorted mask and the perfectly maintained marble statue:

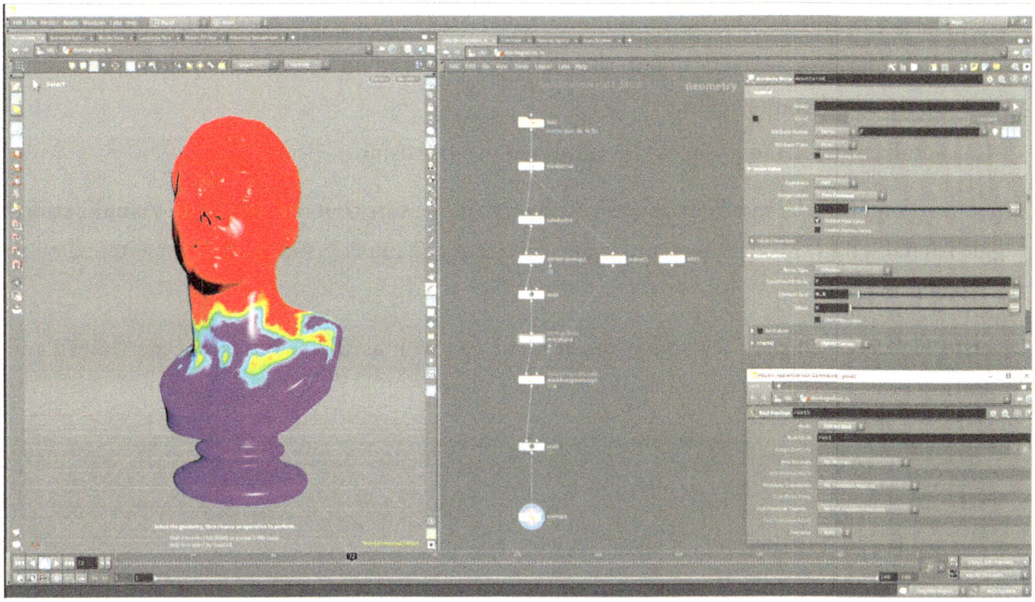

Figure 7.8 – Animated mask attribute

Now that we have an interesting detailed animated mask that we can adjust with artistic control, let's move forward and apply the mesh erosion process by following these steps:

1. Create a **Delete** node after the **Normal** node.
2. Set the **Delete Entity** to **Points** since the mask attribute is stored on points.
3. Set the **Delete Operation** to **Delete by expression**.
4. In the **Filter Expression** box, type `@mask` to delete the parts of the geometry that have a mask value higher than **0**.
5. Add a **Clean** node to remove all the disconnected points and unwanted mesh artifacts after deletion.
6. Add a **mountain** node to distort the edges of the eroded mesh for a more organic look.
7. Turn on the **Blend** checkbox on the **mountain** node to utilize the **Mask** attribute and add noise only on the edges.

8. Turn off **Noise Along Vector** to achieve a 3D distortion noise.
9. Set the **Amplitude** to `0.25` and the **Element Size** to `0.1` to get a smaller noise pattern.
10. Turn off **mask** visualization in the viewport by going into **Node Info** panel and clicking on the **mask** name again.
11. Scrub the timeline to check the animated mesh erosion.

When working with the **mask** attribute, you need to make sure that the **Attribute Visualizations** toggle is enabled in the viewport and make sure that the **mask** visualization is switched on in the **Node Info** panel.

Refer to *Figure 7.9* to see the eroded mesh result, as well as the settings for the **Delete** and **mountain** nodes:

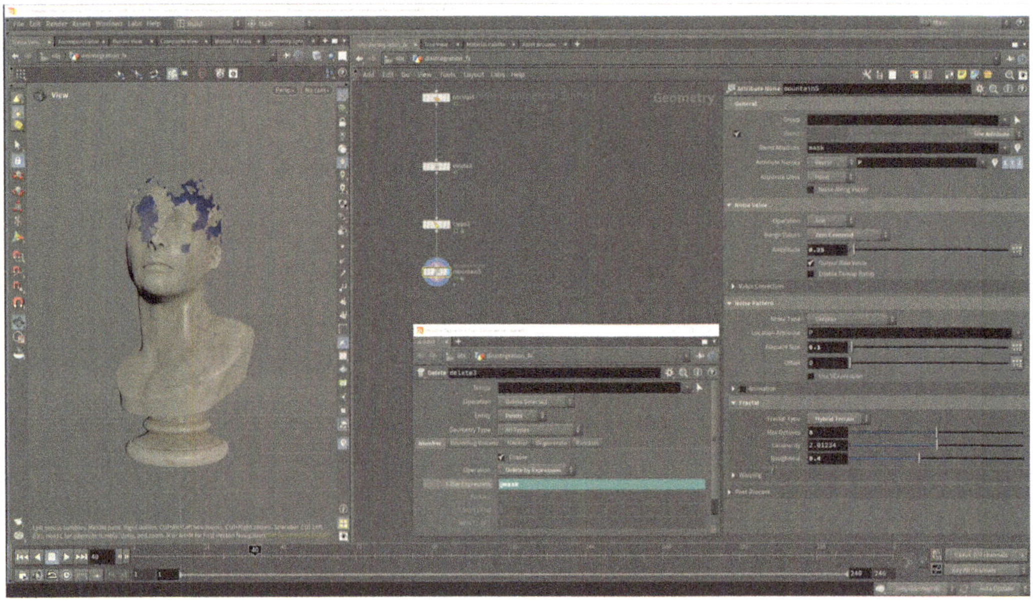

Figure 7.9 – Eroding mesh finalized

In the next section, we will decouple the mask into a new edge attribute and source dissolving particles from the edge of the eroding mesh.

Adding attributes for disintegration source

In the next steps, we will adjust and manipulate the **mask** attribute to get the desired particle emission.

Let's proceed with the following steps:

1. Branch out from the **Normal** node and create an **Attribute Blur** node to smooth the mask and have a wider area for particle emission.
2. In the **Attributes** box, type `mask` and remove **P** to only blur the **Mask** attribute.
3. Add an **Attribute Remap** node after the **Attribute Blur** to remap the mask values into the new attribute that we will use for the emission.
4. In the **Attribute Remap**, set the **Original Name** to `mask` and the new name to `emit`.
5. Visualize the **emit** attribute in the viewport to see the result (see *Chapter 3* for attribute visualization methods).

Refer to *Figure 7.10* to see the updated network view and the **emit** attribute:

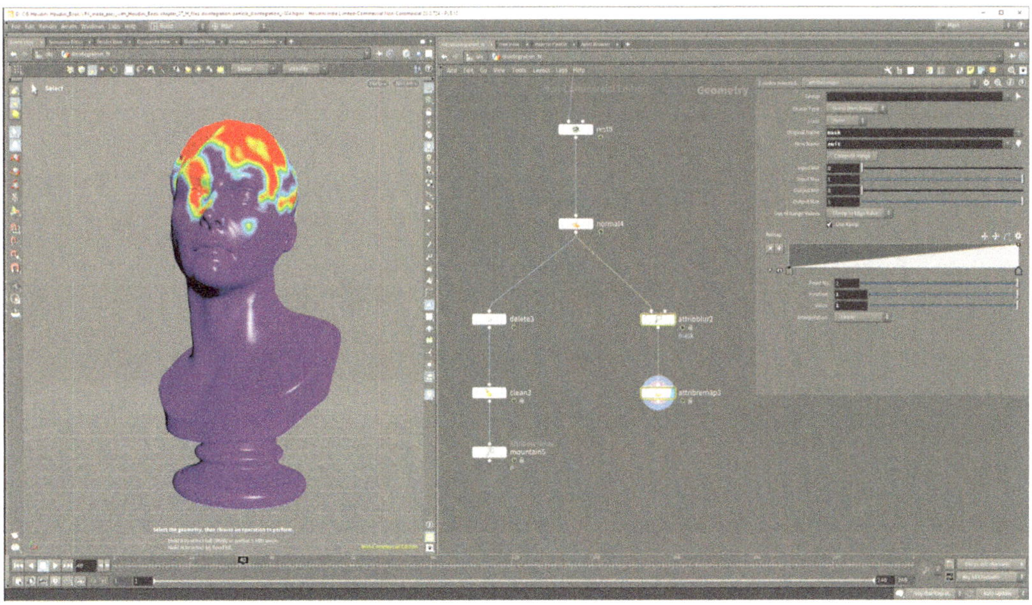

Figure 7.10 – Remapping the mask

As you can see, the **emit** attribute sourced from the mask looks exactly like the blurred mask. However, for correct particles sourcing from the erosion edge, we would need the emit to be concentrated with red values only on the mask edge.

This could be easily achieved by remapping the ramp on the attribute remap by setting the ends of the ramp to level `0` and setting the middle point of the ramp to the highest value. You can create additional points on the ramp by clicking anywhere on the ramp box, or you can choose the **Hill** preset from the ramp menu.

Let's adjust the ramp to remap the emit values to the edge by following the next steps:

1. Click on the little **gear** icon on the right above the ramp's highest point.
2. Choose **Hill** from the preset menu.
3. Notice how the **emit** attribute changed to a thin edge.

Refer to *Figure 7.11* to see the ramp settings and the updated **emit** attribute in the viewport:

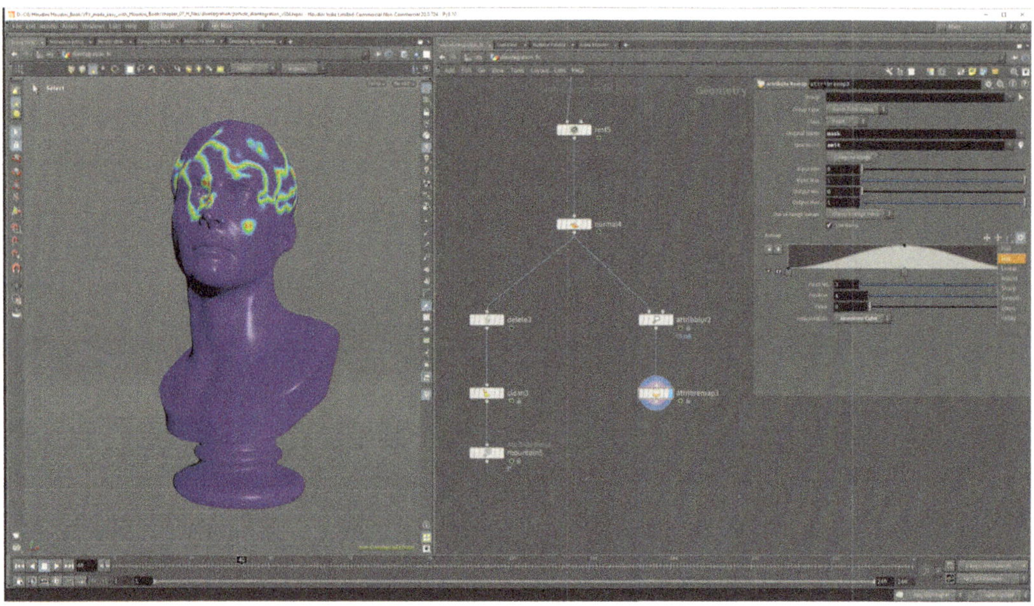

Figure 7.11 – Adjusting the ramp

To achieve better connectivity of particles being sourced from the eroded edge, we need the **Emitter** geometry to have the same distorted positions from the **mountain** node as in the eroded mesh branch.

Thanks to Houdini's procedural nature, we can easily rearrange the place of the **mountain** node that is currently created after the **Clean** node and distorts the edge.

Let's place that **mountain** node after the **Normal** node before branching off to the **Delete** and **Attribute Blur** nodes.

It will look like entangled intersecting polygons at first; however, these bad polygons will be deleted, with the **Delete** node remaining intact down the chain and ignored during the particle sourcing stage.

Refer to *Figure 7.12* to see the updated network with the rearranged **mountain** node:

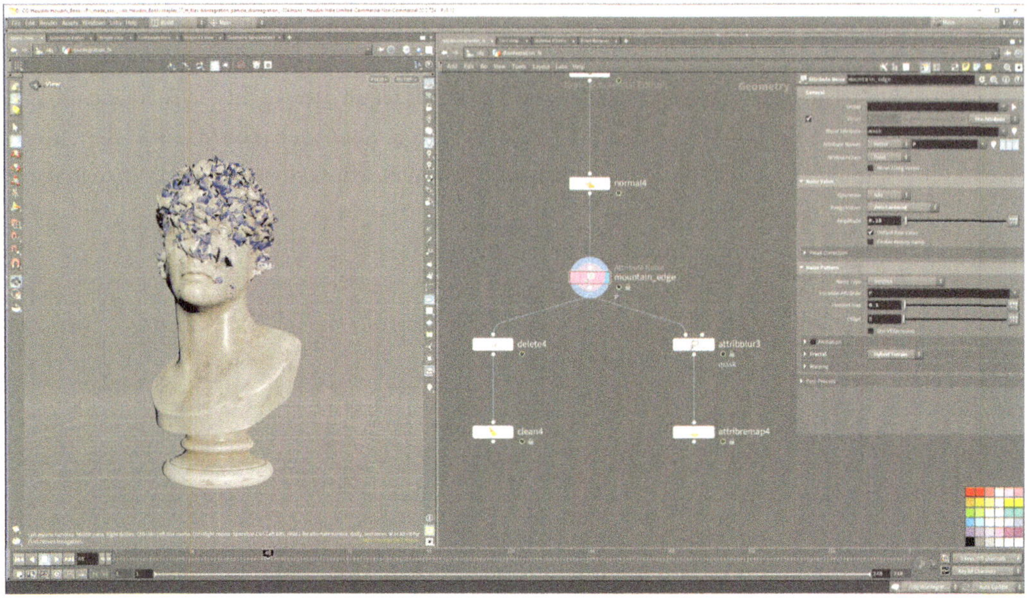

Figure 7.12 – Rearranging the mountain node

We have one more step left before we can start emitting particles, and that is creating an initial velocity to achieve interesting simulation details from the start. For the next steps, we will utilize the **Point Velocity** node to set a base initial velocity for the simulation.

Let's follow the next steps to create the initial velocity:

1. Add a **Point Velocity** node after the **Attribute Remap** node.
2. Enable the **Add Velocity** checkbox to set the initial directional velocity direction.
3. Input a value of 1 in the **Positive X** and **Z** direction to make the velocity directed from left to right with a little push forward off the surface.
4. In the **Basic** tab of **Point Velocity**, the initialization is set to **Compute from Deformation**. This setting will take the distorting surface and calculate the realistic surface noise velocity.
5. Set the **Frame Sample** value to 2 to have better velocity blending and interpolation between frames.

6. Go to the **Curl Noise** tab and enable the **Add Curl Noise** checkbox to add additional initial turbulent swirls for the velocity vectors.
7. Set the **Scale** parameter to `0.25` and **Swirl Scale** to `0.5` to make the swirls smaller and reduce the strength of the curl noise.

Refer to *Figure 7.13* to see the settings of **Point Velocity** and velocity vectors visualized in the viewport:

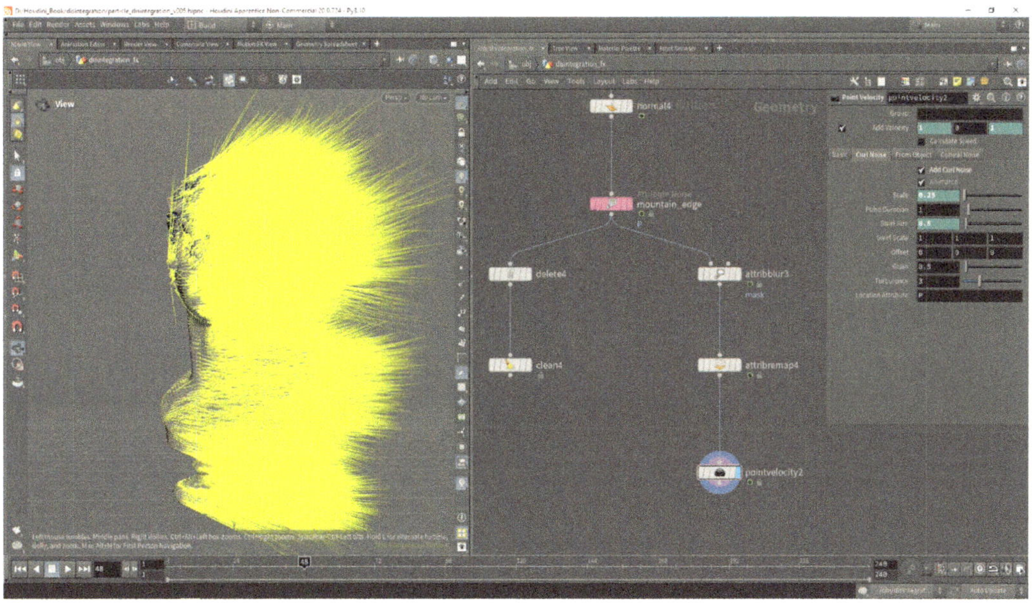

Figure 7.13 – Adding the initial velocity

Moving on, let's start sourcing disintegration particles based on the created attributes.

Sourcing dissolving particles and adjusting simulation

For further steps, we will utilize the **POP Network** node to efficiently source and modify the dissolving particles simulation. If you need to remember any settings or parameter workflows for particles, please refer to *Chapter 3*.

Follow the next steps to start sourcing particles using the **emit** attribute:

1. Create the **POP Network** node through the **TAB Menu** and connect the output of **Point Velocity** to the first input of the **POP Network** node.
2. Click on **POP Source** to adjust the particle emission settings.
3. In the **Source** tab of **POP Source**, click on the **Emission Attribute** box and type `emit` to force the particles to be only sourced from the custom **emit** attribute that we have created.
4. Select the **Scale Point Count by Area** checkbox and set the **Reference Area** parameter to `1` to concentrate all the particles into the surface area of the **emit** attribute.
5. Play the simulation until frame **48** to see the result.

Refer to *Figure 7.14* to see the initial particle emission settings:

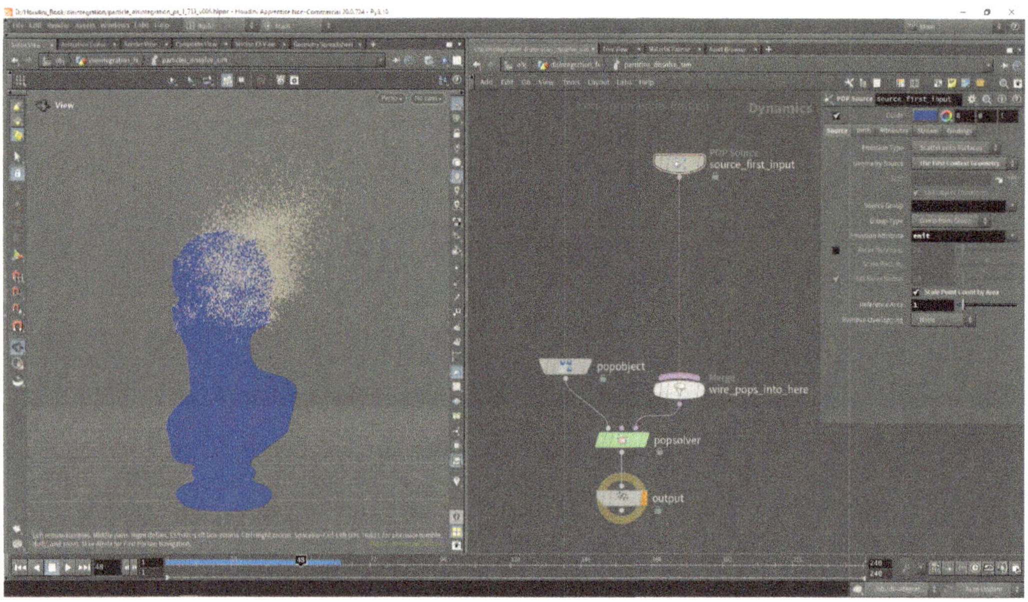

Figure 7.14 – Initial particle emission settings

After playing the simulation, you can see that our setup works and that the particles are sourcing the object color and efficiently being sourced in the direction of the initial velocity. However, for better results, we will need to adjust some source settings in the **Birth** tab.

Follow the next steps to adjust the number of sourced particles and the particle life:

1. Click on the **POP Source** node and go to the **Birth** tab.
2. Set the **Impulse Count** to `1500`, which will force 1,500 particles to be emitted per frame.

3. Set **Constant activation** and **Constant Birth Rate** to `0`, since we will not be using this emission mode (see *Chapter 3* for more details).
4. Set the **Life Expectancy** to `3.5` seconds and **Life Variance** to `0.25` seconds to make the life of particles shorter and add more variance.
5. Set the **Jitter Birth Time** to **Negative** and **Interpolate source** to **Back** for smooth emission without stepping and repetitive artifacts caused by fast motion.
6. Play the simulation until frame **55** to see the result.

Refer to *Figure 7.15* for preferred particle **Birth** settings:

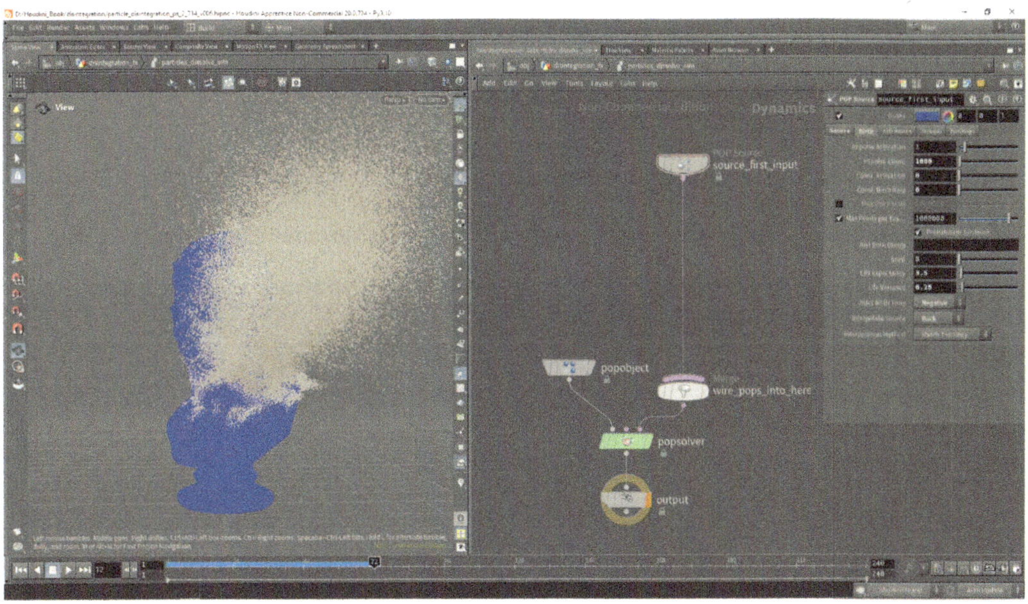

Figure 7.15 – Adjusting the particle source

After implementing these settings, we can now see many more particles and their shorter lifespan. However, the result looks like a very fuzzy and noisy particle cloud. To further improve the result, we will add **POP forces** to have better control over the shape and motion of the simulation.

Let's continue with the next steps to add directing particle forces:

1. Add a **POP Force** node after the **POP Source** node.
2. Set the **Force** parameter value on the **X axis** to 5 to have a stronger wind-like directional force from left to right that will continue to push particles after the emission.

3. In the **Noise** tab of **POP Force**:
    - Set the **Amplitude** to `2.5`.
    - Set the **Swirl Size** to `1.5`.
4. Add a **POP Drag** force after the **POP Force** to simulate air resistance.
5. Set the **Air Resistance** parameter to `0.25` to have a smaller drag.
6. Turn off the **Ignore Mass** checkbox since we will randomize the mass per particle and force each particle to have a varied air resistance according to the particle's mass.
7. Add the **POP Property** node and turn on the **Mass** checkbox.
8. Turn on the **Use VEXpression** checkbox to add mass variance through VEX code.
9. Click on the **dropdown** icon above the expression box and choose to randomize the mass expression preset.
10. Play the simulation until frame **48** to see the result.

Refer to *Figure 7.16* to see the particle force network and mass variance expression:

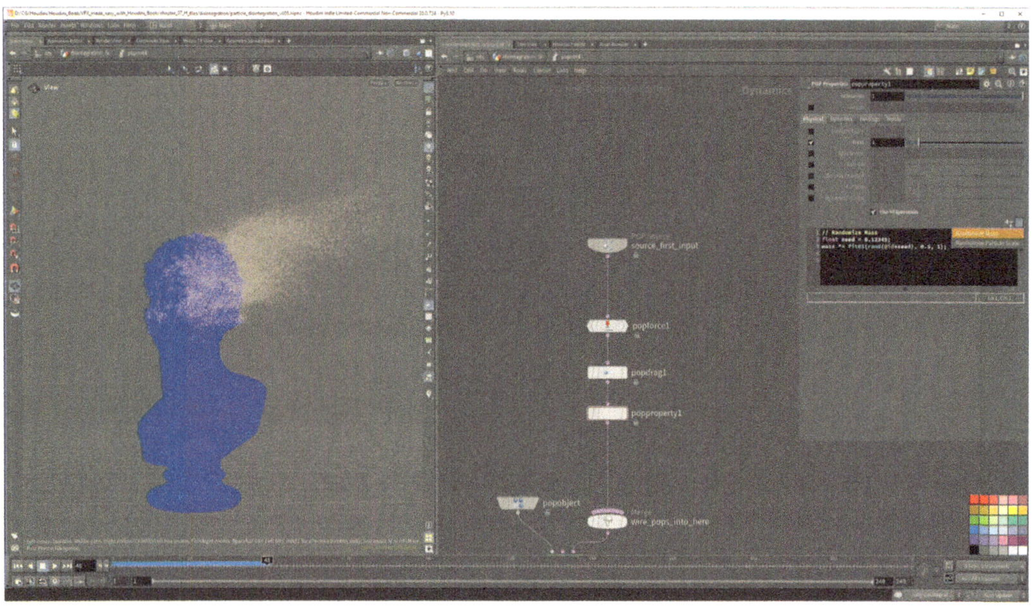

Figure 7.16 – Adding POP forces and mass randomization

Adding a custom collider to the particle simulation

Our dissolve particle system is almost ready. The only further addition that we will make is the **collision geometry** for more realistic results. I also encourage you to add more forces and experiment with settings to direct the particles in the way you like.

Let's continue with the next steps to create the efficient collision geometry:

1. Press *u* on the keyboard to go up to the **obj** level, where we will prepare the 3D object for collisions.
2. Branch out from the **mountain _edge** node and add a **Peak** node to shrink the object that we will use as a collision. Shrinking the object would prevent the newly born particles from immediately colliding and bouncing off the surface and overall will give a more stable and smooth particle flow.
3. Set the **Distance** parameter to `-0.05` to shrink the geometry. Add a **Collision Source** node to add collision properties to the 3D object.

   The **Collision Source** node will give the user two outputs: one for *collision surface polygons* with calculated velocity and the other for the *collision VDB surface* that is the most efficient way for the particles to collide (see *Chapter 4* for more information about VDBs and their benefit of being used as collision volumes).

   For better results, I recommend setting velocity approximation to **None** in the **Geometry** tab. Since the actual object is not physically moving in 3D space and only has surface deformation, which we are already injecting as initial velocity, there is no need to add extra deformation velocity from the collision geometry.

4. Switch to the **Volume** tab to adjust the resolution of VDB volume, which will define the accuracy and quality of the collision surface.
5. Set the **Voxel Size** to `0.025` to increase the resolution of the collision VDB.
6. Create two **Null** nodes for each output of the **Collision Source** node.
7. Name the first **Null** node `OUT_object_collision_geo` and the second **Null** node `OUT_object_collision_vdb`.
8. Double-click on the **POP Network** to dive inside and add the path to the collision output nulls.

Refer to *Figure 7.17* to see the collision preparation setup:

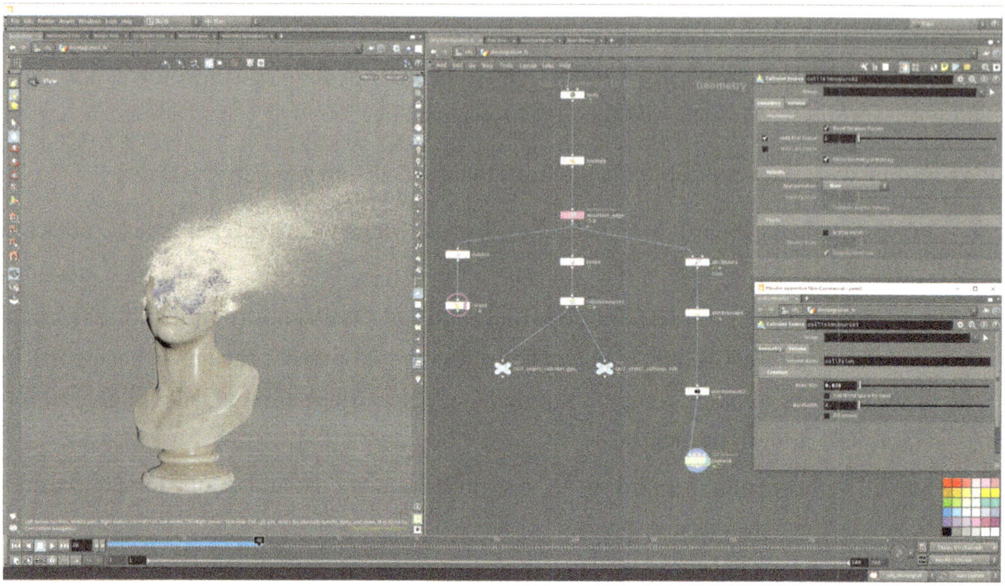

Figure 7.17 – Creating an object collider

During the next steps, we will use a **Static Object** node inside the POP network to link the created collision elements into the particle simulation.

Static Object is a very versatile node that has many settings and properties for static and even deforming colliders. The number of settings might be overwhelming at first; however, the sections and parameters that are needed to produce particle collisions with custom 3D geometry from SOPs are very easy to use.

Let's concentrate on the following sections:

- The **SOP Path** box, where we can link a path to collision geometry output null
- The **Proxy Volume** box in the **Collisions** tab, where we can link a path to the VDB collision volume
- **Collision Volume Creation** mode in the **Collision** tab, which needs to be set to **Volume Sample**, as the collision volume was created outside of the POP network and only needs to be sampled for faster creation

After we connect all the collision output links into the **Static Object**, it needs to be merged after the **POP Solver** by being connected first into the **Merge** node, with the **POP Solver** connected second. This connection order is very important because dynamic objects on the left of the dynamics network will affect the dynamics objects on the right.

Refer to *Figure 7.18* and follow the next steps to connect the **Static Object** collider to the particle simulation:

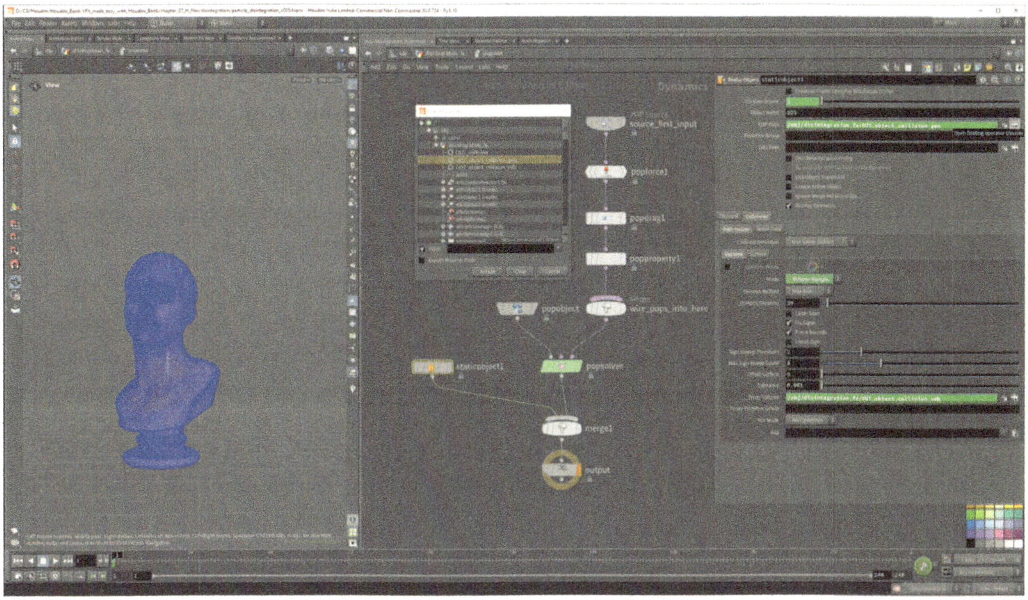

Figure 7.18 – Adding complex colliders

Next, we will link the collision source from SOPs to POPs:

1. Create a **Static Object** node inside of the **Dynamics** network and place it to the left of **POP Solver**.
2. Click on the **Open floating operator chooser** icon on the right of the **SOP Path** box to link the path to the collision geo from the **obj** level.
3. Choose the **OUT_object_collision_geo** node from the **Choose Operator** window.
4. In the **Collisions** tab, change the **Mode** to **Volume Sample**.
5. Connect the path to the **VDB** collision volume in the **Proxy Volume** box by clicking on the operator chooser and selecting **OUT_object_collision_vdb** from the **Choose Operator** window.
6. Add a **Merge** node under **Static Object** and **POP Solver**.
7. Connect the static object first from the left and the **POP Solver** from the right.
8. Connect the **Merge** node to the **Output** node.
9. Play the simulation until frame **60** to see the result.

We now have successfully integrated a custom complex collider that was created outside of the **Dynamics** network. For more advanced scenarios, where you will have the collider actively deforming and changing its position in 3D space, you can enable the **Use Deforming Geometry** checkbox on the **Static Object** node to have the particles collide with a dynamic deforming object.

Another recommended workflow is to pre-cache the collision source outputs so the expensive calculations of VDB volume wouldn't create an overhead on the simulation process.

Additionally, you can also add a ground plane for an infinite ground collider in the same way as in *Chapter 3*.

> Note that whenever you have more than one collider, you will need to merge them using an additional **Merge** node before merging with the **POP Solver**.

You can also adjust the physical qualities separately per collider in the **Physical** tab of each collider to change how much **Bounce**, **Friction**, and other qualities would affect the particles during the collision.

Refer to *Figure 7.19* to see the complete POP network with forces, colliders, and physical settings:

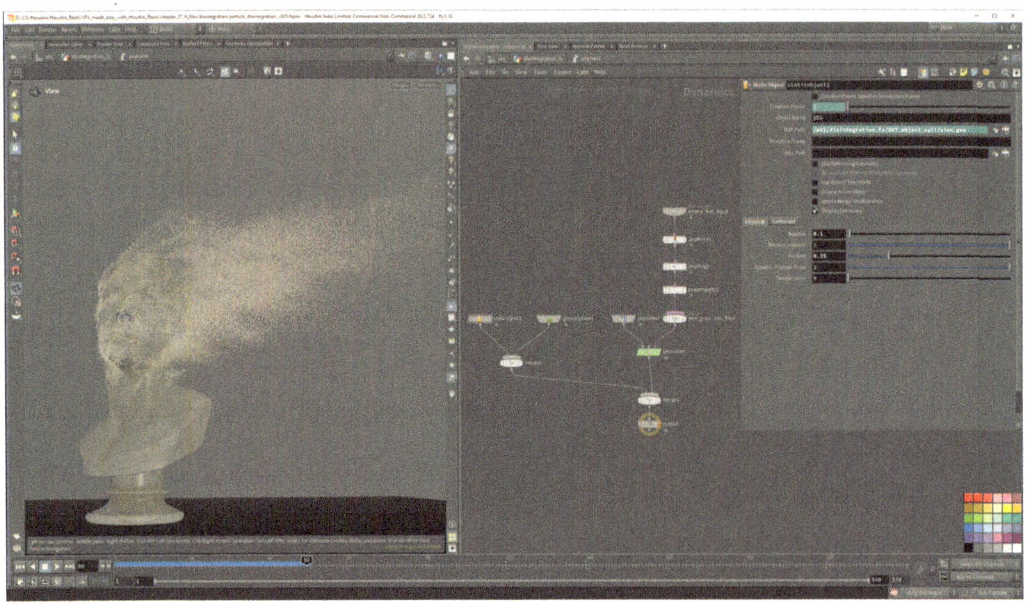

Figure 7.19 – Adding a ground collider and adjusting physical settings

Moving on, let's see how we can create an extra procedural layer that will help to blend the transition between the eroding mesh and emitting particles.

Adding extra procedural layers

Let's jump back to the **Geometry** SOP level to preview the disintegrating particles together with the eroding mesh. Before making a preview, we need to adjust what **POP Network** imports into the **Geometry** level by following these steps:

1. Click on the **popnet** node and go to the **Object Merge** tab.
2. Remove the * symbol from the **Object** box, which is currently importing everything including the collision geometry.
3. Click on the *dropdown* on the right of the **Object** box and choose **popobject**. This will force the **popnet** to only import the particles and their attributes into the **Geometry** level.
4. Add a **Merge** node and connect the particles and the eroding mesh from the **Clean** node into the **Merge**.
5. Play the simulation until frame **60** to preview both the eroding mesh and dissolving particles.

Refer to *Figure 7.20* to see the result and the **popnet** import settings:

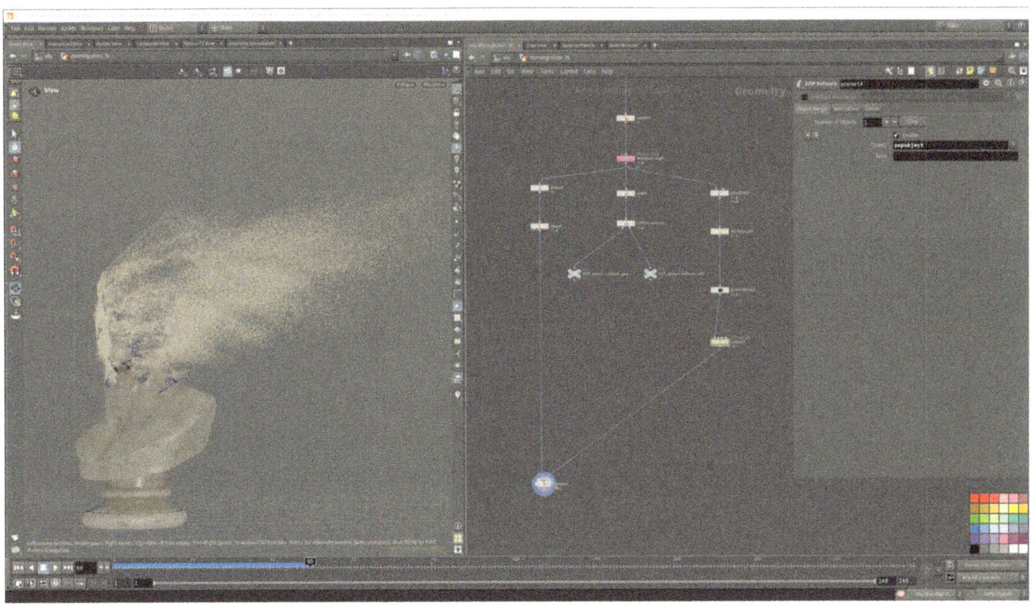

Figure 7.20 – Eroding mesh and particles preview

As we can see, both effect layers are working together; however, there are some significant gaps between the eroding mesh and emitted particles. We can fix the gaps by adding an extra layer of procedurally scattered particles.

Let's follow the next steps to add an extra layer of particles:

1. Branch out from the **Attribute Remap** node that remaps mask into **emit** attribute.
2. Add a **Scatter** node after the **Attribute Remap** and turn off the **Force Total Count** checkbox. Since we will be scattering based on a custom attribute, we will use another scattering method.
3. Select the **Density Attribute** checkbox and type `emit` in the empty box.
4. Increase **Density Scale** to `50000`—you should see a dense point cloud.
5. Add a **Point Jitter** node and set the **S** value to `0.05` after the **Scatter** node to randomize point positions for a fuzzier look.
6. Connect the result of **Point Jitter** into the **Merge** node that combines the eroding mesh and dissolving particles.
7. Preview the updated simulation.

Refer to *Figure 7.21* for the updated look of the three combined layers:

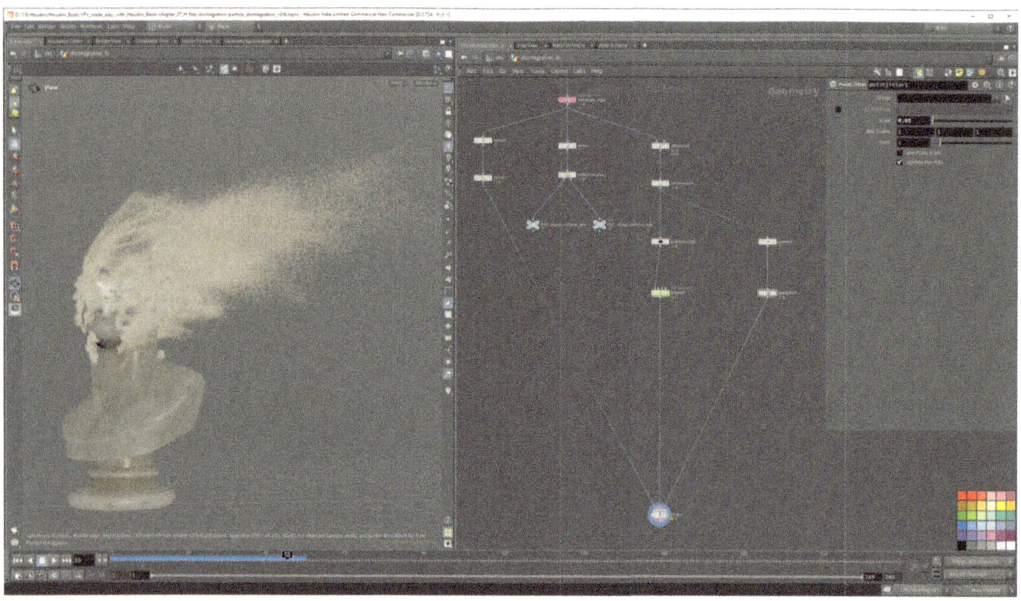

Figure 7.21 – Adding an extra procedural fill layer

Now, we can see much better connectivity between the dissolving particles and the eroding mesh. The extra layer also adds much more realism during the growth of the effect.

To complete this part, I recommend optimizing the dissolving particles layer attributes with **Attribute Delete** and caching all the layers to disk before rendering (see *Chapter 3* for particle optimization and caching).

Before bringing all the effect layers into **Solaris** for rendering, let's create some attributes for the particles by following the next steps:

1. Add an **Attribute Wrangle** node after the cached dissolving particles and write the following expression to create a particle scale:

   ```
   @pscale = 0.0075;.
   ```

2. Add the following expression in the next line to randomize the particle scale based on the `mass` attribute:

```
@pscale *= fit(@mass, 0.5, 1, 0.5, 1.25);
```

3. Additionally, we can fade away the particle scale using the age attribute by adding this expression to the wrangle:

```
@pscale *= fit(@age, 3.5, 0.85, 0.55, 1);
```

Refer to *Figure 7.22* to see the dissolving particle scale attribute:

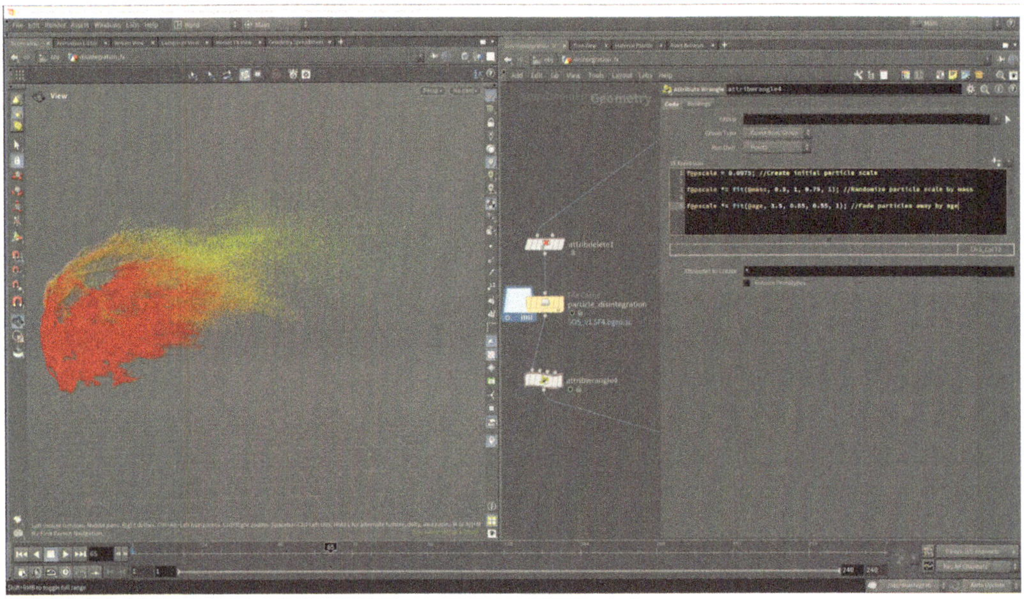

Figure 7.22 – Dissolving particle scale attribute

4. Add an **Attribute Wrangle** node after the extra scattered particle layer and type the following expression in the box: `@pscale = 0.0035;`.
5. Create output **Null** nodes for each effect layer and name them accordingly: `OUT_render_eroding_mesh`, `OUT_render_dissolving_particles`, and `OUT_render_blending_edge_points`.

Next, we will import all the disintegration layer outputs to **Solaris** for lighting and rendering.

Disintegration effect lighting and rendering

Follow these steps to bring all the disintegration elements into the **stage** context for look development :

1. Import all three disintegration layers into **Solaris** with the corresponding **SOP Import** nodes and merge them with the **Merge** node.
2. Add a **Camera** that will frame the disintegration object and particle layers from a nice angle.
3. Experiment with **Karma Physical Sky**, **Sunlight**, and **Dome Light with HDRI** to achieve interesting lighting.
4. For **Environment Dome Light**, I used a free HDRI map downloaded from Poly Haven named `kloppenheim_02` (see the *Technical requirements* section).

Refer to *Figure 7.23* to see the imported geometry objects and initial lighting settings:

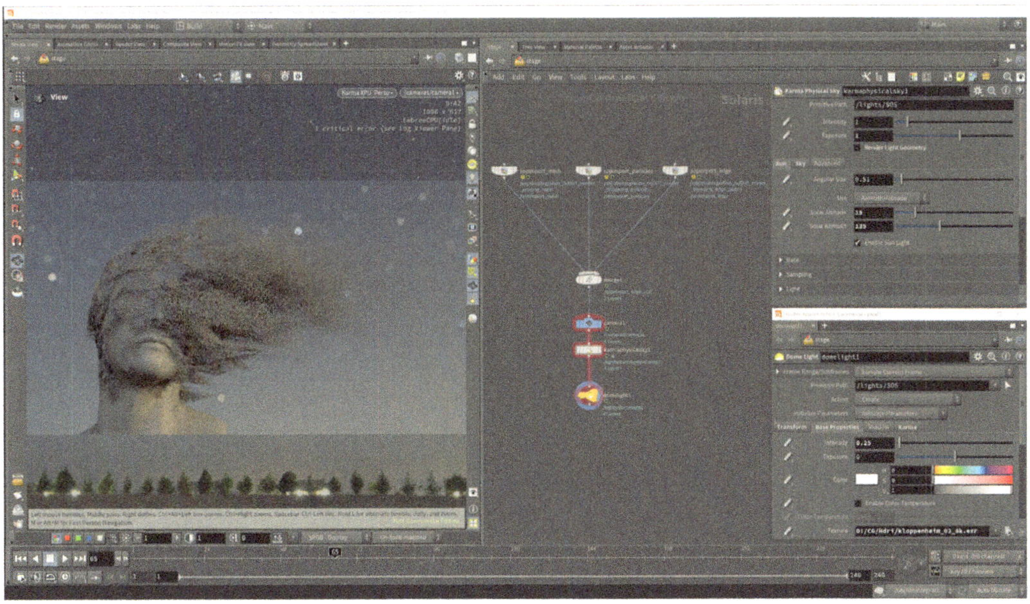

Figure 7.23 – Import to Solaris and lighting

The initial lighting test looks pretty good; however, we can add more realism by creating interesting materials representing the marble surface that will use textures downloaded with the bust asset.

Let's follow the next steps to add materials and textures:

1. Add a **Material Library** where we will create shaders for the effect layers.
2. Dive inside the **Material Library** and create two **Karma Material Builder** nodes for disintegrating objects and dissolving particles.
3. Use the **MtlX PBR Texture Set** node to import and connect the 3D object's textures and connect them into corresponding channels in the material (see the *Lighting and rendering a realistic fire with smoke* section in *Chapter 4*, where this process is described in detail).
4. For the particle material, you can bring in the particle color attribute through **MtlX Geometry Color** node and connect it to the base color of **mtlxstandard_surface**.
5. Play with the **Roughness** parameter on the particles to make the particles less or more shiny.
6. Assign the material using the **Material Linker** node.

Refer to *Figure 7.24* to see the materials and textures network:

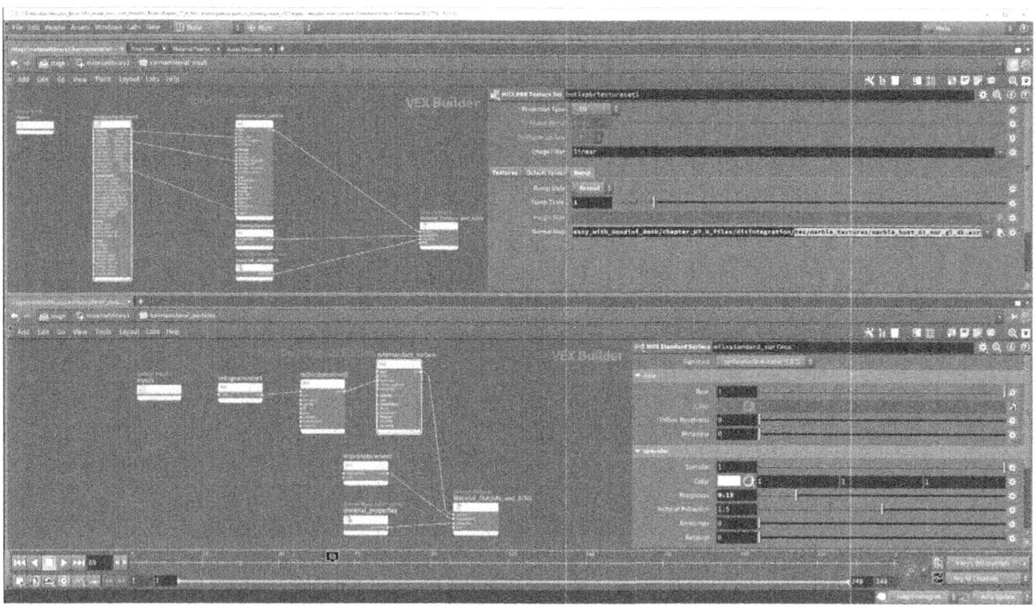

Figure 7.24 – Adding materials and textures

Finally, let's look at the render settings to finalize the disintegration project into a rendered image:

1. Add a **Karma** node and, on the **Rendering** tab, click on the **Camera Effects** subtab.
2. On the **Camera Effects** tab, turn on **Velocity Blur** to achieve realistic motion blur on the motion of particles.
3. Adjust the rendering quality with **Path Traced Samples** (minimum 16 on **Karma CPU** and minimum 64 on **Karma XPU**).
4. On the **Image Output** tab, click on the **Filters** sub-tab and enable **Denoiser** for a noise-free render.
5. Render image sequence to disk using **usdrender_rop**.

   usdrender_rop is a special node in the **Solaris** context that renders your scene. It works kind of like a *render button* for scenes built in the **stage** context using **Universal Scene Description (USD)**. When you press render on this node, it tells Houdini to take everything in your scene (geometry, materials, lights, and camera) and create the final image using a render engine, that is **Karma**.

Refer to *Figure 7.25* to see the final rendered result:

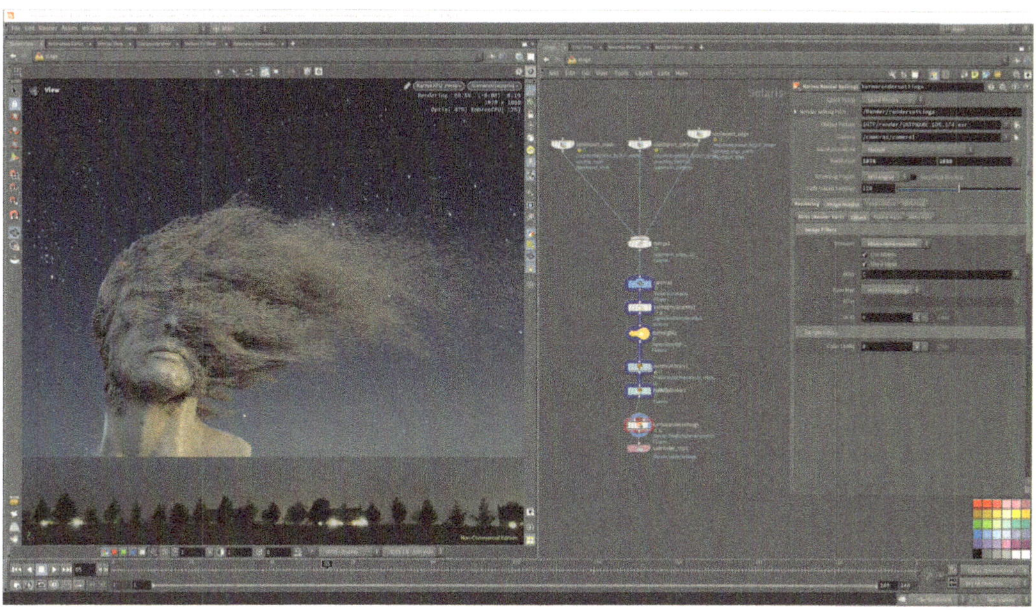

Figure 7.25 – Adding an extra procedural fill layer

Congratulations on creating your first disintegration effect in Houdini!

Summary

In this chapter, we have utilized many workflows for geometry and attribute manipulation using techniques learned mainly from *Chapter 1* and how to create a more complex particle emission and motion by utilizing the particle basics from *Chapter 3*.

Finally, we have shaded, lit, and rendered the entire scene with custom objects, textures, and materials in **Solaris** by utilizing techniques from *Chapter 3* and *Chapter 4*.

In the next chapter, we will continue with our case studies by creating an explosion effect, which is very popular in the world of VFX.

8

Effects Case Study: Explosion FX

In this chapter, you'll learn how to create realistic explosions in Houdini using its powerful pyro tools and node-based workflow. We will build upon the foundational Pyro FX skills introduced in *Chapter 4*, incorporating Houdini's advanced explosion toolset to enhance and expand this knowledge.

By gaining hands-on experience with tools such as **Pyro Burst Source** and **Pyro Solver**, you'll develop a deeper understanding of how to art-direct complex explosions and control their behavior with precision. These skills are essential for producing high-quality, cinematic FX shots that meet the demands of modern VFX and game pipelines.

Here are the main topics that we will cover in this chapter:

- **Pyro Burst Source** tools for explosion elements
- Sourcing additional explosion layers
- Hero explosion build walk-through
- Explosion layers caching, optimization, and output
- Explosion elements shading and rendering

By the end of this chapter, you will be equipped with all the knowledge needed to create a realistic explosion effect in Houdini.

Figure 8.1 shows an example of the explosion effect that we will be creating:

Figure 8.1 – Explosion in Houdini

Technical requirements

A Houdini file with notes is provided in the book's GitHub repository to help you explore and navigate the nuclear explosion setup: `https://github.com/PacktPublishing/VFX-Made-Easy-with-Houdini`.

To view the chapter images in better clarity, scan the provided QR code. It will direct you to a dedicated link where you can take a look at the images.

After completing this chapter, I would also encourage you to experiment with different sourcing methods and settings to create your own explosion from any source of inspiration.

Now, let's jump into Houdini and explore the new explosion tools.

Pyro Burst Source tools for explosion elements

As always, we will start by creating a new Houdini project. We will give it the name `Explosions` and open up an empty geometry container.

You will find all the new explosion tools and presets in the **Geometry** level of the **obj** context. All you need to do is press *Tab* and type `pyro` in the search bar.

Refer to *Figure 8.2* to see the available explosion tools through the **TAB Menu**:

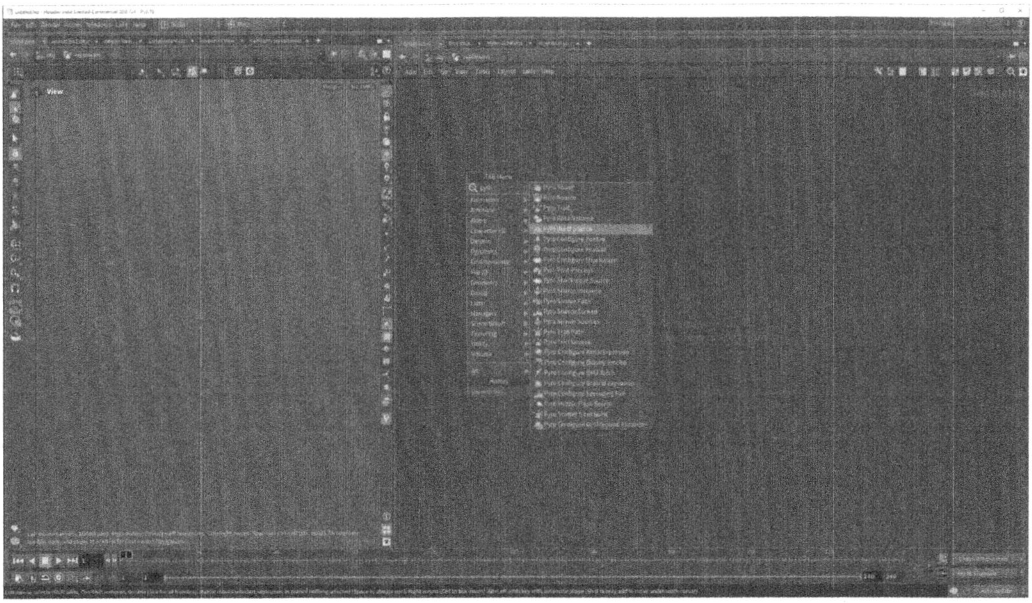

Figure 8.2 – Explosion pyro tools

So far, we have explored the **Pyro Source** and **Pyro Solver** nodes, in the introduction to Pyro FX in *Chapter 4*. **Pyro Source** is a simple node that can help create an emitter for fire and smoke; however, for the complex shapes and motion of the explosion elements, SideFX has created a specific node called **Pyro Burst Source**.

The **Pyro Burst Source node** is a powerful tool designed to generate explosive events by creating particle bursts of density, burn, temperature, and velocity for pyro simulations. It provides a procedural way to define key characteristics of an explosion, such as the intensity, shape, and timing of the bursts.

The **Pyro Burst Source** node also allows artists to control attributes such as burst duration, spread, and randomness, enabling the creation of complex, dynamic effects with precision. Often used in conjunction with other pyro tools, the **Pyro Burst Source** node simplifies the setup of large-scale explosions and offers a high degree of customization for achieving realistic results.

Creating a simple explosion using Pyro Burst tools

Let's follow these steps to create a simple explosion, using the **Pyro Burst** tools:

1. Add a **Pyro Burst Source** node through the **TAB Menu**.
2. In the **Pyro Burst Source** node, click on the **Quick Setups** drop-down menu.
3. Choose the **Pyro Simulation** option.
4. Play the simulation till frame **40** to see the simple explosion fireball.

Figure 8.3 shows the **Pyro Burst** settings and node network:

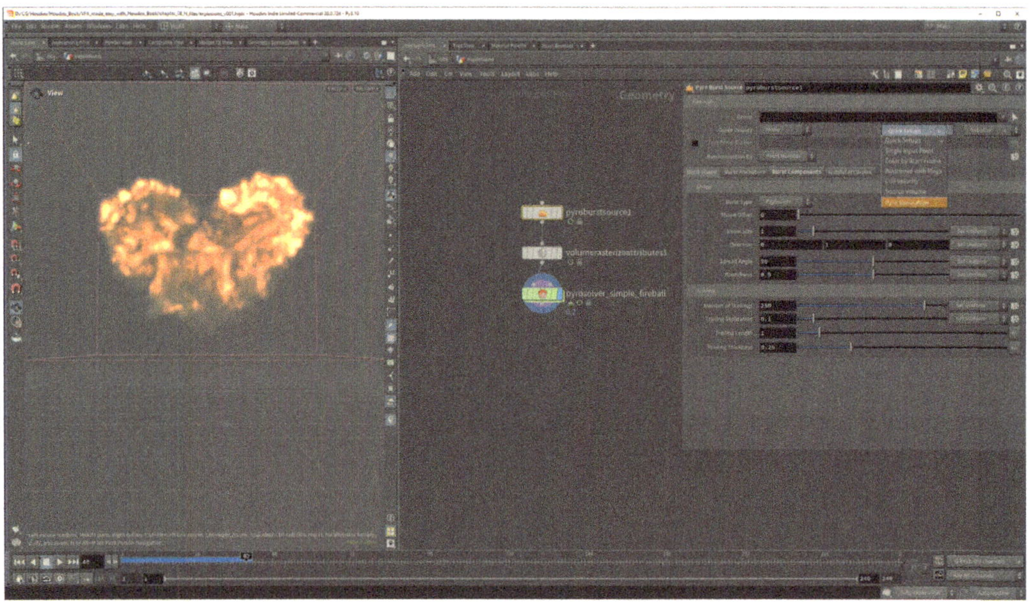

Figure 8.3 – Quick explosion setup

Let's break down what happened under the hood in this simple explosion setup:

1. Placing the **Pyro Burst Source** node is usually the first step for creating the explosive source shape. Currently, the **Pyro Burst Source** node can generate four different explosive sources or burst types:
    - **Explosion**: Designed to generate a variety of explosive-looking shapes
    - **Shockwave**: Designed to generate a variety of initial shapes for different types of shockwaves

- **Blast Rings**: Designed to generate a variety of flat rings expanding along the blast for large explosions
- **Muzzle Flash**: Designed to generate shapes resembling blasts coming from a firearm or powerful explosions bursting into the air

It is important to create a burst type and shape that corresponds to the type of effect you want to create. For example, choose **Explosion** for different types of blasts and explosions with fiery elements, or the **Shockwave** type as a starting point for the impact wave from the explosion. **Blast Rings** can be used to add an additional air impact source, and **Muzzle Flash** can be used as a source to simulate gun bursts.

2. The **Pyro Burst Source** node created an interesting explosive shape that consists of particles with attributes specific to pyro simulation, such as density, burn, temperature, and **v (velocity)**.
3. After choosing **Pyro Simulation Setup** from **Quick Setups** of the **Pyro Burst Source** node, the tool auto-generated two new nodes with settings configured for us:
   - The first auto-generated node is our well-known **Volume Rasterize Attributes**, which converts the burst particles and attributes into a volumetric fields source
   - The second auto-generated node is **Pyro Solver**, which takes all the volumetric source data and applies it to a pyro simulation
4. Additionally, **Pyro Solver** has set specific settings and parameters (explained later in the chapter) controlling the burn expansion, temperature, and detailing to achieve an expanding, quick-rising fireball.

Moving on, we will explore some of the important settings to adjust the explosion source and create a bigger explosion.

Adjusting the explosion source

Before we delve into the details, I suggest using this basic setup as a guide and a good starting point for nodes and settings needed to create a basic explosion. By adjusting just these three nodes (**Pyro Burst Source**, **Volume Rasterize Attributes**, and **Pyro Solver**), we can create many different explosions and add variation very easily.

The **Pyro Burst Source** node has many settings, and I will guide you through the most important tabs and parameters. However, I encourage you to play with the **Pyro Burst** settings and see how different parameters would change the explosion's shape and look.

Now, let's proceed by adjusting some quick settings in **Pyro Burst Source** to make the explosion look bigger and smokier:

1. Select the **Pyro Burst Source** node to adjust the settings in the **Burst Shape** tab.
2. Set **Shape Offset** to 2 to create a different random explosive shape.
3. Adjust the **Roundness** parameter from **0.5** to `0.75` to make the shape more round.
4. Reduce **Trailing Separation** to `0.075` to have more particles in the explosion shape.
5. Increase the **Trailing Length** parameter to 5, so the spiky trails extend back for stronger sourcing.
6. Change **Trailing Thickness** to `0.125` to have thinner and more detailed spike trails.

Refer to *Figure 8.4* to see the **Pyro Burst Source** settings and the updated burst shape:

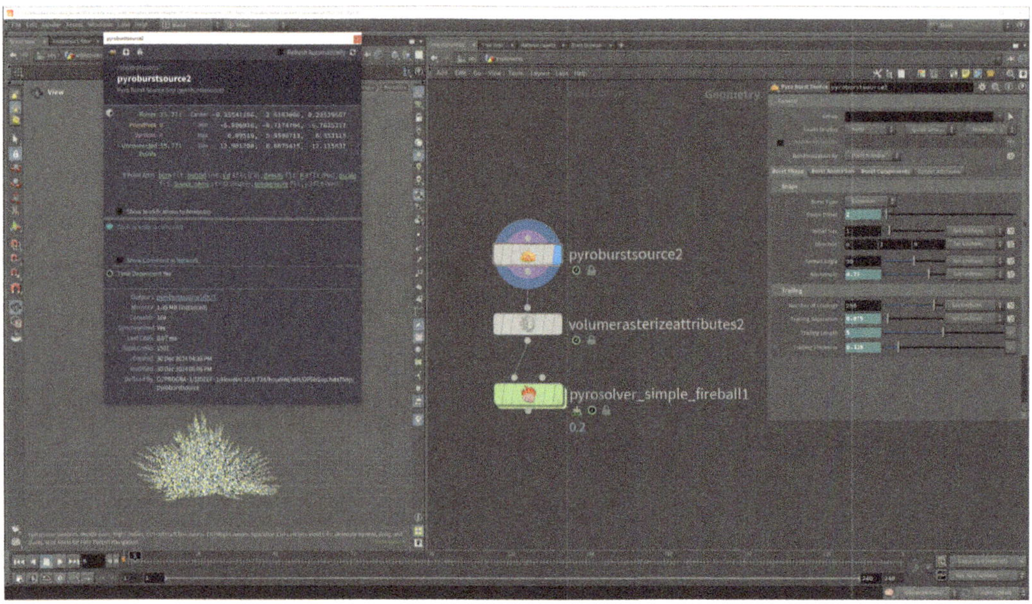

Figure 8.4 – Pyro Burst settings

As you can see in *Figure 8.4*, we have all the important attributes needed for explosion simulation. To continue adjusting our source, we will increase the burst shape expansion and add more smoke to the source attributes.

Let's follow the next steps to add further modifications to the explosion source to make it look bigger and smokier:

1. In the **Pyro Burst Source** node, switch to the **Burst Animation** tab, where you can adjust the **Start Frame**, **Duration**, and **Outward Expansion** properties of the explosive shape.

2. Increase the **Outward Expansion** parameter to 5 to have the explosion expand faster.
3. Switch to the **Burst Components** tab to control the explosion source attributes and their values.
4. In the **Pyro Sources** rollout, you can see all the source attributes in numbered tabs:
    - The *first* tab has the **Density** attribute, which controls the initial smoke density
    - The *second* tab controls the initial **Temperature** value
    - The *third* tab is responsible for the **Burn** attribute, which acts as the fuel that ignites during the explosion
5. Increase **Density Source Scale** by 5, to source more smoke into the simulation.
6. Turn on the **Enable Noise** parameter to achieve variation in the smoky areas of the explosion.
7. Finally, set the display flag on the **Pyro Solver** node and play the simulation till frame **42** to see the updated result. The explosion is now much bigger and smokier.

Refer to *Figure 8.5* to see the updated explosion, compared to the fireball (from *Figure 8.3*) next to it, with the default setup settings.

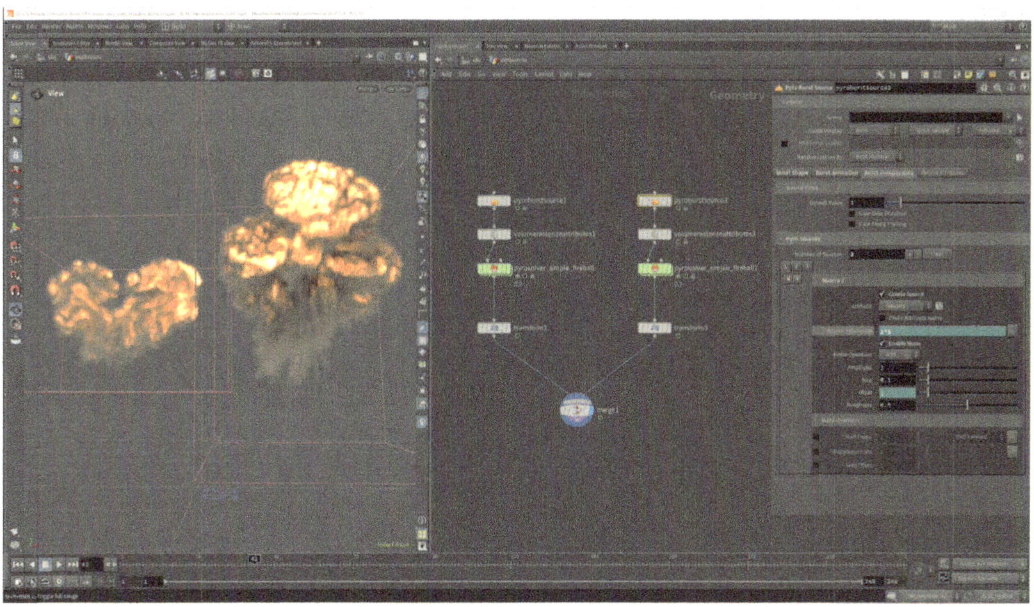

Figure 8.5 – Adjusted fireball

By adjusting just a couple of settings in **Pyro Burst Source**, we have achieved a completely different explosion without even changing the **Pyro Solver** settings. However, for more control over the simulation and explosion behavior, we will now proceed with the **Pyro Solver** node.

> Tip
>
> If you need to refresh your knowledge of pyro simulations and volumetric field basics, I recommend referring to *Chapter 4*.

Before we start exploring the explosion settings in the **Pyro Solver** node, I would like to take a look at the **Volume Rasterize Attributes** node that was automatically created after using **Quick Setups**. As we know from *Chapter 4*, this node is used to convert point-based attributes into volumetric fields that can be used in volumetric simulations.

When we used the quick explosion setup in the **Pyro Burst Source** node, Houdini added a **Volume Rasterize Attributes** node that has all the point attributes linked with the corresponding **Pyro Burst Source**. This auto-linking is very convenient for us as we don't have to manually add all the attributes that we want to convert into volumetric fields. Additionally, every time we adjust the **Pyro Burst Source** node's attributes, the **Volume Rasterize Attributes** node will also update the corresponding fields.

You are also welcome to do everything manually, by placing a **Volume Rasterize Attributes** node from scratch and typing only the list of attributes that you want in your pyro simulation, in a similar way to what we did in *Chapter 4*.

Moving on, we will adjust different parameters in the **Pyro Solver** node to quickly change the shape and look of the explosion.

Adjusting the Pyro Solver node

Let's select **Pyro Solver** and proceed with the following steps to make adjustments to the explosion simulation:

1. In **Pyro Solver**, go to the **Collision** tab to add ground collision.
2. In the **Ground Planes** rollout, set **Y Ground Plane** to **Closed Below 0**. This will force every voxel of the explosion that is below 0 on the *Y* axis to collide with an invisible ground.
3. Play the simulation till frame **40** to see the updated explosion shape.

Refer to *Figure 8.6* to see the simulation settings and updated explosion shape:

Figure 8.6 – Adjusted explosion shape

As we can see, by just adding the ground plane into the simulation, we achieved a much more interesting explosion with a stronger smoke tail and a better fireball shape.

For the next example, we will continue with the same pyro simulation, where we will turn this into a more spread-out ground explosion rather than a fireball. You can copy the three nodes (**Pyro Burst Source**, **Volume Rasterize Attributes**, and **Pyro Solver**) of the fireball setup to the side and continue adjusting the **Pyro Solver** node.

Changing the explosion behavior

To change the explosion behavior from a *fast-rising fireball* to a *spreading blast*, we will be increasing the initial velocity, increasing the fire expansion, and reducing the buoyancy that is responsible for pushing the volume based on the temperature.

Let's continue with the following steps to further adjust the simulation:

1. In the **Pyro Solver** node, go to the **Sourcing** tab and scroll down to the **Velocity** rollout.
2. Change **Velocity Operation** to **Add** to accumulate the source velocity over time.
3. Increase **Source Scale** to `0.75` to have a stronger source velocity injection.

4. Move to the **Divergence** rollout and increase **Divergence** to `50` to have a much higher burning expansion.
5. Switch to the **Shape** tab and reduce **Buoyancy** to `0.1` to make the explosion rise up more slowly.
6. Play the simulation until frame **40** to see the result.

Refer to *Figure 8.7* to see the updated explosion shape and parameters:

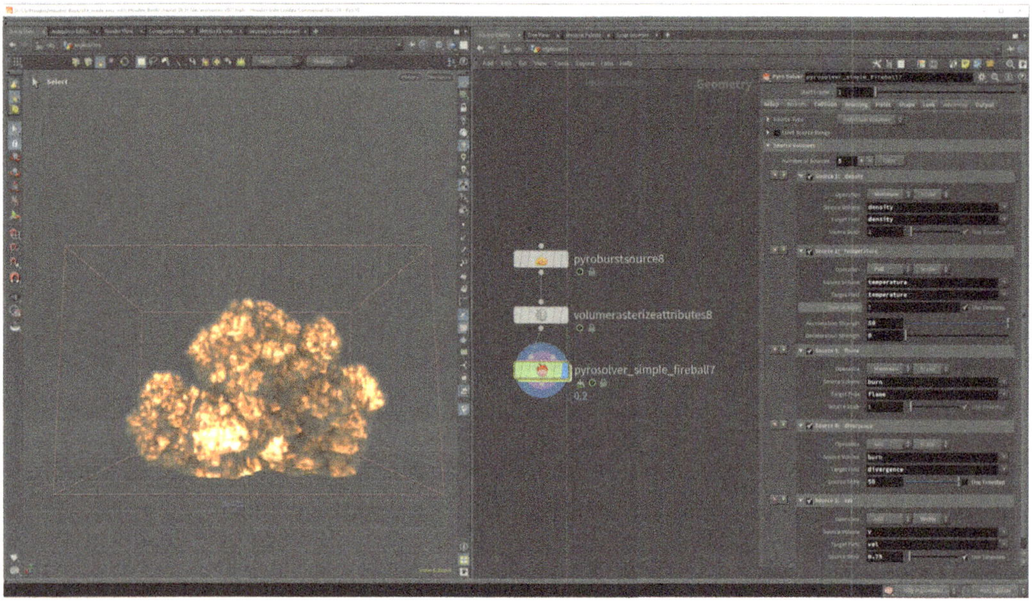

Figure 8.7 – Modifying source volumes

By only adjusting the **Velocity** and **Divergence** source volumes and reducing **Buoyancy**, we have achieved a completely different look. Keeping all this in mind, I encourage you to experiment with these parameters and see how they would change the simulation.

Also, feel free to use a **Transform** node and rotate your explosion around the *Y* axis to see what shapes are generated from different sides and angles.

Before we move on to the next section, I want to introduce a new node called **Pyro Bake Volume**, which can significantly improve the look and quality of the explosion both in the viewport and during rendering, as we'll see in the next section.

Improving the look of pyro explosions

To have more control over the look of pyro explosions, both in the viewport and during rendering, SideFX has created a **Pyro Bake Volume** node.

The **Pyro Bake Volume node** is designed to enhance the visual quality of pyro simulations by applying post-simulation adjustments to volumetric data, such as density, temperature, and color fields. This node enables artists to fine-tune attributes such as brightness, contrast, and color mapping, ensuring the final render aligns with the desired artistic vision.

The **Pyro Bake Volume** node also provides tools for optimizing volume visualization, such as ramp controls for shading and emission parameters, as well as support for adding detail and enhancing the appearance of fire and smoke. Using the **Pyro Bake Volume** node is an essential step in the pyro workflow, allowing for efficient iteration and polished results.

Let's follow the next steps to improve the look of our pyro simulation:

1. Add a **Pyro Bake Volume** node after the **Pyro Solver** node.
2. In the **Smoke** tab, increase the **Smoke Density** value to `25`.
3. Set the desired color of the smoke by using the **Smoke Color** palette or **Color Ramp**.
4. Switch to the **Scatter** tab and enable **Scatter** to map the explosion temperature to emission.
5. Increase **Scatter Intensity Scale** to `1000` to make the emission brighter.
6. In the **Masking** rollout, play with the **Mask Center** parameter for a different look of the explosion core. I have set the value to `0.25`.

Refer to *Figure 8.8* to see the comparison of the explosion look with and without the **Pyro Bake Volume** node:

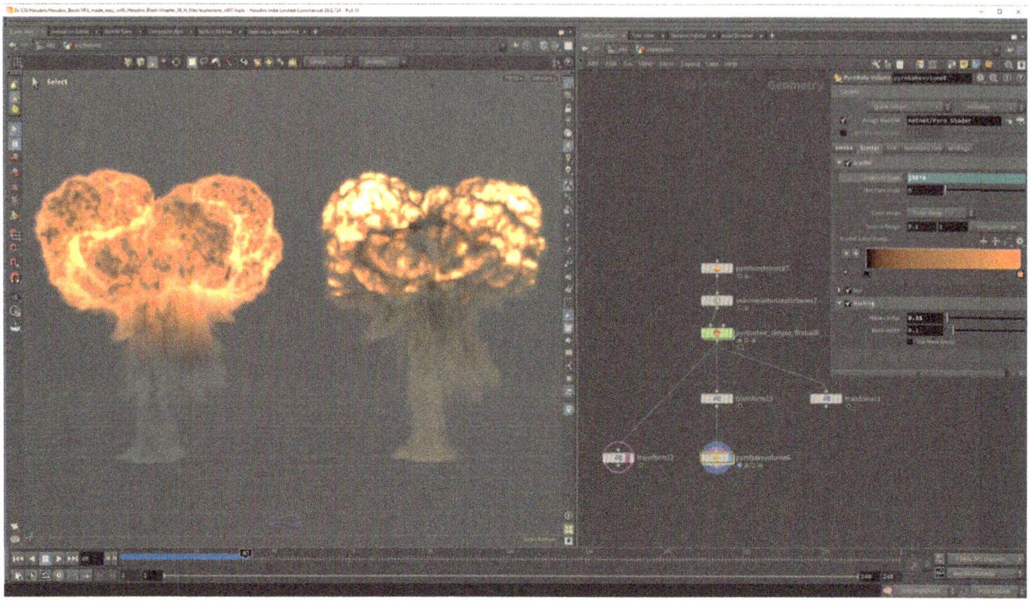

Figure 8.8 – Pyro Bake Volume

As you will notice, **Pyro Bake Volume** gives a much more detailed and realistic look to any pyro explosion simulation.

Usually, the **Density** and **Scatter** options are enough for the final look; however, you can also add a fiery core as an additional layer by enabling it in the **Fire** tab.

Additionally, you can have complete control over the bright, fiery scattered areas by adjusting how the scatter is being calculated. By default, the **Scatter** field is formed from **Temperature** combined with **Density**. However, you can generate a **Scatter** field from any combination of the **Flame**, **Temperature**, and **Density** fields. All of the adjustments to the field mappings are located in the **Bindings** tab of the **Pyro Bake Volume** node.

Refer to *Figure 8.9* to see an example of the **Pyro Bake Volume** node applied to a ground-spreading explosion:

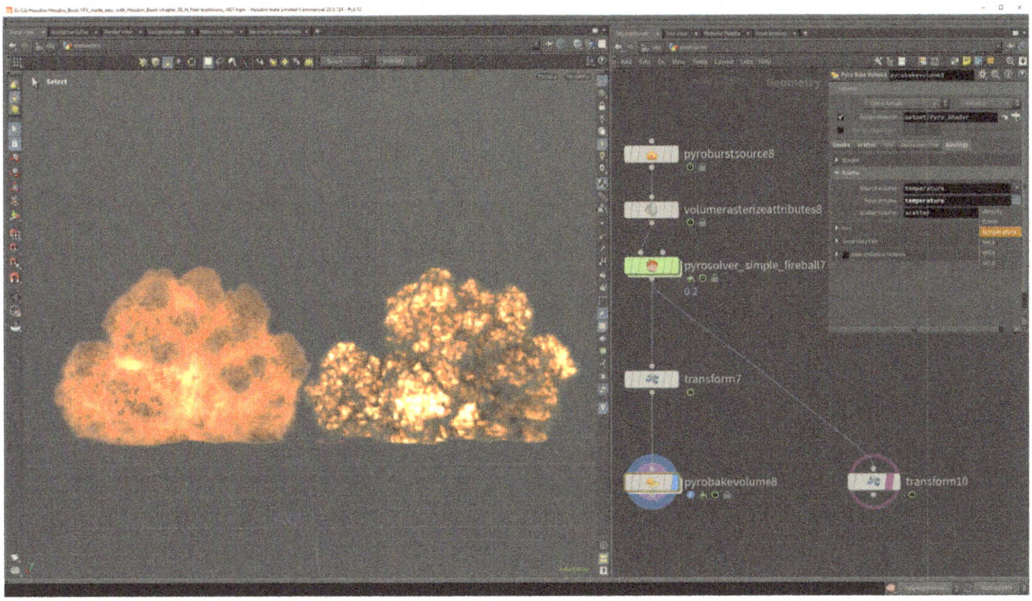

Figure 8.9 – Pyro Bake Volume

As we can see, setting **Pyro Bake Volume**'s **Scatter** fields to be calculated only from **Temperature** resulted in a softer, scattered explosion look.

> Tip
>
> For further learning and exploration of how to create fireball and ground explosion setups, I recommend trying to add **Pyro Configure Fireball** and **Pyro Configure Ground Explosion** setups from the **TAB Menu**. These setups are created by SideFX and are a great resource to learn which settings and parameters can be used to achieve a more advanced explosion.

In the next section, we will explore how to source and simulate other important explosion elements, such as ground dust shockwaves.

Sourcing additional explosion layers

Any fiery explosion on screen can look sophisticated and detailed by itself; however, for more realism and complexity, it is always a good idea to create additional explosion layers. Ultimately, you can add as many layers as you want, consisting of shockwaves, ground dust, blast rings, fiery spark trails, and so on. That said, the second important and most visible layer that can add much more realism and complexity is the **volumetric dust shockwave**.

Let's continue with the following steps to create a dust shockwave source:

1. Create a **Pyro Burst Source** node and set **Burst Type** to **Shockwave**.
2. Enable **Add Shape Noise** to make the circular shape more interesting and broken up.
3. Reduce the **Size** parameter of **Shape Noise** to `0.5` to include smaller details.
4. In the **Point Distribution** rollout, reduce the point **Separation** to `0.05` to increase the particle density in the source.

These initial parameters are responsible for the shaping and particle density of the shockwave emitter. Refer to *Figure 8.10* to see the initial parameters and the shockwave shape compared to the explosion emitter:

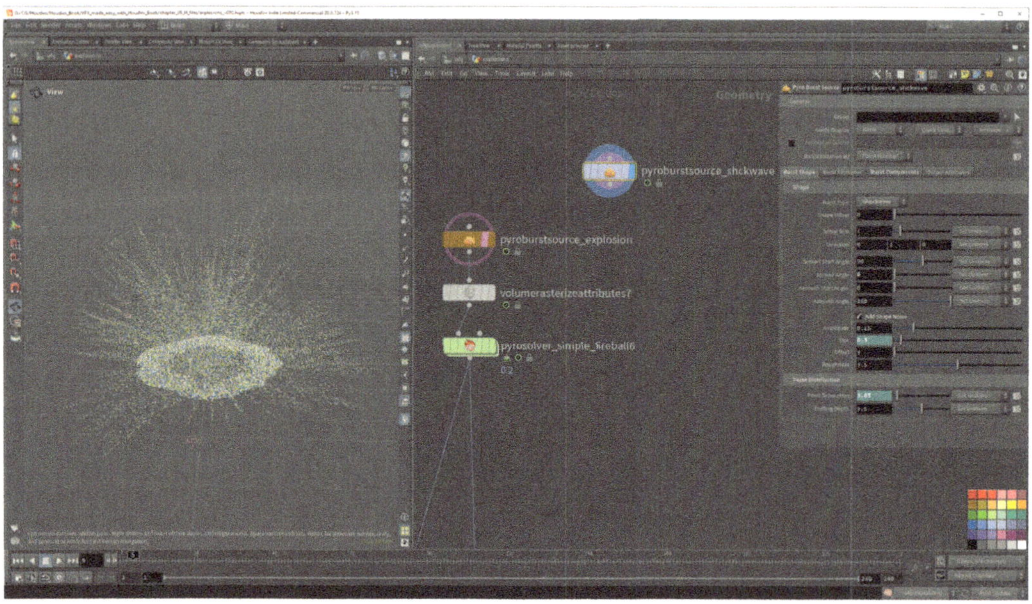

Figure 8.10 – Initial shockwave source

As you can see, currently our shockwave shape is smaller than the explosion source shape, which can lead to unrealistic results if we proceed with this size. We'll fix this in the next section.

Adjusting the animation and expansion of the shockwave source

Generally, the shockwave tends to spread outward at a longer distance than the explosion core. Therefore, it is always a good idea to compare the emitter sizes before simulation.

Let's follow the next steps to adjust the animation and expansion of the shockwave source:

1. In the **Pyro Burst Shockwave** node, switch to the **Burst Animation** tab.
2. Increase **Exterior Expansion** from **3** to 6 to make the shockwave source cover a bigger area.
3. Switch to the **Output Attributes** tab and enable the **Add Velocity Noise** option to add variation for expanding velocities.
4. Switch to the **Burst Components** tab and disable the sourcing of the **Burn** component, as the shockwave will mainly consist of density-based ground and smoke dust.
5. Go to frame **5** and compare the shockwave source with the explosion source.

Figure 8.11 shows the updated shockwave size and settings:

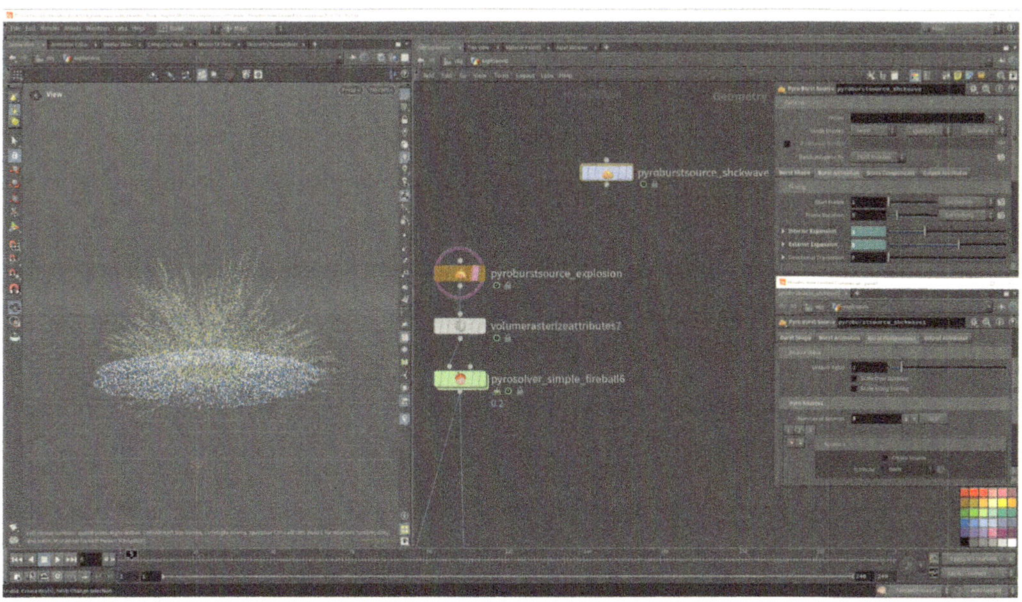

Figure 8.11 – Shockwave burst animation

As we can see, now the shockwave is covering more area and is slightly bigger in radius than the explosion shape. During the simulation, the shockwave will expand even more due to the volume pressure and velocity, which will result in a much more realistic look.

For the next step, let's utilize the **Quick Setups** option on **Pyro Burst Source** and choose **Pyro Simulation** to create an automatic **Volume Rasterize Source** node and **Pyro Solver** with initial recommended settings. As a result, you are going to see a fiery blast circle, which we will turn into a smoky shockwave by following the next steps:

1. Select the newly created **Pyro Solver** and go to the **Sourcing** tab.
2. Increase the **Sourcing Density** value to `10` to source more smoke.
3. Change **Velocity Source Operation** to **Add** and set **Source Scale** to `1` so the shockwave pushes outward with higher velocity.
4. Switch to the **Collision** tab and set **Y Ground Plane** to **Closed Below** to add invisible ground collision.
5. Switch to the **Setup** tab and set **Advection - Reflection** to **Single-Project** to keep the energy of the simulation for a longer time and increase the amount of swirls.
6. Switch to the **Fields** tab and reduce **Dissipation** to `0.01` so the smoke lingers for a longer time after the emission ends.
7. In the **Temperature** rollout, disable **Emit from Flame**, so the shockwave doesn't emit any extra temperature as it wouldn't in the real world.
8. Switch to the **Shape** tab to adjust buoyancy and extra noise forces applied to the shockwave.
9. Expand the **Buoyancy** rollout and enable the **Density Influences Gravity** option, so the shockwave dust starts settling down in the heavier areas instead of rising.
10. Reduce the **Disturbance** value to `15` so the shockwave edges become smoother.
11. Add a **Pyro Bake Volume** node to have more control over the shockwave shading in the viewport.
12. Preview both the shockwave and the previously created fireball to see how both effects work together at frame **48**.

Refer to *Figure 8.12* to see the updated shockwave with the fireball explosion:

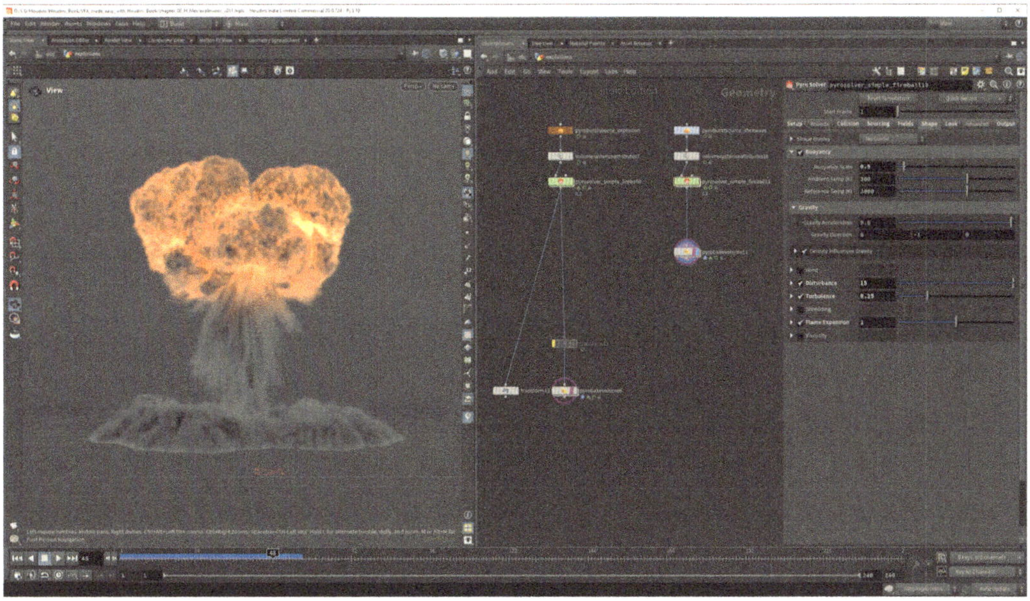

Figure 8.12 – Shockwave simulated with the explosion

All the settings that we have set in the previous steps are usually a good starting point for a realistic shockwave motion. Additionally, I encourage you to play with the **Pyro Burst Source** node and **Pyro Solver** settings to change the look, speed, and area coverage of the shockwave compared to the explosion size that you are creating.

In the next section, I will do a walk-through of a more complex explosion setup, which you can access through the project file.

Hero explosion build walk-through

I recommend utilizing the Houdini file for this chapter (see the *Technical requirements* section) and keeping it open as I guide you through this section to enhance your learning experience.

First, let me explain the term **hero explosion**. A "hero explosion" typically means a big, complex explosion that is the main action or point of interest of any particular scene or story. Usually, hero explosions have many layers and stages that increase in complexity and the amount of interesting details in the shape and motion.

My main source of inspiration for this hero explosion was classic cinematic depictions of large-scale blasts, including iconic mushroom cloud visuals seen in movies and games.

Once you open the Houdini file for this chapter, you will see a geometry container named `explosions`. Inside the container, you will find a hero explosion setup as shown in *Figure 8.13*:

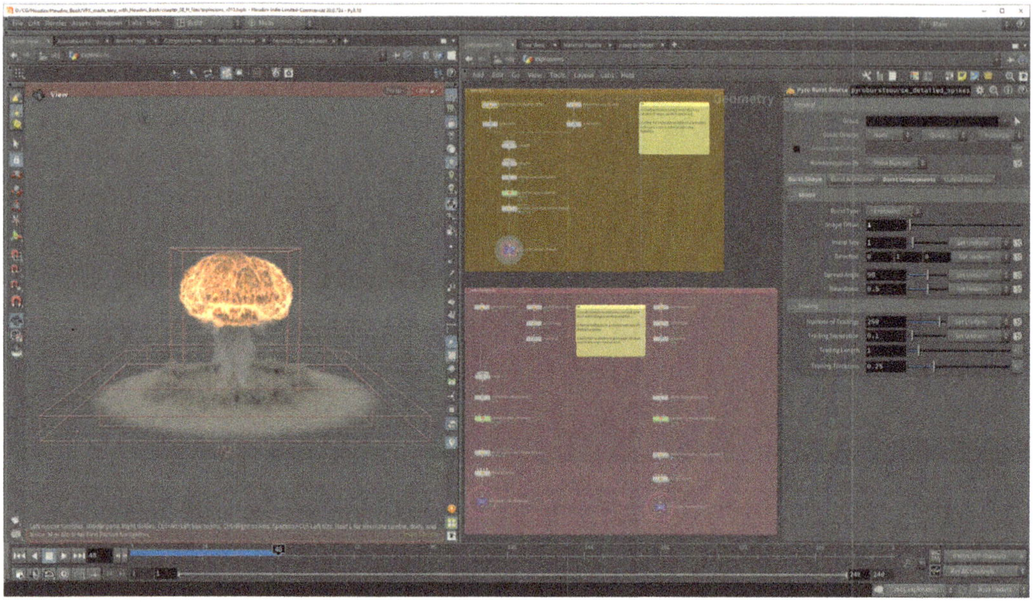

Figure 8.13 – Explosion build walk-through

This explosion setup in the Houdini file uses all the methods and techniques that we have learned about in this chapter and all of the previous chapters. The hero explosion build consists of two main parts:

- The main explosion fireball
- Hero shockwave layers

Let's explore these in the subsequent sections.

Exploring the main explosion build

We will start the walk-through from the orange-colored main explosion build. Refer to *Figure 8.14* to see the network view and the viewport focusing on the main explosion fireball:

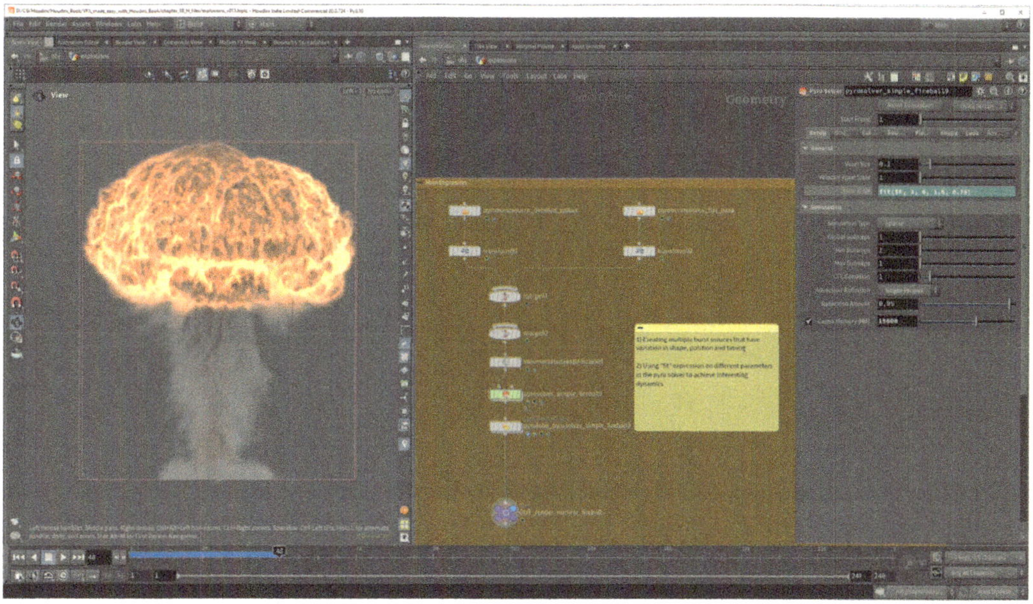

Figure 8.14 – Explosion build walk-through

The main difference between the advanced hero explosion and the one we created at the beginning of the chapter is in the number of source layers. There is also a difference in the shape, size, and procedurally animated settings in the **Pyro Solver** node, which we will go over in this walk-through.

While looking at the explosion setup in the provided Houdini file, you will notice that I'm using two differently shaped **Pyro Burst Source** nodes to achieve a thicker smoke trail and bigger expansion on the ground, which is usually a big feature in a nuclear explosion.

Refer to *Figure 8.15* to see how the source shape translates into a complex fireball:

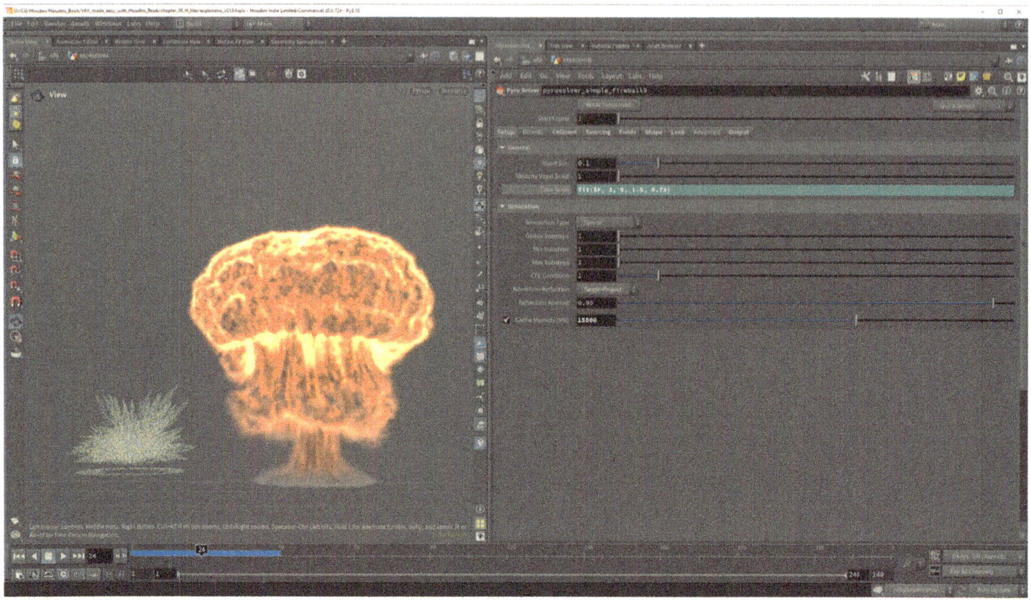

Figure 8.15 – Complex explosion source

You can creatively use two or more differently shaped and timed **Pyro Burst Source** nodes to achieve bigger area coverage and specific goal shapes of the hero explosion that you are aiming to create.

Additionally, you will notice that I am procedurally animating the time scale of the simulation with the help of the following expression:

```
fit($F, 3, 6, 1.5, 0.75)
```

Quick tip: Enhance your coding experience with the **AI Code Explainer** and **Quick Copy** features. Open this book in the next-gen Packt Reader. Click the **Copy** button

(1) to quickly copy code into your coding environment, or click the **Explain** button

(2) to get the AI assistant to explain a block of code to you.

Copy Explain

1 2

```
function calculate(a, b) {
  return {sum: a + b};
};
```


We have already used this expression, utilizing the `fit` function, in *Chapter 3* to set a varying particle scale attribute. In this case, we are using the `fit` expression to animate the time scale parameter from `1.5` to `0.75`. In the provided expression, we are specifying frames `3` and `6` as the start and end frames for the animation, and `$F` is a variable that will return the current frame number.

This technique is quite common for explosions, where we force the explosion to expand and shape faster with an increased timescale in the first three frames, and then the timescale decreases, leading to a slower motion that highlights the scale of the effect.

I encourage you to explore all other settings in the main explosion setup and see how these specific settings affect the shape, size, and timing of the effect.

Tip

Houdini files with setups can serve as a great source of knowledge, and being able to analyze and learn from the setups built by other artists is an important skill that will benefit you on this learning journey. Many of these setups can be downloaded for free from the **SideFX Content Library**: `https://www.sidefx.com/contentlibrary/?category=11&o=-publish_date&page=1`.

Moving on, I will walk you through the shockwaves setup next.

Exploring the hero shockwave layers

The shockwaves setup is very straightforward and was designed to mimic multiple layers of dust, smoke, and air density that kick up after the heavy impact of a large-scale cinematic explosion. It is always important to make the shockwave spread out faster and into a wider area than the main explosion. As can be seen from many examples of explosions in the real world, the bigger the explosion, the bigger and denser the shockwave generated as a result is going to be.

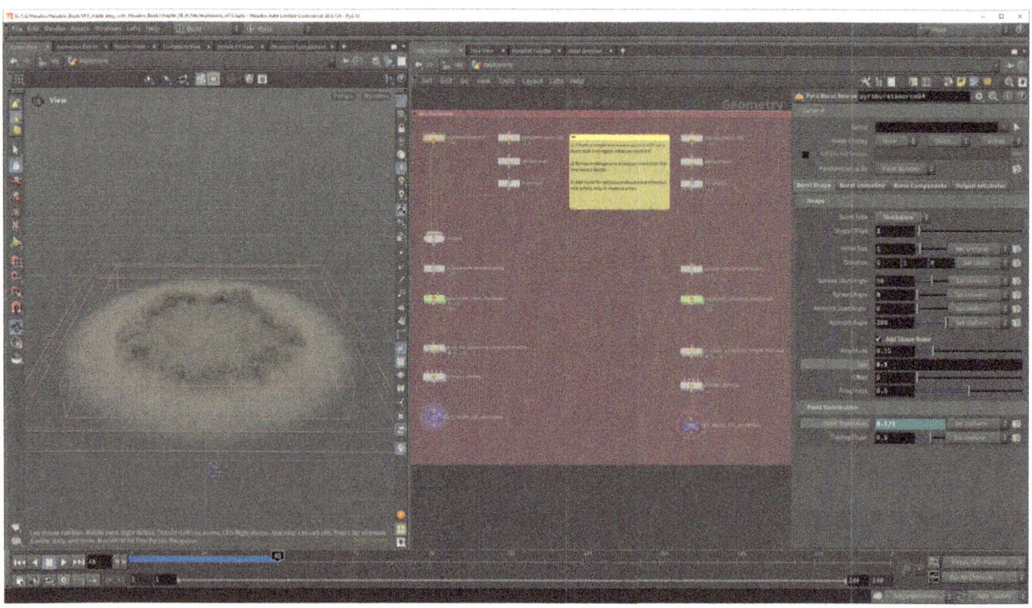

Figure 8.16 – Hero shockwave

For this setup, I have three source layers, as follows:

- The first source layer has the highest density and turbulence because it is the closest to the area where the explosion happened
- The next source layer is much lower in the *Y*-axis spread, is of a reduced density, and serves as a blend with the third shockwave
- The third shockwave layer is very flat but covers a much wider radius and serves to enhance the sense of the scale of the explosion

Refer to *Figure 8.17* to see the three shockwaves layers separated:

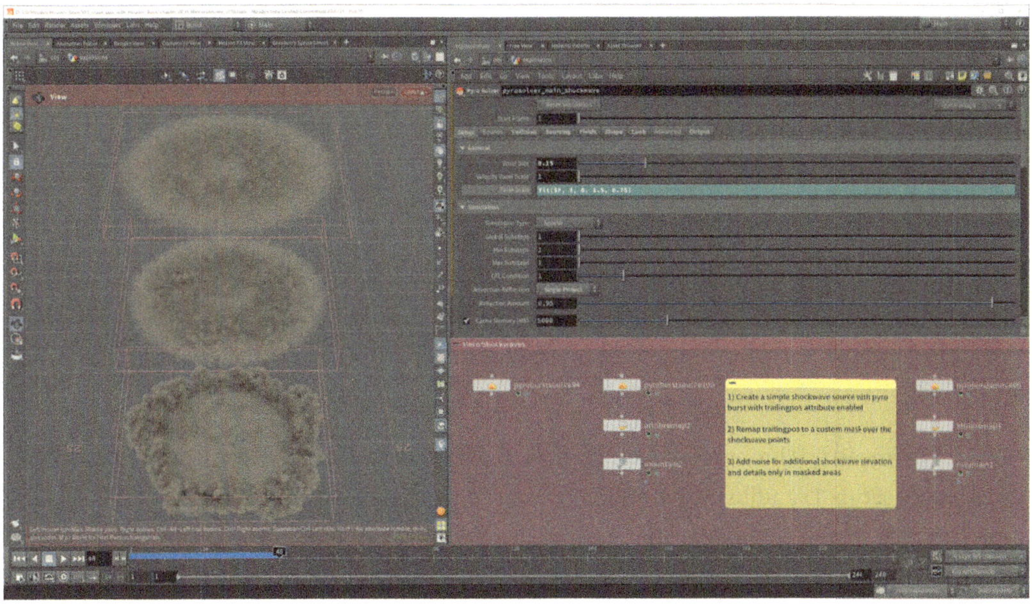

Figure 8.17 – Shockwaves breakdown

I have also placed some notes inside the Houdini file in a yellow box, describing some of the important and unique techniques involved in the setup. Referring to *Figure 8.17*, you can see that I have added an extra procedural noise attribute on the generated shockwave emitter to achieve more interesting height and detailed area variation.

Additionally, you can sharpen the shockwave density volume after the simulation with a simple preset inside the **Pyro Solver** node. The **Sharpen Volume** preset can be found inside **Pyro Solver**'s **Quick Setups** menu (see *Figure 8.18*):

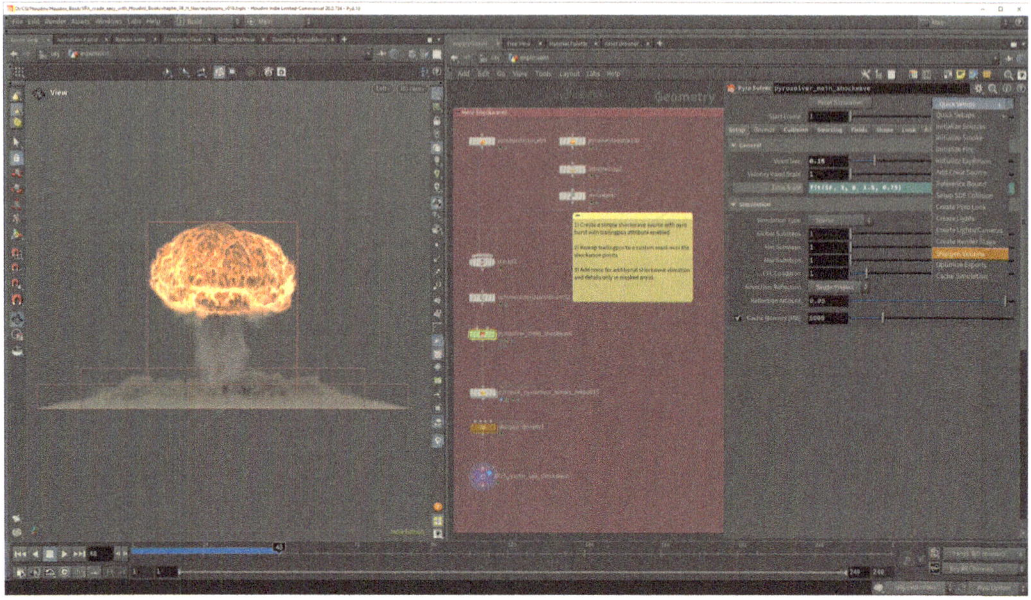

Figure 8.18 – Sharpen volume density

Take some time to go through the file and explore all the ins and outs of the hero explosion and shockwaves setup. Try adjusting the parameters and creating your own variation of the big hero explosion. Use all the techniques that we have learned about volumes, pyro sourcing, and simulations in *Chapter 4* and this chapter to help you in the process.

Next, we will transition to the optimization and caching of the hero explosion layers.

Explosion layers caching, optimization, and output

Once you start dealing with bigger simulations involving multiple layers and high-resolution volumes, optimization, caching, and having enough disc space available become increasingly important.

We are going to utilize the convenient optimization and output settings built into the **Pyro Solver** node before caching. Just like we did in the *Preparing the pyro simulation for output and caching* section in *Chapter 4*, we can navigate to the **Output** tab of the **Pyro Solver** node for each layer of the fireballs and shockwaves and enable the **Convert to VDB** and **Write 16-bit Float Values** checkboxes.

This step will compress and save all the simulation fields in a fast and lightweight VDB format. Additionally, we can save space by enabling the **Resample Volumes** checkbox, which, by default, will operate on the velocity field. Resampling vector volumes can save a lot of caching space since vector volumes store data that takes three times more space than any other float volume.

The resample operation will internally reduce the vector volume resolution by a specific factor provided in **Voxel Size Scale**. Usually, the default number of **2** works well and will save vector velocity volumes with a resolution decreased two times from the original.

Refer to *Figure 8.19* to see the optimization settings:

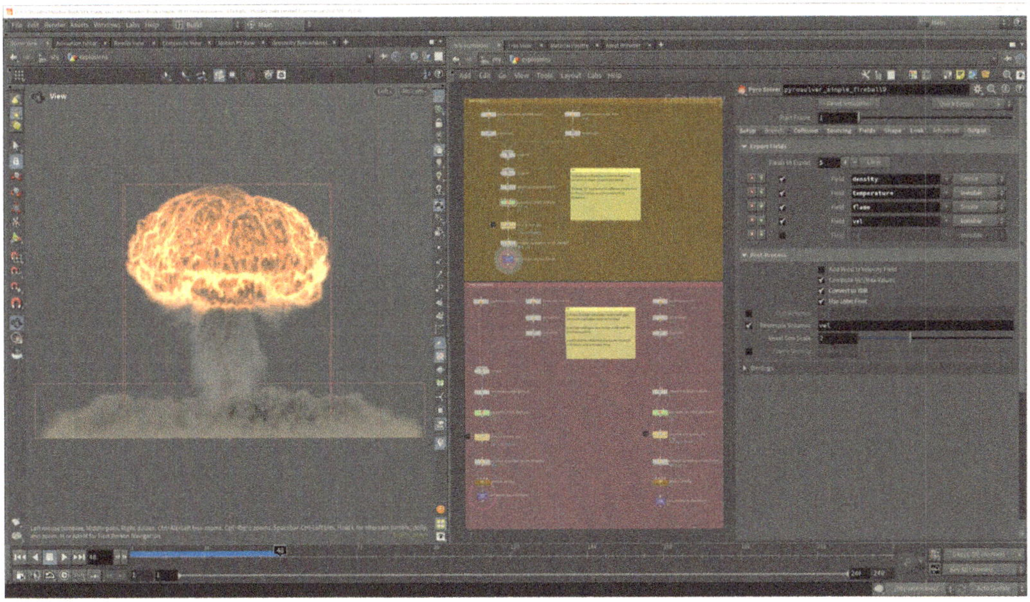

Figure 8.19 – Volumes optimization

Generally, reducing the velocity volume resolution by two times would not have a big impact on the final result, especially with big, slow-moving explosions. Since the **vel** field is only going to be used for motion blur, and the general direction of the vector will stay the same, we can reduce the volume size to save disc space.

Another important technique that I typically use during the caching process is caching the volumes *immediately* after the **Pyro Solver** node and then doing any density sharpening or baking color and emission volumes with **Pyro Bake Volume** after the caching. This approach provides more flexibility during the rendering process to interactively test and adjust all the manipulations to the volumes without having to recache the simulation.

Moving on, let's look at the shading and rendering process of big hero explosions.

Explosion elements shading and rendering

In this final part of the chapter, I will walk you through some areas of interest in the setup for lighting and rendering. I also encourage you to explore all the nodes and settings yourself, since this setup uses all the techniques we learned in previous chapters, especially in *Chapter 4*.

Once we have cached all the pyro simulation layers, as usual, we would transition into the **stage** context for the development of the look and creation of materials, lighting, and rendering. You will find the full **Solaris** rendering setup in the same provided Houdini file (see the *Technical requirements* section), in the **stage** context.

Refer to *Figure 8.20* to see the final render and **Solaris** setup:

Figure 8.20 – Hero explosion rendering

As you will notice, I have added a simple terrain environment for the nuclear explosion to have a more finished and realistic look. This deserted terrain is a simple grid geometry that has a displacement noise from the **mountain** node and an adaptive polygonal subdivision based on the camera's point of view. You can find the terrain setup in the file mentioned in the *Technical requirements* section and explore how it was created. We will explore another terrain-generation method in *Chapter 9*.

Let me briefly break down what is happening in the **Solaris** network:

- All the explosion layers and the ground plane are imported into **Solaris** with the help of **SOP Import** nodes.
- There are optional transformations applied using the **Transform** nodes to better position and stage all the elements together in the scene.
- The camera uses a long lens of 100 mm to mimic how this would be shot in real life and create a sense of a massive explosion happening a long distance from the viewer.
- The lighting is achieved with the **Karma Physical Sky** node, mimicking the late sunset and darker time of the day.
- The strongest light source in the scene is the actual emission from the fireball, which illuminates the shockwave and the surrounding area for a more dramatic look.
- There are three materials in use here:
    - Two of these are simple **Karma Pyro** shaders that use a scatter field that was generated in the **Pyro Bake Volume** node in the explosion setup
    - The last material is a simple shader for the ground with some rough reflectivity and bump mapping for smaller details
- Lastly, the **Karma Fog Box** node creates atmospheric fog and contributes to the story of a nuclear explosion happening somewhere in the deserted terrain. **Karma Fog Box** was also used in *Chapter 1* to create volumetric rays coming from the magic sphere, and in general, it can be used for many interesting fast atmospheric effects.

Overall, these are all the nodes and settings involved in achieving the render that you see in *Figure 8.21* and on the book cover. The main difference in the renders used for the image on the book cover is that I have used some simple color corrections (which are covered in *Chapter 11*) to enhance the final look.

Finally, we have the **Karma Render Settings** node, which is using the CPU render engine, mainly because the interactive light source from the explosion's shader doesn't produce enough illumination when used in **Karma XPU**. I assume that this feature would be further developed and integrated in the next or a later version of Houdini.

Additionally, I have enabled the **Denoising** option in **Karma Render Settings** to have a cleaner render and use only 16 primary samples for faster results. Refer to *Figure 8.21* to see the **Denoising** settings:

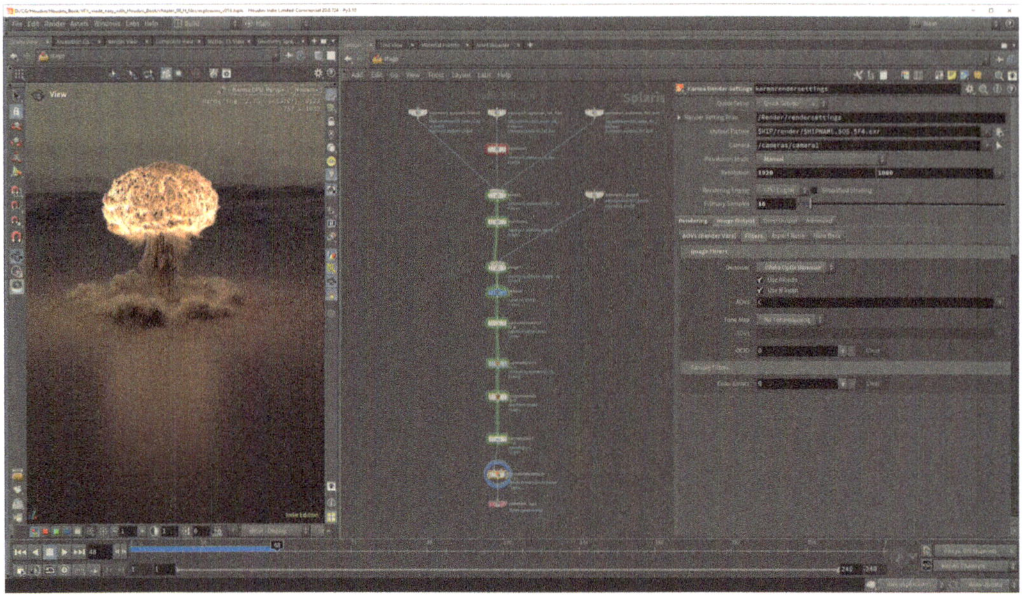

Figure 8.21 – Render settings

Take some time to play with the **Pyro Bake Volume** settings and see how it affects the fireball emission. Adjust the shockwave thickness and density in the materials and try different lighting scenarios, such as daylight or foggy noon.

This wraps up this chapter on explosion case studies. We have opened the door to the world of big explosive pyro simulations, which are often the most captivating and interesting parts of FX.

Summary

In this chapter, we have expanded our knowledge of pyro simulations into the dimension of explosions. We have explored how to source and create different types of explosions and blast elements, as well as practiced different simulation settings and parameters. Additionally, we have broken down the process of creating a complex nuclear explosion scene from start to final render.

In the next chapter, we will dive into our final big VFX project: a large-scale volcano eruption!

This project will utilize all the techniques that we have learned about so far, from *Chapter 1* to *Chapter 8*, including procedural modeling, particles, pyro, destruction, fluids, lighting, and rendering.

Subscribe to Game Dev Assembly Newsletter!

Part 3

Creating VFX Ready Projects

Now that you have explored Houdini's simulation toolset, it is time to bring everything together into complete, production-style projects. In this part, you will work through a large-scale volcanic eruption sequence, combining destruction, smoke, fire, and fluids into one cohesive shot. Step by step, you will model and fracture a crater, layer in secondary destruction, and then add pyroclastic plumes, fiery debris trails, and splashing lava bursts. Once the simulations are complete, you will transition into Solaris to light, shade, and render your scene, preparing every element for a polished final composite.

It is important to note that this project will follow a different approach. Instead of a fully guided, step-by-step breakdown, you will be provided with a ready-made Houdini file. Your task will be to study, review, and analyze the setup in order to replicate and understand the workflows. This reflects real-world VFX studio practice, where artists often need to learn from the work of teammates, and it will help you develop the crucial skill of learning directly from Houdini files.

The part concludes with a set of best practices covering workflow organization, performance optimization, and tips for building a standout demo reel. By the end of this part, you will know how to take an effect from concept through simulation, rendering, and compositing, creating VFX shots ready for real-world production.

This part has the following chapters:

- *Chapter 9, The Big Finale: Part 1*
- *Chapter 10, The Big Finale: Part 2*
- *Chapter 11, The Big Finale: Part 3*
- *Chapter 12, Best Practices for Houdini Artists*

9

The Big Finale: Part 1

This chapter will challenge you to combine all the knowledge obtained from *Chapters 1* to *8* and apply it to a volcano eruption shot created in Houdini from start to finish!

During this and the next three chapters, I will walk you through a complex shot that includes everything from modeling and creating the volcano mountain to simulation destruction, pyroclastic smoke, lava bursts, and particle debris. We'll end it with delving into the full lighting and rendering of the entire scene.

Due to the number of steps and settings involved in the creation of this shot, the *The Big Finale* chapters will serve as a walk-through and guidance through the provided Houdini file, which contains the full setup. For instructions on accessing the Houdini file, refer to the *Technical requirements* section.

On the other hand, it will be beneficial for you to explore and analyze all the finer details and settings of the setup by yourself, as breaking down demo Houdini files from other artists is a valuable skill and an essential part of the learning process.

In this chapter, we'll cover the following main topics:

- Procedural volcano creation
- Fracturing and preparation for destruction
- Big crater destruction
- Secondary destruction elements

By the end of this chapter, you will have learned all the steps involved in creating crater destruction and advanced 3D geometry workflows in Houdini.

Figure 9.1 shows the final rendered version of all the layers in the volcano eruption effect:

Figure 9.1 – Volcano eruption in Houdini

Technical requirements

A Houdini file is provided in the GitHub repository to help you explore and navigate the volcano eruption: `https://github.com/PacktPublishing/VFX-Made-Easy-with-Houdini`.

To view the chapter images in better clarity, scan the provided QR code. It will direct you to a dedicated link where you can take a look at the images.

After completing this chapter, I would encourage you to go through the nodes and workflows in the provided Houdini file and try to recreate them yourself.

Now, let's jump into Houdini and explore the workflows involved in the creation of the volcano.

Procedural volcano creation

Let's open the Houdini file for *part 1* and dive into the `the_big_finale` geometry container. I have split the full setup into three files, containing the elements and effects corresponding to each part, so it will be easier to navigate. The files are named corresponding to different parts, such as `the_big_finale_part_one` and so on.

Each part of the setup is contained in small network boxes (annotated in *Figure 9.2*) with different colors and names. Take some time to zoom into network view and inspect the different network boxes corresponding to the steps of the volcano creation and destruction part.

Refer to *Figure 9.2* for the volcano creation and destruction setup:

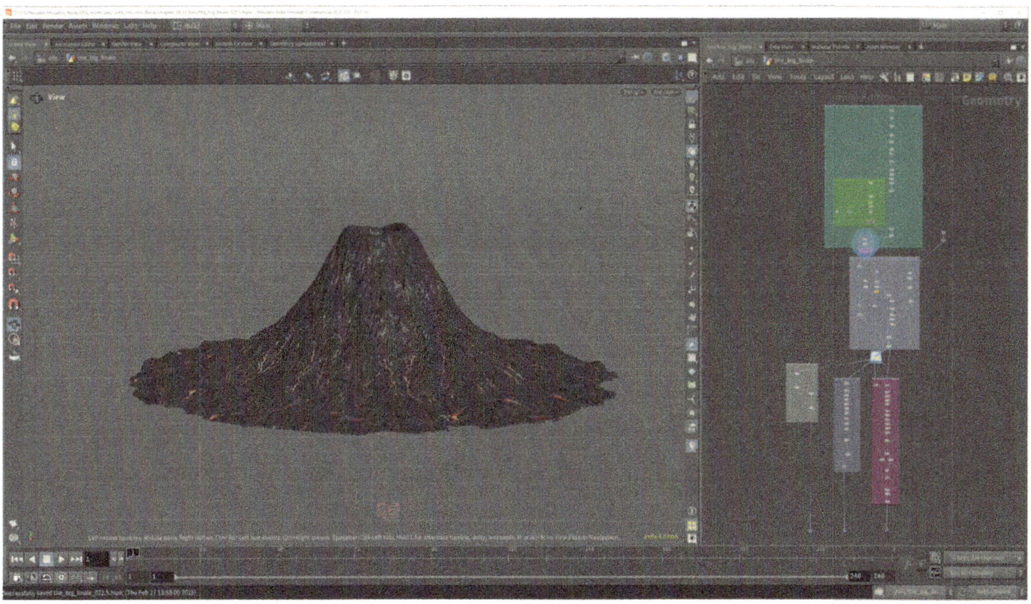

Figure 9.2 – Volcano creation and destruction node groups and networks

First, we will focus on the *green* top network box, named `Volcano model build`. The steps for creating the basic crater and mountain shape are very similar to those used in *Chapter 2* for procedural modeling.

We start by creating the volcano profile outline with the curve tools. We then revolve it into a 3D mesh that we convert into a VDB volume, then add extra details, as we will see in the subsequent steps.

Figure 9.3 shows the breakdown of volcano base model creation, from the outline to the VDB volume stage:

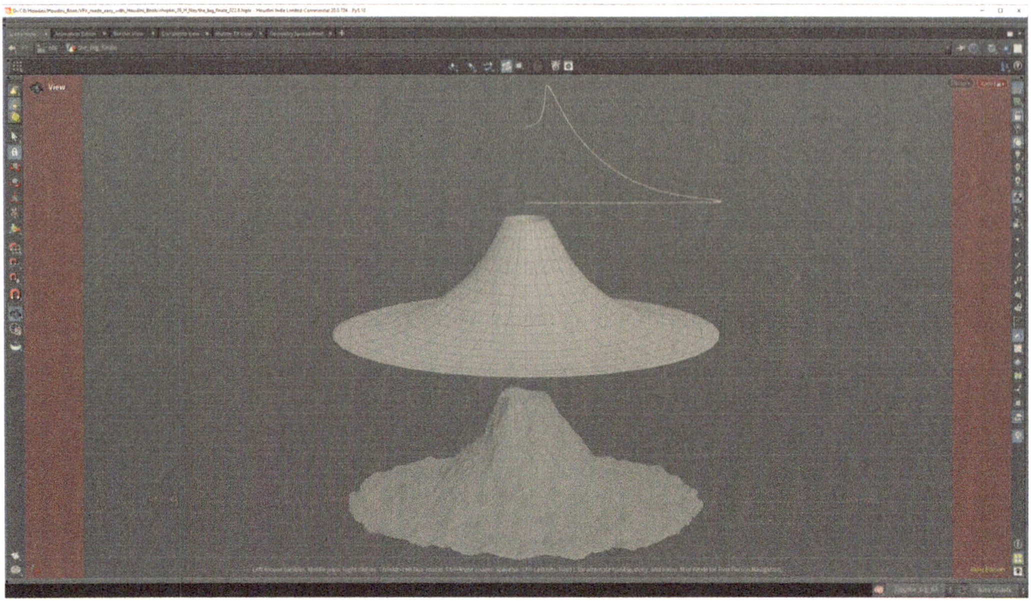

Figure 9.3 – Volcano basic mesh creation

One of the most important things when creating big effects and simulations is to create a *correct sense of scale*. This can be achieved by making the volcano model size close to what it is in the real world. Notice that the volcano model is bigger than any other asset that we worked with. The scale of the volcano will contribute to realism in the simulation and rendering of the effect.

Technically, the shape and level of detail already resemble a volcanic mountain with a crater and are sufficient when rendered from a distance. However, I went ahead and added an extra level of detail by using the terrain tools.

Terrain tools in Houdini are based on height fields. **Height fields** are a type of volume-based terrain system used to create and manipulate landscapes efficiently. Unlike traditional polygon-based geometry, height fields are represented as 2D volumes (grids), where each voxel stores a height value, allowing for lightweight and highly detailed terrain generation.

To convert the volcano polygons into the terrain height field, I have created a **HeightField** node and projected the volcano mesh elevation with the **HeightField Project** node.

After our volcano has been converted into a height field, we can run a terrain erosion process to achieve some of the realistic details that shape the mountains over time. To add terrain erosion, I used the **heightfield_erode** node and froze the erosion simulation result after 10 frames. Since erosion is a simulation process that mimics the terrain formation over time, you can choose any frame to stop the erosion process at that point.

Refer to *Figure 9.4* to see the eroded volcano mountain and erosion node settings:

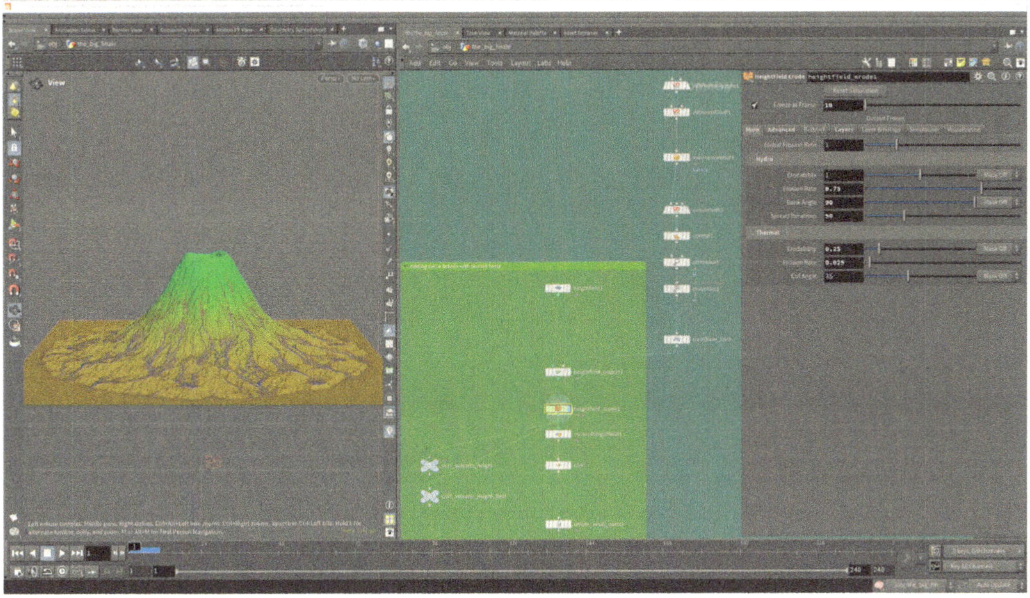

Figure 9.4 – Volcano erosion details

As we can see in *Figure 9.4*, erosion added a lot of interesting terrain details that will contribute to the realism of the volcano mountain even more. The last step after the height field erosion would be to convert the height volume back into the polygonal mesh with the help of the **Convert HeightField** node. I have also added a **Clip** node to delete any flat polygons without elevation or terrain details.

I recommend putting a **File Cache** node after generating the final eroded and detailed volcano model, and saving the result to disc. Caching frequently after heavy operations on the source geometry can reduce memory usage and computational overhead before proceeding to the next steps.

Refer to *Figure 9.5* to see the comparison between the volcano mountain before and after the terrain erosion process:

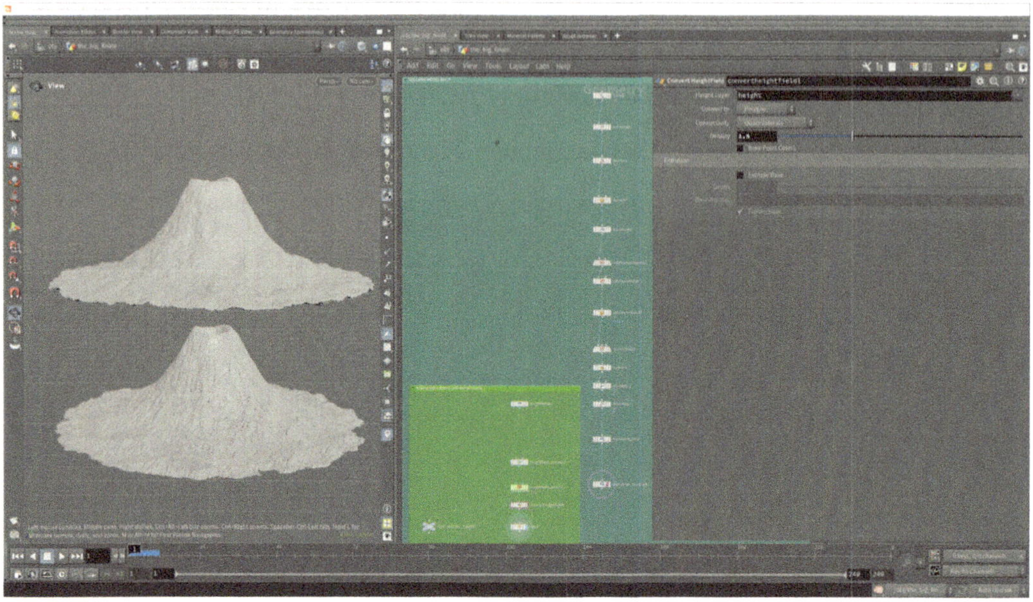

Figure 9.5 – Completed volcano model

In the next section, we will learn how to fracture and prepare the volcano for destruction.

Fracturing and preparation for destruction

After creating the 3D model of the volcano, the next step is to prepare for destruction. Usually, when dealing with large-scale destruction, you should strategically isolate the area that will be destroyed. This is to save time on fracturing and simulation, as well as to put as much detail into the destroyed area as possible.

> Important note
>
> Detailed fracturing of large areas can be a very heavy computational process. Therefore, I recommend switching the viewport update mode to **Manual**. This prevents the viewport from constantly refreshing after every parameter change, which can significantly slow down performance. By updating the scene only when needed, you reduce unnecessary calculations, making it easier to manage large simulations and complex networks efficiently.

In this case, for the purpose of storytelling, I am destroying the crater, with the volcano rock blasting outward, to make the eruption look more impactful. Therefore, it is important to isolate only the top of the crater from the middle and bottom parts.

We can easily shatter the volcano into two parts by using the **Boolean Shatter** operation, which will cut through a custom area containing just the top in the **Bound** node. After the **Boolean Shatter** operation, the top and bottom parts can be easily separated with the **Split** node.

Refer to the provided Houdini file and *Figure 9.6* as a guide to the settings:

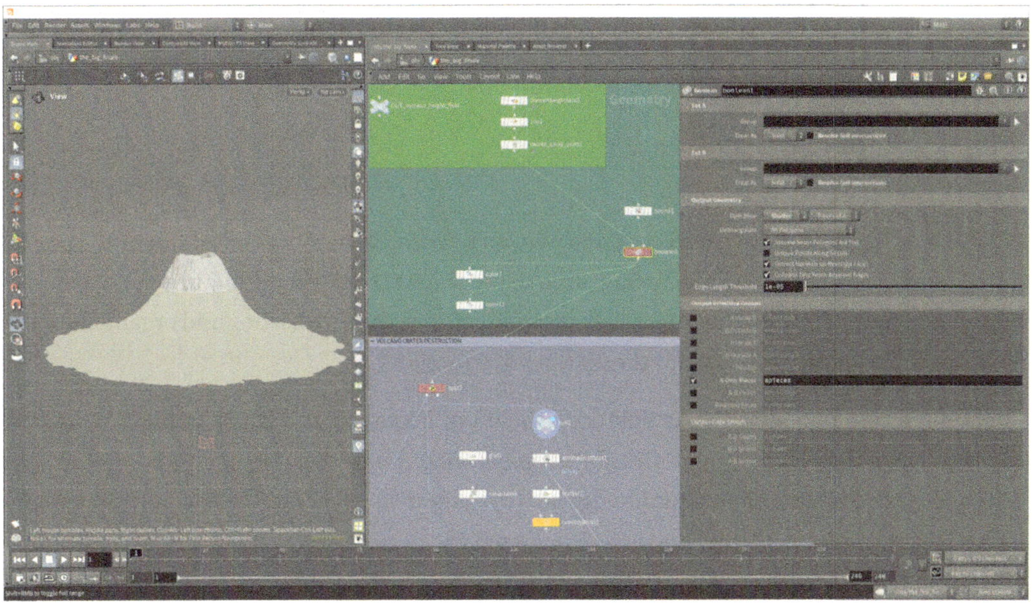

Figure 9.6 – Completed volcano model

After separating the top part of the volcano, we can now create highly detailed fractures concentrated around the crater. For fracturing, I am using the **RBD Material Fracture** node with the **Material Type** mode set to **Custom**. **Custom** mode can give very interesting and organic-looking fractures that should work well for the volcano destruction.

Custom fracturing mode scatters points on the input geometry and copies randomly rotated cutting planes that slice through the object, generating unique fragments. Additionally, I am generating extra cutting planes for the edge area of the crater to generate extra smaller fragments in that area. Those extra cutting planes are generated with a grid that is copied on scattered points.

Tip

I encourage you to play around with the amount of scatter points for the cutter geometry and see how it affects the fracturing shapes and resolution of fragments. With more scatter points, you will get more cuts and a higher number of fractured fragments; however, the process will get slower and heavier.

Refer to *Figure 9.7* and the **RBD Material Fracture** node in the provided file to see how the fracturing setup works:

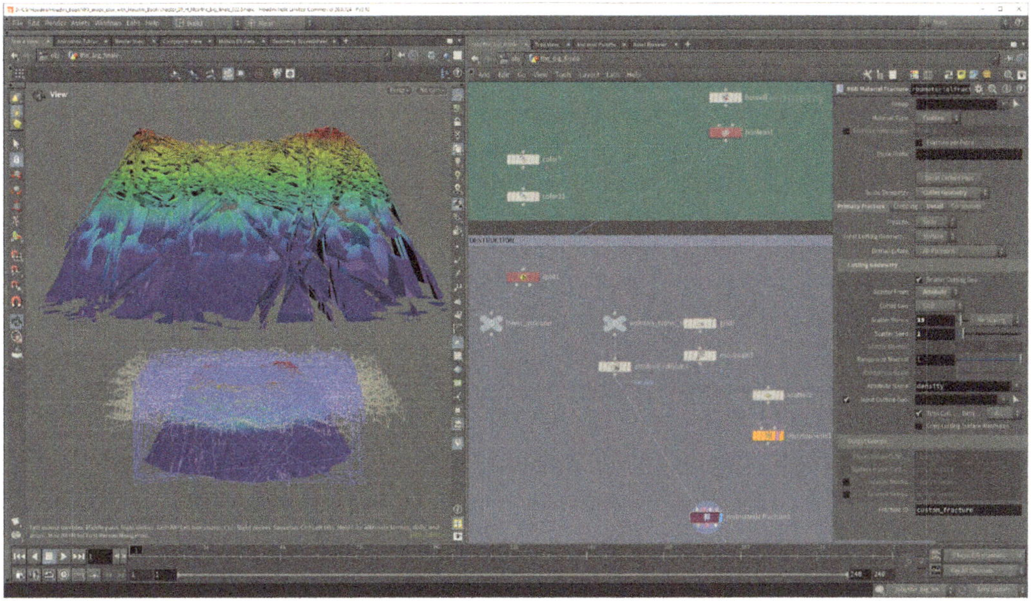

Figure 9.7 – Volcano fracturing

In the top section of the screenshot in *Figure 9.7*, you can see all the fractured fragments spread apart and, on the bottom, you can see the volcano crater with cutting planes. I have also colored the fragments based on the cutting density for better visualization.

I recommend putting a **File Cache** node after generating the fractured fragments and saving the result to disc. Caching frequently after heavy operations on the source or fractured geometry can reduce memory usage and computational overhead before proceeding to the next steps.

After creating the fragments, I created initial **Velocity** vectors pointing outward from the center of the object. **RBD Bullet Solver** will use these vectors on the fragments to push them outward with a force that would mimic a blast.

Previously, in *Chapter 4*, we mainly covered how to create rigid body simulations of the objects affected only by gravity. In this project, I am injecting specific **Velocity** vectors to guide the motion better and make the crater fragments explode outward.

> Important note
>
> Note that with this workflow, instead of using any RBD constraints, I'm just going to activate the crater area fragments to blast outward based on the initial velocity.

Velocity vectors are created from the **Normal** attribute of the sphere that is custom-placed inside the crater. By default, the normal vectors of the sphere point outward, and when transferred onto the volcano surface with the help of attribute transfer, they can work perfectly as outward velocity blast vectors.

Additionally, I have added some noise and variation to the transferred vectors, as well as adjusted the vector magnitude to decrease to 0 as the vectors get further down from the crater area.

I encourage you to experiment with the **Velocity** vector's magnitude and noise settings and see how it will affect the motion of the fragments in the simulation.

Refer to *Figure 9.8* and the provided file's node network as a guide:

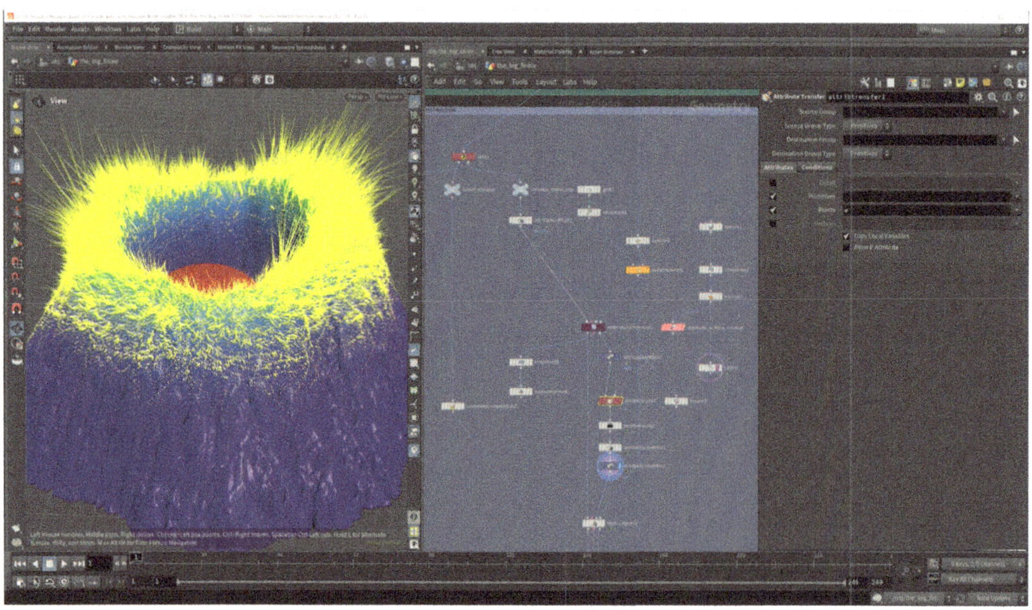

Figure 9.8 – Fragments' initial velocity

After creating the initial blast velocities, the final step of fracturing and preparation is using the **RBD Configure** node to convert the polygonal fragments into packed primitives that are optimized for destruction and set the active simulation area using custom bounds.

The **active simulation area** refers to an area where fragments will be affected by simulation forces, that is, velocities, and will have a dynamic motion. Any area that is not active will be *static* and act as a collider. Under the hood, the active area is defined by an integer attribute called **active**.

To make a custom active area, I have created a **Bound** node that captures just the top fragments of the crater. Once the **Bound** node is connected to the last input of the **RBD Configure** node, the **Active** checkbox, along with the **Use Bounds** checkbox, needs to be enabled to activate only the fragments that are inside the custom bounds.

I have also enabled a guiding display in the **RBD Configure** node that assigns a *green* color to the active fragments and a *black* color to non-active fragments.

I encourage you to play with the **Bound** node and increase or decrease the area that activates the fragments involved in the destruction.

Refer to *Figure 9.9* to see the active fragments area:

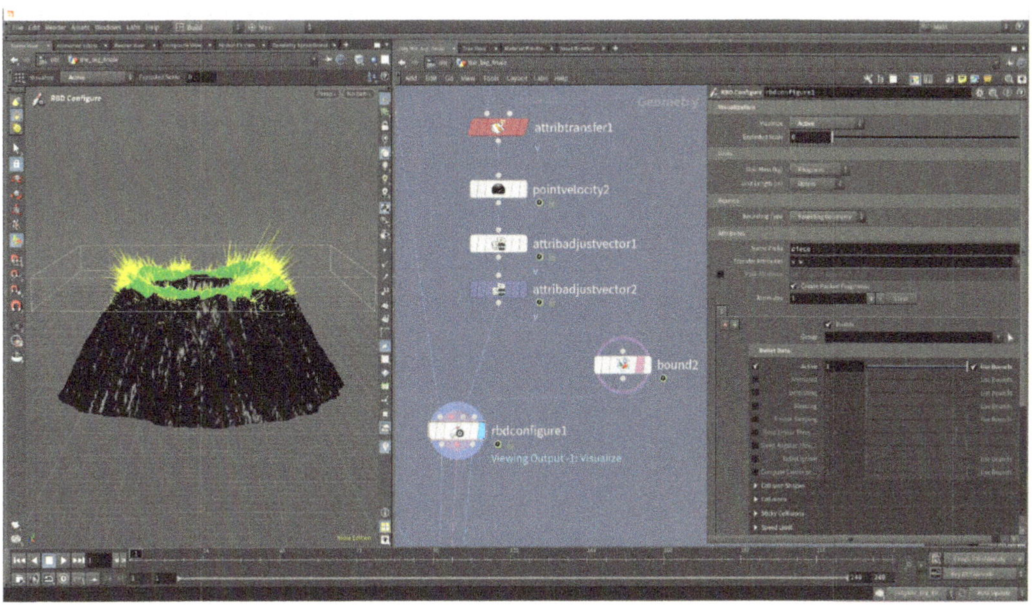

Figure 9.9 – Active fragments area

Moving on, we will learn how the **RBD Bullet Solver** node simulates the fractured fragments into a crater blast.

Big crater destruction

The destruction phase, involving **RBD Bullet Solver**, is perhaps the simplest of all the other effects for this project. Since a lot of preparatory work was put into the fracturing, creation of the initial velocities, and custom active simulation areas, **RBD Bullet Solver** worked with the default settings with everything plugged into it.

The only additional modification I made was to toggle on the built-in **Drag** and **Drag Spin** forces to add air resistance and make the fragments feel heavier. These settings can be found in the **Forces** tab of **RBD Bullet Solver**. I have used the lower non-fractured volcano geometry as a collider for the simulated fragments.

After the RBD simulation was complete, I used the **RBD I/O** node to cache the simulation to disc. The **RBD I/O** node is basically the same as the **File Cache** node, with the ability to cache additional elements, such as constraints, simulation fragment centroid points, and fragments, in different resolutions. Caching these additional elements can be useful as valuable data to drive secondary simulations.

Refer to *Figure 9.10* to see the RBD simulation of the volcano fragments:

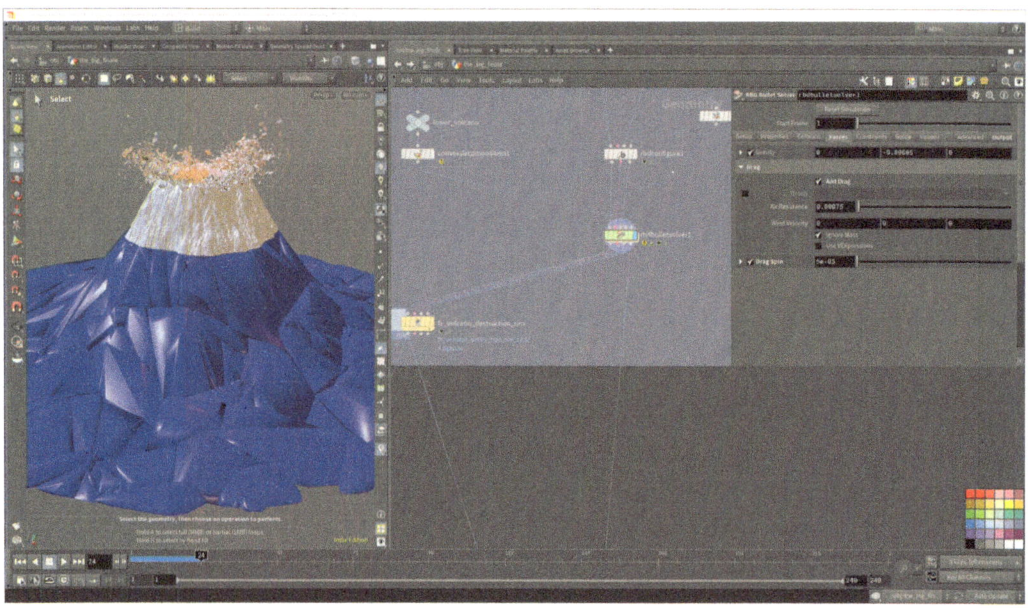

Figure 9.10 – Volcano RBD destruction

An important thing about the lower volcano collider is that it has to be prepared in a specific way for the fragments to collide correctly.

Since the fastest collision shape generation for **RBD Bullet Solver** is the **Convex Hull** method, objects that have any curvature or bend will have a convex collision shape that will ignore the curvature. This can lead to unrealistic-looking collisions where the fragments will be floating over the concave areas of the collider.

To solve this problem, it is recommended to use a **Convex Decomposition** node. The **Convex Decomposition** node in Houdini is used when you need to approximate a complex shape with multiple convex hulls for better collision detection. Since physics engines (such as **Bullet** in Houdini) perform best with convex collision shapes, the **Convex Decomposition** node helps optimize collision accuracy and performance.

Refer to *Figure 9.11* to see the optimized lower volcano collision shape that was created with the help of the **Convex Decomposition** node:

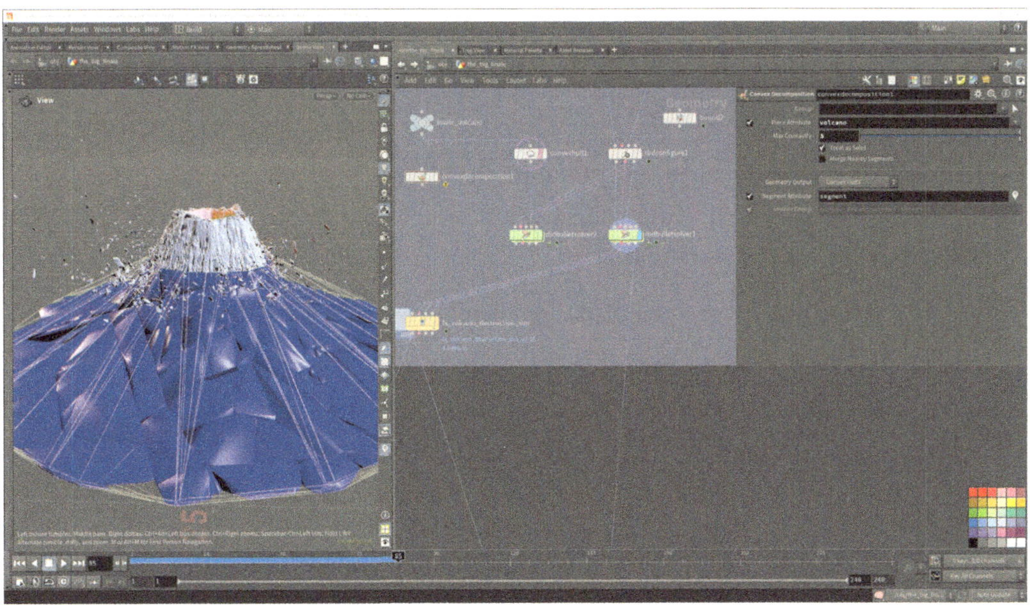

Figure 9.11 – Volcano complex collision solver

Moving on, we will explore the creation of additional destruction layers with debris and particles in the next section.

Secondary destruction elements

After creating the main volcano destruction simulation, we can add secondary destruction elements for more details. There are different ways to add secondary elements such as debris, dust particles, and fragment trails. Whenever I need to create any of the secondary destruction layers, the **Debris Source** node comes to the rescue.

The **Debris Source** node is used to generate emission points for secondary debris effects in destruction simulations. It analyzes fractured or animated geometry to detect exposed edges, moving pieces, and impact areas, creating points that can drive particle systems for dust, rubble, or small debris.

With controls for density, velocity thresholds, and emission modes, this node helps add realism by producing dynamic, physics-driven debris that enhances the detail of rigid body simulations. It is commonly used in VFX and games to create more immersive destruction effects.

You can create one or multiple debris sources for different debris layers. The points generated through the **Debris Source** node will result in a very realistic debris emitter that creates emission points at the time when the fragments detach. It has the ability to delete emission points at any time during their life attribute.

The **Debris Source** node can be used to drive additional particle simulation, or pyro simulation to generate dust kicks, trailing dust, and smoke, as well as tiny debris particles following the motion of the main destruction simulation.

Refer to *Figure 9.12* as well as the provided Houdini file to see how the debris source can be used to generate extra destruction and eruption elements.

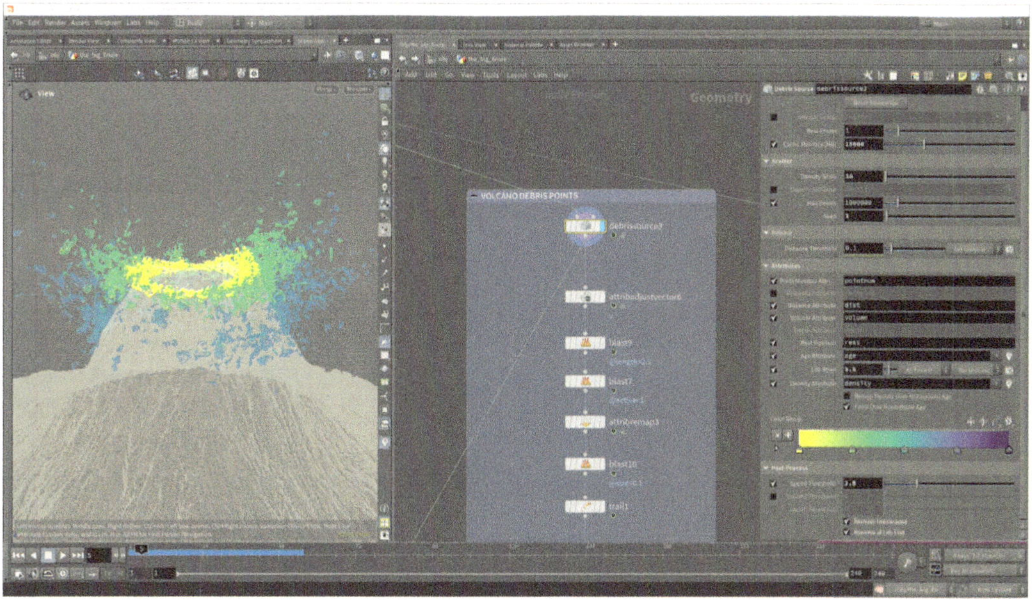

Figure 9.12 – Debris Source settings

In the volcano destruction file, I am using two separate **Debris Source** nodes:

- One to generate the procedural particle trails after the small fragments
- Another to generate emissive blast particles that are usually seen in erupting volcanoes

Most of the **Blast** nodes after the **Debris Source** node are used to isolate smaller fragments based on their velocity and density.

Refer to *Figure 9.13* to see the procedural and POP simulation-based secondary destruction elements:

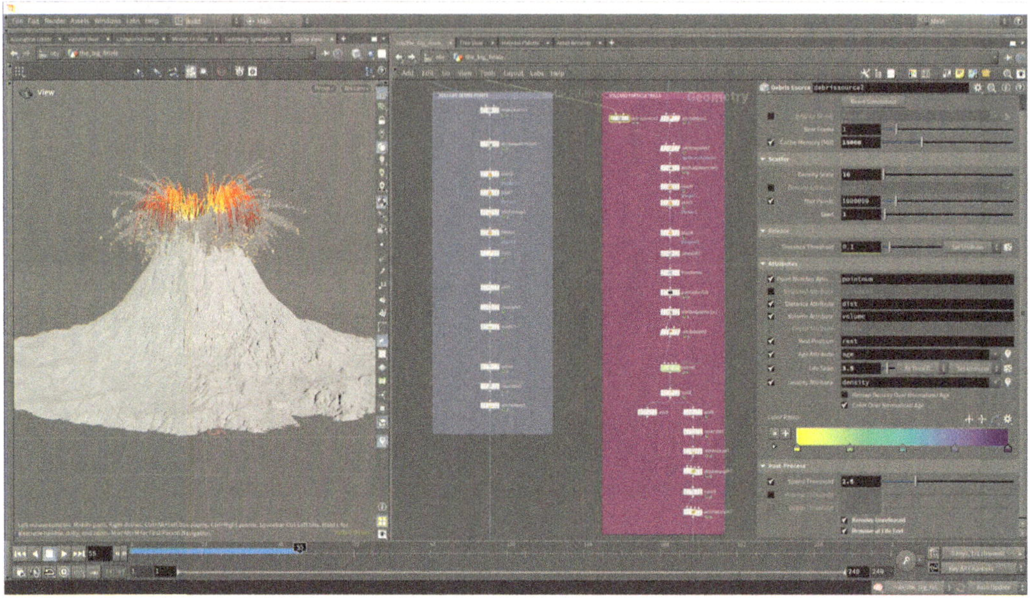

Figure 9.13 – Secondary destruction elements

In the next chapter, I will expand this further by using a **Debris Source** node to create a source for pyroclastic fiery trails coming from the larger fragments.

I encourage you to use the provided Houdini file and explore the **Debris Source** node, as well as experiment with additional secondary elements generated through particle simulation and procedural methods to add more details to the existing destruction elements and take the visual complexity to the next level.

Summary

In this chapter, we have explored different workflows for more advanced procedural geometry creation and destruction. The workflows were introduced through your independent exploration of the provided Houdini file, and the chapter served as a quick guide—this approach can be more beneficial than the step-by-step approach.

One of the fastest and most proven ways to learn is by analyzing and studying the setups and parameters created by other artists. This approach also encourages you to experiment with settings and learn problem-solving independently.

In the next chapter, we will continue with the volcano eruption and learn how to create large-scale fluid simulations in a real-shot scenario.

Subscribe to Game Dev Assembly Newsletter!

We are excited to introduce **Game Dev Assembly**, our brand-new newsletter dedicated to everything game development. Whether you're a programmer, designer, artist, animator, or studio lead, you'll get exclusive insights, industry trends, and expert tips to help you build better games and grow your skills. Sign up today and become part of a growing community of creators, innovators, and game changers.

`https://packt.link/gamedev-newsletter`

Scan the QR code to join instantly!

10

The Big Finale: Part 2

In this chapter, we will continue the walk-through of the volcano eruption effect and add more simulation layers for the crater smoke plumes, fiery debris trails, and lava bursts emanating from the crater.

To successfully follow the creation of these simulation layers, I recommend revisiting *Chapter 4* and *Chapter 8*, which cover the creation and parameters of pyro effects. Additionally, it's a good idea to revisit *Chapter 6*, which covers fluid parameters. This will help us with the bursting lava creation.

We will also add some additional complementary effect layers for light smoke at the base of the volcano, which we will build using particles and volumes.

Similar to the previous chapter, this will be a walk-through of the setups that can help you study and independently work with the provided Houdini file with the full effect.

Here are the main topics that we will cover in this chapter:

- Creating pyroclastic crater plumes
- Adding fiery pyro debris trails
- Simulating splashing lava bursts
- Meshing lava fluid simulation

By the end of this chapter, you will know how to add big-scale pyroclastic and fluid simulations to a realistic effect shot.

Figure 10.1 shows the final rendered version of all the layers in the volcano eruption effect:

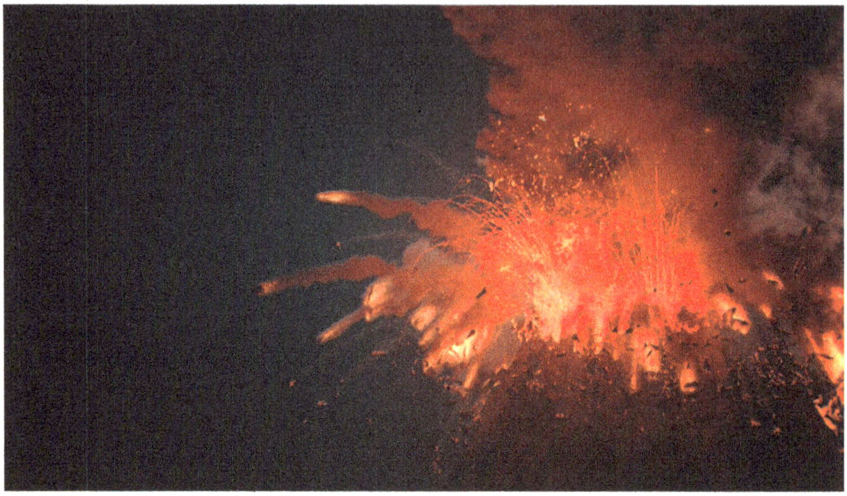

Figure 10.1 – Pyroclastic and fluid effect elements

Technical requirements

I will be using **Houdini version 20.5** moving forward for this project. Please download a production build of 20.5 to proceed. Here's the link to the download page: `https://www.sidefx.com/download/`.

A Houdini file is provided in the book's GitHub repository to help you explore and navigate the volcano eruption: `https://github.com/PacktPublishing/VFX-Made-Easy-with-Houdini/tree/main`.

To view the chapter images in better clarity, scan the provided QR code. It will direct you to a dedicated link where you can take a look at the images.

After completing this chapter, I would encourage you to go through the nodes and workflows in the provided Houdini file and try to recreate them yourself.

Now, let's jump into Houdini and explore the workflows involved in the creation of the effects.

Creating pyroclastic crater plumes

Let's open the Houdini file for *Part 2* and explore the `the_big_finale` geometry container. To make navigation easier, I've divided the full setup into three separate files (`the_big_finale_part_one`, `the_big_finale_part_two`, and `the_big_finale_part_three`), each one aligned with the elements and effects covered in its respective section.

Within the file, you'll find the setup organized into neatly labeled and color-coded network boxes. Take a moment to zoom into the network view and examine these boxes—they represent the key stages in building the pyroclastic plumes and lava burst effects.

Refer to *Figure 10.2* to view the setup for volcano creation and destruction:

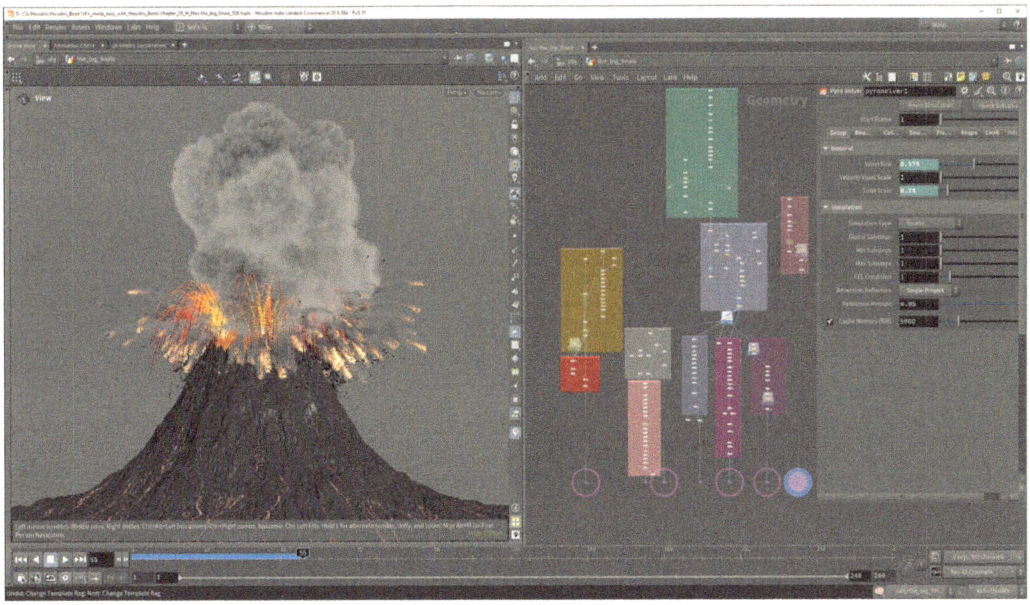

Figure 10.2 – Pyroclastic plumes and lava bursts setup

First, we will focus on the *dark pink* network box, named **VOLCANO MAIN SMOKE SIM**. The steps for creating the pyro plumes emitter are very similar to those used in *Chapter 4*, describing the introduction to pyro effects.

We start by creating a simple **Sphere** node and then transform it into a crater. Then, we utilize a **Pyro Source** node with **Volume Rasterize Attributes** to turn the sphere into a pyro emitter. Additionally, I have distorted the source shape with **Noise** for a more interesting emission and added **Initial Velocity** to push the smoke out of the crater faster.

One of the key settings to achieve big, dense plumes is to inject smoke expansion from the density source – this is controlled by the **divergence** field in Houdini. Everything else is controlled inside the **Fields** and **Shape** tabs to make the smoke dissipate more slowly and get affected by **Wind**, **Disturbance**, and **Turbulence** for extra details.

After the simulation, I have used **Pyro Bake Volume** to have better control over how the smoke looks, as well as to add **temperature**-based emission near the source.

Refer to *Figure 10.3* to see the breakdown of the dense pyro plumes setup:

Figure 10.3 – Dense pyro plumes

Take some time to study the **MAIN SMOKE SIM** setup in the provided Houdini file. I would also encourage you to go ahead and recreate the smoke plume effect from scratch once you have studied all the nodes and parameters involved.

Moving on, we'll create fiery debris trails in the next section.

Adding fiery pyro debris trails

Let's shift our focus to the *dark purple* **VOLCANO PYRO TRAILS** network box. You will find that I am reusing the points from the **Debris Source** node from the previous chapter to generate sources for fiery trails.

One of the key elements is that we only want to source the fire and smoke from the biggest and fastest debris pieces. Therefore, in the **Debris Source** node, I am using the **Speed Threshold** and **Volume Threshold** parameters to limit the source only to the specific areas of the destruction sim.

Refer to *Figure 10.4* to see the **Debris Source** settings that are specific to the fiery trails source:

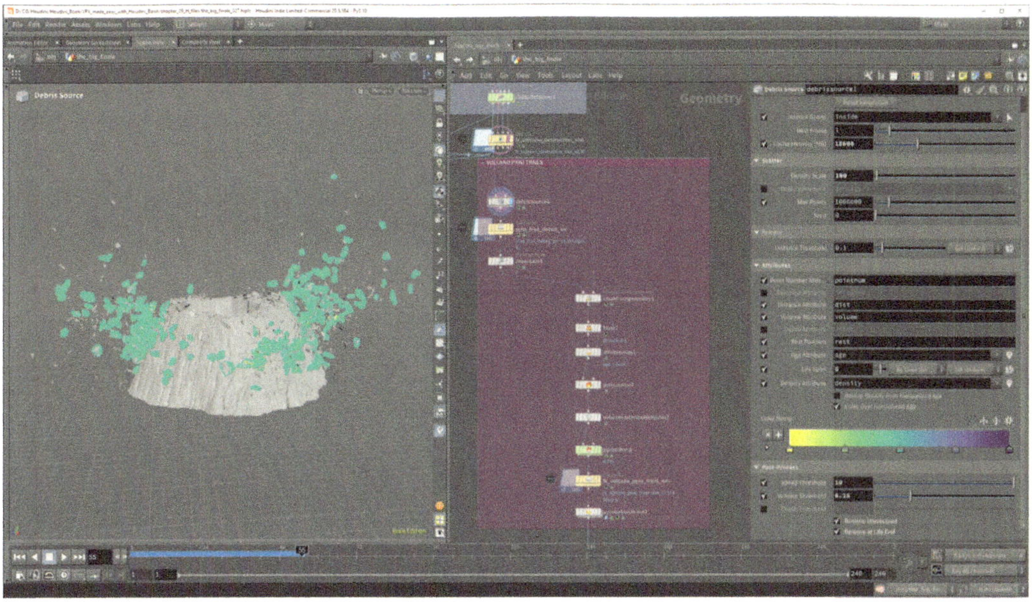

Figure 10.4 – Fiery trails source

In *Figure 10.4*, note that the *green* areas are only capturing the biggest and fastest fragments, and all the smaller fragments will be ignored for the smoke emission.

Another important step is to make sure that we don't source fire from the debris pieces very close to the volcano's surface. This helps avoid a very concentrated fire and smoke area and only keeps the fiery trails nicely spread on the fragments in the air. This is my personal preference, as I didn't want to have a lot of fire and smoke by the crater, since they were covering the lava bursts and the crater too much.

I am using the **Mask From Geometry** node to mask out the fragments close to the crater and volcano surface and then deleting those with the **Blast** node.

After we are happy with the emission area of **Debris Source**, we can utilize the **age** attribute and remap it to burn in a way that will generate much more burn and flames at the tip of the fragment and fade off into a smoky trail.

The rest of the setup uses the same principles and logic as any other pyro simulation that we have built previously. We will then add **Pyro Source** and **Volume Rasterize** attributes to prepare the pyro emitter. Finally, we will use the trusty SOP-based **Pyro Solver** to simulate the fiery trails.

Refer to *Figure 10.5* to see the debris pyro trails simulation result:

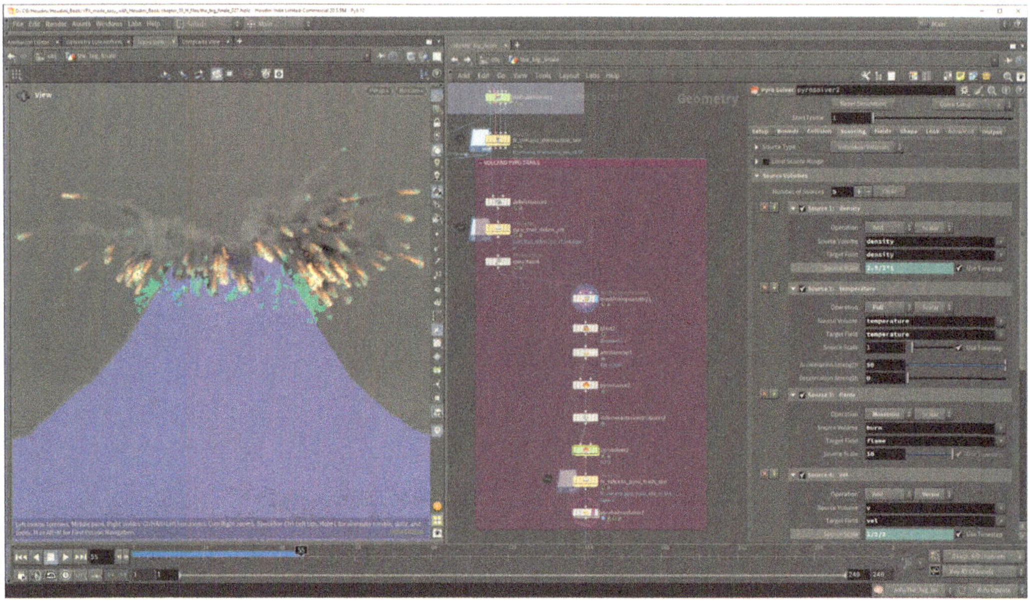

Figure 10.5 – Fiery debris trails simulation

In the next section, we'll learn how to create the bursting lava splashes.

Simulating splashing lava bursts

You will find the sourcing and simulation setup for the lava bursts in the *orange* network box, named **VOLCANO LAVA SIM**.

Refer to *Figure 10.6* to view the network box of the bursting lava:

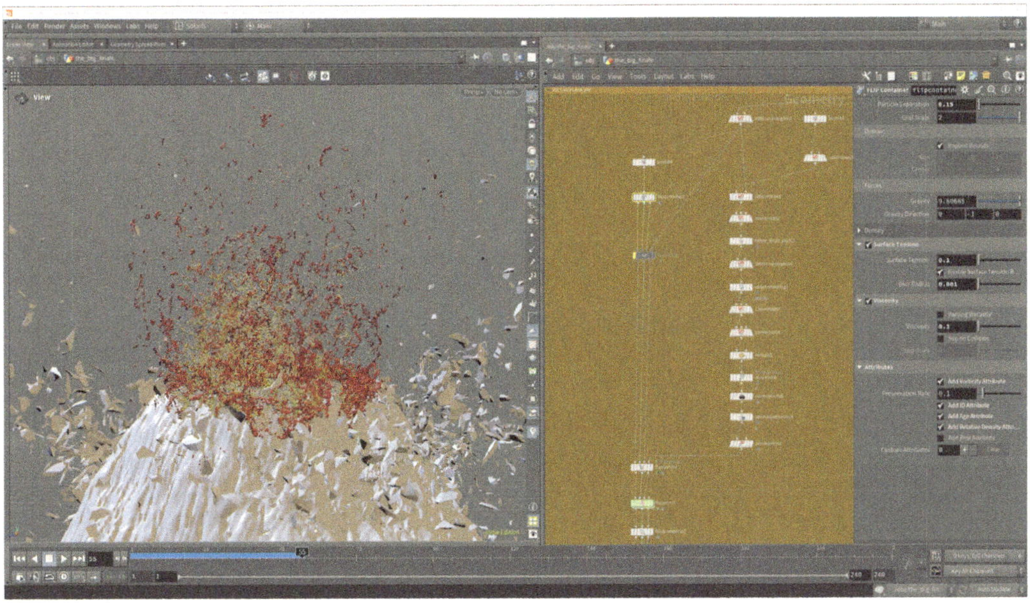

Figure 10.6 – Lava bursts simulation setup

Let's explore what is happening on the very right of the network box, where we create the source for the lava pool. I'm using a combination of volume **VDB** operations to isolate the top part of the crater and fill it as an enclosed volume.

After creating the lava pool, I am adding different **Noise** patterns both to the position and velocity to make the emitter shape more interesting and dynamic from the start. I recommend examining the different noise settings I have used on the **volumenoisefog1** and **mountain6** nodes by clicking on them individually to see the resulting emitter shape.

Figure 10.7 shows the result of the emitter shape before the simulation:

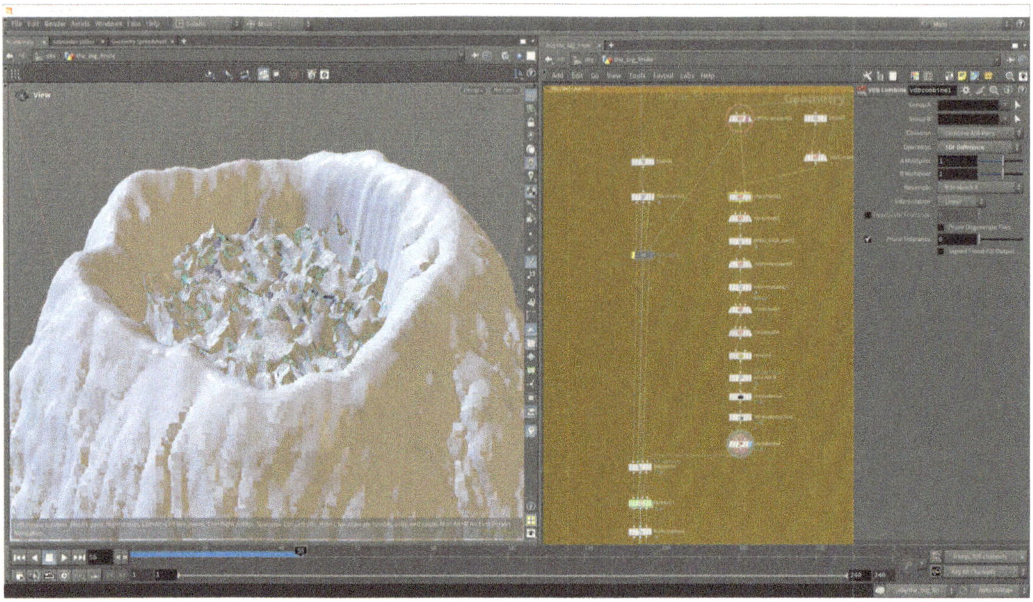

Figure 10.7 – Lava emitter shape

For the next steps, I have created a **FLIP Container** node matching the size and dimensions of the volcano crater. I have also adjusted the **Bound** node, responsible for calculating the crater boundaries, by making it bigger, so the domain of the lava simulation will be big enough to capture big, bursting splashes.

After the **FLIP Container**, I have added the **FLIP Source** node where I'm plugging in the result of the lava pool geometry emitter as the last input. You can refer to the *FLIP fluids sourcing methods* section in *Chapter 6* to remind yourself how the structure of the FLIP simulation works.

Finally, I am adding a **FLIP Solver** node that is also loading a height field of the volcano for a more optimized collision. I didn't change many settings on the **FLIP Solver**, aside from changing the **Velocity Transfer** setting to **Splashy** to get more dynamic splashing bursts.

The last step for the lava simulation will be to add a **Fluid Compress** node and cache the fluid particles to disk. We will then use these cached particles for meshing in the next network box.

Refer to *Figure 10.8* to see the **FLIP Solver** settings and the initial splashing particles result:

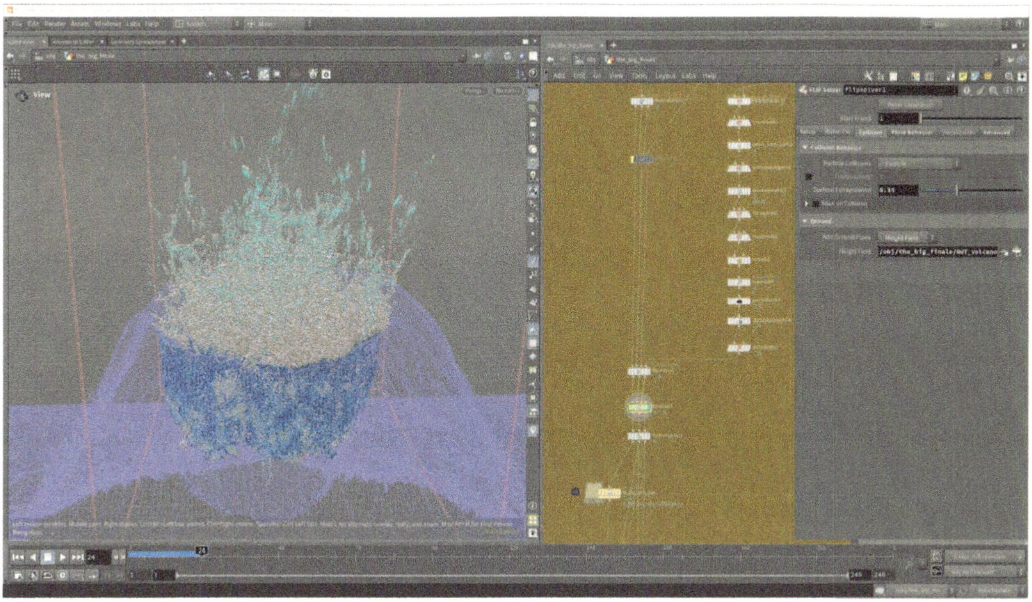

Figure 10.8 - Lava emitter shape

After caching the lava particles to disk, we can move on to meshing and setting some important attributes such as **Color** and **Emission**.

Meshing lava fluid simulation

You can find the meshing *red* network just under the **VOLCANO LAVA SIM** network box. The process is simple and straightforward; the only additional element that I have added is the **Attribute Blur** node. I've used it to blur the point positions of the fluid particles to achieve a more clustered look. I am also reducing **Particle Scale** to make the lava tendrils and droplets look thinner.

After this, I'm using the **Particle Fluid Surface** node with the **Spherical** meshing method for more details. I am coloring the lava particles based on their **Velocity** value with a color ramp inside the **Particle Fluid Surface** node as well.

Finally, I am adding a **Smooth** node to make the mesh thinner and smoother and achieve fine droplets.

Refer to *Figure 10.9* to see the lava meshing network and result:

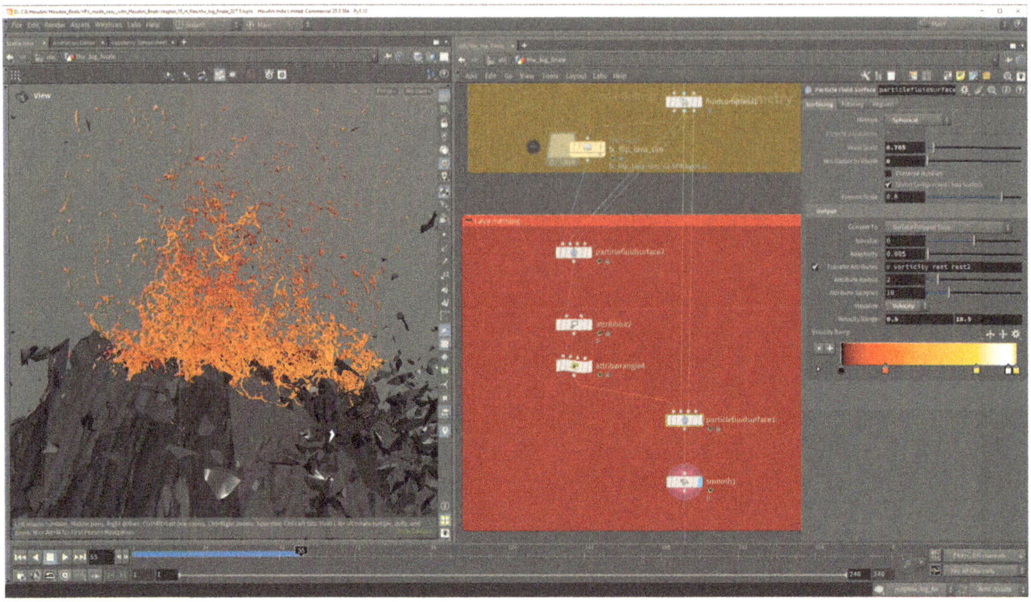

Figure 10.9 – Lava meshing

With this, you can see how we can achieve a much bigger fluid splash resembling chunky lava by still utilizing the simple SOP-based FLIP simulation techniques learned in *Chapter 6*.

That brings us to the end of simulating the pyro and lava fluid elements. Now, it's your turn to dive deeper and make the most of what you've learned.

I encourage you to open the Houdini file provided in the GitHub repository and take some time to explore how each element was created, from the sourcing of the pyro and lava to the simulation techniques used throughout the scene. Look closely at the following aspects:

- Node networks
- Parameter settings
- Overall structure of the setup

Once you're familiar with how everything works, try recreating the simulation in a fresh Houdini file. Use the original file as your reference, but challenge yourself to rebuild it from scratch.

This hands-on practice is one of the best ways to reinforce your understanding, build confidence, and start developing your own workflow.

In the next chapter, I will cover how to prepare all the elements for output into the stage for lighting, shading, and rendering.

Summary

In this chapter, we explored a variety of workflows for tackling more advanced pyro and fluid simulations. At this point, you have probably noticed that the core process is usually the same: create an interesting source shape, add velocities, forces, and simulate. Rather than walking through each step, you were encouraged to dive into the provided Houdini file and use the chapter as a quick reference. This kind of hands-on exploration can often be more valuable than following a step-by-step tutorial.

One of the best ways to learn is by studying how other artists build their setups—looking at the nodes, parameters, and structure of a scene. It not only helps you understand the logic behind each decision but also pushes you to experiment and develop your own problem-solving skills.

Up next, we'll continue working on the volcano eruption and bring all the elements together with lighting and rendering.

11

The Big Finale: Part 3

This chapter serves as the culmination of everything you've learned throughout the book. In this final chapter, we will bring all the elements of the volcano eruption effect together and prepare the scene for rendering. You will learn how to organize and export your simulation geometry, import assets into Solaris, and set up a rendering-ready environment. We'll cover essential steps such as configuring lights and cameras; creating and assigning materials to different elements such as smoke, lava, and debris; and adjusting render settings, including **Arbitrary Output Variables** (**AOVs**), for compositing flexibility.

To follow along smoothly, it's recommended to revisit previous chapters, particularly those covering shading, lighting, and rendering for particles, pyro, fluids, and 3D assets (see the sections on rendering in *Chapters 2, 3, 4*, and *6*). Additionally, you can look at some real volcano eruption references online, as the visual characteristics of each element will inform how we shade and light them.

We'll also look at the final stage of the pipeline: rendering the AOV layers and compositing them together to produce a polished cinematic shot.

Here are the main topics that we will cover in this chapter:

- Preparing geometry elements for rendering
- Importing everything into Solaris
- Setting up lights and cameras
- Creating materials for different elements
- Configuring render settings and AOVs
- Compositing all the layers together

By the end of the chapter, you'll have not only simulated a complex volcanic eruption in Houdini but also lit, rendered, and composited it into a complete, production-ready sequence.

Figure 11.1 shows the final rendered version of all the layers in the volcano eruption effect:

Figure 11.1 – Rendering all the elements

Technical requirements

I will be using **Houdini version 20.5** moving forward for this project. Please download a production build of 20.5 to proceed: `https://www.sidefx.com/download/`.

A Houdini file is provided to help you explore and navigate the volcano eruption: `https://github.com/PacktPublishing/VFX-Made-Easy-with-Houdini`. After completing this chapter, I would encourage you to go through the nodes and workflows in the provided Houdini file and try to recreate them yourself.

To view the chapter images in better clarity, scan the provided QR code. It will direct you to a dedicated link where you can take a look at the images.

Let's jump into Houdini and explore the workflows involved in rendering the final scene.

Preparing geometry elements for rendering

Let's open the Houdini file for *Part 3* and explore the `the_big_finale` geometry container. To make navigation easier, I've divided the full setup into three separate files (`the_big_finale_part_one`, `the_big_finale_part_two`, and `the_big_finale_part_three`), each one aligned with the elements and effects covered in its respective section.

Within the file, you'll find the setup organized into neatly labeled and color-coded network boxes. I would like you to focus on the big *purple* network box at the bottom of the full volcano setup. This network box has output nodes for every element and effect that we have previously built. Take some time to inspect each output and the setup it leads to, for a better understanding of the scene elements.

Figure 11.2 showcases the complete network with render outputs:

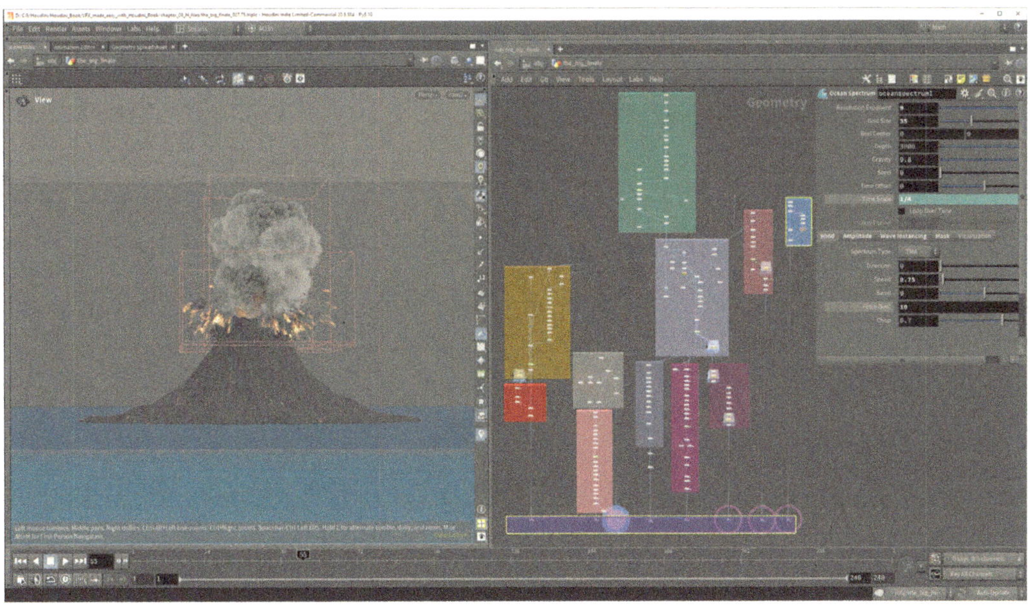

Figure 11.2 – Complete scene overview

You will also notice that I have added a quick water surface to make the environment and shot more complete. The setup can be found in the *blue* network box, and I will do a quick walk-through on how it was created.

The creation of the ocean surface has two main parts:

- Surface generation
- Water waves displacement

In the first part, I created a large plane grid to define the area of the water, and then I used a **Remesh to Camera** node to add adaptive resolution. This means that the node will create a lot more polygons in the area of the plane that is in the camera's field of view.

Refer to *Figure 11.3* to see the node tree and result:

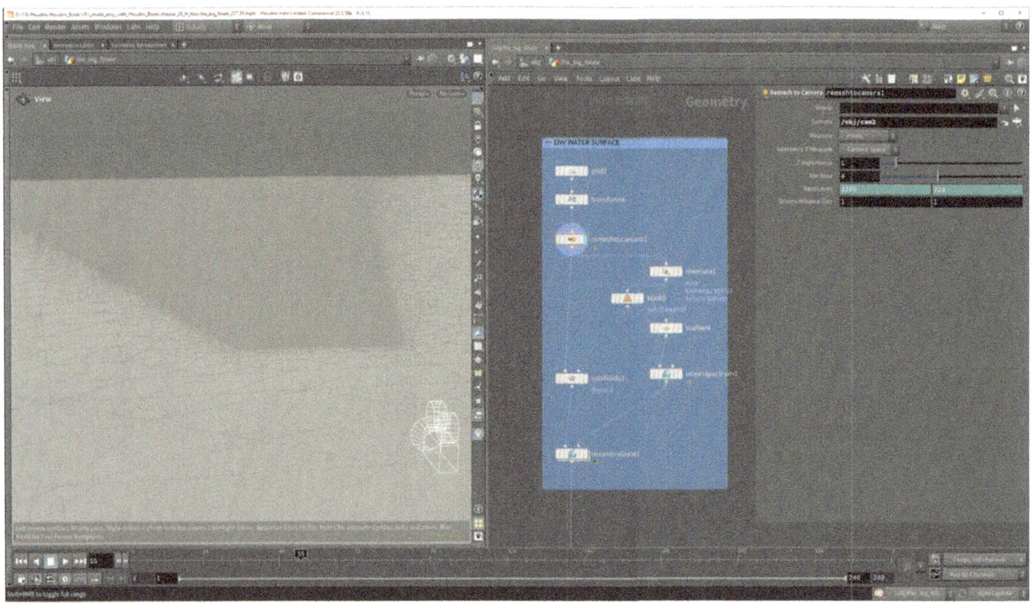

Figure 11.3 – Remesh to Camera

In the second part, I scatter points on the dense area of the grid, and these points will act as wave instancing points once plugged into the **Ocean Spectrum** node. **Ocean Spectrum** and **Ocean Evaluate** are parts of the **Ocean** tools in Houdini and are used in combination with other, more advanced techniques to create realistic water and ocean surfaces.

In a more advanced workflow, I would save the spectrum in a separate file and use it to displace the surface through the ocean material. However, to keep things simple, I will use the **Ocean Evaluate** node to perform the displacement right on the 3D geometry.

Ocean Evaluate will take the input grid and displace it in the areas of the instanced wave points. **Height Direction**, **Frequency**, and many other wave parameters can be found in the **Ocean Spectrum** node.

Refer to *Figure 11.4* to see the water surface mesh after the **Ocean Evaluate** node:

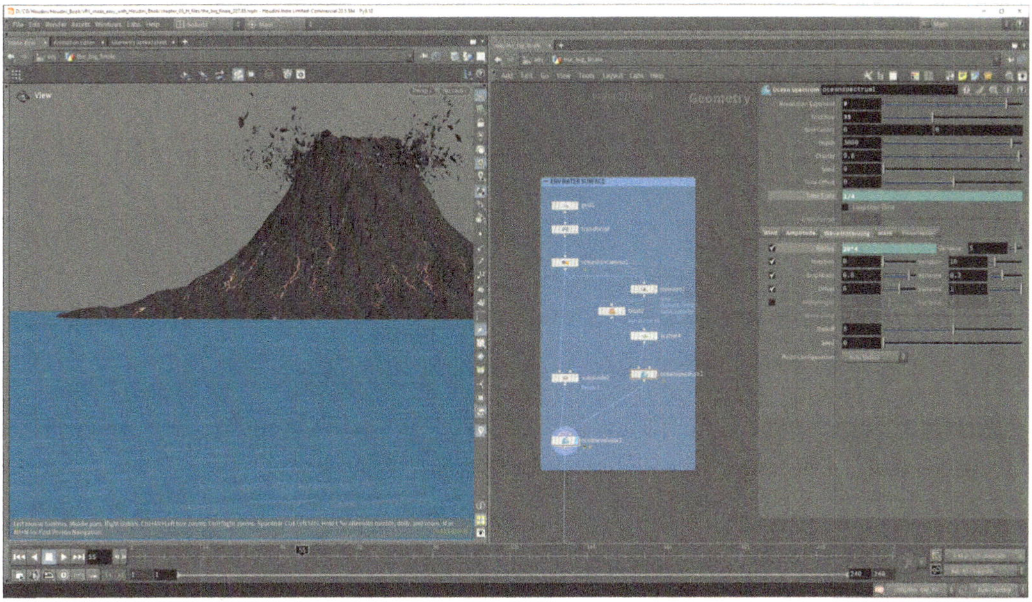

Figure 11.4 – Grid with ocean waves

With this, we are now ready to move on to the next section, where we bring all the elements into Solaris for lighting and rendering.

Importing everything into Solaris

For the next steps, let's switch to the **stage** context and inspect the shading and lighting and rendering network.

Refer to *Figure 11.5* to see the viewport and network of the setup:

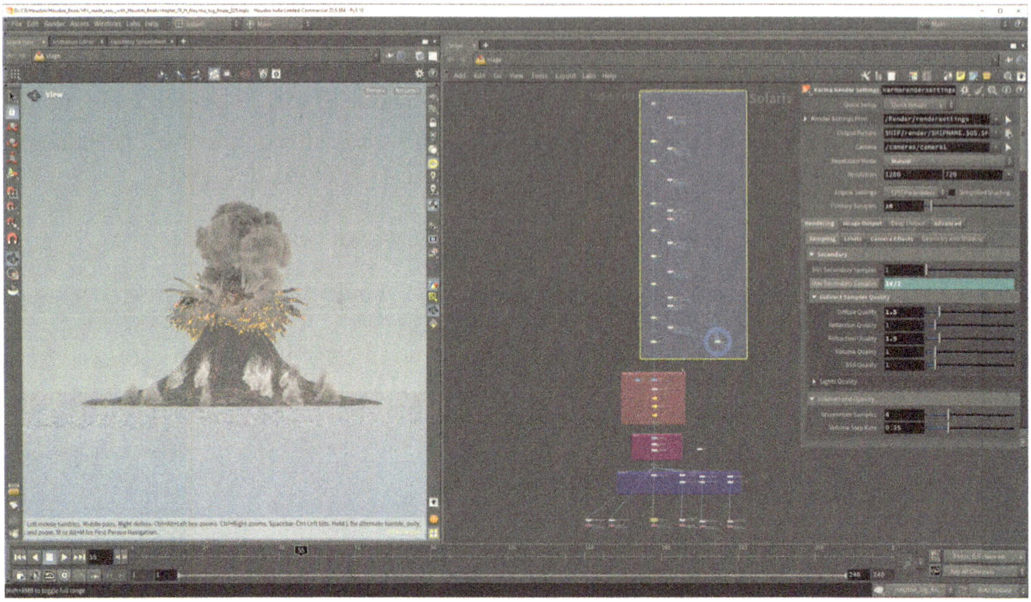

Figure 11.5 – Rendering network

In *Figure 11.5*, you can zoom into the first network box with the *yellow* outline. Here, you will see all the elements being imported with the help of **SOP import** nodes.

If you have a powerful machine with more than 64 GB of RAM and a high-memory GPU, you can just merge all the SOP imports, and carry out the look development, lighting and rendering on all the elements together, and then render all the layers together with a **Cryptomatte** workflow for further control and separation in compositing.

It is important, however, to know how to optimize and set the scene in a way that not all the elements will be loaded at the same time, especially if you don't have a powerful machine. For this purpose, I have created multiple **Switch** nodes that are created to assist in configuring the elements we want to render separately.

The general workflow is to connect each layer as a second input to the **Switch** node and utilize the **Select Input** box of the **Switch** node with this expression: `@switch_element_name`. This way, the **Switch** node will be set to `0` and will not load any geometry by default, unless the expression link is triggered to `1`.

Refer to *Figure 11.6* to see the **Switch** node for the volcano geometry and water surface:

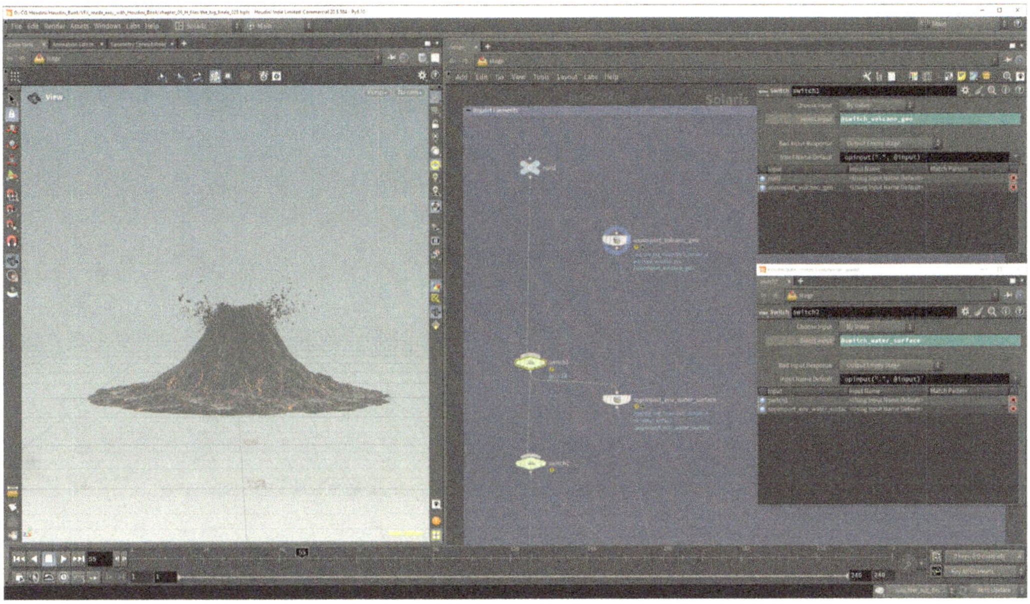

Figure 11.6 – Enabling geometry load based on Switch

Later, we will use the **Edit Context Options** node right before the **Render** settings to load only the element we need for the current render pass.

The **Edit Context Options** node will understand the `@switch` expression, so the only thing you need to do is type the same `@switch_element_name` of the corresponding layer in the **Option Name** box and set **Option Type** to **Number**. This way, by setting the number to either `1` or `0`, the geometry will or will not go through the **Switch** node.

Let's refer to *Figure 11.7*, where the **Option Name** values are the same as in the **Input** box of the corresponding **Switch** nodes. Only **Volcano Geo** and **Water Surface**'s **Option Value** fields are set to 1, therefore making them visible and renderable in the scene.

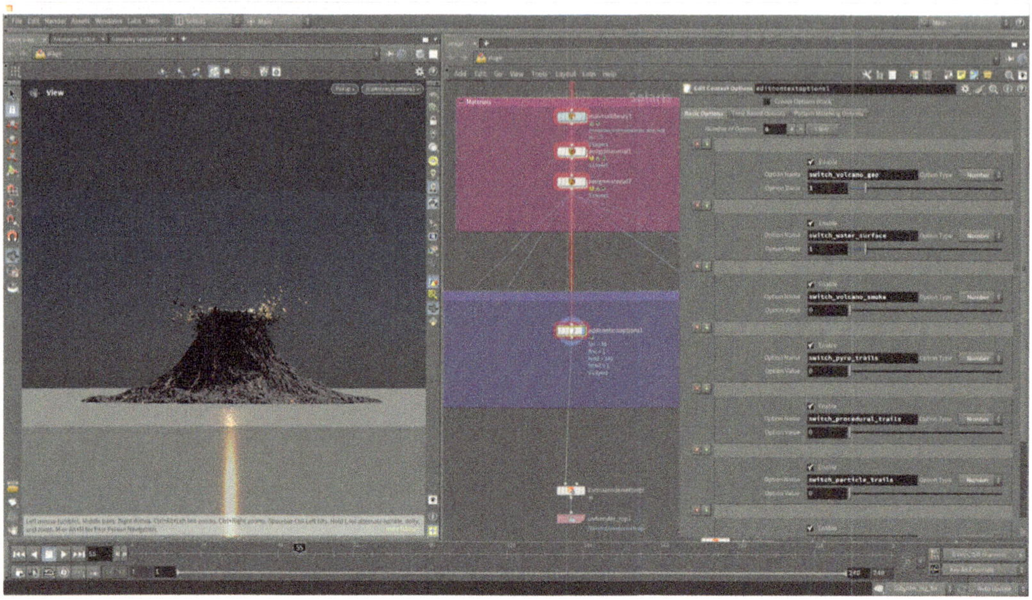

Figure 11.7 – Context options

This workflow is very powerful when working with big scenes and elements. One benefit is that you can easily set separate render elements with unique render qualities and render settings. This also allows for testing materials and lighting by only loading specific elements, which will speed up the process and reduce memory usage and computational overhead.

Edit Context Options can be placed anywhere after the **Switch** nodes. For this example project, I have added it right before the **Karma Render Settings** node.

Moving on, we'll see the setup for the shot camera and scene lighting in the next section.

Setting up lights and cameras

I have created a long lens camera for this shot to make the sense of scale realistic. **Long lens cameras** are essential for achieving realism in large-scale visual effects scenes because they mimic the way real-world cinematographers capture distant or massive subjects.

Long focal lengths naturally compress perspective, making vast environments, towering structures, or explosive simulations feel grounded and believable. This compression reduces the exaggerated depth often caused by default wide-angle views in 3D scenes, helping to convey the true scale and weight of effects such as mountains, volcanoes, or city-wide destruction.

By using long lenses, artists can match real-world cinematic language more closely, ensuring their VFX shots integrate seamlessly into live-action plates and resonate with the visual expectations of film audiences.

Refer to *Figure 11.8* to see the camera focal length and network box:

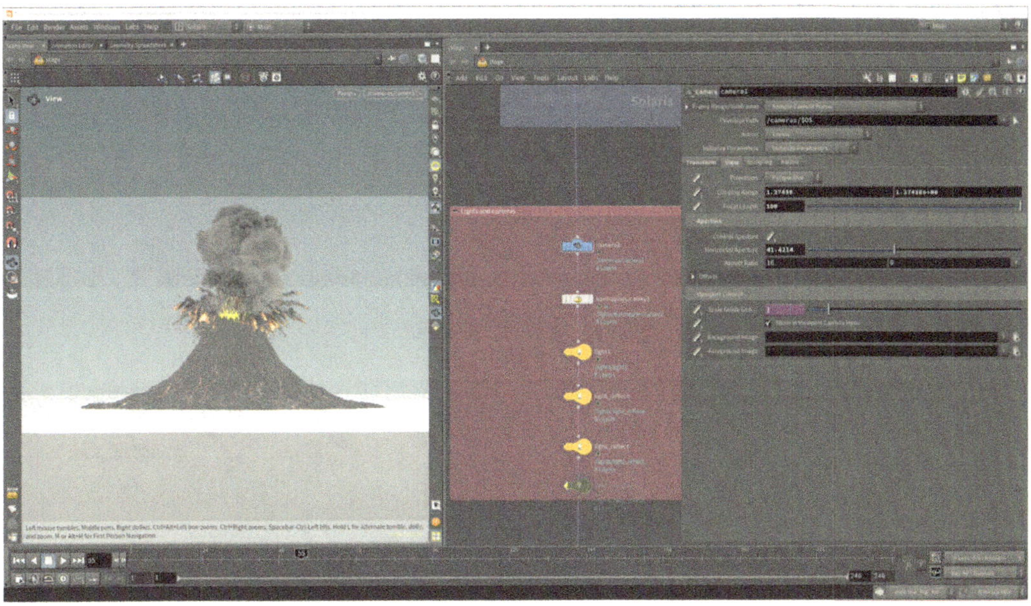

Figure 11.8 – Camera settings

For the lighting, I decided to create an outdoor dusk scenario, with the help of **Karma Physical Sky** and supporting **Sphere** lights to make the main illumination source come from the crater.

An interesting thing to note is that each light can be set to contribute to different things, such as **Diffuse** color and **Reflection**. I encourage you to experiment with the **Light** contribution settings to get more control over the scene lighting.

Additionally, I have added **Geometry Light** properties to emissive elements such as **Lava** and **Pyro Trails** through the **Render Geometry Settings** node.

Refer to *Figure 11.9* and *Figure 11.10* to see the light's effect on the geometry:

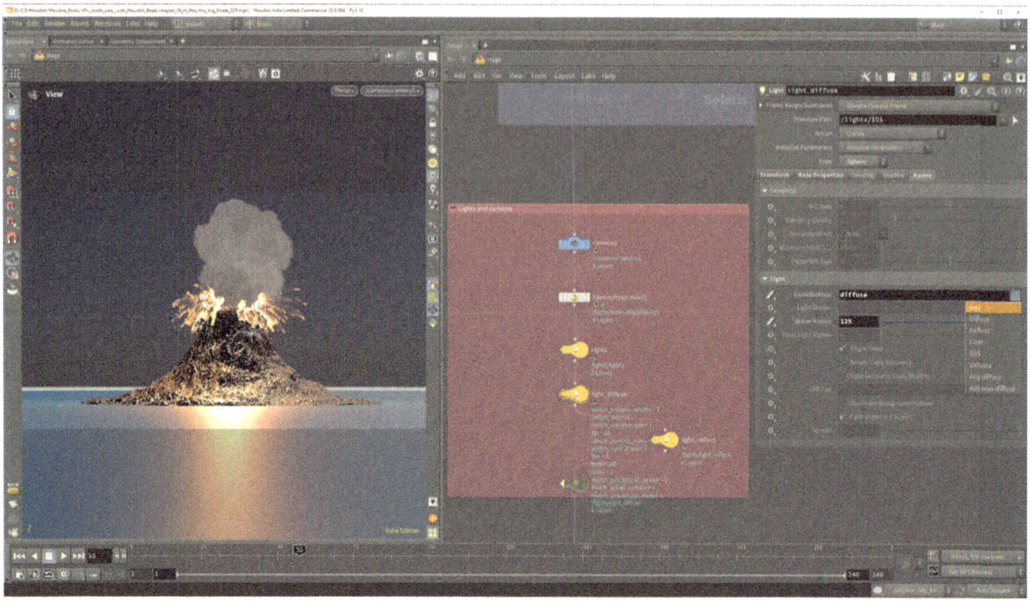

Figure 11.9 – Light contributions

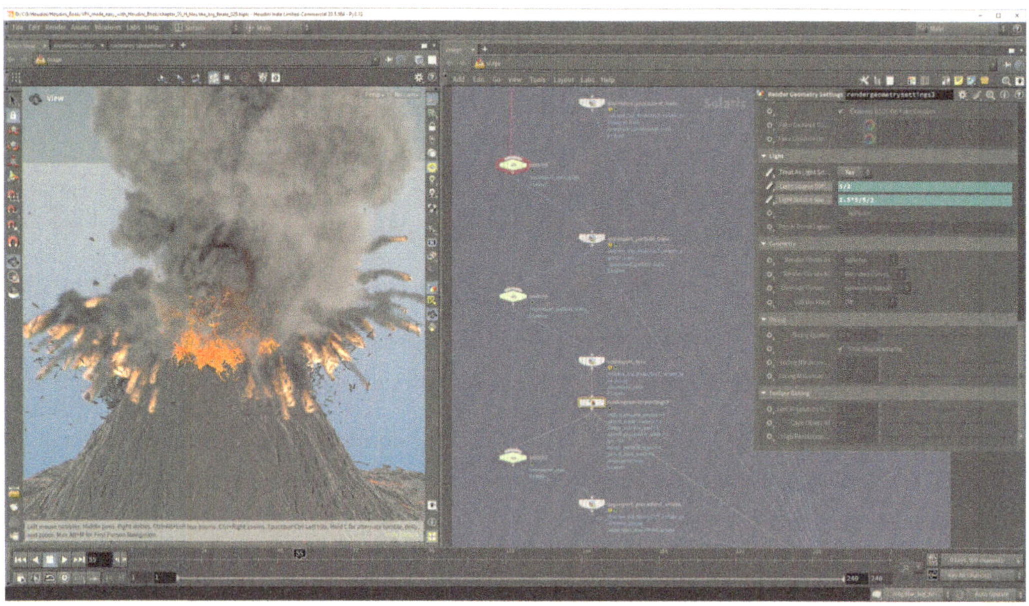

Figure 11.10 – Geometry light property

Quick tip: Need to see a high-resolution version of this image? Open this book in the next-gen Packt Reader or view it in the PDF/ePub copy.

The next-gen Packt Reader and a **free PDF/ePub copy** of this book are included with your purchase. Scan the QR code OR visit `packtpub.com/unlock`, then use the search bar to find this book by name. Double-check the edition shown to make sure you get the right one.

Take some time to inspect different elements and how they react to the individual scene lights. You can also try to create different lighting scenarios representing daylight or sunset.

In the next section, we'll move on to the materials' setup.

Creating materials for different elements

You can find the materials' setup inside the *purple* network box. All the materials are created inside the material library by using the same techniques described in the shading and rendering section of every project we did in the previous chapters. They are then applied to the corresponding elements through the **Material Assign** node.

Figure 11.11 shows how the material layout and assignment are set up:

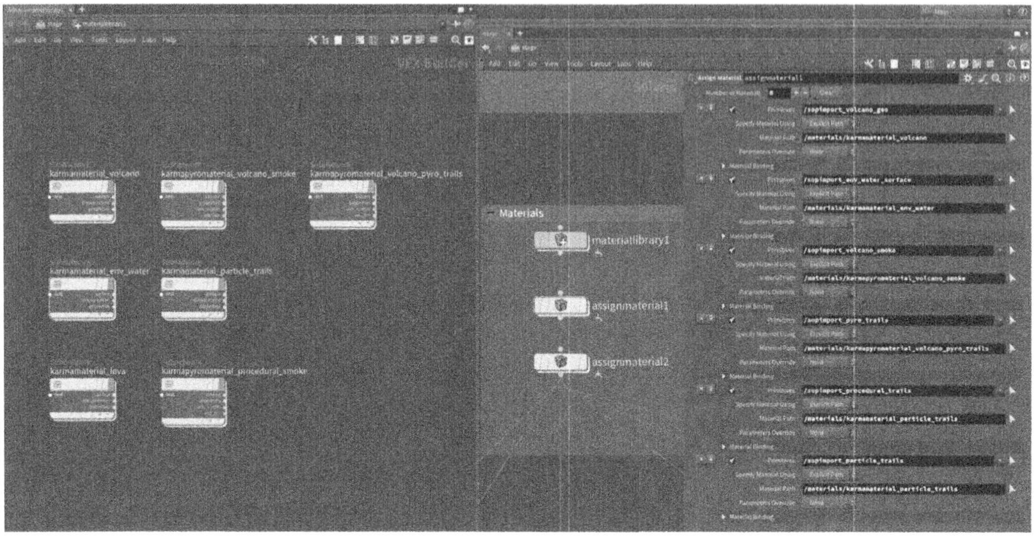

Figure 11.11 – Material library and assignment

Dive in and explore the individual settings used to create shading of different surfaces and FX elements. You can also revisit *Chapters 1* and *3* for reference on creating particle materials and attributes, as well as *Chapters 2*, *4*, *6*, and *8* to get a refresher on creating materials for hard surface, volumes, and liquids.

Moving on, we'll learn how to render all elements into a final image.

Configuring render settings and AOVs

For the final render, I am using **Karma CPU** with lower primary samples and a denoising workflow.

On average, the rendering times for this scene ranged from *10 to 30 minutes per frame*. If you would like to benefit from faster renders using **Karma XPU**, you will need to have a powerful graphics card with more than 10 GB of VRAM memory, since the scene is heavy and contains lots of elements.

The following example is a part of intermediate to advanced workflows for managing bigger scenes and complex effects layers. In the example, we separate multiple elements using the **Edit Context Options** switches to load and render fewer elements at the same time. While selecting which elements to switch on in **Context Options**, you can also add extra elements that can be reflected in the rendered surface and make them only visible in reflections or refractions with the help of the **Render Geometry Settings** node.

Zoom into the *purple* network box named **Render Elements** and inspect the example setups where I show how volcano geo, water surface, and pyro elements can be separated. The main nodes to be inspected are **Edit Context Options** and **Render Geometry Settings**.

Refer to *Figure 11.12* to see how the water surface gets rendered separately while still reflecting the non-visible volcano and the pyro emissive elements:

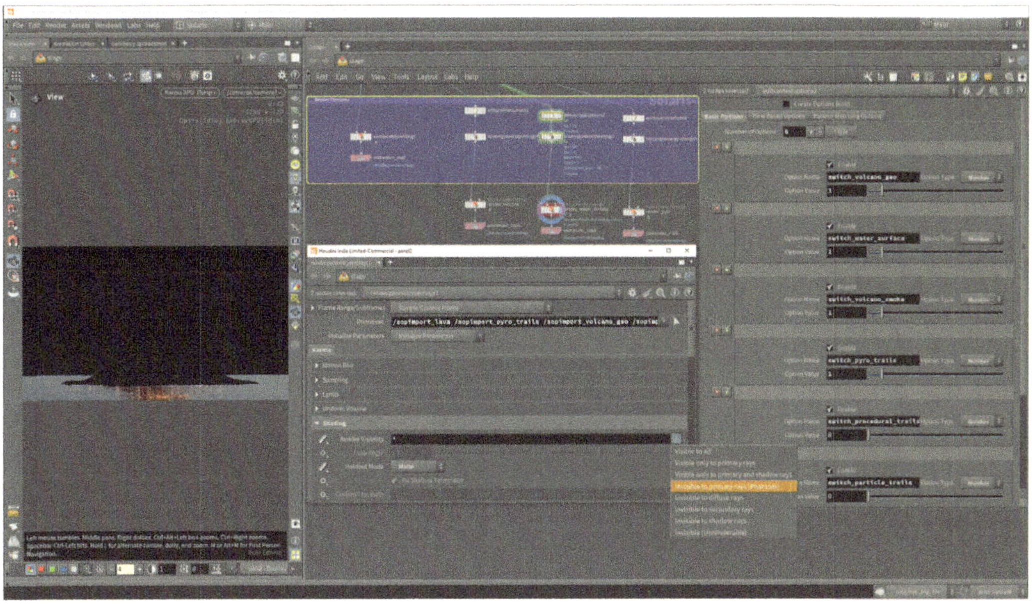

Figure 11.12 – Rendering separate layers

A key takeaway from the setup is the use of visibility switches. These are applied to the main object to be rendered and to all objects that will be visible in reflections. In this case, the water surface is the main renderable object, and the volcano with pyro layers needs to be visible only in reflections. Therefore, the switches for those objects are set to 1.

Now, to make the volcano and the pyro layers only visible in reflections, and be cut away from the rendered layer, we need to select them in the top **Primitives** box of **Render Geometry Settings** and set **Holdout mode** to **Matte**. Additionally, if you don't want to cut them out from the image and just render through reflection visibility, you can set **Render visibility** to **Phantom**.

Render Geometry Settings is a very powerful node that lets you set and override many important scene parameters per object or object groups. By default, all the parameters will not be accessible and will be grayed out. To make a parameter editable, you can click on the little **circle** icon next to the parameter and choose the **Set or Create** option.

Refer to *Figure 11.13* to see an example:

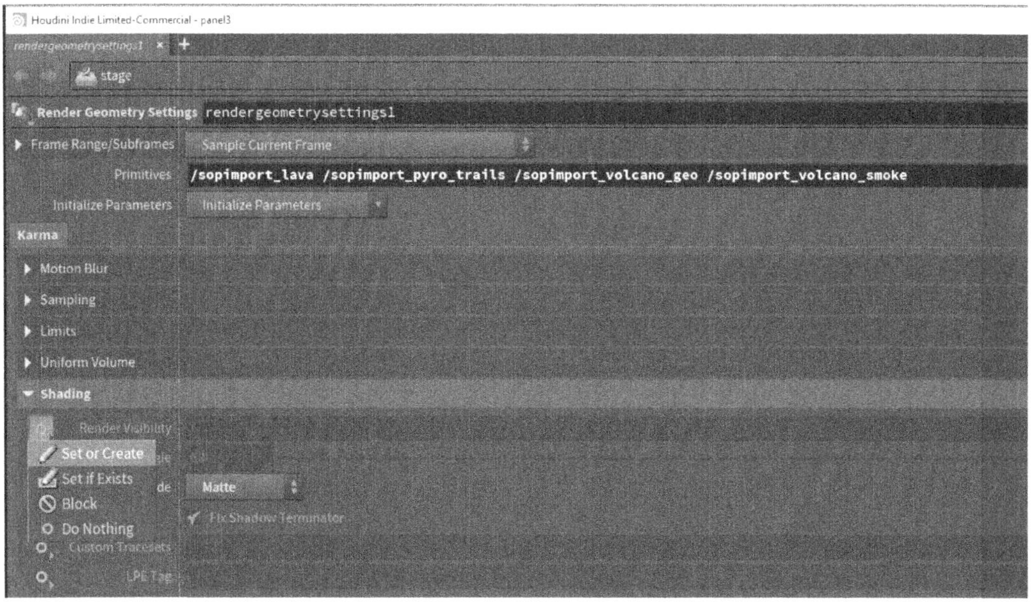

Figure 11.13 – Rendering geometry settings

The benefit of this workflow is that you can set custom render visibility and render settings per separated layer, which gives more flexibility and control. It also lets you break down complex scenes into smaller, renderable elements.

Another option would be to render all the elements together and use specific render layers, or **AOVs**. AOV settings can be found in the **Karma Render Settings** node in the **Image Output** tab.

Figure 11.14 shows the **AOVs** menu and all volcano layers:

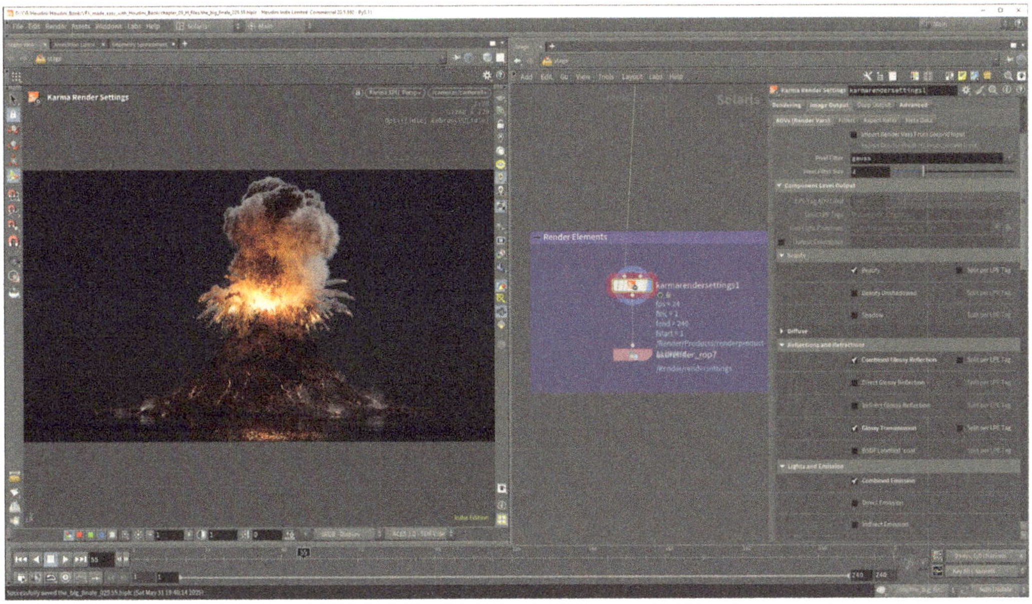

Figure 11.14 – AOVs menu

Take some time to inspect the AOVs that I have selected in the parameters pane. Usually, we want to be able to control different components of the surface after rendering, so the most common AOVs are diffuse for color, reflection, transmission, emission, and volume.

In addition to this, you can also add more technical AOVs, such as **Cyptomatte** or **Crypto Material**, to get each rendering element assigned with a color ID, which can be useful to separate them later in compositing. You can preview different AOVs directly in the viewport by using the **Viewing Output** icon on the right edge bar of the viewport.

Refer to *Figures 11.15* and *11.16* to see the AOV viewport preview, and some of the most common AOVs combined into one image:

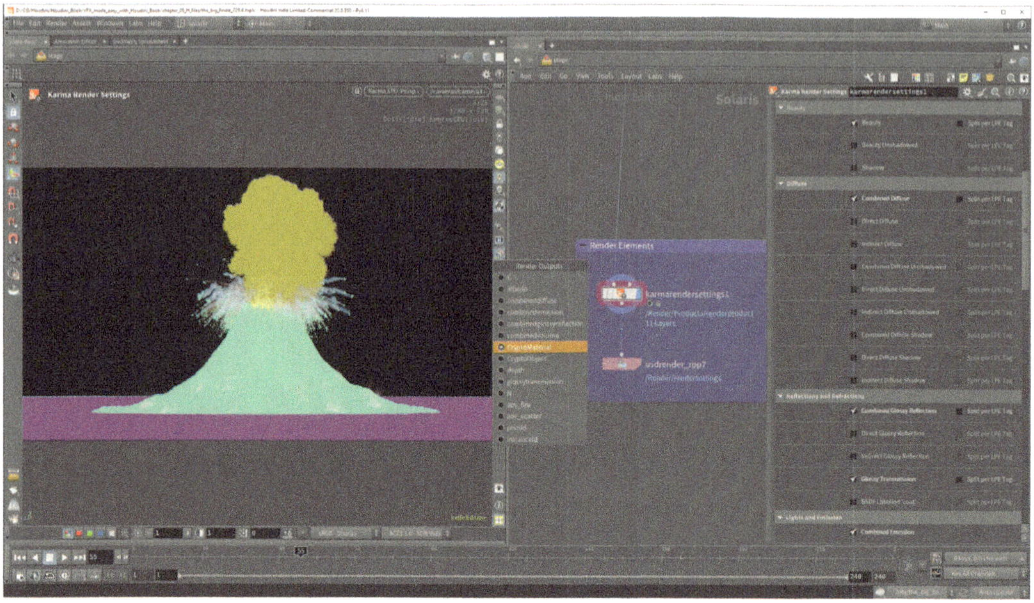

Figure 11.15 – Preview AOVs in the viewport

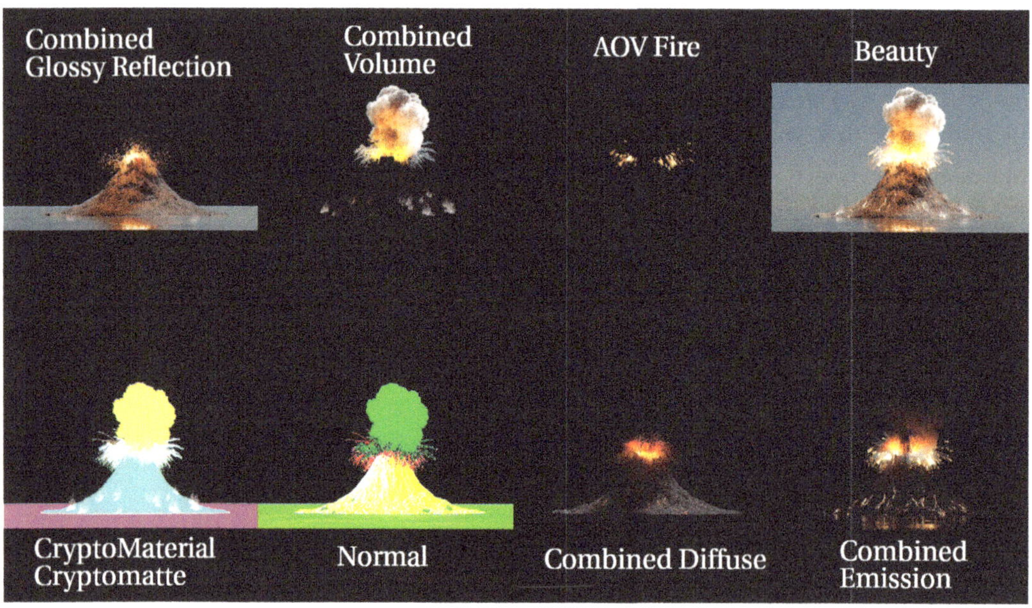

Figure 11.16 – Breakdown of the most common AOVs

Finally, I encourage you to inspect the **Karma Render Settings** nodes to see the parameters used to render the scene. I have set the parameters to render with **CPU** and **XPU** separately in different nodes. You will also notice that I am using a denoising workflow with the help of **Albedo** and **Normal** AOVs. Most of the render settings are the same as the ones we were using by the end of each chapter to render our scenes.

Refer to *Figure 11.17* to see the final image and **Karma Render Settings**:

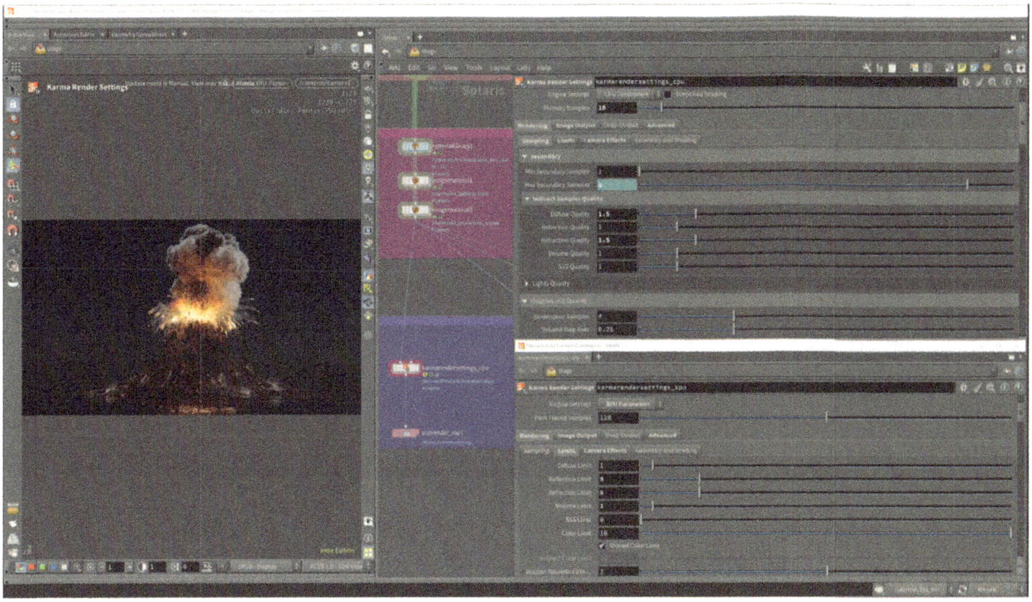

Figure 11.17 – Rendering the final image

Moving on, we'll learn how to do quick compositing and color corrections.

Compositing all the layers together

We can compose all the rendered elements and do some color corrections for a more cinematic look right inside Houdini! Moreover, Houdini 20.5 comes with a completely new image processing upgrade to the previous **IMG/COPs** context, which is called Copernicus.

Copernicus introduces a powerful node-based system for image compositing and texture creation directly within Houdini. While its long-term goal is to provide full compositing capabilities, the current release focuses on a robust set of nodes for general image processing and procedural texture generation. Artists can perform tasks such as color adjustments, blurs, masks, and blending operations, making it ideal for look development, texture work, and integrating image-based workflows into Houdini's procedural pipeline.

You can find a simple example of how to composite elements and do some basic color corrections inside the **copnet_compositing _example** node.

Refer to *Figure 11.18* to see the **Cop** node location:

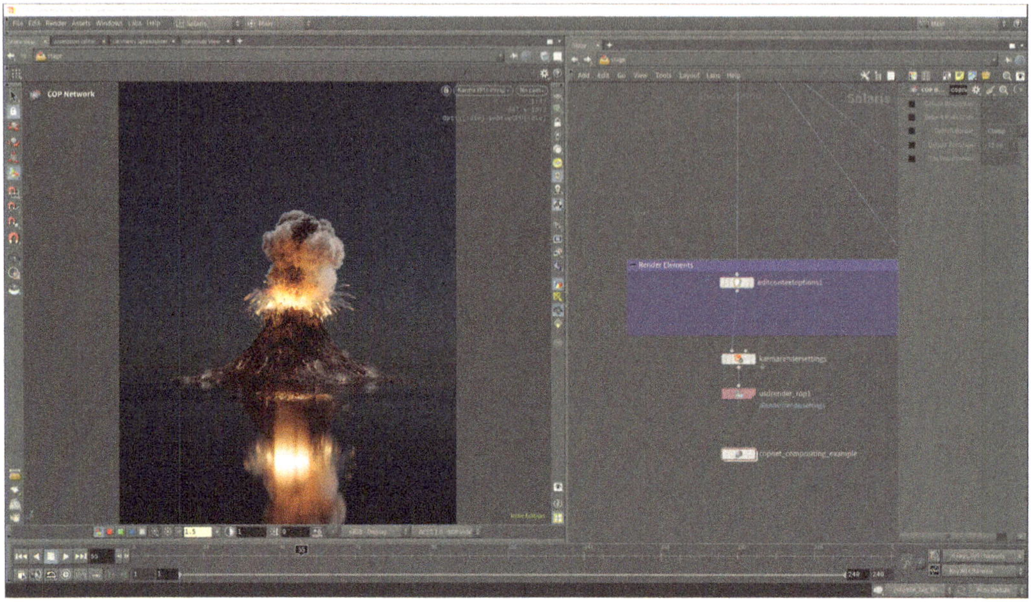

Figure 11.18 – Copernicus compositing

Once you double-click on it, you will see a simple network that I encourage you to explore and have fun with. You will also need to switch to **Composite** view at the top of your viewport. The main idea is that you import the rendered image through the **File** node on the left side of the network, then do some compositing/color corrections, and output the final image from the right with the **ROP Image Output** node. All the nodes can be accessed through the **TAB Menu**, just like in any other Houdini context.

Refer to *Figure 11.19* to see the compositing network:

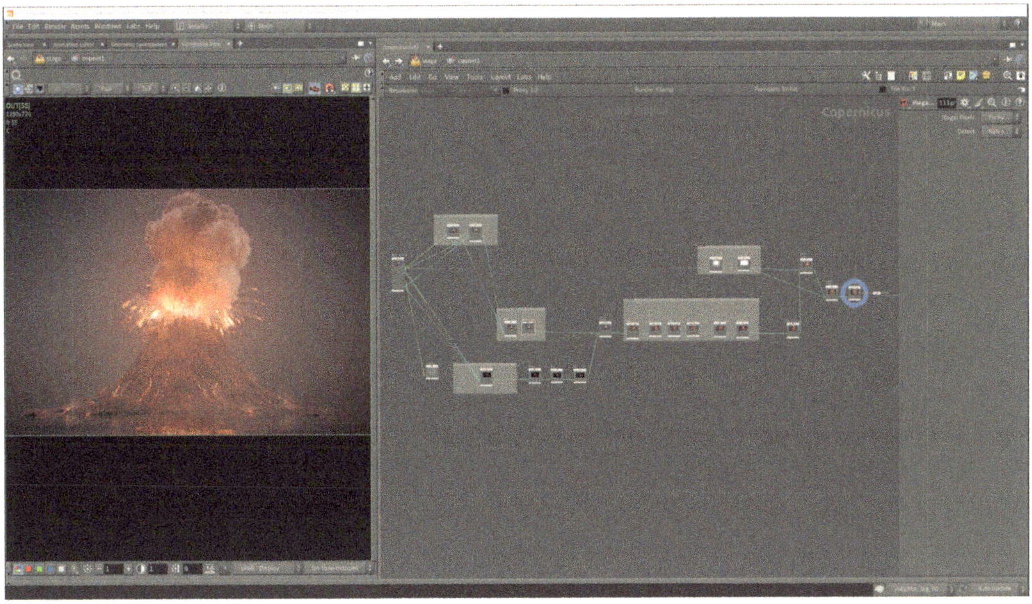

Figure 11.19 – Copernicus compositing

This wraps up the overview and guide through the big finale volcano eruption project.

Summary

In this chapter, we explored the final stages of the VFX pipeline by preparing our volcano eruption scene for rendering and compositing. You learned how to organize and export geometry, import elements into Solaris, set up lights and cameras, assign materials to different components, and configure render settings, including AOVs for greater compositing control. We wrapped things up by compositing all the rendered layers into a cohesive image, ensuring a polished, cinematic result.

By now, you've seen how Houdini's procedural nature extends from simulation to final pixel. Rather than following every step, you were encouraged to explore the provided Houdini file and use this chapter as a reference for your own rendering workflows. This hands-on approach mirrors how many professionals work by reverse-engineering, adapting, and experimenting.

Completing this chapter means you've built up a full-shot FX workflow from the ground up: from shaping a source and simulating pyro and fluids all the way to lighting, rendering, and compositing. You now have a solid foundation not just in using Houdini but also in thinking like a procedural FX artist, breaking down complexity, solving problems creatively, and owning every stage of the process.

In the next chapter, we'll explore best practices to streamline your workflows and ensure your projects are production-ready, and finish with practical tips for creating an impactful demo reel.

12

Best Practices for Houdini Artists

As you complete this journey through Houdini FX fundamentals, it's crucial to carry forward not just technical skills but also professional habits that will improve your workflow, optimize your scenes, and make your work production-ready.

This chapter consolidates essential best practices across procedural asset building, simulation types, shading, lighting, and rendering in **Solaris**, and concludes with demo reel guidance for junior artists using Houdini 20.5 and upward.

Therefore, in this chapter, we'll cover the following main topics:

- Setting up an organized workspace
- Optimizing procedural FX workflows
- Shading, lighting, and rendering in **Solaris** (**Karma**)
- Best practices for creating a demo reel

Technical requirements

To view the chapter images in better clarity, scan the provided QR code. It will direct you to a dedicated link where you can take a look at the images.

Setting up an organized workspace

Before jumping into simulations, it's worth taking the time to build a clean, organized project just like the pros do in big VFX studios. A well-structured workspace not only helps you stay focused but also saves hours of confusion later when you're dealing with dozens of nodes, caches, and renders. Whether you're working solo or collaborating with others, having a solid system in place makes your work easier to follow, easier to update, and easier to share.

In studio pipelines, organization isn't optional; it's the *backbone* of every project. Artists from different departments (modeling, FX, lighting, and compositing) all need to access the same files and understand how everything connects.

A clear project layout ensures the following:

- Consistent file paths (for geometry, textures, and renders)
- Smooth handoffs between departments
- Less time spent hunting for missing files
- Better compatibility with render farms, asset tools, and version control

To support a structured workflow, you can utilize Houdini's native project structure.

Using Houdini's project structure

Luckily, Houdini gives you a head start with its **File** | **New Project** feature. Instead of building folders manually, this option creates a ready-made project structure with all the essential folders just like you'd find in a professional VFX pipeline.

Here's how you can use the **New Project** feature:

1. Go to **File** | **New Project**.
2. Choose a project name and folder location.
3. Houdini will automatically create a set of folders, as shown in *Figure 12.1*:

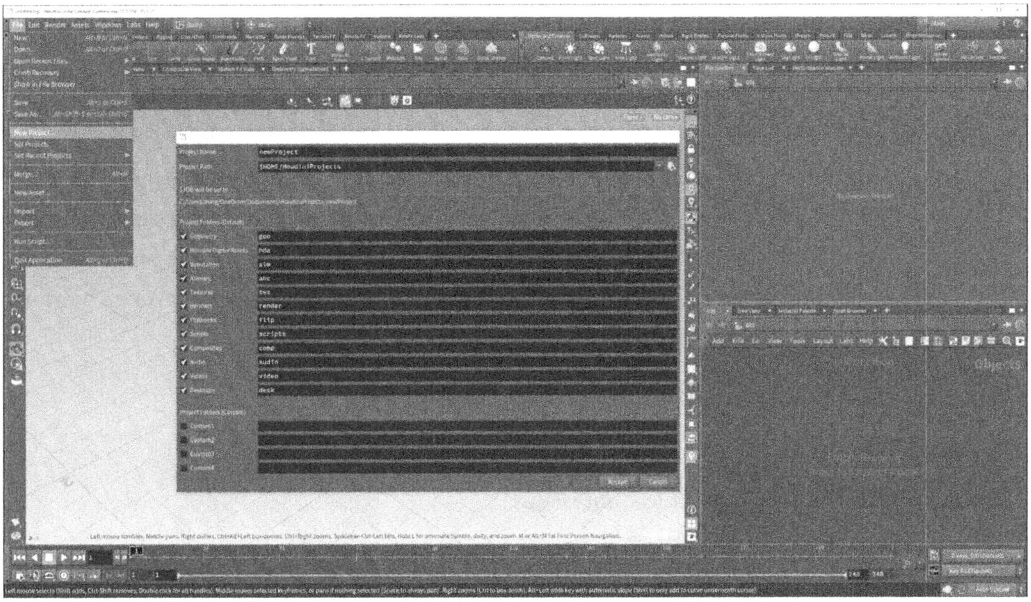

Figure 12.1 – Project folder structure

By keeping things in their proper folders, you stay organized and reduce the risk of overwriting files or breaking file paths. When naming files that will be saved to disk in the form of render or cache, use clear and versioned names such as `lavaSim_v03.bgeo.sc` or `volcanoRender_v05.exr`. This helps track changes and makes it easy to go back if something breaks.

Clear naming conventions inside Houdini

Inside your Houdini scene, naming matters just as much. Instead of leaving nodes as `null1` or `transform2`, give them meaningful names, such as the following:

- `OUT_lava_geo`
- `SIM_smoke_trails`
- `CACHE_debris_v01`

This might feel like extra work at first, but it makes your scene much easier to read, especially if you return to it months later (or someone else needs to pick it up).

Some simple tips worth considering are as follows:

- Group related nodes into colored network boxes, labeled by function (e.g., `Smoke Sources`, `Collision Setup`, etc.)
- Prefix important nodes that export data with tags such as `OUT_`, `CACHE_`, or `EXPORT_`

Keeping the node network clean and readable

As your Houdini scenes become more complex, your node networks can grow into large, intricate webs of interconnected elements. Especially in FX work, where simulations, sources, forces, and caches often live side by side, networks can quickly become overwhelming if not properly maintained. Hence, organizing your node network is essential not only for clarity but also for working efficiently and collaborating with others.

A well-structured node layout helps you do the following:

- Understand and navigate your setup at a glance
- Quickly identify and troubleshoot issues
- Make updates or changes without getting lost
- Hand off your project to others with minimal confusion

In the subsequent sections, we'll look at some best practices to help keep your networks clean, readable, and professional.

Use colors and shapes

Houdini allows you to assign custom colors and shapes to nodes, making it easier to distinguish different types of tasks visually:

- Use distinct colors for key node types such as caches, exports, sources, or simulations
- Change node shapes (accessible via right-clicking, then selecting **Flags** | **Shape**) to indicate outputs, key effects stages, or important junctions in your network

This simple visual coding helps reduce cognitive load when working in large graphs and allows for faster navigation.

Group with network boxes

Network boxes are one of the most effective tools for organizing related nodes. Select a group of nodes, such as a smoke sourcing setup, a velocity injection section, or a collision prep area, and press *Shift* + *O* to create a network box around them.

Here are some best practices to keep in mind for network boxes:

- Name each box clearly (e.g., `Pyro Source Setup`, `Forces and Velocities`, `Mesh Export`, etc.)
- Use soft or muted colors to differentiate sections without overwhelming the view
- Collapse unused boxes to simplify the visual layout when focusing on specific parts of the setup

Network boxes turn a sprawling node graph into structured, modular sections, which are easier to manage and document.

Refer to *Figure 12.2* to see an organized network in comparison to a non-organized one:

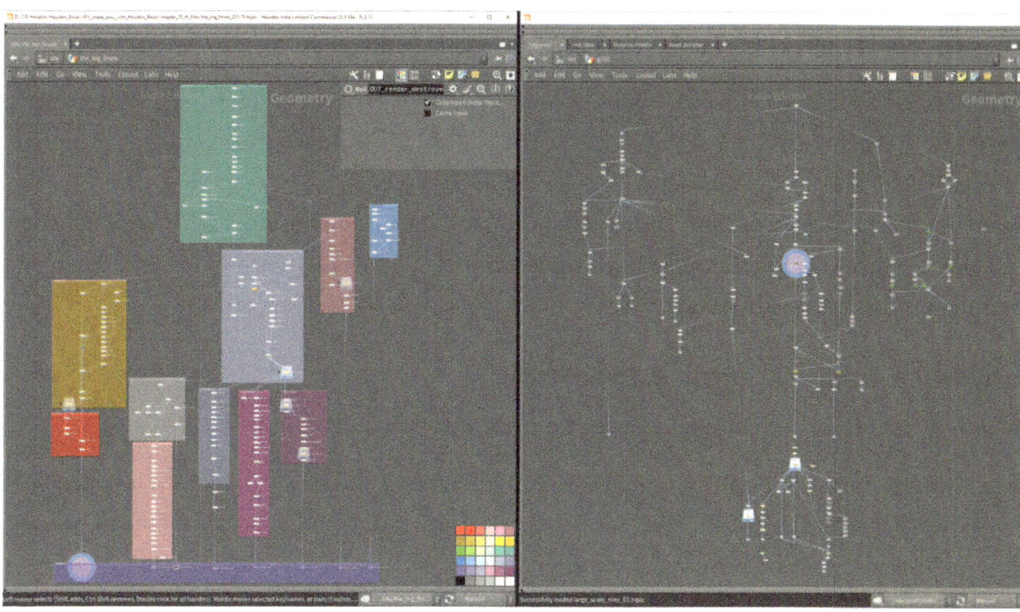

Figure 12.2 – Organized network (left) vs. a non-organized network (right)

Leave notes and visual cues

Adding comments to your network can be extremely helpful, especially for complex setups. You can use the following:

- Sticky notes to explain how a section works or why a certain approach was taken
- Labeled **Null** nodes positioned as visual bookmarks or separators within the flow of the network

These annotations can serve as reminders, guides, or documentation for yourself or anyone else reviewing the file later on.

By organizing your networks with naming, color, grouping, and notes, you make your setups more understandable, scalable, and production-ready. In professional studios, clean node graphs are not only expected, they're essential. Treat your network layout as a reflection of your workflow: structured, intentional, and easy to follow.

In the next section, we'll look at the best practices for optimizing procedural FX workflows.

Optimizing procedural FX workflows

As you move through the different stages of building your FX shots in Houdini, balancing creative freedom with technical efficiency becomes key. Houdini's procedural nature gives you incredible flexibility, but that power comes with responsibility, especially when preparing effects for rendering, collaboration, or delivery. Whether you're working on smoke, fire, particles, destruction, or fluids, these best practices will help you maintain clean networks, optimize performance, and produce production-ready results.

Emitters and FX element setup

When setting up emitters for your effects, keep these principles in mind:

- **Keep emitters simple and purpose-built**: Use clean, low-res geometry that's specifically shaped for the effect you're creating. A sphere with noise can drive a fireball, while a custom curve can act as a lightning source.
- **Emit what you need, not more**: Control emission density, velocity, temperature, or activation using attributes. Start with the minimum necessary, and layer in complexity as needed.
- **Add variation with noise or animation**: Avoid static, repetitive effects. Apply animated transforms, turbulent noise, or time offsets to make the emission feel dynamic and natural.

Figure 12.3 shows a comparison of a good emitter shape with variation versus a bad emitter shape:

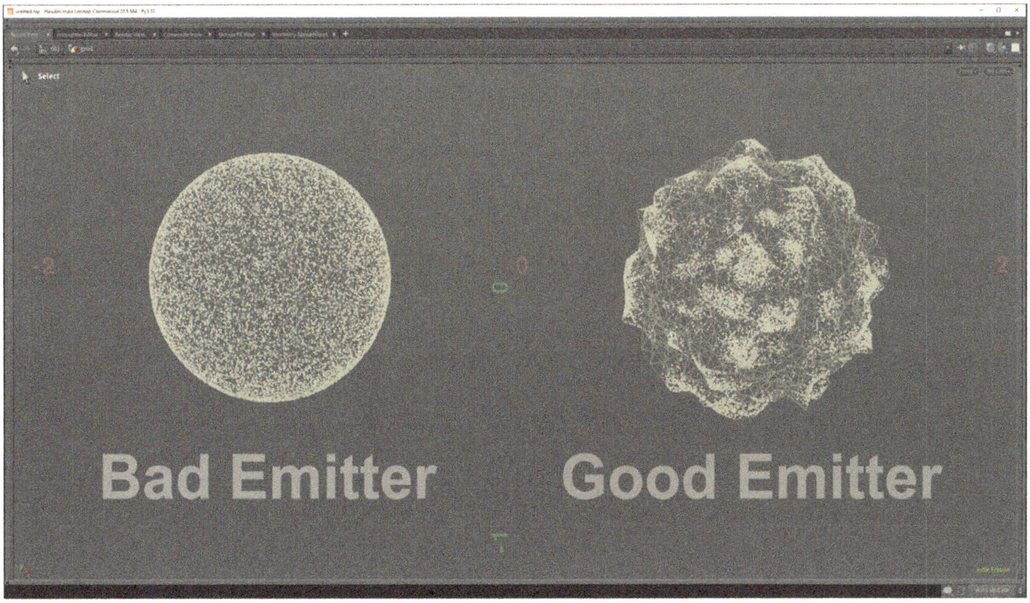

Figure 12.3 – Emitter comparison

A broken-up emitter shape, such as a fractured or noise-displaced surface, produces significantly better simulation results compared to a plain primitive. The added surface variation introduces natural irregularities in the source, leading to more dynamic, realistic motion right from the start. This enhances solver interaction, creates richer secondary behaviors, and reduces the need for artificial turbulence or post-sim tweaks.

In contrast, unbroken primitives generate flat, uniform sources that often result in lifeless or overly symmetrical simulations, offering limited art-directability. A detailed emitter is essential for achieving high-quality, production-ready FX.

Particle effects (POP FX)

For particle-based effects, these practices will help you keep control while achieving natural, dynamic results:

- **Emit with intention**: Tailor particle **Lifespan**, **Speed**, and **Direction** settings to the story and timing of your shot.
- **Use forces in layers**: Combine forces such as **POP Wind**, turbulence, and **POP Drag** for more believable movement. Stack small effects instead of relying on one heavy force.

- **Control particle count**: Begin with a low count for lookdev. Increase only when the motion is working and you're ready for final-quality output.
- **Attribute-driven behavior**: Attributes such as **age**, **life**, **pscale**, **Cd**, and custom floats/vectors can drive motion, transitions, rendering, and shaders. This allows fine control without overcomplicating the solver.
- **Cache in stages**: Split caching into emission, motion, and rendering passes. This allows reuse, faster debugging, and more efficient rendering.

Figure 12.4 shows magical particles emitting from the hammer and forming complex and interesting shapes:

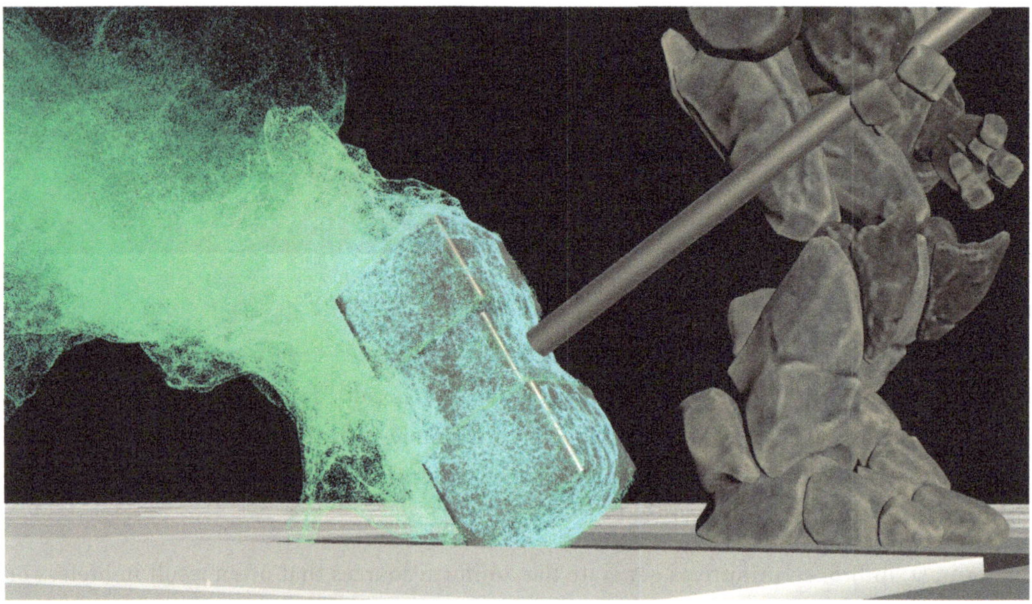

Figure 12.4 – Interesting particle emission combined with forces

In *Figure 12.4*, notice the variation in color, emission areas, and different forces applied to this particle simulation.

Pyro FX (smoke and fire)

When working with smoke and fire, these best practices will help you achieve efficient, realistic, and cinematic pyro effects:

- **Shape before you simulate**: Your emission source and initial **velocity** field determine 80% of the final look. Spend time sculpting these before running long sims.

- **Use Sparse solvers**: Houdini's **Sparse Pyro Solver** is faster and more memory-efficient—ideal for both high-res and iterative sims.
- **Control temperature and fuel carefully**: Use ramps and masks to guide temperature decay, fuel burn, and dissipation. Artistic control over field shaping is crucial for cinematic fire and smoke.
- **Visualize fields constantly**: Use the **Visualize Volume SOP** or **Volume Slice** tools to monitor the **temperature**, **velocity**, **fuel**, and **density** fields. This helps debug issues such as over-dissipation, directionless motion, or overly diffused flames.
- **Break down explosions into layers**: Use staggered sources and multiple field emitters (**blast core**, **fire plume**, and **shockwave**) to build complexity. Each component should serve a purpose.
- **Post-process for cinematic quality**: Use **Pyro Bake Volume** and **Volume Sharpen** to enhance the shape, colors, and breakup. Add detail without the cost of high-resolution simulations.

Figure 12.5 shows a complex explosion with multiple burst fireballs and a shockwave:

Figure 12.5 – Pyro explosion bursts and shockwave

In the scenario shown in *Figure 12.5*, combining pyro explosions with RBD destruction simulation will produce even more realistic results.

Destruction FX (RBD)

To create controlled, believable, and production-ready destruction effects, follow these practices:

- **Use constraints and material properties**: Using glue constraints, soft constraints, and hard constraints paired with material presets gives better realism. Customize **Strength**, **Breaking Threshold**, and internal **Glue** logic for control.
- **Fracture based on impact logic**: Avoid uniform patterns. Use masks, distance fields, or collision proximity to guide more realistic cracking and breakage.
- **Apply initial velocities**: Fracture pieces should inherit motion from the impacting object or explosion. This adds realism and energy to the breakup.
- **Activate fragments when needed**: Inactive fragments save processing and add realism. Use impact triggers, bounding boxes, or custom attributes for activation timing.
- **Cache everything in stages**: Break destruction into phases:

    1. Fracturing
    2. Constraint setup
    3. Simulation
    4. Post-process transformations

    This keeps things manageable and easy to revise.

Figure 12.6 shows a complex destruction combined with pyro dust:

Figure 12.6 – Fracturing and destruction

Destruction simulations achieve greater realism when the input fractured model incorporates multiple material types and layered structures. Additionally, including a range of detail scales, such as *large*, *medium*, and *small*, within the simulation enhances visual complexity and physical believability.

Small-scale water FX (FLIP)

When simulating splashes, drips, or sprays, these practices will help you achieve realistic small-scale water effects:

- **Use small particle separation for detail**: Water drips, splashes, and fine sprays benefit from higher resolution. You can test the motion quickly with low to medium resolution; however, pushing the resolution higher will always produce more realistic details and meshing results.
- **Emit only where needed**: Use bounding boxes, collision masks, or **Camera Frustum** tools to emit particles only in visible areas.
- **Keep forces subtle**: For small-scale interactions, use light gravity, low turbulence, and moderate drag. Overpowered forces break the realism.
- **Mesh efficiently**: Use the VDB-based **Particle Fluid Surface** SOPs with **Smoothing** and **Dilation** controls. Mesh only the necessary regions to avoid wasting time on distant or hidden splashes.

Figure 12.7 shows an example of a small-scale liquid splash:

Figure 12.7 – Liquid splash with high surface tension

Procedural FX and attribute-driven workflows

To make your effects scalable and adaptable, employ these principles:

- **Use attribute-driven techniques:** Drive simulation behavior using attributes such as **age**, **Cd**, **velocity**, **density**, or custom fields. This allows you to vary intensity, timing, shape, or material behavior without manual animation.
- **Leverage procedural noise**: Add variation and breakup with procedural noise functions, such as **Perlin Noise**, **Worley Noise**, or **Curl Noise**. Use them to modulate motion, shape, or attributes across particles and volumes.
- **Keep your FX modular**: Structure your FX into clear layers: **Source**, **Velocity**, **Solver**, and **Post-Process**. Keeping modules separate makes them easier to debug, replace, or reuse in other shots.

Cache optimization and data cleanup

Efficient caching and clean data management are essential. These practices will help keep your simulations lighter, faster, and easier to work with:

- **Cache in stages:** Don't wait until the end to cache often. Cache emission separately from forces or collisions. Use `.bgeo.sc` or `.vdb` formats for efficient file sizes and compatibility.
- **Clean up attributes**: Use **Attribute Delete** SOPs to remove unnecessary data (e.g., temporary attributes, simulation artifacts, etc.). This reduces cache size and speeds up rendering.
- **Compress volumes**: Use volume compression options when writing VDB caches. Lower voxel precision (where acceptable) and remove unused fields to reduce disk space and load times.
- **Use checkpoint caching for large sims:** In heavy simulations, cache checkpoints periodically. This allows you to resume a sim if it crashes, without rerunning everything.

Figure 12.8 shows an example of multiple effect layers that are cached separately and combined after for the final render:

Figure 12.8 – Caching and combining multiple FX layers

By following these best practices across FX types, caching, and procedural workflows, you'll produce more efficient, adaptable, and professional-quality effects. Houdini rewards structure and clarity if you think modularly and build with intention. Your setups won't just look great, they'll be fast, flexible, and ready for the demands of a production environment.

Shading, lighting, and rendering in Solaris (Karma)

Shading, lighting, and rendering are where our Houdini scenes truly come to life, turning raw geometry into cinematic visuals. In this section, we'll focus on building a strong visual foundation, from crafting convincing materials to setting the right mood with thoughtful lighting. You'll also learn how to work efficiently with Karma's powerful rendering tools so you can iterate quickly and achieve professional, polished results.

Let's have a look at the best practices:

- **Start with simple scenes**: Test your scene and iterate with a camera and lighting first, then add materials and any additional rendering effects such as fog, depth of field, and motion blur. Test rendering scenes with *everything on* can be very slow and hard to iterate on or troubleshoot any rendering issues.

- **Learn to create a variety of surface types**: Study common surfaces such as concrete, metal, glass, skin, and wood by using **MaterialX** shaders, focusing on key parameters such as roughness, specular, subsurface, and displacement.
- **Experiment with different lighting setups**: Start with **Dome lights** for HDRI-based ambient lighting, and **Physical Sun & Sky** for outdoor natural light. You can then create additional shaped lights (sphere, rectangle, etc.) for more control.
- **Use Karma XPU**: **Karma XPU** is great for fast lookdev previews and iterations quickly with lower sample settings before final renders. Additionally, you can use the denoising functionality to achieve clean renders with fewer samples and render time.
- **Understand and organize render passes (AOVs)**: Render passes such as diffuse, specular, emission, and cryptomatte give flexibility in compositing.

Figure 12.9 shows a rendered scene with multiple materials, simple dome lighting, and denoising:

Figure 12.9 – Rendering different elements together

Finally, let's move on to demo reel/portfolio best practices.

Best practices for creating a demo reel

Creating a strong demo reel is one of the most important steps in showcasing your skills and landing opportunities as an FX artist. This guide offers practical tips to help you present your work clearly, professionally, and in a way that highlights your strengths.

From choosing the right shots to structuring your reel effectively, these best practices will help you stand out in a competitive industry:

- **Keep it short**: Aim for 1 to 2 minutes maximum. Your best work should be front-loaded and no filler included. Each shot must earn its place and show diversity in skills.
- **Avoid dragging shots or repeated effects**: A reel with 3 or 4 strong, concise projects often makes more impact than one packed with unpolished material.
- **Break down shots**: Include visual breakdowns of your FX process. Show wireframes, simulation passes, AOVs, or viewport-to-render transitions to communicate how your effect was built. For instance, if you created a tornado, show the particle sim, velocity field, volume source, and final render. This reveals both your creative and technical command.
- **Label your work**: Indicate your specific contributions for each shot. Use clear lower thirds or overlay titles, such as `FX Only`, `Lighting and FX`, or `Sim + Shading`. Also, list tools used, such as Houdini, Nuke, Redshift, and so on. Recruiters often review reels in silence, so make your labeling concise and informative without relying on narration.
- **Final polish**: Use high-quality renders, accurate motion blur, and clean compositing. Avoid raw viewport captures or unfinished sims unless labeled clearly. You might work on blockbuster-level content, but if your reel lacks polish, it could be overlooked. Treat it like a finished product ready for clients.
- **Host professionally**: Upload your reel to a clean, ad-free platform such as **Vimeo** (`https://vimeo.com/`) or your personal site. Use a simple interface, enable easy downloads, and include contact info and a link to your résumé. Avoid cluttered **YouTube** channels or **Instagram** pages. A professional presentation builds trust and confidence before it even hits play.

By following these best practices, you'll not only streamline your Houdini workflows but also build habits that will serve you in real-world production environments. As you continue beyond this book, keep experimenting, stay curious, and refine your artistry with every project you take on.

Summary

In this chapter, we explored essential best practices for Houdini artists, focusing on how to build a strong foundation in procedural workflows. Key topics included organizing node networks for clarity, working non-destructively, and maintaining clean scene structures. We also emphasized the importance of learning by experimentation, breaking down complex problems into smaller steps, and gradually developing confidence with Houdini's powerful toolset. By following these principles early on, artists can build efficient habits that scale well into more advanced projects and professional workflows.

VFX Made Easy in Houdini was written with one core belief: that learning Houdini can be easy, fun, and deeply rewarding. My goal throughout this book has been to demystify the procedural approach and show that, with the right structure and mindset, anyone can create powerful, flexible, and production-ready effects without needing to master every node or have advanced programming skills.

Whether you're just beginning or building upon prior related experience, I hope this guide has helped you develop both confidence and curiosity. The techniques covered, from procedural modeling to lighting, rendering, and FX, are designed to give you a solid foundation that you can continue to grow and adapt to your own creative goals.

Remember, Houdini isn't about knowing everything; it's about thinking systematically, solving problems creatively, and iterating with purpose. With patience and play, you'll find that proceduralism isn't just a technique, it's a mindset that opens doors across VFX, games, and beyond.

Keep exploring, keep experimenting, and most importantly, *enjoy the journey*. You're now equipped with the tools and perspective to go even further.

13

Unlock Your Book's Exclusive Benefits

Your copy of this book comes with the following exclusive benefits:

Next-gen Packt Reader

AI assistant (beta)

DRM-free PDF/ePub downloads

Use the following guide to unlock them if you haven't already. The process takes just a few minutes and needs to be done only once.

How to unlock these benefits in three easy steps

Step 1

Have your purchase invoice for this book ready, as you'll need it in *Step 3*. If you received a physical invoice, scan it on your phone and have it ready as either a PDF, JPG, or PNG.

For more help on finding your invoice, visit `https://www.packtpub.com/unlock-benefits/help`.

Note

Did you buy this book directly from Packt? You don't need an invoice. After completing Step 2, you can jump straight to your exclusive content.

Step 2

Scan this QR code or go to `packtpub.com/unlock`.

On the page that opens (which will look similar to *Figure 13.1* if you're on desktop), search for this book by name. Make sure you select the correct edition.

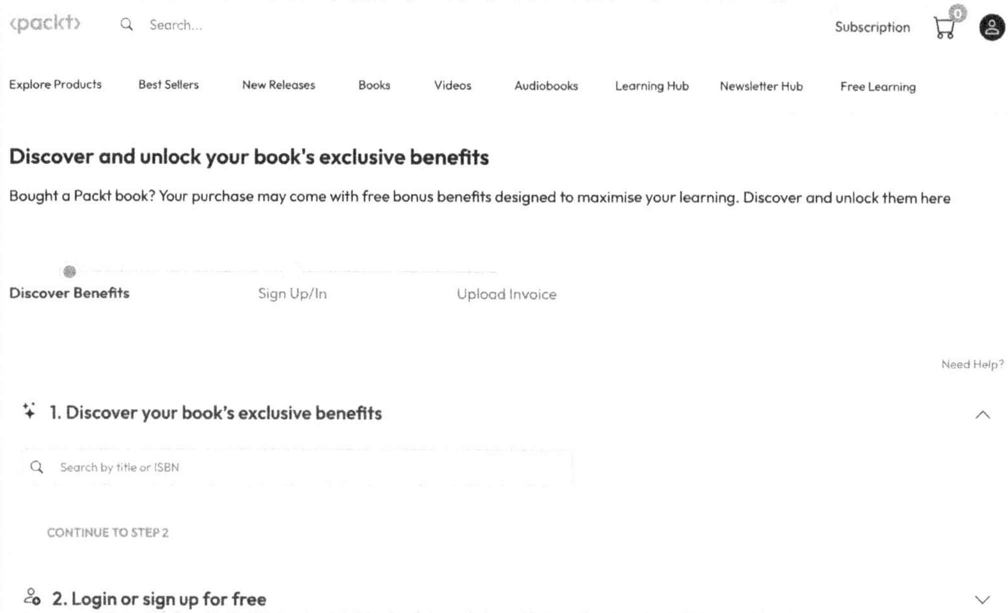

Figure 13.1 – Packt unlock landing page on desktop

Step 3

Once you've selected your book, sign in to your Packt account or create a new one for free. Once you're logged in, upload your invoice. It can be in PDF, PNG, or JPG format and must be no larger than 10 MB. Follow the rest of the instructions on the screen to complete the process.

Need help?

If you get stuck and need help, visit `https://www.packtpub.com/unlock-benefits/help` for a detailed FAQ on how to find your invoices and more. The following QR code will take you to the help page directly:

Note

If you are still facing issues, reach out to `customercare@packt.com`.

www.packtpub.com

Subscribe to our online digital library for full access to over 7,000 books and videos, as well as industry leading tools to help you plan your personal development and advance your career. For more information, please visit our website.

Why subscribe?

- Spend less time learning and more time coding with practical eBooks and Videos from over 4,000 industry professionals
- Improve your learning with Skill Plans built especially for you
- Get a free eBook or video every month
- Fully searchable for easy access to vital information
- Copy and paste, print, and bookmark content

At www.packtpub.com, you can also read a collection of free technical articles, sign up for a range of free newsletters, and receive exclusive discounts and offers on Packt books and eBooks.

Other Books You May Enjoy

If you enjoyed this book, you may be interested in these other books by Packt:

Unity 6 Shaders and Effects Cookbook, Fifth Edition

John P. Doran

ISBN: 978-1-83546-857-9

- Understand the principles of shaders, along with how to work in Shader Graph
- Harness URP and HDRP packages for efficient shader creation
- Enhance game visuals with modern shader techniques
- Optimize shaders for performance and aesthetics
- Master the math and algorithms behind the commonly used lighting models
- Transform your game's atmosphere with the Post Processing Stack
- Develop sophisticated shader effects by leveraging fragment shaders and grab-pass techniques

Learn Blender Simulations the Right Way, Second Edition

Stephen Pearson

ISBN: 978-1-83620-005-5

- Create a realistic campfire simulation with sparks and motion blur
- Simulate a chaotic explosion using smoke, fire, and particle effects
- Implement Fluid simulation for a waterfall with waves and foam
- Use the Soft Body system to simulate a sphere moving through obstacles
- Apply Cloth physics to animate a waving flag attached to a pole with ropes
- Master the Rigid Body system to create a Rube Goldberg machine-like animation
- Animate painting effects and raindrops using Dynamic Paint
- Combine multiple simulation effects to create a burning effect animation

Packt is searching for authors like you

If you're interested in becoming an author for Packt, please visit `authors.packt.com` and apply today. We have worked with thousands of developers and tech professionals, just like you, to help them share their insight with the global tech community. You can make a general application, apply for a specific hot topic that we are recruiting an author for, or submit your own idea.

Share your thoughts

Now you've finished *VFX Made Easy with Houdini, First Edition*, we'd love to hear your thoughts! Scan the QR code below to go straight to the Amazon review page for this book and share your feedback or leave a review on the site that you purchased it from.

`https://packt.link/r/1835882919`

Your review is important to us and the tech community and will help us make sure we're delivering excellent quality content.

Index

Symbols

A

B

C

D

M

N

O

P

Made in the USA
Monee, IL
15 September 2026

63035031R00230